Seen and Heard in Mexico

THE MEXICAN EXPERIENCE
William H. Beezley, series editor

Seen and Heard in Mexico

Children and Revolutionary Cultural Nationalism

ELENA JACKSON ALBARRÁN

University of Nebraska Press   Lincoln and London

To Noel Lewis

CONTENTS

ILLUSTRATIONS

ACKNOWLEDGMENTS

I am indebted to many friends, colleagues, mentors, and acquaintances for their many contributions in the process of researching, writing, and publishing this book. First and foremost, at the University of Arizona Bill Beezley saw the seeds of this project take root and grow from a semester paper, to a master's thesis, to a dissertation, to the manuscript in its current form. His mentorship and support were instrumental in making the process a rewarding one. I am also grateful to Bert J. Barickman and Kevin Gosner for lending their support—and withholding overt expressions of skepticism—to my pursuit of this highly ephemeral dissertation idea in its embryonic stage. The BQ chapter of the PEO philanthropic organization provided generous funding, which along with support from the Marshall Foundation facilitated a year dedicated to writing the dissertation. Subsequent research trips were funded in part by the generous support of the Faculty Research Fund of Miami University's Department of History.

In Mexico City a year of research was immeasurably enriched by the companionship and *comadrazgo* of Susanne Eineigel, with whom I shared a living space, travel adventures, archival triumphs and travails, *tianguis* runs, a rigorous *telenovela* schedule, and endless hours of conversation about Mexican history. The indomitable Carmen Nava Nava not only opened her impressive home library but also provided expert navigation among the city's flea markets, antique bazaars, and used bookstores, helping me turn up untold treasures. Alberto del Castillo Troncoso and Beatriz Alcubierre both shared their expertise in child-related research topics. Claudia Agostoni welcomed me into her weekly seminar on health and education at the Instituto de Investigaciones Históricas at the Universidad Nacional Autónoma de México, where I was fortunate to be immersed in some of the top scholarship on these themes in the country. And a happenstance research consultation with Susana Sosenski over coffee at the Instituto Mora blossomed into a lifelong friendship and professional collaboration. Fellow researchers in Mexico generously shared some of their relevant archival finds: Gretchen Raup Pierce, Emily Wakild, Thom Rath, Stephen Neufeld, María Muñóz, Michael Matthews, and Claudia Carretta all helped make research a collaborative experience. Both Susan Deeds and Tracy Goode provided hospitality and good cheer, fostering a sociable community among researchers. Ryan Kashanipour was always at the ready with advice, some of which I heeded. In Washington DC Kelly Quinn and Damon Scott doled out logistical support and libations. And perhaps the most influential friendship and scholarly collaboration has been forged over a long graduate career marked by several shared research trips with Amanda López. In our various Mexico City sublets, and over hours of metro travel together, we hashed out theories—historiographical, apocryphal, and metaphorical alike—that have informed our mutual scholarship, pedagogy, and friendship in unspeakably enriching ways.

The work of a historian would be impossible without the often-invisible, heroic labors of the librarians and archivists that maintain, organize, interpret, and deliver materials that can be fragile, ephemeral, and challenging to classify. The library staff at the Biblioteca Lerdo de Tejada remains unparalleled in their polite efficiency in delivering rare items from their outstanding collection. At the SEP, Roberto retrieved box after box of documents with great dispatch and a good dose of cutting humor. The permissions staff at the Archivo General de la Nación, and in particular Fabiola María Luisa Hernández Díaz, worked swiftly and efficiently to facilitate the procurement of authorization for many of the images that appear in these pages. Likewise, Jorge Fuentes Hernández at the SRE archive helped me to track down and digitize other images in a timely manner. The Isabel la Católica branch of Café Jekemir sustained nearly daily breaks between archives, thanks to its potent brew and cheerful service.

Once the treasure hunting was done, many people contributed to improving the organization and expression of ideas that followed. Elise Dubord, Áurea Toxqui, Justin Castro, Drew Cayton, Tatiana Seijas, and José Amador all read sections and provided critical feedback. Miami University graduate students in history and English graciously (or perhaps patiently) read and discussed one of the chapters, and Cheryl Gibbs in particular provided concise comments. I have benefitted enormously from the guidance, critical feedback, and comments on both written and presented versions of sections of this project from Mary Kay Vaughan, Ann Blum, Eileen Ford, Bill French, Stephen Lewis, and John Lear, scholars with whom I feel humbled to have shared some intellectual space. Kelsey Vance masterfully improved the poor quality of many of the archival images that appear in this book. At the University of Nebraska Press, the editorial staff has been incredibly professional and communicative, making the process of publishing such a long-term project a true pleasure to see through in its final stages. First Heather Lundine and then Bridget Barry were wonderful editors and reassured my every doubt. I thank copy editor Annette Wenda in particular for her acute attention to detail, which saved me from some potentially embarrassing oversights.

On a personal note, the attention to the visual culture and the aesthetic sphere that thread through parts of this book reveals a sensibility toward art and art history fostered in me since childhood by Peggy Jackson, a lifelong artist and art history educator. It has been a rare pleasure to be able to seek consultation about the history of art education from none other than my mother. I have also been buoyed by the love and support of my father, Lewis Jackson, as we empathized in late-night conversations about the challenges of writing a book. I have also benefitted from the wisdom of my father-in-law, Tom Miller, who has shared his vastly accumulated trade secrets from the publishing world. My mother-in-law, Regla Albarrán Miller, has also shared her advice and insight about literature. Shelley Hawthorne Smith kept me both grounded and afloat, for which I am eternally grateful. Other family members Acacia, Martha, Keith, Brian, Leo, and Katie have brightened my life and withstood my absence from family events when research, writing, and conference presentations took me in other directions.

Two very important fellows have made it possible to write a book while maintaining a household, a job, and some sanity. When I did not get the research funding necessary to sustain a year in Mexico, Juan Carlos Albarrán supported me by delivering mail under the Tucson sun, even while completing his own graduate degree. On his visits to Mexico, he uncomplainingly assumed the mantle of my research assistant, helping me frantically transcribe documents before an archive's planned closure for a long holiday or the onslaught of an impending *aguacero*. Given my tight research budget, he was compensated only by *churros*. On late-night writing sessions, he stayed up with me in solidarity. That this book came to completion is largely a testament to his steadfast partnership. Lastly, Noel Lewis Albarrán came into being as the manuscript took its final form. He has grown up alongside this project. His presence in my life has dramatically revised what I thought was a historically sound understanding of children and has led me to question and nuance my interpretations of nearly every section of this book. But more than anything else, he has been a delightful, kind, beautiful reminder of the way our lives are greatly enriched when we slow down and stoop down to allow children to be seen and heard.

Seen and Heard in Mexico

Introduction
Seen and Heard in Revolutionary Mexico

> My home is the Women's Penitentiary. I sleep on a woven mat on the floor. The clothing that I have is one pair of jeans, one cotton shirt, one jacket, and leather shoes. . . . The toys that I have I made myself at school: a grasshopper, a see-saw, a hobby horse, and a crocodile. I practice marbles, the harmonica, and the cup-and-ball. . . . My mother treats me well; she neither beats nor scolds me, and my teacher is kind, and I learn from her in a friendly and caring way. I am not satisfied with the way that I live.
>
> —ENRIQUE GÓMEZ HERRERA, child autobiographer in Guanajuato, 1937

> It takes a long time to become young.
>
> —PABLO PICASSO, Cannes, France, 1966

Enrique Gómez Herrera awoke each morning on his straw mat on the floor of his mother's cell in the Women's Penitentiary in Guanajuato, where she was serving a twenty-year sentence for the murder of her older daughter's abusive husband.[1] Daily, Enrique bathed and dressed his younger sister and then donned his only set of clothes and set out from his prison home for school, where he attempted to integrate himself into a classroom of his peers. In an autobiographical essay solicited for a collection of Guanajuato schoolchildren's personal experiences, Enrique dutifully relayed the expected hallmarks of childhood: a catalog of his toys, his siblings, and the adults and institutions that shaped the contours of his young life. Despite the extreme circumstances that distinguished him from other children his age, he strained to provide a normalizing narrative of his life. His painful awareness of social difference coexisted, in this short excerpt, with an equally acute sense of the contemporary definition of a normal childhood in revolutionary Mexico. Unlike many other unfortunate children living unconventional lives in a time of growing national attention to children's well-being, Enrique's story saw public dissemination—not only as a contribution to the eighty-four-page anthology *Voces Nuevas* published in Guanajuato by former state education director Francisco Hernández y Hernández but also in excerpted form in a review for Mexico City's daily *El Universal Gráfico.*

That his plight interested anyone at all suggests an aperture, during the two decades following the Mexican Revolution, in which children gained consideration as viable social actors, cultural critics, and subjects of reform. During a period that scholars have come to define as a child-centered society, children became central to the reform agenda of the revolutionary nationalist government—and the recipients of the largest percentage of the national budget. Despite the rhetorical, sentimental, and material attention heaped upon children in the 1920s and 1930s, historians have a remarkably flimsy sense of how children themselves experienced and perceived the onslaught of resources and consideration. The reproduction of Enrique's story in the national press tugged at the public's heartstrings and confirmed the critical position of the article's author that questioned the leftist intellectual tendency to romanticize the proletarian classes, a waning fashion by the late 1930s. But it also serves as a document—imperfect, edited, and excerpted, to be sure, but a document nonetheless—that captures a moment in which a child took the time to evaluate his own living circumstances as compared to the national standard. Countless snippets of children's experiences culled from the archives in the form of letters, stories, scripts, drawings, interviews, presentations, marginalia, and homework assignments all attest not to the uniform Mexican childhood envisioned by revolutionary ideologues but rather to varied and uneven childhoods all formed against a monolithic backdrop of cultural nationalism.

The Symbolic Child and Real Children

National identity formation in modern Mexico took place in waves, and each wave resulted in the consolidation of a set of collective memories that more or less corresponded to generations. Since independence, official attempts to cobble together a set of national symbols, beliefs, images, and practices from the country's diverse population met with lukewarm public reception; in many cases, the spontaneous and streetwise popular versions of national identity that characterized festivals, parades, games, and entertainment corresponded more authentically to the visions that Mexicans had of themselves.[2] For children, the sensory power of animated dolls, voices emitted from an electrified box, and the hustle and bustle of bodies in parades and demonstrations contributes to a sense of collective identity more than the political affiliations and institutional memberships that adults use to organize themselves into social groups.

Alongside evolving discourse that signaled the symbolic child as a measure of the strength of nascent Mexico's heartbeat, real and living children thrived and languished along with the nation's sputtering welfare. Heeding the astute observations of sociologists of childhood, we would do well to attend to the rhetorical power of "the child," but not to confuse this singular device with the conditions and experiences of "children"; in most cases, political references to "the child" bore little resemblance to individual children's lives.[3] As diverse and often disparate visions of the emerging nation competed, unifying symbols emerged to forge political peace. Appeals for the welfare of "the child" were among the earliest and most conciliatory. But official representations of the child often failed to materialize into programs and policies that would lead to the meaningful incorporation of real children into the nation-building project.[4] At the core of this study lies an interrogation of the tension, historical and historiographical, between the symbolic child and the real child.

Since the independence era, officials relied increasingly on tabula rasa tropes of children as metaphors for constantly reconfigured projections of the imagined nation. While the politics may have shifted, the child remained at the core of moral, religious, medical, and educational debates—a facile symbol of hope and regeneration recalled by Liberals and Conservatives, reformers and caudillos alike.[5] Over the course of two centuries, cycles of war followed by national reconstruction yielded mounting efforts to define and institutionalize the abstract concepts of nation and citizenship. In particular, the expansion of public education during the period of Liberal rule known as the Restored Republic (1867–76) offers an instructive comparison to the decades examined here. Amid an environment still fraught with competing ideologies, the Liberal ruling elite identified young children as the source material for their nation-building project. The 1867 Law of Public Instruction undermined the persistent power of the church as a socializing agent by replacing religious education with "moral education" in Mexico City, a legislative coup quickly adopted by many states in the federalized education system. Although nineteenth-century Liberals had identified the desirable avenues for citizen building, and made the tentative first steps toward creating the institutions that would convey their project, not until the postrevolutionary years was the state able to transmit a comprehensive and uniform "idea of nation" to schoolchildren through a centralized educational system.[6] Yet for much of the nineteenth century, while children enjoyed symbolic presence at the center of moral, religious, medical, and educational debates, a distinctly child-oriented popular culture did not emerge until 1870, with a rise in the publication of children's books and magazines. Notably, the children's magazine *La niñez ilustrada* (1873–75) sought to put enlightened ideas about child citizenship (as the "producer, reproducer, citizen, and soldier of tomorrow") into the hands of middle- and upper-class children. Even then much of this Mexican children's literature, though newly liberated from its Europhile roots, saw limited dissemination among the upper classes.[7] Furthermore, the vast majority of child-oriented cultural production persisted in treating the child as a symbol of loftier political ideals or, at best, an object of socialization.

As early as the era of Porfirio Díaz (1876–1911), emerging government discussions identified the child as an active citizen and resulted in educational policy reform. The *niño activo* was the twentieth-century heir of the Liberal-era *hombre positivo*, evidence of expanding definitions of Liberalism and democracy from the Constitution of 1857 to the Constitution of 1917. The medicalization of childhood and expansion of public health and hygiene initiatives during the Porfirian era helped to mobilize the child as the object of state concern. In particular, hygienists focused their energies on regulating conditions in the public schools, the physical conditions of which offended their sensibilities and jeopardized the auspicious developmental start to citizenship desired for Mexican children.[8] Porfirian education implemented a positivist belief in the perfectibility of the population only in uneven fits and starts, as attested by historian Mílada Bazant. In some exceptional cases progressive teachers (public and private alike) implemented innovative pedagogical strategies designed to inspire political and social action among young children.[9] In general, educational officials during the Porfiriato did strive to make curricular materials more appealing and age appropriate for their intended audiences, and textbook analyses of the time reveal a tendency to activate the child reader as a civic actor.[10]

Understandably, little information exists about the rhetorical treatment of and educational policies for children during the tumultuous years of the Mexican Revolution. During the decade-long upheaval, the rotating doors of Chapultepec Castle, the seat of the presidency, meant that little meaningful consolidation of ideas and practices about childhood took place. From Chihuahua to Guerrero, children from across the social spectrum were swept up as soldiers or camp followers, saw their families irrevocably broken apart, or were whisked away to exile. Resources were depleted, and modes of conveying them were disrupted. Childhood for many in this decade was defined by great deprivation, violence, prostitution, homelessness, and general lack of structural or institutional attention. An estimated 1.5 million Mexicans perished in the revolution that waged from 1910 to

1920, decimating the population and eliminating an entire generation of productive men of working age. By the time the conflict came to a close, these experiences amounted to a denial of childhood for a generation of Mexicans. During the 1920s and 1930s, then, the revolutionary officials set out to rectify this cultural gap and endeavored to reconstruct a nation divided by three decades of dictatorship and crippled by a decade of civil war. They sought to replace that generation with active citizens who supported the ideals documented in the forward-thinking Constitution of 1917, forged by constitutionalist delegates over arduously debated sessions in Querétaro.

Revolutionary-era lawmakers, professionals, and governors believed firmly in the possibility of constructing the ideal citizen from birth, through the balanced application of sound pedagogy, firm ideology, and modern medicine. The intellectual sector saw increasing importance assigned to children as the theme of various national and international conferences on children, most notably the Pan-American Child Congresses (Congresos Panamericanos del Niño). Viewed from above, the rhetorical and symbolic prominence of children in policy making seemed little more than an intensified continuation of positivist concerns for the health and hygiene of the national population.

But for a brief window of about twenty years from 1920 to 1940, and ranging in form and intensity, child-centered reforms accompanied a meaningful incorporation of children into political and civic culture. The revolutionary era offered new opportunities for the child to serve as an active member of society in his or her own right, and not simply as a future citizen. Both the governmental and the private sectors undertook a project of expanding the scope of childhood through the creation of new locations, activities, and media outlets. At the same time, as a result of the initial mission of the revolution to expand participation in the construction of the nation, young people from rural, poor, or indigenous backgrounds now, and for the first time, were recognized as children, whose modern childhood deserved the locations, activities, and media outlets that pressed into their communities.

The culture of childhood changed notably in these decades, in an evolution from the symbolic child to the actively engaged social citizen. Efforts transformed the role of the child from that of an individual bounded by the family to that of a member of the classroom, the community, the nation, and a transnational generation. The hallmarks of childhood presented in this study—puppet shows, radio, art curriculum, extracurricular organizations, and Pan-Americanism—gained nearly universal recognition as formative components of a cross-section of society. Children who participated in these new opportunities found themselves in a community that bisected the long-standing social categories of race, class, and gender and one that transcended geographic boundaries. Given the new, improved, and restored communications technologies that corresponded with this period, the resulting generation shared more cultural references than any one previous. Many children growing up in these optimistic years enjoyed unprecedented access to their peers through opportunities afforded by official educational initiatives, new and improved media technologies, and new forms of children's popular culture. Yet, as the following chapters will suggest, the officially produced model of the ideal child shifted from the 1920s to the 1930s, suggesting changing attitudes about the roles that children from different social and ethnic classes ought to play in revolutionary Mexico.

President Alvaro Obregón founded the Ministry of Public Education (Secretaría de Educación Pública [SEP]) in 1921, and the various agencies within the burgeoning institution introduced many new forms of interaction and consumption to children. Revolutionary governments through this agency launched educational expenditures to an all-time high, averaging 10 percent of the budget from 1921 to 1940, reaching its apex during the Cárdenas administration at nearly 14 percent.[11] In its first years the SEP blossomed under the talented, ambitious José Vasconcelos, who served as secretary of education from 1921 to 1924 and pointed the agency in the direction it would take for two decades. Forging a unified society from diverse cultural or geographic groups began at the level of rural education, where schoolteachers instilled the unifying concepts of patriotism and language.[12] Vasconcelos's successor, José Manuel Puig Casauranc (1924–28), exhorted schoolteachers to enjoy the privilege of working with children, whom he considered fresh, clean material not yet molded into the sad, contorted souls of adults.[13] The dissemination of the revolutionary cultural nationalism espoused by Vasconcelos and fellow ideologues found fertile soil in the elementary classrooms popping up in the countryside.[14]

In the early 1920s the *indigenismo* that flooded creative and academic production in the intellectual spheres resulted in a primary school curriculum, intended largely for urban, middle-class schoolchildren, that reified the rural indigenous population as the holders of authentic nativist sentiments. Yet these idealized depictions that valorized indigenous culture did not make their way into the pages of textbooks trucked by burro into the ever-expanding frontiers of the rural education mission. Rural children in the 1920s did not read textbooks in which the protagonists looked or lived like them. In fact, up until a National Assembly mandate in 1930, the Ministry of Public Education had separate departments for schools classified as rural, semiurban, and urban. In 1930 these classifications held, but politicians deemed the respective curricular distinctions unconstitutional and declared that Mexican children should all study from the same textbooks and be held to the same program of "progressive work."[15]

While a linear characterization of the uniform emergence of a new model of active childhood culminating in the presidency of Lázaro Cárdenas would be overreaching, evidence does point to a convergence of political idealism, policy, and practice between 1934 and 1939. A 1934 reform of constitutional Article 3 officially eliminated all distinctions between schools and ushered in an experimental but brief era of socialist education, championed by Cárdenas. The advent in socialist education marked a shift in the model of the ideal Mexican child from the aesthetic to the political, as the romantic indigenous type gave way to the *niño proletario*, or the proletarian child. The intended audience migrated as well; the government saw the burgeoning young population in the countryside as a wealthy resource to tap for the collective good of the national economy. Textbooks began to promote ideas of group citizenship over individual citizenship and promoted productivity at all levels, from the kindergartens to the state governments. Socialist education's stated goals were to transform social institutions, to achieve a better distribution of wealth, to eliminate religiosity in the classroom, and to bring the proletariat to power.[16] The proletarian child was ideally situated to bridge the gap between this radical new educational movement and his parents, seen as perhaps too entrenched in structural oppression to mobilize on their own accord. The *niño proletario* lost currency by the end of 1939, as Cárdenas conceded to pressure from religious activists to curtail the secular, anticlerical overtones of the socialist education agenda.[17]

Regardless of these pedagogical and ideological trends that brought with them compelling social models of idealized Mexican childhood, the integration of children across the nation into the revolutionary family occurred much less cleanly. Post-revisionist historians of education caution us against confusing the SEP's intent with the actual outcome of its educational initiatives.[18] Although these historians have focused their energies on the experiences of schoolteachers and community members that negotiated top-down mandates with state and municipal officials, the application of their method is instructive for the history of childhood as well. Not all children were exposed to official constructions of the symbolic child, and reasons for this abounded: some could not afford to attend school because they were needed to work at home, others attended so irregularly as to render a tiered curricular program meaningless, teachers often filtered official material according to personal beliefs or for time constraints, Catholic families withheld children from schools deemed too radically anticlerical, and middle- and upper-class urban children measured government-produced educational material against the myriad competing influences that they consumed in internationally produced children's literature. These factors and more make it impossible to outline a single contour of revolutionary Mexican childhood. To recognize the plurality of Mexican *childhoods* that were possible in an era that celebrated monolithic expressions of cultural nationalism means to recover stories both of children who conformed enthusiastically to models of the day and of those who found themselves lamentably outside of the circle of benefits that modern Mexican childhood offered to an elite few.

In effect, many children gained access to a newly constructed social category—Mexican childhood—one of a pantheon of national types erupting in popular and official culture. Beginning in the heady decade of the 1920s, the state virtually sanctioned national stereotypes into a set of icons, characters, and motifs that could be readily identified by Mexicans and foreigners alike as *lo mexicano*. In the process intellectuals and elites distilled the diverse national population into a single set of tropes carefully selected from an idealized past and projected it on the nation's walls, textbook covers, and collective memory.[19] New national types celebrated by some and derided by others included the *charro*, the *china poblana*, the proletarian, the rural schoolteacher, the *india bonita*, and the *chica moderna*. As a result of the proliferation of these stylized types, children shared more common cultural references than before. Yet even the powerful ties of unifying icons did not prevent these new generations from emerging stratified into levels of socioeconomic inequality that mirrored the past and foretold the future direction of the revolution. On the one hand, universal childhood ostensibly was available to all Mexicans. On the other hand, at the operational level, many children accessed these cultural forms on uneven terms or were denied them altogether. This was the consolidtion of the generations that would construct, constitute, and live through the Institutional Revolutionary Party's (Partido Revolucionario Institucional [PRI]) Mexico.

The revolutionary child trope and its attendant child-based reform agenda did not resonate with equal force across the population. Children growing up after the revolution experienced an undoubtedly nationalist curriculum, cultural milieu, and rhetoric that formed their identities as members of a collectivity. But they also saw, heard, and tasted the global influences that coexisted, sometimes uneasily, alongside a highly idealistic emerging cultural nationalism. As chapter 6 demonstrates, boys who joined the Mexican chapter of the Boy Scouts in the 1930s navigated the complicated terrain forged by nativist and international forces. Sometimes, these influences would seem at odds with one another: how to encourage membership from poor, indigenous members into a troop while at the same time requiring that they adhere to the British-run organization's stringent uniform mandates? And as the child artists in chapter 2 poignantly and repeatedly remind us, artistic innovations from countries such as Japan simply appealed more powerfully to some than the aesthetic styles derived from ancient indigenous motifs, supposed in the 1920s by government art educators to be inherent in Mexican children. The Mexican Revolution, therefore, did not hold a monopoly on the fickle allegiances of its children.

Counternarratives of Childhood in Revolutionary Mexico

As we have seen, the institutional framework of the SEP allowed it to be one of the dominating forces defining officially sponsored ideas of modern Mexican childhood. Others have fleshed out the complex evolution of this institution that, along with land reform and labor organization, proved to be the most powerful and influential tool wielded by the revolutionary government.[20] This is not a history of the SEP, nor is this a history of a comprehensive socializing campaign spearheaded by a monolithic government. The government was not monolithic, nor was the campaign comprehensive. Contradictions between programs under the same government agencies, and between different administrative officials, prevented the existence of any government leviathan.[21] Furthermore, the SEP did not provide the only model for civic engagement.

The Catholic Church, long accustomed to holding sway over children's moral instruction in their formative years, strongly resented the government's rapid encroachment upon children's education. Since the colonial period, the church had dominated the domain of child socialization. Even in the Liberal heyday of the Reforma (1855–76), the church successfully promoted and disseminated curricula that ran counter to the official educational materials.[22] Despite the heady momentum enjoyed by revolutionaries, a strong and persistent conservative counternarrative persisted during these decades that assailed reformers for their overt politicization of the child, their attacks on traditional gender and family roles, and their staunch policy of secularization. By the twentieth century direct attacks from the revolutionary government, particularly during the Calles administration, rather than effectively cutting off religious education, drove many urban Catholic schools underground and undercover, functioning in a diminished capacity with the support of a devout middle class.[23] Anticlerical legislation such as the 1926 law that banned crucifixes and altars from the classroom fueled the radical Catholic-based Cristero movement growing in opposition to the revolutionary government, in a program of retribution that occasionally turned spectacularly violent.[24] Despite the constitutional requirement for secular education, Catholic schools and religious education persisted.[25] Children were deployed as symbols in the conservative backlash—a discourse that countered government propaganda and curriculum through church publications, pamphlets, and editorials in the conservative press. Religious organizations promoted many child-centered initiatives—such as children's magazines, recreation centers, youth groups, summer camps, and long-distance correspondence—that paralleled those in the school system sometimes as independent programs and sometimes as an alternative to similar government programs.

As early as 1921 the Catholic children's periodical *La Vanguardia* had identified José Vasconcelos as the most corrupting influence on Mexico's youth. Editors published diatribes to their child audiences, warning them of the dangers of being seduced by an "imbecile and brute" who did not recognize Agustín Iturbide as the father of independence and who promoted "official atheism."[26] Such periodicals were often free and provided literary competition with—or complements to—officially promoted children's literature such as Vasconcelos's own compilation, *Literatura clásica para niños*, a collection of classic folk- and moral tales from around the world. While Catholic publications dedicated many of their pages to doling out dour condemnations and stringent prohibitions of cultural activities (since the movies incited adolescent homicide and suicide, and the Young Men's Christian Association [YMCA] promoted antisocial Protestantism, few church-approved activities remained for children), the spiritual life did offer its thrills for children as well. In the face of anticlericalism, a wave of "crusades" swept the nation's parishes in the early 1920s, and children turned to youth groups for social activities. Members of the Children's Eucharistic Crusades (Cruzada Eucarística de los Niños), established in the Colegio Francés in Mexico City, displayed enraptured responses to poignant Old Testament sermons.[27] In June 1923 six hundred children in Angamacútiro, Michoacán, enacted a pilgrimage to the local cemetery to honor the image of the Christ of the Sacred Heart, bearing standards that proclaimed the Cristero motto of *¡Viva Cristo Rey!*, erupting into spontaneous proclamations of joy upon arrival.[28]

Perhaps even more appealing than those activities organized by the church hierarchy were spontaneous expressions of popular piety, many of which featured children (or representations of children) as protagonists. In the village of San Francisco Ixpantepec, Oaxaca, a region largely outside of the major Cristero-government battleground, the apparition in 1928 of the Virgin Mary to a young indigenous girl named Nicha coincided with a series of natural phenomena that resulted in a surge of pilgrims and a substantial measure of ecclesiastical debate.[29] The rise to fame in the late 1920s and 1930s of a so-called child healer in the northern state of Nuevo León, known as the Niño Fidencio, lured even the staunchly anticlerical Plutarco Elías Calles for a medical consultation in 1928 (during the throes of the *Cristiada*, or Cristero revolt). Fidencio was far from a child; rather, his androgynous appearance and effeminate demeanor lent him the moniker. Perhaps his nonthreatening designation as a "child" made his miraculous brand of healing more palatable to the statesman. Regardless, the association of innocent youth and divine inspiration provided models of exceptional childhood that the religious sector could embrace and promote among children that competed with revolutionary nationalist representations. This counternarrative of alternative models of childhood, sometimes reactionary and sometimes proactive in nature, deserves a great deal more depth of study. The sources consulted here admittedly do not do justice to the many versions of childhood that did not fit the revolutionary nationalist model.

An illustration of the tenor of revolutionary detractors demonstrates recognition of the symbolic power that children had in making a political appeal to the public. Ardent demands, voiced by fictionalized child protagonists of a 1924 editorial in the conservative Mexico City daily *El Universal Gráfico*, jabbed pointedly at the excesses of the rapidly unionizing labor sector: "No more cod liver oil! Double servings of dessert! Keys to the pantry! Death to soap, combs, and other instruments of inquisitional torture! Mandatory daily lollipops! One dozen toys every week! Death to the *patria potestad*!"[30] The author of this metaphorical account, a frequent contributor of counter-revolutionary critiques working under the pseudonym Jubilo, described the secret proceedings of a newly formed children's syndicate. The union's young members, ranging in age from babbling newborns to twelve-year-olds flirting with cigarettes, gathered in resistance to the tyranny of parental and institutional control. A precocious nine-year-old boy assumed authority and rallied the diverse juvenile crowd with a reminder of the centuries of oppression endured by children at the hands of adults. He warned parents that if they did not meet these demands, the children would go on strike; they would cease to be sons and daughters and become absorbed instead into the homes of indulgent sterile and single adults longing for children to spoil. A reporter approached the boy and asked if he feared any negative reaction from his parents for his involvement in political organization. He wryly replied that no, he was an orphan—a ward, after all, of the ultimate expression of *patria potestad*: government welfare institutions. Having successfully rallied his comrades, the young leader smugly inserted his finger into his nose and left the meeting.[31]

The counterrevolutionary camp had deployed its own version of the symbolic child that impugned the morally incorruptible proletarian child ideal. At first glance Jubilo's editorial characterized unionized laborers as narcissistic children with infantile demands that undermined their long-term well-being. They snubbed their benefactors and naively thought themselves capable of self-rule. He wrote the column at a crucial moment in the history of labor, when membership in the official union, the Regional Confederation of Mexican Workers (Confederación Regional Obrera Mexicana [CROM]), expanded exponentially as its organization became more tightly centralized around the corrupt figure of labor leader Luís Morones. His article provides more than the obvious political backlash against the radicalization of labor. There is much to be discovered about the ways that conservative political and religious organizations deployed images of children as well as propaganda for children as part of their antirevolutionary foment. The tenacity of these sentiments articulated alongside the mainstream left-leaning discourse contributes to the national tension between the Eagle (state) and the Virgin (church) that characterized much of the revolutionary period.

Read through another lens, Jubilo's editorial speaks vividly to the visibility of children as social and political beings in a moment when revolutionary reforms rendered children viable social actors. Beyond the political metaphor, the children in the story came alive with youthful interests: candy, recreation, and freedom from restraints. These fictional children seized upon the politically charged atmosphere of collective action to draft a set of demands that reinforced their status as children, both physically and socially removed from the adult world. Jubilo's editorial, while fanciful and satirical, reflected a historical moment in which the concept of childhood underwent dramatic changes, created by both the goals of the Mexican Revolution and the global emergence of a modern model of childhood.[32]

Historical Actors and Cultural Liaisons:
Negotiating Children's Agency

The history of childhood, an academic pursuit spawned in the mid-twentieth century, has sought to define the parameters of human experience as shaped by collective ideas about age. At the core is the assumption that children are not full-fledged members of society relative to adults. Philippe Ariès inaugurated the field with his classic *Centuries of Childhood,* in which he argued that medieval society did not conceive of childhood as a distinct social category, an assertion supported largely by visual representations of children as miniature adults in medieval art.[33] Pioneering explorations of the changing social value of children have led to the inclusion of age as a category of historical analysis. The field currently enjoys a revival that places children at the center of historical inquiry. Among others, Colin Heywood, Peter Stearns, and Paula Fass contributed to the development of childhood studies by placing the study of childhood within a global context, revising Ariès's beleaguered assertions to account for cultural, geographic, and temporal variations.[34] To this end I take up the challenge issued by Steven Mintz for scholars to adopt a "bifocal" approach to the history of childhood: to meld adult-centered histories with those that privilege the voice and views of the child.[35]

This work forms part of the wave of scholarship examining the revolutionary programs of the 1920s and 1930s in which attention to social conditions takes priority over structural explanations in evaluating efforts to achieve the revolution's goals. The emergence of cultural history in the mid-1990s lay the foundation for research that brings top-down, government-produced history back into scholarly discussion without leaving the everyday people out. The effort to achieve cultural revolution resulted in the introduction of agencies and institutions but moved far beyond the sphere of government influence, as individuals began to fuse their own interpretations of citizenship with the official campaign. Pioneers in the study of popular culture examined festivals, material culture, and everyday behavior and found examples of the ways individuals affirmed or critiqued officials and society's status quo. This study, following the cultural history approach, examines the interaction among and negotiations between government officials and their intended audience: children.

Scholars of nationalism, as it emerged in Mexico, as elsewhere, have rightly turned to a scrutiny of the prevailing intellectual discourses and then to the institutions designed to translate rhetoric to policy. A recent study of nineteenth-century nationalism in education by Beatriz Zepeda convincingly demonstrates the need to move beyond the official and oppositional articulations of nation to the role played by institutions (namely, state-sponsored public education) in their dissemination. A close look at the institutions reveals the limits of the state's power to reach its target audience, as highly publicized proclamations and promises often fell flat in practice or as propagandistic textbooks saw negligent distribution.[36] Studies of the concerted programs of citizenship formation that characterized the highly centralized nationalist regimes of Juan Perón in Argentina and Getúlio Vargas in Brazil engage in rich analysis of the textbooks and cultural production for children intended to guarantee their loyalty to their respective nations.[37] But some of the best scholarship on the troubled relationship between nationalist ideas and practice stop short of what is perhaps the most diffuse and least understood of processes: individual reception of nationalism. I intend to nudge the examination of the transmission of nationalism into the admittedly murky waters of historical inquiry, in which children are not simply socialized by the state and its institutions but rather respond to mandates for social citizenship in diverse ways. This project requires refocusing the lens of history on the individual and validating the power of cultural reception as powerful components in the dialectic of nation building.

In my efforts to foreground the voices, experiences, and perceptions of children, it might appear that the role of parents, educators, and institutions has a diminished importance during the revolutionary decades. This most certainly is not the case. The integral role of individuals and structures in carefully and consciously governing, shaping, or transforming children's lives has been well documented by historians of modern Mexico, among which most recently the impressive works of Ann Blum, Susana Sosenski, Alberto del Castillo Troncoso, Nichole Sanders, Elsie Rockwell, Claudia Agostoni, and Mary Kay Vaughan stand out.[38] Without an understanding of the physical and rhetorical sites of interaction between the government officials and those individuals and social groups that they sought to reform, assist, educate, or heal, an investigation into the experiences of children that navigated these systems would be meaningless. Although it is not my intention to treat childhood independently from the histories of gender, women, and welfare to which it has been inextricably linked, the diversity of children's experiences merits an in-depth examination that privileges a view from below. Children did not spend all of their time in their mothers' arms or under the watchful gaze of their teachers or on the other end of a police inquisition. My intention is to move children from the aesthetic to the political realm in an analysis recently undertaken by other scholars of citizenship.[39]

Envisioning children as citizens requires extracting the term from its political definition and engaging with its multiple subjectivities. One of the limitations often encountered in deploying this term is the conflation of citizenship with the nation-state, a relationship that becomes problematic when considering children, who are often dependent upon the nation-state's institutions for their welfare and well-being, yet who (usually) cannot participate directly in its political apparatus through voting or official representation. I situate this cultural history of childhood among the burgeoning studies of citizenship, both as process and as practice. For the children in these pages, citizenship meant meaningful (even if occasional) inclusion in any of a number of interrelated and overlapping systems: the classroom, the virtual community of radio listeners, public civic performances, church organizations, and more. Sometimes meaningful inclusion in one group put the child at odds with another community to which he or she belonged, revealing the everyday contingency of citizenship practice. Citizenship is not a permanent quality bestowed upon children; it is in a constant state of redefinition and negotiation. In these cases, as scholars of "unexpected citizens" have begun to reveal, we see that children are not merely the product of the prevailing ideological or discursive systems under which they come of age; rather, they engage with those ideas and discourses in ways unforeseen by administrators, intellectuals, and other adults.[40]

Writing the history of revolutionary Mexican childhood requires the identification of the historical actors that contributed to the social and political milieu. These actors are tiered, but as I will demonstrate, their influence did not flow solely from the top down. At the top of the pyramid looms the head of the revolutionary state: pronouncements by the consecutive presidents helped listeners to imagine the symbolic child. Calles and Cárdenas in particular gave a name and a shape to that new national type. At the second tier a transnational class of professionals emerging from the heyday of positivism contributed scientific justifications for policies aiming to improve and modernize backward elements of society. At the third tier the agencies of the revolutionary state—chiefly the SEP but also the Department of Public Welfare (Beneficencia Pública)—operationalized the rhetorical flourishes and professionalized knowledge into concerted programs for child development, including provisions for the collaboration of the proverbial village. At the fourth tier, and operating at cross-purposes with the government agencies, the Catholic Church and its adherents provided parallel programs to counter the revolutionary and international influences bearing down upon them. And finally, the fifth tier, and the emphasis here, is that of the children who participated in or were the subjects of the programs, studies, and models enacted by the levels above them. Discourses and actions flowed between and among these tiers. The relationships between these actors also shifted from the mid-1920s to the 1930s. For example, the rise of transnational influences (such as commercial sponsorship by foreign-owned companies in children's magazines that promoted economic nationalism among its readership) and foreign-based organizations (such as the Boy Scouts adapted to the Mexican context) received tacit, if not overt, support from the state, suggesting shifting ideas of how to make cultural nationalism a modern phenomenon.

The cultural history of twentieth-century Mexico has enjoyed a surge in recent decades, enriched by historians who have explored the quotidian experiences of sectors of society over-looked by revisionists: environmentalists, performers, Afro-Mexicans, teenagers, gays and lesbians, expatriates, industrial workers, and Catholic activists, among other groups.[41] All of these studies have contributed discursively to a working defi-nition of citizenship, as a category both defined by Mexican contemporaries and applied by historians. The placement of children at the center of revolutionary reforms, rhetorically and literally, has received short shrift in scholarship of the era; in many of the excellent monographs mentioned above, chil-dren appear only when they are in trouble (institutionalized, unhealthy, in physical or moral peril, or as political mascots).[42] The present study revises this oversight by placing children rightly at the center of Mexico's revolutionary narrative.

Children further confuse the already muddled definition of citizenship. Barring political rights, what is the fullest way that we can expect children to meaningfully behave as citizens? In its early years, the revolution purported to uphold the full-est implementation of Liberal philosophy, extending member-ship in the nation to all Mexicans. Revolutionary citizenship did not equate voting rights—these were legally denied to all women and effectively denied to a vast number of indigenous men. In fact, revolutionary citizenship seemed to have much less to do with the rights and benefits due to the nation's mem-bers and more to do with the civic duties and responsibilities owed to the *patria* in exchange for the privilege of membership. The Children's Moral Code of 1925, intended for elementary schoolchildren to memorize and recite at the start of each day, summarized the government's expectations of the populace in eleven "laws" regulating behavior and social attitudes.[43] Once again, the existence and brief implementation of this pledge suggest only the ideal at best. Nevertheless, the vast scale and rapid pace of child-oriented programs, literature, services, and education during the 1920s and 1930s underscore the assertions made by scholars of childhood that children's exclusion from political rights does not mean they are excluded from political *life*.[44] In fact, the cases here suggest that children can actually become political *agents*—with a range of self-consciousness. And even in the many cases in which children served as unwitting political pawns, as we shall see, mimicry became a practice, as other children watched their peers allegedly gain a political voice. Studying citizenship practiced by children, then, allows us to expand our definition of what it means to participate meaningfully in the construction of a nation, from above and below, from within and from the outside.

This book is as much about the origins of memory as it is about the construction of the modern Mexican state or the analysis of childhood as a category. As theorized by Maurice Halbwachs in his ruminations on the collective memory of the family, the common past of the Revolutionary Family formed the baseline sensory and material experiences from which a new citizenry matured.[45] Jane Eva Baxter noted that most adults do not recall how they experienced the world as a child. In her work as an archaeologist of childhood, she sifts through the material remains of a past occluded by both time and the elements to restore to modern understanding the relationships between children, their toys and tools, and the communities in which they lived.[46] Rooting through twentieth-century archival materials turns up its share of dust, though it is not nearly as gritty an endeavor. Nonetheless, a concentrated focus on recovering the historical remnants left by children—whether by their own hands or languishing between the lines of adult-produced histories—can be equally rewarding, as it allows us to piece together childhoods forgotten not only by history but perhaps even by the grown-up children themselves in their later years.

Following the path paved by other historians, my main preoccupation here is to recover, to the extent possible, children's individual and collective efforts to process, editorialize, or repro-

duce the cultural values and tenets of citizenship conceptualized for them by the revolutionary government. Every historical
voice that enters the record suffers some form of mediation,
in the form of either self-editing, official censorship, or subtle
manipulation of fact through interpretations of a third party.
Children's history is no different. Their documents, even when
written in children's own hands, often have suffered one or
all of the above modifications from the pure intentionality of
thought. In any case, children's heightened visibility, especially
in the publicity that accompanies nation-building projects, merits a closer inquiry of the records that they left behind.

Recent scholarship has attested to the dynamic nature of
child socialization rather than the more structuralist version
promoted by sociologist Norbert Elias in his influential tome
The Civilizing Process.[47] In the chapters that follow I trace the vari-
able expressions of individuality—and conformity—that children produced through their interactions with new forms of
media, technology, and popular culture. The respective contexts
of art classes, radio, puppet shows, student organizations, and
political rallies resulted in varying degrees of creative maneuver for the children participating in them. While children's
educational radio programming emitted uniform content to
all listeners, the radio itself relieved parents and teachers of
supervising duties and afforded children more autonomy in
their interpretive responses to the shows. Although the rigid
guidelines of the official art curriculum dictated form, art pupils
enjoyed considerable leeway in their choice of subject matter.
Furthermore, as suggested by Foucault, within a highly super-
vised space one experiments with and develops new skills for
self-expression. The number of child matriculates in Open
Air Painting Schools (Escuelas de Pintura al Aire Libre) who
went on to artistic careers testifies to the permanence of some
of these cultural programs.[48]

There will always be intangibles that leave a historian of
childhood unsatisfied with her work. The task of trying to measure the power of cultural forces on the impressionable minds
and unchecked imaginations of young people seems daunt-

ing. How could we access that fleeting sensation felt by a street child leafing through the pages of a discarded *Universal Ilustrado* upon seeing a printed photograph of a popular paperboy "type"? How would that sensation compare to the role-playing fantasy temporarily experienced by a wealthy urban child dressing as a *china poblana* for the local charity festival? What did Otomí children in rural Tlaxcala envision when they listened to descriptions of unknown technologies come crackling across the airwaves on their newly installed community radio? These diverse, hypothetical experiences illustrate that the nature of nation building was uneven, multivalent, fragmented, and overlapping. It did not produce a single outcome, but there were common threads that held together the fragments, and there were enough of them to begin to bind the revolutionary generations together in meaningful ways.

New technologies introduced during these decades paired with new ideologies that ruled children's physical spaces and social interactions. New codes of conduct emerged, framed as revolutionary citizenship. As we will see, these new networks of sociability were enacted immediately following the revolution. Just as immediately, new conduct became reinforced, internalized, and identified as the standard of normativity. Adherence to freshly scripted revolutionary civic behavior paved for some children the path to distinction. Conversely, the failure to behave according to the revolutionary script—a condition usually informed by lack of access—relegated certain groups of children to the margins of modern Mexican childhood. The blueprint for a twentieth-century political culture that rewarded party allegiance began to be etched in children's cultural domains of the 1920s and 1930s.

I make a particular effort to identify the extent to which historically marginalized children experienced official campaigns of cultural nationalism differently from their urban, nonindigenous counterparts. In some unique cases, this difference took the form of a more intense and concerted effort to reform indigenous children into the mestizo Mexican ideal, while in other cases *indigenista* reformers set these children on a pedestal that soared far above the often grim realities of their day-to-day lives. To this end I strive to recapture, and validate, the fleeting experience of childhood. In the process, by insinuating their perspective into the rich tapestry of revolutionary Mexican history being spun by historians of women, the middle class, conservatives, bureaucrats, educators, politicians, indigenous people, teenagers, and other individuals and social groups, we can begin to better understand the extent and limitations of the abstract concepts of democracy and citizenships as they were lived by twentieth-century Mexicans.

Structure and Organization

This book explores the relationships between adult-produced rhetoric and policies that placed children at the center of plans for creating new revolutionary citizens in the period from 1921 to 1940, the establishment of new agencies to achieve this goal, the adaptation of the new mass media to the campaign, the influence of transnational models of modern childhood, and the responses of children to these multivalent cultural forces. The revolutionary campaign created a popular cultural and educational program in which children interacted with other children on local, national, and international levels, as they learned and contributed to ideas about citizenship and nation.

Chapter 1 outlines the structural framework within which children became more visible and vocal in the public eye and constitutes the adult-centered side of this book's binary. I explore adult-produced rhetoric and policies emerging from two institutional hallmarks in the history of modern Mexican childhood in 1921: the First Mexican Congress of the Child (Primer Congreso Mexicano del Niño) (as well as the Pan-American Child Congresses in which Mexico subsequently participated) and the creation of the Ministry of Education. Intellectuals and politicians involved with these institutions placed children at the center of plans to create new revolutionary citizens. Lawmakers, professionals, and governors attempted to construct a homogeneous generation of citizens through the balanced application of sound pedagogy, firm ideology, and modern medicine.

Adults transformed public space to heighten the visibility of the (healthy) child and assumed new rhetorical styles that refashioned the child as a metaphor for the nation's future—not a new formula but rather a tried-and-true metaphor infused with fresh revolutionary buzzwords. Revolutionary officials consciously attempted to create a homogeneous generation of revolutionary citizens from the top down, through the professionalization of child-related fields, the transformation of public space, the reiteration of visual motifs in public art, and the dissemination of an official bureaucratic language that placed children at the center of reforms and public policies.

Chapters 2, 3, and 4 explore three different cultural domains funded by the Ministry of Education that contributed to forging a sense of generational unity among children. The expressions of cultural nationalism embodied in puppet theater, radio, and art magazines, respectively, introduced new cultural references that united children from across the country. As each chapter demonstrates, children responded uniquely to each of these programs en masse, sometimes in unexpected ways. A close look at children's interactions with these three new cultural offerings also reveals the persistence of familiar patterns of inclusion and exclusion.

In chapter 2 I examine the project of constructing a national aesthetic from the bottom up through the Ministry of Education's art education program. Spearheaded by Adolfo Best Maugard, with the implementation of his indigenous motif-based curriculum, *Método de dibujo*, in the public schools in 1921, and transformed by Juan Olaguíbel through the children's art magazine *Pulgarcito*, children learned to reproduce distilled tropes of their cultural heritage and natural surroundings. As a free, government-funded publication with nationwide dissemination from 1925 to 1932, *Pulgarcito* reveals the uneven process of nation building made evident by disparities in participation levels from urban and rural child contributors. *Pulgarcito* was unique in its nearly entirely child-produced content; its pages abound with children's commentary, both textual and visual, of the changing world around them. The national art curriculum—with *Pulgarcito* as its main evangelist—incorporated excursions and natural observation into the lesson plans, with an emphasis on iconic natural sites such as the volcano Popocatépetl. Art instructors encouraged the creation of an indigenist, social realist, Mexico City–centered aesthetic, which children dutifully reproduced in the magazine and in art competitions. Mexican children earned fervent international acclaim for their uniformity and thematic cohesion in their design and illustration, as their drawings won competitions around the world. Yet the pages of *Pulgarcito,* and especially the letters to the editor, reveal the disjuncture between urban and rural children (and, by definition, between middle-class and impoverished children), both in their access to forms of popular entertainment such as *Pulgarcito* and in the expectations that revolutionaries had of the two classes of children. The social inequalities apparent through an analysis of the seemingly innocuous art program paralleled the growing disenfranchisement of the rural poor in the wake of the promise of revolutionary reform.

From 1932 to 1965 itinerant puppet theater Teatro Guiñol, conceptualized by socialist intellectuals, sponsored by the Ministry of Education, trucked out children's versions of revolutionary ideology to rural elementary schools. Focusing on the most heavily funded decade of the 1930s, in chapter 3 I analyze the transcripts of the plays, correspondence between the puppeteers and upper-level bureaucrats regarding performances, letters from schoolteachers detailing children's responses, and drawings of the puppets by the children who observed the plays. Children's reactions to the plays reveal a disconnect between the production and the reception of these puppet shows, suggesting weaknesses in the state's top-down dissemination of cultural nationalism. While children's drawings may well have been filtered by adult editorial interventions, they nevertheless constitute genuine—and rare—firsthand responses to official programs intended for their benefit.

Radio emerged in the 1920s against a backdrop of new or newly available technological innovations, including the typewriter, the elevator, and the electrified trolley car. In chapter 4

I describe the children's radio programming from the official Ministry of Education station XFX and argue that radio technology tightened the web connecting children in urban and rural areas and pushed young imaginations to conceptualize common experiences shared with invisible friends. Radio transformed the cultural landscape by adding a new sensory component to the feeling of collective identity described by Benedict Anderson in his discussion of print media. Children wrote letters to the program editors in response to the children's shows; sometimes they complied with the assignments and activities suggested to them over the airwaves, but just as often they contested the terms of their participation, demonstrating a keen awareness of their relative social positions among their peers. The letters, penned in the children's own unsteady hands, contain self-reflexive references to socioeconomic status, age bias, national politics, civic engagement, and capitalist values. They suggest a surprising degree of civic engagement and class consciousness on the part of children and shed a sliver of light onto children's reception of universal education programs broadcast nationwide.

Chapters 5 and 6 explore the processes of internalizing and exporting the above-described tenets of cultural nationalism by tracing children's involvement in national organizations and international organizations, respectively. They demonstrate, in the first case, the logistics involved in learning something as abstract as love for one's country and, in the second case, the mechanisms by which children learned to express this new brand of nationalism abroad through membership in international organizations. In chapter 5 I explore extracurricular activities with national coverage that allowed children to sample political life through participation in children's conferences, literacy campaigns, student councils, and antialcohol manifestations, all of which bore the bureaucratic trappings that would be expected from those with adult participants. First, I argue that the visibility of children in public spaces contributed significantly to the expansion of the definition of democracy. Second, I make a parallel connection between the rapidly bureaucratizing Mexican state in the 1930s—with the consolidation of the ruling official political party, the National Revolution Party (Partido Nacional de la Revolución [PNR])—and the hierarchical structures that emerged in children's organizations. As the previous chapters suggested, inequalities and ruptures pervaded the top-down cultural programs intended to unify the generation; in this chapter I systematically dismantle the myth of cultural nationalism. National children's organizations during the 1930s bore the bureaucratic hallmarks of exclusionism, hierarchies, and classism that mirrored those becoming evident in the political culture of the revolutionary years and foreshadowed the future of twentieth-century Mexican social stratification.

In chapter 6 I expand my analysis to the international sphere, as Mexican children began to participate in transnational—and primarily Pan-American—exchanges among schoolchildren through the Junior Red Cross, pen-pal exchange programs, and the Boy Scouts. Membership in organizations with an international scope allowed Mexican youth to see themselves as part of a hemispheric family, united by a common race and common colonial heritage. Through their letters, presence at international conferences, individual travel experiences, or exchange of cultural goods (including charity goods, drawings, telephone conversations, and national scrapbook albums), participating children exported a version of Mexican cultural nationalism. Self-conscious expressions of a collective identity based on membership in a nation—and the symbols, images, and histories upon which this identity is constructed—are encoded in these materials exchanged between groups of schoolchildren. Meanwhile, global youth identities, and the attendant reaffirmation of gender norms, made their mark on the Mexican national chapters. The ideologically charged "proletarian child" trope, held aloft in particular by the Cárdenas administration as the revolution's most powerful agent, teetered unsteadily alongside that of the young modern global citizen, a white Western middle-class ideal normalized in the propaganda emanating from the international headquarters of these Anglophile organizations.

As I dip into these varied cultural programs available to revolutionary children, I intend to demonstrate the gradual changes to childhood that evolved from the didactic nativism of the 1920s (demonstrated in the development of the visual arts program and the educational goals of children's radio programs) to the modernizing nationalism of the 1930s (evident in the bureaucratizing tendencies of school organizations and the popularity of the Boy Scouts and the Red Cross). These changes reflect evolving conceptions of the role that children ought to play in the nation. Throughout these two decades children responded as children will: with ambivalence, with delight, with unexpected fervor, and with lackadaisical resignation. Children like Enrique, writing from his home in the women's prison, capture that tension between the ideal and the mundane. Some embraced the socializing goals as if according to a script and became modern Mexican revolutionary citizens. But others—many, or even most—adapted the revolutionary government's cultural initiatives alongside other powerful influences of family, the agricultural calendar, foreign popular culture, and the church to construct their own version of what it meant to be Mexican.

CHAPTER ONE

Constructing Citizens

Adult-Produced Science, Space, Symbolism, and Rhetoric for the Revolutionary Child

What a beautiful spectacle, that after ten years of incessant divisions between brothers and persecutions among groups of Mexicans, after ten years of combat and blood, as though arising from the ashes and purified by fire, men of science are gathering to treat academically the instruction, the hygiene, the surgery, the medicine, and the beauty of the child.

> —JOSÉ VASCONCELOS, opening speech of the First Mexican Congress
> of the Child, *El Universal,* January 2, 1921

We students should intervene in the decoration and setup of our classrooms, to perpetuate in our own style something of our national identity.

> —CONSUELO DURÁN, HERLINDA REYNA, and ROMÁN HERNÁNDEZ,
> child delegates at the First Conference of Child Peasants and Workers,
> *El Nacional,* October 18, 1936

In perhaps a fated turn of events, the newly elected president, Álvaro Obregón, fell ill on a winter evening in 1921 when he was scheduled to deliver the inaugural address of the First Mexican Congress of the Child. In his stead José Vasconcelos, at the time head of Bellas Artes and the National University, issued poetic opening remarks that suggested the redemptive power of the child in the wake of a devastating decade of bloodbath. In less than a year Vasconcelos would take charge of the Ministry of Education, created in October 1921, arguably the most influential government bureau in the early twentieth century. Vasconcelos himself would take the first steps in expanding the school system into the rural reaches of the country, creating and implementing a national curriculum, with the goal of teaching every child what it meant to be Mexican. To that end Vasconcelos and a cadre of intellectuals (many among his cohort in the Ateneo de la Juventud, the generation of intellectuals that bridged the positivist *científicos*—nineteenth-century scientific advisers to Porfirio Díaz—and the revolutionary ideologues) used the First Mexican Congress of the Child to spearhead a movement that placed the child at the forefront of the long process of national reconstruction. This official gathering marked the beginning of a rhetorical and conceptual shift in the definition of childhood, both in Mexico and around the world. Intellectual, visual, and physical spaces opened up to make room for the child in society—albeit a symbolic child distilled to a handful of idealized characteristics. In the decades that followed Vasconcelos's opening salvo, revolutionary officials became both more professional and more concerned with children, especially in educational programs, creating what family historian Ann Blum has called a child-centered society in the 1920s and 1930s.[1] By the end of the Cárdenas administration (1934–40), the heyday of the proletarian child, child-centered official rhetoric and reforms had become institutionalized to the point of rendering them autocratic and stagnant.

Confronted with a frustrating dearth of firsthand accounts from children, scholars have posited that the only way to study the child is through the official discourses, images, and strategies employed by adults to construct their worlds.[2] To the contrary, I argue that an approximation of children's experience that privileges the child's voice is possible, and I dedicate most of the rest of this book to the child's perspective growing up in a society ostensibly tailor-made for their personal success and physical well-being. Yet understanding what it was like for children in the 1920s and 1930s to grow up as embodiments of the revolution requires an overview of the official discourse produced by adults that governed their world and the ways these adults refashioned Victorian and Porfirian ideas about children in the decades of revolutionary social reforms. Adults provided the rhetorical devices, and constructed the physical spaces, into which the new Mexican child must now fit.

The adult-produced sources consulted here constitute the leading ideas about children that emerged after 1921. Revolutionary officials produced an overwhelming body of documents, legislation, and propaganda during these decades with the intention of instructing the adults on raising the nation's children. Striving to replace the decimated population with a productive, ideologically committed generation, officials imagined an ideal revolutionary child and disseminated the image among the nation's mothers, schoolteachers, and community members. Sampling this literature reveals not just the institutional reform that marked this new child-centered era but the accompanying ideas about age—and attendant categories of race, class, and gender—that drove these reforms.

Congressional deputies debated educational reform programs that disclosed their ideas about biological age as it related to social roles and their decisions to build parks transforming the urban landscape specifically to include the child. Proceedings from the First Mexican Congress of the Child and the Pan-American Child Congresses—especially the one hosted by Mexico in 1935—not only disclose an explosion in the number of agencies and institutions designed specifically to socialize and perfect the child but also indicate that these agencies provided new professional opportunities for women by virtue of their state-sanctioned authority of issues relating to children. Specialized government publications and radio bulletins on child care and hygiene supplemented the educational programs and institutional reforms to ensure that adults aligned home life with the government campaign to construct the ideal citizen. Finally, presidential collections contain thousands of letters from average citizens who repeated the new rhetoric, reflecting at once the internalization of the public campaign for the revolutionary child and an astute use of this rhetoric for personal goals. Taken as a whole, these sources indicate a consensus among adults across social and economic classifications that the child belonged primarily to the nation. This abstract "nation" composed of myriad individuals with diverse backgrounds and authority levels existed most clearly in rhetorical treatments of the child.

Beginning in the early 1920s, officials strove to construct universal childhood through a common set of experiences and to subject it to a standard measure of normalcy defined by biology. Despite these efforts, the ideal childhood remained an exclusive category. As professionals honed their vision of young citizenship, differentiated models of childhood emerged: the *protected childhood,* a middle-class vestige of the nineteenth century, persisted alongside its emerging binary of the *endangered childhood.*[3] Street children, working children (forced into early adulthood out of economic necessity or as a result of abandonment), and non-Spanish-speaking native children were targeted for reform to become the ideal children that professionals conjured up in conferences and debates. The stark socioeconomic differences that marked these competing versions of childhood evolved with the revolution. By the onset of Lázaro Cárdenas's administration, a new official model had emerged that rendered these distinctions irrelevant by overtly glorifying the working class: the *proletarian childhood.* The proletarian child, a political and rhetorical device, evolved hand in hand with the implementation of the Socialist School (Escuela Socialista) in 1935 and became the unofficial mascot of events surrounding the 1935 Pan-American Child Congress.

The conscious construction of childhood during these decades reminds us that adults owned the means of producing and disseminating knowledge; they operated the press, enforced legislation, and wrote the curriculum. Adults created the parameters within which the successive generations came to understand themselves as citizens. Lest this chapter create the impression of structural determinism, future chapters will delve into the complexities of children's growing self-awareness and responses to government and popular child-centered culture within this political climate. As we will see, the discourses, institutions, and physical spaces conceptualized for the socialization of revolutionary children did not produce clean or uncontested results. Nevertheless, the present chapter examines the science, the geography, the visual, and the rhetorical treatments of children that adults produced as a framework for understanding parameters in which multiple and contested citizenships were forged.

Each section below follows a roughly chronological trajectory that traces evolving official and popular treatments of childhood through the first decades of the twentieth century in different cultural domains created by adults, extending back and forward from 1920 to 1940. First, this chapter explores the professionalization and development of official attitudes about children as they emerged and evolved in the postrevolutionary decades, in particular by comparing and contrasting two high-profile conferences in 1921 and 1935. Second, it describes the way that reformers carved out physical spaces for children in response to scientific conclusions drawn by health and educational experts at these intellectual gatherings. As a result, these decades saw a transformation of city parks, school patios, and welfare institutions, newly designed to place children in the scrutiny of the public eye. Third, it examines the degree to which the Mexican public absorbed, employed, and negotiated rhetorical treatments of the symbolic child through their petitions to agents of the state. Finally, it reviews the ways that government officials and artistic intellectuals deployed rhetorical and visual tropes of the proletarian child as a national redeemer. While not strictly linear, the structure of this chapter should demonstrate the eventual emergence by the mid-1930s of a more politicized, though still idealized, understanding of revolutionary childhood.

Science: Conferences and the Professionalization of Pediatric Knowledge

The turn of the century marked the heyday of scientific approaches to pediatric knowledge worldwide. In the United States the Progressive Era (1890s through the end of World

War I) ushered in a spate of social reforms that regulated children's health, hygiene, labor, education, and upbringing. Much of the legislation targeted the urban poor and immigrants; in the best of cases reformers looked upon these groups with compassion, although often they assumed a mission to civilize the perceived "dangerous classes."[4] Porfirian positivists and American Progressives constituted the transnational intellectual milieu, a generation of social science intellectuals who exchanged and mutually informed national policies on both sides of the U.S.-Mexico border. While Mexican professionals responded to Western scientific trends, adapting them to a nationalist discourse of constructing a modern mestizo nation, the period before the Americanization of social sciences (1930s–45) allowed Mexicans to enjoy a sliver of the global spotlight as an innovator in forging a modern nation.[5] A wide range of citizen-building campaigns targeted women, children, and the family in the early twentieth century.[6] Mexico emerged from its revolution enthusiastic to embrace a post–World War I era and join other modern nations that sought to expand the civic participation—if not full citizenship rights—of their historically marginalized populations. This section traces the evolution of scientific knowledge produced about and applied to Mexican children in the professional sphere.

The nineteenth century saw the rise of positivism—science-based methods of social improvement—with agents of hygiene focused on institutions for improving sanitary conditions. The Porfirian schoolhouse in Mexico City had as its goal the separation of the child from the home. In fact, schoolteachers literally washed the home off the children when they crossed the school's threshold, and the schools served as an enclosed fortress, completely distinct from children's familiar domestic spaces.[7] Following the revolution, officials reversed the division of home and school and sought instead to bring both of these sectors in alignment with the revolutionary program. They carried this out most notably through the practice of social pediatrics and the 1929 introduction of home hygiene inspectors, concerned not just with children's illnesses but also with their place in the concentric human circles of the family, the class-room, and the community.[8] In the revolutionary era scientific treatment of children acquired a strongly nationalist character administered by new professionals in the fields of eugenics, puericulture (the science of child care), pediatrics, and psychology. The overhaul of the educational system purported to draw the family into public education and extend the government's effort to sanitize institutions into the home.

A cadre of child specialists emerged who shared an intellectual continuity with the *positivistas* trained in the Porfirian era (1876–1911). Scientific knowledge about the child flowed from European techniques such as psychometrics and phrenology and acquired a Latin American flavor after being steeped in Vasconcelos's "cosmic race" ideology of mestizo racial fusion at the pinnacle of the human racial composite, a philosophy he developed over the course of his tenure as minister of education.[9] The shift toward the child-centered approach to social hygiene received a boost from the 1924 Geneva Convention on the Rights of the Child; by ratifying the agreements postulated in this international summit, Mexican officials positioned their nation among the foremost countries making economic and intellectual investments in the youth.[10] A comparison of two major child-related conferences—the First Mexican Congress of the Child in 1921 and the VII Pan-American Child Congress in 1935—suggests the evolution of the professional treatment of children from one steeped in positivism to an attempt to foster meaningful civic engagement.

The touchstone event marking the revolution's commitment to children's health and hygiene came in the 1921 First Mexican Congress of the Child, financed and presided over by Dr. Félix Palavicini and sponsored by the government of Álvaro Obregón.[11] The First Mexican Congress of the Child brought together the country's best and brightest professionals in a three-week show-case of strategies to prevent and correct any social, physical, or mental deviance among children. Professionals expounded on numerous topics in six sections: Eugenics, Education, Pediatric Surgery, Pediatric Medicine, Hygiene, and Legislation.[12] Presentations outlined the successes and goals of the school lunch and free milk programs, the problems presented by children working alongside their parents in the markets, the creation of farm schools, ways to combat child delinquency, and legislation regarding child labor, among other themes.[13] As a testament to its success, the event resulted in a second congress in 1923. Still, these early efforts established the child as a barometer of the nation's health. Integration of children into civic life had not yet entered the picture. The tenor of this conference stemmed directly from the Porfirian-style scientific approach to children, keeping in sight the end goal of perfecting the national population.

Palavicini's position as editor of the national daily paper *El Universal* also ensured favorable—and ample—coverage of the conference proceedings so that readers nationwide could be kept abreast of the progress of the revolutionary political elites. Months in advance of the conference's inauguration, Palavicini began to run public surveys about the significance of a professional gathering on this topic and published the enthusiastic acclaim in heady anticipation of the event. The children featured in the conference announcements, which Palavicini published almost daily, embodied the clean, cared-for, happy, lighter-skinned, middle-class ideal that the meeting sought to establish as the national standard (fig. 1).[14] Palavicini's public canvasses both documented and fomented popular support for one of the revolutionary government's first professional initiatives in collaboration with the professional elites from the private sector. *El Universal* also benefited from a hearty dose of self-promotion, as Palavicini's charitable generosity in sponsoring the event did not go unattributed. Thus, the Porfirian paradigm of an alliance between government and intellectuals based on scientific "positive verification" had been restored, only this time draped in revolutionary rhetoric.

The congresses yielded a number of empirical studies and programs designed to quantify and perfect the child. Foremost, the presenters pursued normalcy, which could be determined only upon achieving total knowledge of the child. At

EL CONGRESO MEXICANO DEL NIÑO

1. *El Universal*, February 1920. Courtesy of the Biblioteca Miguel Lerdo de Tejada.

the congress physician Rafael Santamarina laid out the benefits of a comprehensive profile of the normal Mexican child—
the only other available models at the time were from French
children—as a tool against which to measure children's psychology and biology.[15] Santamarina followed a brand of nationalist eugenics popular in Latin America that valued the mestizo
race above the Anglo ideal (though still privileging Hispanic
physiognomy over indigenous characteristics). At the core of
his inquiries was a belief in the rigidity of categories of age as
biologically determined stages of development.[16] Bolstered by
the publicity and impetus generated at the congress, the following year Santamarina launched the long-term diagnostic
Study of the Mexican Child (Estudio del Niño Mexicano) to
quantify physical and mental development across a sampling
of the nation's children for the purpose of pinpointing areas
of improvement.[17] Daily, over the course of the study, nurses
brought carefully selected middle-class students from the public
school system—those deemed to be "normal" in every sense—to
the offices of the Ministry of Public Health (Secretaría de Salubridad Pública), where medical officials conducted a series of
tests adapted from international sources.[18]

Building upon the momentum gained over four years of accumulating data, in 1925 Santamarina established the Department of Psychopedagogy and Hygiene (Departamento de Psicopedagogía e Higiene) as an agency of the SEP. Children's Hygiene Centers (Servicio de Higiene Infantil) began opening their doors around the country as outposts of the government initiative to ensure that mothers were supplementing federal care of their children's health. The Ministry of Public Health sought to closely supervise mothers, especially those from humble backgrounds, in child-care issues, including hygiene, breast-feeding, home ventilation, and meal preparation.[19] The SEP, for its part, became increasingly vigilant over the architectural aspects of the classroom, in an effort to provide proportionally perfect accommodations—utopist, some argued—so as not to hinder learning through any physical impingement of the child's workspace.[20] In all of these efforts, remnants of positivist quantitative approaches became infused with a new revolutionary purpose in the pursuit of the perfectibility of the child.

A global shift in social and political treatment of children had been evolving since World War I and saw its most strident expression in the 1924 Geneva Declaration of the Rights of the Child. Though not legally binding, this document ratified by the League of Nations was the first to articulate the legal and personal rights of children and did so by placing the physical and emotional welfare of children in the hands of the nation-state. Across the globe countries that considered themselves modern began to revise the more clinical treatments of children that had prevailed in the nineteenth century and began to develop programs and institutions (both within the ambit of the state and run by private organizations) that promoted the idea of the child as an active citizen. These transnational ideas meshed well with the democratizing auspices of the revolutionary administrations in Mexico.

By the 1930s, though, eugenics-based approaches began to give way to the power of cultural nationalist discourses that sought to activate the innate potential of working-class children. Over the course of the 1920s and 1930s, Mexico sent delegates to the Pan-American Child Congresses and hosted the prestigious international event in 1935, when winning the bid against its continental counterparts to host the seventh annual conference represented a major victory for the revolutionary government of Lázaro Cárdenas.[21] The high-profile hosting duty allowed Mexico an opportunity to express Cárdenas's populist preference for the working classes in the context of modern approaches to fostering nationalism and to articulate this program to an international audience. U.S. delegate Katherine Lenroot, in her inaugural speech contextualizing the selection of Mexico, pointed to the country as the best positioned to bridge Latin and Anglo-Saxon civilizations and lauded the nation's advances in the protection of children (though she awkwardly praised the country for its conscious preservation of the "high level" of culture from the motherland, Spain, while actively pursuing the "development" of indigenous culture).[22] Enjoying the international limelight, conference delegates officially designated the week of the conference as the Week of the Child (Semana del Niño) and supplemented conference sessions with an array of public cultural events, charity drives, and festivals either featuring children or arranged for their benefit.

The executive committee made certain not to disappoint visiting delegates and supplemented the weeklong academic panels with various activities to showcase national advances in child welfare. Participants enjoyed elegant banquets at the city's upscale eateries, toured the most modern welfare facilities, and, in most scripted fashion, interacted with the young beneficiaries of the revolutionary programs. Mexican delegate Rosaura Zapata, serving at the time as inspector of kindergartens, organized a festival in the Parque Lira, in which kindergarteners from the Tacubaya neighborhood lined the leafy walkways dressed in various regional costumes, tents exhibited the classroom carpentry and artisan workshops taught in kindergartens, and a puppet show delighted everyone present. The exhibition featured the very young children's artistic prowess, and photographs of the event show primly dressed children proudly showing off their paintings of national landscapes,

2. A kindergarten class proudly demonstrates their art in the Parque Lira in an exhibition of Mexican schoolchildren's successes for the visiting international delegates to the Pan-American Children's Conference, 1935. AGN Fototeca, Archivo Fotográfico Díaz, Delgado y García, Caja 55/17.

while other "proletarian children" dressed in overalls demonstrate class-appropriate brick-building techniques to a crowd of international delegates (figs. 2 and 3). Delegates also visited Santamarina's Child Hygiene Centers, the milk distribution center in downtown Mexico City, and a government-run children's home. One day trip introduced visitors to the three- to six-year-old residents of the new, modern Coyoacán orphanage, the Casa de Cuna. The children's well-being, and by extension the state's beneficence, was on display for the delegates, as the small scrubbed and pressed government charges performed folkloric songs and dances that surpassed expectations for their tender age. From the Casa de Cuna, the delegates proceeded to the Tlalpan children's home Casa del Niño, where children—aged six to twelve—received residential vocational education. Director Rafael Sierra Domínguez greeted the conference del-

3. "Proletarian children" dressed in overalls demonstrate their manual labor abilities in Parque Lira for the Pan-American Child Congress, 1935. AGN Fototeca, Archivo Fotográfico Díaz, Delgado y García, Caja 55/17.

egates, inviting them to observe the efforts of the Department of Public Welfare (Beneficencia Pública) in its daily struggle to secure the future for those children who lacked the support of their families.[23] The visitors were also treated to a sampling of local lore and ritual in a reenactment of ritual human sacrifice at the Teotihuacán pyramids just outside Mexico City.[24] The stylized ceremony, staged against the impressive archaeological ruins in the hot desert sun, must have posed a striking contrast to the ultramodern buildings filled with robust children whom the delegates met during their stay in the city. The children provided a reminder of the great civilizing strides the revolutionary government had accomplished for the welfare of its citizenry, performed against the physical remnants of a distant past rife with savage disregard for human life.

At the VII Pan-American Child Congress, the number of Mexican delegates—with an impressive representation from women—far outstripped their Pan-American counterparts.

The professions still divided along gendered lines—men in the hard sciences, medical fields, and organizing committee and women in areas of pedagogy and child care—but women's presence in the conference marked a significant departure from the male exclusivity of the Porfirian positivist days.[25] The conference provided new opportunities for women to engage in professional development and public policy working through organizations such as the National Association for the Protection of Children (Asociación Nacional por la Protección de la Infancia) and the Society for the Protection of Children (Sociedad Protectora de la Infancia), often sponsored by Mexico's first ladies. These child-centered professional activities created one of the early platforms for women to exercise political power in the wake of the 1916 Feminist Conference in Mérida, Yucatán, and leading up to women's suffrage process that culminated in the national right to vote in 1954.[26] In the face of increasing attention to children as a group that merited political action, women gained leverage as public figures and experts by taking advantage of their role as primary caretakers to claim places in the institutionalization of child welfare and welfare policy reform.

The Pan-American Child Congresses revealed the changing paradigm of child welfare by the 1930s that placed the child, and not the family, at the center of reform and policy initiatives. Recalling an emphasis on individual rights as clearly stated in the Liberal constitution of 1857, introducing the *child* as an individual reflected the interpretation of individual rights and the expanded concept of citizenship promised in the revolutionary Constitution of 1917. A strong thread of continuity from the Porfirian era still emphasized building the national family by pairing the woman with the government in a joint effort to raise the nation's children, corresponding to a time in which the state assumed a role in the family triangle by redefined masculinity (and models of fatherhood) as being associated with labor outside of the home. Increasingly, even the mother found herself nudged from the equation. Conference delegates turned to the child as a model, a member of his or her family, classroom, and community, perfectible almost wholly through guidance by medical, psychological, and educational officials.

Government officials strove to become the main authority rearing the child, with mothers as the recipients of official information, acting as government agents in their own homes. The revolutionary government continued to rely on child internment rather than offering social services directly to needy families and suggested an unwillingness to relinquish the child entirely to the care of mothers.[27] Instead, mothers brought their children to government offices such as the Child Hygiene Centers for medical care and advice. Some mothers read the *Mexican Mother's Book* (*Libro para la madre mexicana*), promoted by First Lady Aída Rodríguez in 1933, and learned the official, middle-class version of correct child rearing. Inspectors evaluated domestic circumstances to ensure that women met the national standards for cleanliness. Women entered into a relationship with these officials in raising the child, but not on equal footing and not with trust in their maternal instinct.

Both the First Mexican Congress of the Child and the VII Pan-American Child Congress attest to the development of a child-centered revolutionary society. A comparison between the two suggests that between 1921 and 1935, state officials had configured the child as an idealized metaphor for the nation but had made strides toward rendering the child visible, both to the national and to the international public, as proof of Mexico's progress toward modern nationhood. An examination of the transformations to public spaces that accompanied the knowledge generated and shared in these conferences suggests the ways that children began to be "seen" by the state.

Space: Patios, Parks, Playgrounds, and the Public Visibility of the Child

The public sphere, a space for convergence and debate among private individuals interested in public issues, is a necessary reference point for understanding citizenship practice. Jürgen Habermas's now classic treatment of the public sphere transcends physical spaces and legal categorization, operating instead as a set of implicit and explicit rules that make consensus possible.[28] But physical spaces function as a crucial facet of the public sphere, in that they render visible and attempt to regulate desired (and undesired) behaviors associated with the common good. Inspired in part by the professional child-related events of the early 1920s, government officials, to construct the new citizen, created new locations where the child could be observed, measured, and guided by trained child specialists.

An expanded concept of the ideal school extended the classroom into the building patio and grounds. Parks and playgrounds cropped up around the city, and recreational equipment became subject to scientific scrutiny of their contributions to molding the child's physical development. Stadiums and theaters changed from locations for adult entertainment to spaces with the dual purpose of allowing children to perform national identity and to showcase their physical fitness. These reworked public spaces all contributed to the more public role of children, increasing their visibility and function as members of the national community. They also subjected children to the scrutiny of the public at large, wards of "the collectivity,"[29] and not just limited to the specialized purview of professional experts.

The industrial era throughout the world ushered in a transformation in the landscapes of children's lives, through alterations in architecture and material culture designed to regulate and socialize.[30] Public spaces designed specifically for children, limited to welfare institutions and fortress-style schools during the Porfiriato, swelled in the 1920s and 1930s to reflect the expanding social role that the child assumed during this time. In the early revolutionary years the primary concern seemed to be the creation of educational and recreational spaces in which children could be closely monitored. Even as modifications to urban space invited the symbolic child into the public view, transgressive childhoods continued to be shielded from sight. The 1926 creation of the Juvenile Delinquency Tribunal (Consejo Tutelar de Menores) sought to remove undesirable children from their high-profile presence in the streets. The unsavory persistence of child street vendors and paperboys, then, complicated authorities' public projections of a healthy, modern state embodied by children on swing sets and led to a series of labor and penal codes designed to remove these social elements from public view.[31] For those children who did not conform to the standards of health and normalcy, institutions such as the Children's Hospital (Hospital Infantil) and the children's wing of the La Castañeda mental institution (Pabellón Infantil) (discussed in more detail below) not simply institutionalized them but also provided them with age-appropriate activities and environments so that they could catch up with their "normal" peers who performed calisthenics in the National Stadium.

Scientific knowledge produced about children since the Porfiriato, notably in the fields of hygiene and psychopedagogy, triggered visible changes to the physical boundaries of childhood. The hygiene discourse emerging from the neopositivist professional conferences such as the First Mexican Congress of the Child in 1921 mandated that the healthy child spend more time outdoors, and early revolutionary officials actively transformed the geographies of civic spaces to fit the idea. Fresh air and sunshine, maintained the Ministry of Public Health (Departamento de Salubridad Pública), would make children's bodies more resistant to inclement weather and would purify their blood.[32] Furthermore, for postwar societies such as Mexico, a healthy child playing in areas of the city recently soaked in blood and marred by gunfire presented a poignant metaphor for regeneration, a necessary therapeutic step toward national healing.[33] Nevertheless, the creation of, and subsequent public debates about, designated children's areas in Mexico City's public parks suggests that early revolutionary discourse about children still treated children as symbolic, as objects of public preoccupation over the health and hygiene of the nation, rather than as individuals with rights.

Public discussion over the creation of children's recreational areas in public parks provides a barometer of collective attitudes about childhood and concerns about children's corruptibility. Early revolutionary rhetoric about children placed the responsibility of child rearing on the community, and tensions arose surrounding the moral declension that this community exhibited compared to the ideal. The solution seemed to be in age segregation: keeping innocent children apart from corrupted adults. Municipal debates in 1922 centered on the transformation of Mexico City's Alameda Park from an elite promenade to a family-friendly democratized gathering place. Councilmen believed that the construction of a children's park merited the effort required to procure supplemental contributions from private charity organizations to offset the tremendous cost of providing amenities, such as equipment and sufficient lighting. In the Alameda children's park, maintaining a moral environment took precedence. Smoking and cursing were prohibited, and the humble people were expected to maintain the cleanest visage that could be expected of people of their means. Councilmen expressed the greatest concern over six allegorical statues of women that they feared had an adverse impact on the youth due to the eroticism that their neoclassical forms exuded. Councilman Zapata expressed that the statue *Pain* evoked nothing of the sort in the impressionable youth—on the contrary, she inappropriately inspired them to tremble with premature erotic pleasure. Unfortunately, added Councilman Ramos, the statues' proximity to the children's area caused adult passersby to succumb to their influences and commit unmentionable acts of immorality on or near the playground equipment.[34] Likewise, a newspaper editorial bemoaned the trend observed in Chapultepec's children's park of adult couples using the swing sets, slides, seesaws, and climbing gyms for courtship activities, thus committing the double crime of depriving young onlookers of their designated recreational area and exposing them to lustful scenes that corrupted their sensibilities. Of course, the author of the article suggested the usual remedy: the construction of yet another area in the park designated specifically for lovers to carry out their romances.[35] Children's play and the space that it occupied became the subject of public concern and aroused public discussions of age and morality.

In city centers legislators began to carve children's playgrounds out of the green parks already designated as leisure areas for the general public.[36] In Chapultepec Park, the giant emerald at the heart of the capital city, a civil engineer proposed a scenic children's train to run around the perimeter of the zoo; the three-kilometer track bore two five-car trains, with sides secure enough to keep the young passengers safe, yet low enough not to obscure their view of the park and zoo.[37] Eventually, Chapultepec boasted an entire children's park complete with playground equipment that became an auspicious place to display and observe children. The space yielded its intended outcome: a self-regulating urban population, in which citizens (not necessarily parents) kept close vigil over the children at play. Ostensibly merely a place for children to conduct safe, invigorating play, these parks became veritable Foucauldian observation decks for those preoccupied with health and order. One concerned citizen penned a letter to the editor of a daily newspaper decrying the consistent presence of four apparently sick children and their indifferent guardians at Chapultepec's children's park; the children coughed and sneezed all over the swing sets, spreading contagion to the healthy children who played after them. The author of the letter suggested the creation of yet another segregated park area—one for sick children, so that they would not mingle with their healthy friends.[38] The quarantined park never materialized, but the letter suggested that both children and their health status had become the object of public scrutiny through the creation of age-specific play spaces.

As the epistemology of childhood shifted in the late 1920s to consider the nationally constructive potential of harnessing children's energies, the first, and most obvious, place to move children's activities to outdoor settings was the schoolhouse. The internationally renowned model school Francisco I. Madero became one of the first to implement their successful model in publications such as the government-published monthly magazine *El Niño*, which featured specialized knowledge about children's health and well-being and enjoyed national and international distribution.

As the implementation of the constitution's Article 3 extended free, obligatory, and secular education farther out into the countryside, the image of the formal schoolhouse underwent drastic modifications. Schools represented the most visible outposts of the revolutionary regime in many rural communities and allowed for the exchange of ideas among local authorities, parents, and schoolteachers.[39] Rural schoolteachers, often facing local hostility, had to be more resourceful and creative in constructing a learning environment that embodied the ideal "active school" model inspired by U.S. pedagogue John Dewey and an early model for the successive Rational School and Socialist School experiments in the 1930s. The newly designed school centers had the greatest impact on the youngest schoolchildren, those who spent the most time on the school grounds. Many rural children, already accustomed to spending most of their time outdoors, discovered that the retooled school system drew their agricultural productivity away from their parents' home plots and into the confines of the expanded school grounds, for the benefit of the collective community. The shift in ownership over children's "labor" did not come without protest from parents, who saw a percentage of their household economy shift to the hands of the state. Wary of complaints, the national curriculum carefully couched children's activity in the language of essential revolutionary values; children learned and practiced "production, thrift, hygiene, cooperation, corporatism, and gender roles."[40]

One way to foster a sense of ownership was by encouraging children to become directly involved in the construction of the educational spaces carved into their community. *El Maestro Rural* and other SEP circulars and publications insisted that children should have a role in their education, including the shaping of their grounds and building. Road building and educational reform in Tepoztlán, Morelos, for example, transformed the physical spaces of childhood. Education resulted in a marked generation gap, as these locations offered children new activities and new ideas about their role in society. The modern school grounds, and the reiteration of their revolutionary significance in the pedagogical material circulated to rural schoolteachers, allowed rural schoolchildren to envision themselves

4. Girls decorating the walls of their school building, 1928. *High School Service* (American National Red Cross) 5, no. 1 (1928). Library of Congress.

in the same schoolyard as the rest of the country.[41] In many cases, children helped to construct the school buildings with their own hands as part of an official initiative cementing in a literal fashion the community's relationship with the school.[42] One photograph from San Luís Potosí in 1926 shows a group of about a dozen school-age boys led by an adult, climbing ladders, hauling bricks, and spreading mortar on the municipality's new school building.[43] Stewardship followed ownership. Children, such as the girls pictured here in 1928 (fig. 4), decorated the walls of their schools with murals depicting local scenery and according to the nationalist motifs in vogue (discussed more fully in the following chapter).[44]

To attest to the aspiring universality of the expanded schoolyard and its merits, rural schoolteachers sent photographs to the SEP from municipalities in Querétaro, Michoacán, Tlaxcala, Nayarit, Guerrero, Tamaulipas, and Chiapas of their students engaged in revolutionary educational activities in orchards, carpentry workshops, gardens, and sewing rooms. Complying with contemporary social hygiene mandates that fresh air and outdoor locations fortified the body and the soul, schoolteachers moved classrooms to the patios and natural areas surrounding the schoolyard. In the patios children bathed and groomed younger students and practiced basketball, calisthenics, sports, animal husbandry, and agriculture. School patios became transformed into multiuse spaces, as can be seen in the photograph of a boy and a girl giving a haircut to a younger student as others play basketball on the court in the background. In the distance henhouses, workshops, and other huts for vocational training line the patio (fig. 5).[45] A photograph of schoolchildren from the Escuela de Santa Catarina in Querétaro shows boys and girls in sombreros gleefully buried up to their knees and elbows in dirt, as they prepare the terrain on the other side of the school walls for cultivation. The soil, freshly tilled by the oxen and plow being manned by older students in the background, appears ready for the children to plant the school garden. Another photo from Tlaxcala shows kindergarteners diligently planting carrots in an area enclosed by chicken wire, presumably adjacent to the Escuela Federal Tipo (fig. 6). One questions whether cultivation could possibly be considered a novelty for these rural schoolchildren and what motivated such delight at such a mundane chore that, assigned at home, represented centuries of drudgery. These photographs, taken by cultural missionaries, urban schoolteachers stationed by the SEP in rural outposts, and sent to the minister of foreign relations as part of a propaganda package about the success of Mexico's active school model, underscore the metaphor of the child as a seed planted in the revolution's fertile soil. The visibility of these children and their presence on municipal grounds suggest that the adult community ought to bear responsibility for their ideological and physical maintenance to ensure that they flourish as citizens.

In the 1930s the introduction of a European innovation—the industrially manufactured playground—heralded yet another transformation of children's public spaces. Reforms of urban

5. Barber class, Tlaxcala, 1932. Archivo Histórico de la Secretaría de Relaciones Exteriores.

parks and school grounds had already placed children's play in the public domain, and now by directing it on modern apparatuses (or rustic approximations of iron structures) adults created semipermanent monuments to childhood. Recreational equipment, or playground structures, placed children squarely

6. Kindergarteners planting carrots at the Escuela Federal Tipo, Tlaxcala, 1932. Archivo Histórico de la Secretaría de Relaciones Exteriores.

on display and under public observation in the school yards and public parks that figured at the hearts of many communities. The designation of a sanctioned place for play, conceptualized and implemented by adults, signals the simultaneous recognition of the value of recreation in a child's life and the need to structure it, creating a veritable "paradox in the modern discourse of play."[46] Playground structures also offered the facile promise of controlled, easily measured physical normalization according to a (European-generated) universal standard.

Not every child could afford to play the right way. Something as innocuous as play also implied conspicuous consumption, as well as a good measure of understanding of specialized child developmental theory. Ideally, parents learned through editorials in the national press, children should play outdoors at every opportunity, barring inclement weather; if well shod in shoes with rubber soles, children could even play outside with light moisture. The best activities put every muscle to work and employed manufactured equipment such as bicycles and skateboards.[47] Properly employed playground equipment exercised children's muscles, essential foundations for a healthy revolutionary citizenry. In her recommendation before the

VII Pan-American Congress about appropriate forms of play, schoolteacher María Elena Chanes called for the construction of as many parks as possible featuring playground equipment; in communities with fewer resources workshops should build the equipment. Furthermore, Chanes suggested that play equipment be segregated by age groups, so that children under eight would not be hurt or overpowered by their older classmates on the equipment. While her ambitious recommendations bordered on being utopian—she argued for the universal inclusion of swimming pools among standard playground equipment—they revealed the trend among child experts that emphasized the physical development of the child in age-appropriate arenas.[48]

Playground equipment and other outdoor accessories touted in magazines promoted a middle-class childhood based on the idealized European model. In the 1930s the SEP received ample advertisements from New York gymnastic equipment manufacturer the J. J. Vellvé Company. The cover of the catalog that featured sturdy metal swing sets, merry-go-rounds, and slides bore testimony from a municipal authority in Guatemala who claimed that the playground equipment installed in their central plaza was the best investment the municipality had ever made. Unpeopled photographs staged pristine swing sets as a blank slate upon which a healthy young body could be forged. The catalog, written in Spanish, advised that children naturally sought physical recreation, and if their energy was not directed toward such stationary equipment as that pictured, children ran the risk of seeking destructive outlets for their rambunctious instincts.[49] Significantly, in response to a letter from an enterprising Latin American representative of Mr. Vellvé's company, head of the Department of Rural Education Rafael Ramírez proclaimed that rural schoolteachers would not be placing an order for modern equipment, because they and the children were engaged in employing local primary materials for the construction of their own recreational apparatuses.[50]

Surely enough, photographs from a schoolyard in Ziráhuato, Michoacán, depicted children frolicking on seesaws and swinging on swing sets resembling those in the catalog but made of

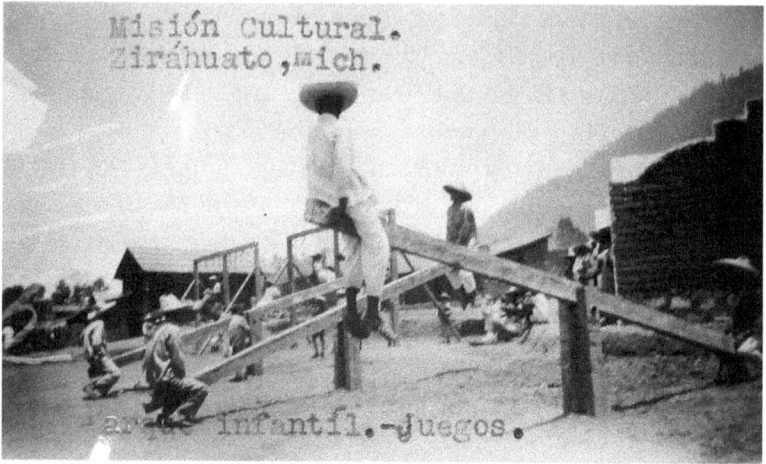

7. Locally made playground equipment in Ziráhuato, Michoacán, 1932.
Archivo Histórico de la Secretaría de Relaciones Exteriores.

roughly hewn pine beams (fig. 7). Mr. Vellvé likely would not have approved of the raucous use of the equipment compared to the proper behavior exhibited by the tidy U.S. children in his catalog. In the photograph from Michoacán, adults looked on as children scamper over the beams, twist their swings to the top of the set, and even pile up two to a swing. One adult even appears to be clambering onto a swing occupied by a child, in clear disregard of the suggested age segregation proposed by Profesora Chanes (fig. 8).[51] In another photo schoolchildren from Querétaro crowd around the ladder of a slide, jostling for position, as three children descend down the front, inhibiting the intended freeing sensation of sliding down alone. Nevertheless, the cropping up of local approximations of modern play structures in remote areas suggests a pervasive cultural shift in the way people saw and used their public spaces. Photographs such as these allow a glimpse into rural communities' reception of official social hygiene propaganda. On the one hand, the erection of an ad hoc rustic version of the catalog swing set demonstrated an attempt to conform to the standards of public health as it related to child's play. On the other hand, the apparent disregard for its intended use reveals that

Misión Cultural. Parque infantil.
Pueblo de Zaráhuato. Mich.

8. Locally made swing set in Ziráhuato, Michoacán, 1932. Archivo Histórico de la Secretaría de Relaciones Exteriores.

official social hygiene mandates often broke down at the local level, as human agency trumped the social engineering power that imported equipment symbolized.

The case of children residing in the General Insane Asylum (Manicomio General), commonly known as La Castañeda, represents a clear example of the way that changing scientific knowledge about the child resulted in transformations of institutional space in the first half of the twentieth century. As we have seen, changing scientific conceptualizations of childhood resulted in evolving transformations of physical spaces intended to yield the desired outcome. Some children did not conform to the ideal of the healthy child playing in the watchful public eye and had to be confined to institutions that would restore their normalcy and convert them into productive citizens. Disadvantaged, unwell, or unstable children had long been relegated to orphanages and welfare institutions run primarily by the church, later assumed by the government.[52] For much of the nineteenth century children with social or physical deficiencies received the same care and accommodations as adults.[53] In the revolutionary period administrators of welfare institutions that traditionally housed adults—such as the prison and the insane asylum—recognized that the best form of rehabilitation was to re-create the environment that children outside of institutional walls experienced.

La Castañeda first opened its doors in 1910, counting twenty-seven children under the age of fifteen among its residents. For the first fifteen years of operation the number of child residents exploded into the hundreds, but they received no special accommodations or age-specific treatment.[54] Not all of the children had mental deficiencies; some accompanied their institutionalized parents, and others were children of La Castañeda employees.[55] Nevertheless, many suffered from observable problems—dementia, epilepsy, aggression, and even alcoholism—that required long-term, professional treatment. During the asylum's early years, children ate the same foods, slept in the same quarters, and engaged in the same activities as adults. The First Mexican Congress of the Child triggered a new awareness of children's special needs based on distinct developmental stages. Reigning pediatric knowledge dictated that children required open spaces, fresh air, and constant stimulation for optimal development. Accordingly, La Castañeda administrators made alterations to children's accommodations. The administration issued a memo stating that the staff needed to treat the children more like children. They reorganized the personnel schedule so that adult supervisors could provide more consistency and stability, more closely approximating the experience of a live-in nanny than a series of hospital nurses on rotating shifts.[56]

In 1927 the Department of Public Welfare constructed a children's ward (Pabellón Infantil) of La Castañeda, furnished with smaller beds, desks and chairs, educational toys, gardens, playgrounds, a squash court, and open-air patios for calisthenics and dance with piano accompaniment.[57] Administrators sent out requests for donations to fill the children's quarters with the accoutrements of a "normal" middle-class childhood available at the posh Palacio de Hierro department store: a radio, a typewriter, board games and puzzles, coloring books, arts and crafts material, and balls for different sports. They wanted their interned children to be up to speed on the Europhile canon of children's literature compiled by José Vasconcelos that was quickly becoming requisite reading for cultural references of the generation: the Grimm brothers' fairy tales, Hans Christian Andersen, *Aladino* and other children's magazines, and Vasconcelos's own compilation, *Lecturas clásicas para niños*.[58] Blueprints of La Castañeda designated children's areas that resembled the bustling open-air schoolyards more than a stuffy welfare institution.[59] The courtyard had areas designated for handball, open-air classrooms, piano, exercise, and horticulture and boasted plenty of open space for play. The emphasis on attaining an agreed-upon national standard of childhood accelerated children's classification into target groups. Within the children's ward itself, staff divided children into "educable" and "uneducable" groups based on the severity of their mental incapacity. By 1932 administrators added a clinic, the Children's Psychiatric Ward (Pabellón de Psiquiatría Infantil), for diagnosis and therapy under the guidance of Dr. Matilde Rodríguez Cabo, with the goal of civilizing even the most deeply challenged children.

In the space of a few short years, administrators transformed the ward into a more child-friendly institution. La Castañeda's children gained skills to participate outside the asylum walls in public events that allowed them to sample "normal" childhood activities. Children under treatment engaged in many of the same activities as public school children: excursions, music, drawing, physical education, small-scale agriculture, livestock care, and handicrafts.[60] The Department of Public Welfare hosted fund-raisers, festivals, and parades that featured children from welfare institutions both as participants and as beneficiaries of the events. In 1931 La Castañeda children participated in the antialcohol campaign, attended puppet shows, and performed gymnastics demonstrations in Chapultepec Park, all hallmarks of modern Mexican childhood. They also produced and transmitted a live radio broadcast—presumably the first broadcast by mentally disabled children in the world.[61] These activities afforded "abnormal" children the opportunity to participate in the national culture that tied them to the other members of their generation with invisible strings. During the 1920s and 1930s La Castañeda underwent the visible transformations of institutional space that reflected its changing orientation toward child rehabilitation. Even within the walls of an institution designed to regulate the process of normalization through heightened vigilance, administrators and staff at the asylum gradually began to treat children as beings socially distinct from adults in accordance with the evolving scientific discourse about children. In the 1940s federal funding began to taper off, and La Castañeda closed its doors in 1968. The efforts made over the life of La Castañeda to mainstream elements of national culture into the institutional lives of the youngest inmates offered many public opportunities to showcase that national identity could be learned and performed, even by the feeblest members of society.

The changing geography of schoolyards, playgrounds, and institutions in the 1920s and 1930s reflects how officials adapted the national landscape to the increasingly active young population. Scientific knowledge produced about children during these years triggered visible changes to the physical boundaries of children's lives. In the early years of revolutionary reform, city planners and educational reformers created physical spaces for children in the public sphere to facilitate collective anxieties about the socialization of the nation's youngest wards. Many of these transformations took place in highly visible areas of urban centers, where children's health and hygiene would fall under the watchful eye of the national community. Rural areas adapted locally constructed versions of these officially mandated reallocations of public space, yet in some cases the didactic and social engineering of these outdoor spaces lost its instructional power as villagers did not conform to the age-specific designations. By the 1930s scientific discourse began to conceptualize the child as an active citizen, and school grounds and extracurricular spaces cropped up to meet the new social needs of an increasingly active youth. A new aesthetic and rhetorical treatment of children during this era accompanied the changes to parks, patios, and courtyards, as the child became an increasingly visible and conceptual figure in the daily lives of adults.

Rhetoric: The Symbolic Child in Popular Discourse

The rhetorical and aesthetic reconfiguration of the child originated in large part from the established cultural authorities:
they were transmitted through presidential proclamations,
professional organizations, the print media, and public art.
Adults at all levels of society, regardless of positions of power,
responded to the change in the cultural tide. Everyday citizens
petitioned for favors and donations in letters to governing officials. In these letters average men and women employed language about children that reflected official language, taking
administrators and governors to task in their revolutionary
responsibility to ensure the well-being of future leaders.[62] The
abstract concept of a monolithic and impermeable government
began to crumble, as individual bureaucrats found themselves
fielding—and often denying—tangible requests for the staples
and commodities deemed necessary to raise properly a revolutionary generation. Some letter writers cut directly to the core
of early revolutionary health and hygienist discourse about
children that prevailed in the 1921 First Mexican Congress of
the Child. Francisca L. de Garces, director of the SEP school
breakfast program, wrote urgently to President Obregón that
their supplies of milk had dried up. She cautioned that if he
did not want to imperil the productive forces of future laborers, he would immediately replenish their kitchens. Obregón's
personal secretary passed the message to José Vasconcelos, who
immediately approved the request and sent the milk on its way.[63]
Perhaps this appeal directly to the rhetorical core of the revolutionary mission found its mark in the hearts of its purveyors.

Adoption requests to orphanages, particularly the government-
operated Casa de Cuna, provide a glimpse into the ways that
adults insinuated collectively held ideas about childhood into
their language. They also reveal the hopes, desires, or expectations that an additional child in the household would fulfill.
Childless adults, in adoption requests, wove intricate tales of
the idyllic family that they envisioned creating. They inserted
references in their letters to the activities and environment that

the ideal child of the newspaper competitions ought to experience and that they would strive to provide. As Ann Blum has described more fully, adoption petitioners contributed to the revolutionary social and political consensus on family identities and their relationship to the Revolutionary Family that was being forged in the public sphere.[64]

Social workers investigated the potential environments that would substitute government care and sought material and environmental cues in prospective parents' homes that would support the ideal childhood promoted by professionals. Fortino Macias, a self-proclaimed humble citizen and senator, had already adopted four-year-old Pedro and five-year-old Esperanza from the Casa de Cuna in 1924 when he wrote requesting permission to adopt an additional child who had won his heart when he and his wife were at the orphanage adopting the other two. In his solicitation Macias claimed that the adoption of this third child would round out his patriotic duty to take in disadvantaged children and would earn him his stripes as a good father raising future citizens. Upon scrutinizing his background credentials and letters of recommendation, the social worker discovered that Macias was not a senator at all. He worked in the senate—as an assistant to the senate accountant. His humble home featured only one bed for the newly expanded family, and conditions gave the social worker the impression that the children lacked even the bare commodities necessary for their well-being. She marveled that the Macias family would want to bring yet another child into a household that seemed incapable of supporting the most recent arrivals. The Casa de Cuna administrator endorsed the social worker's assessment in a firm denial of the request for an additional child.[65] His dubious motives notwithstanding, Macias did his best to present himself and his household as favorable for raising a child. His language suggested his awareness that raising children constituted a patriotic duty and that, being childless, he somehow was not complying with his civic obligations. Furthermore, his inflation of his employment status suggested that he remained unconvinced that a low-level bureaucrat would be deemed capable of raising a child. Gainful employment in politics seemed like a more bona fide career. By exaggerating his credentials, Macias acknowledged that he could be eliminated in the selective process. Many such petitions echoed Macias's reconstituted version of the interconnected roles of the orphan, the household unit, and the state.

The adoption process reflected public and private discussions about government-conferred motherhood and fatherhood.[66] Adoption petitions contained evidence of public reception of the ideal revolutionary child model. The letters submitted revealed popular desires and imaginations about children. Those seeking to add children to their lives cobbled together an ideal domestic unit based on the perceived social roles a child should fulfill. The stilted language of propriety sometimes employed in adoption requests scantily veiled considerably less honorable intentions for bringing unrelated children into their homes— often as a free source of domestic labor. One woman placed a request to adopt an older girl, about twelve or thirteen, who would be sturdy, quiet, and hardworking. Almost as an afterthought the woman included that she promised to raise the girl (already presumably nearing womanhood) as her own daughter and provide her with the direction necessary to be a productive citizen. Clearly, this woman sought an extra helping hand around the house.[67] In examples like the latter case, which abound, petitioners often inserted revolutionary rhetoric about the child into their pleas, expecting a favorable response in exchange for their collaboration with the state welfare project.

In other petitions to revolutionary administrators, parents and teachers included children in language that presumed an ideological commitment on the part of the letter's recipient to honoring redistributive promises, all in order to make concrete material requests. Adults took to heart the presidential promise that the revolution would take care of the children. Manuela Torres, a widowed mother of three from Tampico, wrote directly to President Abelardo Rodríguez in 1932 that although she was willing to fight for her children's daily bread, she had reached the end of her rope. She implored him to send her a sti-

pend to make ends meet. Her request was denied.[68] Many of the
requests clustered around January 6, Three Kings' Day (Día de
los Reyes), when parents with enough means showered children
with toys and sweets. Ernesto Finance, president of the Committee for Children of Actors (Comité Pro Hijos del Actor) of
the Mexican actors' union, also wrote to Rodríguez, reminding
him that because of tough economic times, not all parents had
the resources to provide a toy for their children on the holiday.
He implied that when the parents fell short, the government
ought to step in. Finance ended on a confident note, expressing
his firm belief that Rodríguez would honor such a noble cause
for the benefit of child actors. His request, also denied, belied
a belief that children deserved more than just sustenance. In
a similar letter María Luisa Mena wrote to the president to say
that her children had suffered tremendously over Christmas,
seeing all of the new toys that their peers received—would they
have to suffer the same fate this Three Kings' Day? She plied
the president for a bit of joy for her children. In a postscript she
noted that she had three boys and three girls, a helpful hint
in case the president or his secretary planned on doing some
personal gender-specific toy shopping. Not surprisingly, her
request was denied.[69] Her language insinuated socioeconomic
difference that persisted after the revolution, and she upheld
her children as examples of the daily suffering still sustained
by many Mexicans. Relying on the assumption that *children*, if
not she herself, deserved to live in a fair society, she levied her
request directly with the highest government authority.

As these petitions have suggested, parents and teachers began
to articulate their children's entitlements beyond the scope of
material items for sustenance. As the revolutionary era progressed, letter writers demonstrated greater comfort in claiming
abstract citizenship benefits from the state, including entertainment, emotional health, and happiness. Nicolás Chavero,
director of a children's theater group in Teotihuacán, found his
company short on supplies for the upcoming Christmas charity party for the poor children in the municipality and sent his
plea on their behalf to President Rodríguez. The disadvantaged

youth, he reminded the president, were the compelling force behind the *patria*, the future self-sacrificing campesinos. The shortages these children suffered only fortified their ideological convictions. Nevertheless, Chavero argued, they deserved their "*fiestecita*" as much as any other child, a sweet spot to savor when life delivered only challenges.[70] These supplicants acknowledged that poor children were symbols in the formation of a collective national identity based on class struggle. Yet they also suggested that children represented more than an ideological symbol—children of all social classes deserved recreation, directed attention, and age-appropriate celebrations. To these petitioners, the responsibility to provide all of this fell on the national government.

Yet other petitioners mobilized the new social capital of the symbolic child to garner political favor or to forge a personal link to the Revolutionary Family's patriarchs. Children appeared as devices by which some letter writers transparently attempted to reinscribe their unflagging devotion to the head of the nation and by association to the *patria*. The founder of the Cruz Gálvez School for Boys in Sonora wrote a letter to President Calles thanking him for the donation of five hundred pesos for Christmas (Calles was a longtime patron of the Cruz Gálvez schools in his home state and sent some of his older children there for schooling); the money made it possible to equip their baseball team, an outdoor activity that promised to mold a robust and vigorous group of children, who in the not too distant future would form joyful homes of their own and never forget the name of their kind benefactor.[71] That those five hundred pesos could be credited for the fruitful procreation of a generation of Cruz Gálvez alumni might be a stretch, but the petitioner did not hesitate to make this leap. In one instance Adalberto Argüelles, apparently a forgotten former associate of President Emilio Portes Gil, coyly begged forgiveness for interrupting the president's valuable time in a contrite announcement of the birth of his first son. In his letter Argüelles deemed the long-awaited arrival of a male offspring—a "small citizen"—to be worthy of the president's attention. He seemed particularly pleased that his son had arrived at the fortuitous moment in which his "old friend" Portes Gil found himself in the elevated position of guiding the destinies of the *patria*, a good omen that ensured his son's lifelong devotion to the country. Taking a page from the biblical story of young Samuel, promised by his barren mother into the service of God at birth and literally deposited as a child at the temple, Argüelles stated that he wanted to take advantage of this minor distraction to announce that it would be his pleasure to place this small citizen at the president's orders and promised to inculcate him with respect and affection for Portes Gil.[72] Through this instance of sycophantic *compadrazgo*, or expression of spiritual kinship, Argüelles evoked a rather literal interpretation of the Revolutionary Family metaphor by placing his firstborn in the service of the nation's father.

Image: The Redemptive Proletarian Child

Former president Plutarco Elías Calles gave an oft-cited proclamation in the city of Guadalajara in 1934 on the eve of incumbent Lázaro Cárdenas's administration, in which he minced no terms as he rendered the nation's children the property of the "revolution." In this iconic discourse Calles famously envisioned the nation as a Revolutionary Family, a metaphor that has since been broadened to refer to the way that the revolutionary state restructured its role in the private family.[73] He confirmed the government's ongoing commitment to secular education, but he stripped away layers of bureaucracy and pedagogy that clouded debates over education to reveal his core concern: children.[74] Calles's private family life did not reflect his adamant stance on nationalist education (his younger children did not attend the nationalist public schools he so fervently promoted but rather went to private schools, first in Mexico, and later in Los Angeles),[75] but his public conviction strengthened the discursive power of the child as a public figure, an object of and a metaphor for revolutionary reform. The new rhetorical treatment in the 1930s of an idealized child—previously articulated by officials such as José Vasconcelos, Felix Palavicini, and others—was not confined to the official sphere but became a recognizable trope in public discussions and public art. People changed the way they saw and spoke about children, whether affection toward children within the private embrace of the family circle changed with the public tide or not. This section examines the emergence of a symbolic child that began to consolidate in the official and visual language of the 1930s, even as the revolutionary government institutionalized educational and social reforms designed to streamline future Mexican citizens' success, health, education—and conformity.

Prior to the 1930s the construction of a visual panorama of romantic national types remained devoid of political meaning (with a heavy proclivity for a Victorian-styled, middle-class, whiter ideal). This extended to visual reproductions of children, photographic or otherwise. Even as the symbolic child figured more prominently in the language of politicians, visual representations of children exploded through advances in photography, mass media, and public art. In the late nineteenth century technological developments in photography made studio portraiture available to those with means to capture their child's likeness for posterity. By the turn of the century photography became accessible to an even broader swath of the social spectrum. As photographs replaced paintings, more people could afford to display their progeny in a frame. Changes to printing-press technology meant that images could be mass-produced and distributed in the print media. Images of children moved from being a commodity—a signifier in the colonial era of social status, pure lineage, and healthy genes—to an object in the public domain, reprinted in newspapers and magazines and viewed in cafés and parlors around the country.[76] Photographs of rotund cherubs appeared in the print press in the 1920s as part of a rash of competitions to boost the eugenicist model of robust health. Magazines *El Hogar* and *Jueves del Excelsior* and *El Universal,* the same paper that sponsored the First Mexican Congress of the Child, hosted competitions and circulated the winning images to underscore the importance of an essential generation that would replace the dead revolutionaries. With health suddenly a quantifiable goal, endless variations of the Healthy Baby Contest (Concurso del Niño Sano) sprang up. From the Porfiriato to the 1920s, the public image of the child transformed from a romanticized Victorian ideal of innocence to a militarized, politicized metaphor for the revolution.[77] Both treatments of children relegated them to visual cultural symbols, evocative of public sentiments, or political propaganda.

The onset of Cardenista social reforms in 1934 politicized images of children. In particular, the September 6, 1934, revision of Article 3 made class consciousness an intentional part of the national curriculum, branded for the first time as the Socialist School. In the 1930s a new archetype emerged in the national pantheon: the proletarian child. The premise of Cárdenas's socialist turn was that the revolution had not yet reached the protagonists of the armed movement: the glorified, anonymous proletariat. Unofficially, authorities came to rely on the newly devised social type of the proletarian child to galvanize support of the working masses, and it emerged as a poignant symbol that reinvigorated a revolutionary movement fading away from its flashy idealistic years. The proletarian child, then, emerged after the revolution as a politicized product of generations of class warfare that, because of his vulnerability as a child, felt even more acutely his parents' social marginalization.[78] The 1935 VII Pan-American Congress, its offshoot for children (Primer Congreso del Niño Proletario, discussed in chapter 5), and the 1936 publication by self-styled revolutionary poet Jesús Sansón Flores of a small volume for and about the proletarian child, *El niño proletario: Poemas clasistas*, contributed to the general shift toward a newly politicized model of childhood at the core of the nation's identity. Ostensibly writing for a child audience, Sansón Flores effectively defined the new social type for a general Mexican public. "From the moment your life became flesh within the fertile womb / ... Your condition as a slave was fertilized," he informs the eponymous "Niño" in one poem. "You are not even master of the dirt that you tread! You were born already sold!"[79]

The ideological elevation of the proletarian child as a highly political, stylized image in the leftist intellectual sphere does not suggest that all vestiges of scientific quantification dissipated in the Cárdenas era. In fact, the Department of Psychopedagogy commissioned a 1937 comprehensive study of the biological characteristics of "proletarian schoolchildren," basing their conclusions on a set of data garnered over a year of observing elementary-level students at the Ramón López Velarde School in the Mexico City working-class neighborhood of Colonia Obrera, a population deemed by the researchers as representative of the social class in question. Through a compilation of socioeconomic statistics, anthropometric measures, psychological assessments, and measurements of intellectual aptitude, the researchers crafted a profile of the proletarian child that further reified this social type by suggesting uniformity across individuals. Yet the study also served as a justification for the urgent intervention of the state on their behalf, noting the vast disadvantages of this population in access to educational and nutritional resources.[80] In this way the government relied on this research report based on traditional methods of quantification, in conjunction with an official program that reified the symbol of the proletarian child, to fortify its redistributive agenda and to preempt potential critiques from conservative detractors.

Parallel to the rhetorical shift during the Cárdenas period that politicized the proletarian child, this new social trope took the form of flesh, as demonstrably physical features became associated with the new revolutionary redeemer. By the 1930s the brand of competitive parenting moved away from eugenics and toward a social mobilization of the working classes by seeking out demonstrable "proletarian" characteristics in babies and showcasing these as exemplary. In Saltillo, Coahuila, the guidelines for the 1935 Healthy Proletarian Child Contest (Concurso del Niño Sano Proletario), sponsored by the SEP and the local chapter of the Rotary Club, made explicit that raising strong children was a mother's transcendental duty. Mothers rose to the challenge presented to them by educational and government officials and entered five thousand children in the first round of a healthy baby competition at the Bellas Artes palace. The ultimate prize went to the mother who, through abnegation and sacrifice, produced the child strong enough to tackle the future challenges of leading the nation.[81] These contests, then, suggested that the physical traits identifiable during infancy foretold abstract social behavior such as citizenship and revolutionary nationalism. Presumably, such children would not even need the playground structures prescribed by revolutionary officials.

While photography claimed to document objectively the health and civic behavior of the revolution's children, the burgeoning art movement—headed since the 1920s by a bohemian crowd considerably more politically radical than the governing authorities from whom they took their public art commissions— took liberties with the use of the child's image as a symbol within their social realist pantheon of secular messiahs. Chief among them, Diego Rivera etched lasting images of an ideal, proletarian, revolutionary child on the collective imaginary. The didactic nature of Rivera's social realist work—public canvasses crammed with mestizos and Indians engaging in nationalist productivity and acting out a sweeping Marxist national narrative—provided a visual reiteration of the language of social inclusion in the Constitution of 1917. Most important, Rivera's murals appealed to an illiterate population of mestizos and Indians who saw their skin tones, clothing style, and activities reflected alongside national icons such as Benito Juárez and the eagle and serpent. For example, Rivera's 1932 lithograph *Sueño* (Sleep) portrayed Indians peacefully at rest after a hard day's work; his idealized style softened the rough-hewn traditional clothing, and the predominance of children conflated indigenousness with innocence and purity.

The limitations of muralist art as a propaganda tool have been well noted. First, the majority of the murals, though technically public domain, were housed in courtyard atriums behind the daunting walls of converted colonial fortresses where the average citizen on the street did not view them daily. Second, most of the murals were in Mexico City, far from the gaze of the outlying campesinos, fishermen, and subsistence farmers whose labor constituted the national canvas. Yet Rivera's role as a public intellectual and his extremely prolific artistic career launched his proletarian tropes into other venues that, given the rapid massification of revolutionary propaganda, made his art as universally recognizable as possible in the revolutionary era. His illustrations (and sometimes commentary) adorned popular rural school textbooks, the bilingual magazine *Mexican Folkways*, rural schoolteacher monthly *El Maestro Rural*, socialist magazine *El Sembrador*, Communist Party newspaper *El Machete*, and other publications with nationwide circulation.[82] Facsimiles of his murals appeared in children's magazines, textbooks, and circulars with such frequency that even those who were never exposed to the scale and grandeur of the original murals became familiar with their content and style.

Rivera populated his murals with children, an inclusion so notable that it spawned exhibits and literature addressing *los niños de Diego* as a genre.[83] Rivera painted his children with a nativist, indigenist emphasis on their features: almond-shaped eyes, brown skin, braids, bare feet, muslin overalls, straw hats, and often seated on the woven straw *metate* used by Indians. In his 1934 *Niña Sentada* (Kneeling child), a *café con leche*–skinned, sweet-featured indigenous girl kneels on the *metate* woven for the marketplace or a siesta. Her idealized regional costume is pristine, her shiny hair perfectly combed into a traditional twist of braids atop her head. Her rounded and healthy features and prominently figured hands remind the viewer of her working potential. Much like the mestizos and Indians who saw themselves in murals, children viewing the art saw themselves as protagonists in the newly illustrated national history. Children were more likely to pay attention to art that included other children, their objects, and their activities, and thus would be more likely to emulate some of the activities that Rivera's fictional characters carried out at the service of the nation. In the impressive murals commissioned by Vasconcelos that decorate the three levels of the SEP building's inner courtyard, Rivera's children receive textbooks distributed by a middle-class woman, practice writing the alphabet, listen attentively to their rural schoolteacher, sing revolutionary *corridos*, listen to the radio, and prepare piñatas for patriotic festivals. Vasconcelos and Rivera saw no better way to impart nationalism to the next generation than to provide them with illustrative models, and the murals projected a visual backdrop to Calles's 1934 proclamation.[84] The inclusion of children in Rivera's epic pictorial as socially active beings expanded the idea of citizenship to more members of society, a symbolic step toward the democratizing promises of the Constitution of 1917.

As we have seen, the political, intellectual, and artistic elite all contributed to state-sponsored initiatives to figure the symbolic child prominently before the eyes and ears of the nation as a metaphor for the massive renewal project purported by the revolution. Visual representations of children evolved from aesthetic to political, drawn along by the scientific and rhetorical tide of the official sector. Certainly, the educational and welfare reforms that accompanied those projects proceeded at an uneven pace and along a rockier path. Yet evidence from letters, editorials, petitions, and solicitations suggests that many Mexicans acknowledged and engaged with this new symbol that the state had placed before them.

Conclusions

From the 1920s to the 1930s the child emerged in new physical and rhetorical spaces and became a powerful symbol by which to justify and measure the social reforms that swept the nation. The rise of professionalized pediatric fields in the early 1920s prepared the national soil for a heavily funded, multifaceted child-centered state program, one that formed the foundations of what would become some of the twentieth century's most influential government bureaus: the Ministry of Education (and its Fine Arts Department and the Department of Psychopedagogy and Hygiene) and the Ministry of Health (and its Department of Public Welfare). The presidency of Lázaro Cárdenas accelerated the symbolic role of the child, forging a new revolutionary hero and political actor out of what had been an object of sympathy, affection, and scientific reform. The proletarian child emerged in the mid-1930s as an avenger of class injustice—indignant but childlike enough to provide Cárdenas with a bit more latitude in his more radical socialist reforms that marked the first years of his administration. The symbolic child had become an indelible presence in the official language and imagery, and real children had been brought into the public sphere so intentionally that Cárdenas had only to lean more heavily on this established social trope in order to push a more radical reform agenda.

That petitioners addressed so many of their letters directly to the president rather than to municipal authorities or local representatives of government agencies (although petitions to administrators at all levels of government certainly abound) suggests a literal application of the rhetorical treatment of children that marked the era. Evidence for the penetration of the new discourses of childhood comes through in the language these everyday citizens employed in their letters. In their official correspondence many Mexicans absorbed the language of Calles's Grito de Guadalajara and turned the tables, placing their children in the charge of the revolution. Whether they reproduced this language in the streets or at their homes remains unknown. What their letters do suggest is that many people saw the revolution as synonymous with the governing head of state and entrusted him with the care of their family as promised in political speeches and visually reinforced through murals and art. Through their petitions they acknowledged the power of the revolutionary promise that a paternalistic state would meet the needs—often government defined—of its citizenry.

Although petitions to the government reflect only a sampling of adult-produced responses to the symbolic weight of the child in revolutionary discourse, taken alongside the transformations of public space to accommodate children they demonstrate a cultural change that positioned the child as more central, more entitled, more active, and more productive. As adults changed their ideas about children, new spaces of engagement emerged in which children could participate in the reconfiguration of a revolutionary nation. Many children remained outside of the parameters of reform. But unprecedented numbers of children participated in the new cultural spaces offered to them and engaged with new models of education, citizenship training, and national identity with varying degrees of enthusiasm and understanding. The following chapters examine these transformed childhoods in the 1920s and 1930s, children's interaction with and reception of new physical spaces, technology, cultural forms, and media outlets that cobbled from the nation's youth a generation of revolutionary citizens.

CHAPTER TWO

Pulgarcito and Popocatépetl

Children's Art Curriculum and the Creation of
a National Aesthetic

By means of a children's magazine called *Pulgarcito*, advocate of untrammeled art . . . pupils from Sonora to Chiapas are getting acquainted.

— EMMA REH STEVENSON, "Mexico's Story in Color" (1928)

A drawing published in *Pulgarcito* will be contemplated by all of the artist's colleagues, who will express their admiration for that fortunate child.

— *Pulgarcito* editors, February 1926

The glossy centerfold of the March 1931 issue of the children's art magazine *Pulgarcito* bore a full-color facsimile of Father Miguel Hidalgo's 1810 insurrection, as depicted by fourth grader Ramón Romero from Atzcapotzalco, Distrito Federal (DF). Rendered with childlike yet stylized simplicity, Hidalgo (recognizably clad in a belted long purple frock) faces the viewer, surrounded by a cast of faceless peasants, all dressed in sombreros and white clothing and brandishing farm implements as weapons (fig. 9). Two details catch the reader's attention: instead of the standard of the Virgin of Guadalupe, Hidalgo bears the Mexican *tricolor* flag, and all of the insurgents are faceless. Young Ramón's drawing echoes the social realist technique perfected by the Mexican muralists gaining international visibility at the time of painting generic, anonymous, and repetitious figures to capture the sense of the proletarianization of

9. *Pulgarcito* centerfold by child artist Ramón Romero, 1931. *Pulgarcito,* March 1931, n.p.

the revolution. By applying the conscious aesthetic strategy to populate his depiction of the independence movement with the anonymous masses, Ramón demonstrates an awareness of the revolution in art, washing his gray city with vibrant color and bringing themes of class struggle and racial justice into the public imaginary. Furthermore, his historically erroneous inclusion of the national flag, whether an oversight or a purposeful insertion, infuses the 120-year-old event with contemporary political commentary.

Beginning in the early 1920s schoolchildren like Ramón learned to draw Mexico. Through a revision of the education curriculum vigorously funded by the Ministry of Education, children came to identify both nationalist content and the ideologically sound techniques with which to depict it. By now many are familiar with the fusion of cosmopolitan influences and nationalist revolutionary art that began to adorn Mexico's public buildings by the three great muralists—Diego Rivera, José Clemente Orozco, and David Alfaro Siqueiros—in the service of the revolutionary state's promotion of cultural *mestizaje*.[1] Less is known about the profound impact of the art education program at the elementary school level that provided children with a template for painting their nation that ran parallel to this highly publicized public art initiative. As Rivera's epic historical narratives, Orozco's tortured allegories, or Siqueiros's mesmerizing repetition propped up the revolutionary programs on a grand scale, little fingers reproduced the new visual vocabulary in their notebooks and on their classroom walls. This chapter examines Mexican children's role in promoting an aesthetic shift in the art world, beginning in Mexico and emanating outward. On paper and on walls, modern nationalism met timeless culture, as children learned modern ways to inscribe pre-Columbian motifs on material surfaces and the collective memory alike, producing for the first time a nationalist art. The resulting "Mexican style" of drawing forged by government-appointed art officials in the 1920s persists in the decoration of pottery, tapestries, and other artisanry in today's art markets, curio shops, and official National Council for Culture and the Arts (CONACULTA) outlets.[2] Through their avid participation in Mexico's art curriculum, children learned and reproduced an official version of nationalism that resulted in a distinctly Mexican style and defined the visual culture of a generation.

The construction of a national aesthetic through the art education program spearheaded by Adolfo Best Maugard began with the implementation of his indigenous motif-based curriculum *Método de dibujo* in the public schools in 1921 and was transformed by Juan Olaguíbel through the children's art magazine *Pulgarcito*. *Pulgarcito* was unique in its nearly entirely child-produced content; its pages abound with children's commentary, both textual and visual, of the changing world around them. As a free, government-funded publication with nationwide and international dissemination from 1925 to 1932, *Pulgarcito* reveals the uneven process of nation building made evident by disparities in participation levels from urban and rural child contributors. The national art curriculum of the public education system—with *Pulgarcito* as its main evangelist—incorporated excursions and natural observation into the lesson plans, with an emphasis on iconic natural sites such as the volcano Popocatépetl. Art instructors encouraged the creation of an indigenist, stylized, Mexico City–centered aesthetic, which children dutifully reproduced in the magazine and in art competitions. In this way *Pulgarcito* contributed to a national visual culture that, increasingly, leaned toward a monolithic view of Mexico as painted by its acclaimed artists and as reproduced by its children. Mexican children earned fervent international acclaim for their uniformity and thematic cohesion in their design and illustration, as their drawings won competitions around the world.

Yet the pages of *Pulgarcito*, and especially the letters to the editor, reveal the disjuncture between urban and rural children (and, by extension, between middle-class and impoverished children), both in their access to forms of popular entertainment like *Pulgarcito* and in the expectations that revolutionaries had of the two social groups. Even the curriculum's reification of the volcanoes that ring the Valley of Mexico as preferred subject matter prioritized the nation's geographic center as the primal source of visual national identity. Likewise, *Pulgarcito* forged a sense of imagined community for those children across the nation who drew, read, and participated in it by providing some tangible points of common engagement and shared visual references. Nevertheless, the way that the magazine editors structured contributors' participation alienated some of the children on the periphery and favored those living in the country's urban cultural core. In this milieu *Pulgarcito* editors and art educators constructed indigenous children problematically as doubly possessed of innate talent, but as designated purveyors of the "pain of their race," and not as consumers and citizens in a modern Mexico. The history of *Pulgarcito* reflects a growing dichotomy that emerged between the modern child and the rural child, despite the existence of new media that sought to tie them together as compatriots of a common heritage and destiny. The social inequalities apparent through an analysis of the seemingly innocuous art program paralleled the state's persistent ambivalence toward the rural poor in the wake of the promise of revolutionary reform.

Adolfo Best Maugard and the Art Curriculum in the Public School System, 1921–32

Congressmen debated the nature of public education according to Article 3 of the revolutionary Constitution of 1917, exhorting the inclusion of Civic Instruction and Patriotic History (*Historia Patria*) in the curriculum; they noted that history should elicit an emotional response in schoolchildren, with an emphasis on symbols, heroes, and great men; it should reach children's hearts rather than their brains.[3] Thus, every child, regardless of race or class, would possess the uniform set of cultural references required to consider him- or herself Mexican. Under such nationalizing auspices, the SEP emerged as the most powerful, furthest-reaching, best-funded government agency in the decades following the revolution. The best way to emblazon images of foundational myths on the minds of the nation's children, according to José Vasconcelos, was through the implementation of a nationalist art program. Vasconcelos served as secretary of public education from 1921 to 1924. Despite the short tenure, his promotion of the arts created a twentieth-century visual legacy. He had conceptualized and implemented a canon of children's literature for young citizens that drew from classical Greek, Indian, and other international models, designed to both internationalize and educate the Mexican child as a literate, modern being.[4]

Vasconcelos's effort to fund the arts is perhaps best known in terms of his sponsorship of the aforementioned muralists Rivera, Orozco, and Siqueiros. Yet while Vasconcelos retained a rather conservative vision of the pictorial function of art in documenting the social revolution, the artists he commissioned radicalized art as a politicizing, socializing tool. Feeling alienated from the socialist-tending political milieu, Vasconcelos left his post as the secretary of education in 1924, and the muralist project that he spearheaded during his tenure burgeoned in his absence. Within the short space of a few decades, the muralists established a visual interpretation of Mexican history and culture that became emblematic of the new revolutionary social order. Mexican muralists fixed a romanticized indigenous past alongside utopic visions of an industrialized mestizo future on the walls of public buildings beyond Mexico City to Detroit, Chicago, San Francisco, and New Hampshire.[5] International support and collaboration with Mexican art education innovators helped to bolster the ideological underpinnings of the curriculum. In the United States the link between the artful and the useful resulted in the handicrafts movement of the late nineteenth and early twentieth centuries that sought to render artists out of craftsmen.[6] International collaboration defined the movement as it evolved in Mexico, featuring Franz Boas, Carleton Beals, Edward Weston, Anita Brenner, and Waldo Frank among a generation of art and anthropology enthusiasts.[7]

Diego Rivera, more than most, painted epic historical narratives that paid closer attention to storytelling than realism, an intentionally naive style often characterized as "social realism." Though trained classically in Europe and capable of painting realist art worthy of gilded frames, Rivera chose to develop a two-dimensional, almost cartoonish style, making liberal use of bright primary colors and reducing many of his figures to stylized ethnic types, against which readily recognizable historical figures stood out in relief. Even as child artist Ramón Romero likely based his drawing of Hidalgo's insurrection on Rivera's trademark social realist techniques, Rivera himself touted Mexican children's art as unparalleled in its ingenuity and adherence to revolutionary ideals.[8] Among the muralists Rivera in particular intended his work to be instructive, accessible even to the illiterate masses in their blatant socialist didacticism.[9] The use of a childlike style of painting, or intentionally naive technique, infantilized their intended viewers, further underscoring the colonial metaphor of Indians as children.[10]

Adolfo Best Maugard spent much of the 1910s studying the designs and motifs of Mexico's native societies to discover what he considered the essence of the Mexican aesthetic. He studied anthropology in New York under Franz Boas and art in Paris alongside Diego Rivera. As a young graduate student Best Maugard was influenced by his colleague Manuel Gamio, an anthropologist whose foundational text *Forjando Patria* (Forging a nation) jump-started the cultural nationalist movement. Gamio believed in the emotional power of "authentic" pre-Hispanic symbols and icons, and he believed that the national population needed to be visually trained to consider indigenous art, artisanry, architecture, and aesthetic production as elements of high culture surmounting their Greek and Roman counterparts.[11] For Best Maugard, Gamio's anthropological inspiration consolidated into a concrete project to create a nationalist art curriculum when he accompanied Vasconcelos on a pilgrimage to Tehuantepec, a coastal region of the southern state of Oaxaca considered to be a timeless cultural epicenter.[12] This trio of Mexican culture makers—Vasconcelos, Best Maugard, and Gamio—conflated indigeneity, primitivism, and childhood with both innocence and authenticity. Though patronizing, this approach opened a cultural space for both children and native people to assert a degree of authority, as their aesthetic productions enjoyed a reputation as purely intuitive representations of an elusive national spirit.

Perhaps tellingly, Best Maugard conducted much of this research while living abroad, where the pre-Columbian designs that caught his attention gained luster through both their historic and their geographic distance. Upon his return to Mexico, he quickly became a rising star, earning prominence through his role organizing, decorating, and choreographing the highly stylized Noche Mexicana centennial celebrations in 1921. Though fraught with political intrigue and uncomfortable social friction, the resulting events orchestrated by Best Maugard featured a folk-indigenous version of national patrimony, literally setting the stage for an era of state-sponsored artistic indigenism.[13] His stylistic novelty notwithstanding, Adolfo Best Maugard shared with Vasconcelos a tendency toward a didactic and formulaic pedagogical approach to cultural nation building, one based on the meticulous study of ancient visual forms. Even as Mexican legislators reconfigured the government to reflect the broad-based social inclusion that the revolution had promised, educational officials intended the nationalist art project to be a unifying principle in the still quite diverse regional, ethnic, and socioeconomic components that competed to define Mexico. Vasconcelos created the Department of Drawing and Handicrafts (Sección de Dibujo y Trabajos Manuales)[14] in 1922—a section of the Fine Arts Department—as a civilizing vehicle for the generation that was to replace the decimated population with productive citizens. Vasconcelos placed Adolfo Best Maugard at the head of this new department from 1922 to 1924. The drawing method that Best Maugard implemented in Mexico City elementary school curricula provided a brand-new aesthetic: modernist while at the same time distinctly Mexican. Although his method eventually came to be seen as stagnant and repressive, at this critical juncture of the early 1920s, it served the important purpose of contributing to national rehabilitation through the collective erasure of the revolutionary decade's grim violence.[15]

During his tenure Best Maugard utilized the Department of Drawing and Handicrafts—part of a curriculum that already boasted a hearty emphasis on vocational training, civics, and hygiene—to oversee the inclusion of technical drawing, illustration, pattern design, and handicrafts in the public education curriculum nationwide. The pedagogical principle that good design built upon the most childlike, simplistic forms provided ample justification for the inclusion of a national art program as part of children's development. This heavily didactic project swapped out a set of aesthetic norms deemed outdated—namely, those based on European models—with another, equally exclusive, visual vocabulary that defined national identity. Best Maugard saw the child as an intellectual metaphor for primitive mankind; harnessing their "infantile and ingenuous" creativity early on would allow officials to guide the artistic maturation of children and thus usher in an age of modernity informed by ancient wisdom.[16] Despite the relentless influence of art educators bearing down on the artistic production of the nation's children, they tapped into the innate creative power of children and strove to maintain ambiguity between playing and drawing in order to channel children's best efforts into a Mexican national aesthetic.[17] The resulting effect was an infantilized, simplified, and stylized visual culture, strongly influenced by young artists and emulated by some of the most prodigious contemporary adult artists.

In the spirit of Hobsbawm's "invented traditions," art educators sought to construct an aesthetic that drew from local techniques and resulted in something quintessentially Mexican.[18] To this end painter and art theorist Adolfo Best Maugard concocted a systematic method for drawing that left a permanent imprint on artistic production from its adoption in 1921. His thorough reinvention of how to draw the world also had implications for the way that an entire generation *saw* their world. Through the arena of drawing he contributed to efforts pursued by a cohort of artists working to "ethnicize" the country's visual culture.[19] His visual legacy, as carried out by the countless students who drew, painted, and designed under his instruction, remains firmly embedded in the popular art, artisanry, and design found in today's marketplaces across the country.

In keeping with the rising spirit of revolutionary nationalism, Best Maugard argued that Mexicans should not look to European styles for inspiration but rather should produce art and design based on popular experience and tradition. This nativist approach relied primarily on Aztec symbols culled from the ruins of pre-Hispanic monuments, pottery, and codices, from the observation of which Best Maugard came up with a set of simple, stylized versions that should form the basis of all drawings. After extensive research based on the anthropological models of the day, he identified seven primary motifs unique to Mexican iconography: the spiral, the concentric circle, the *m* arc, the *s* link, the undulating line, the zigzag, and the repeated straight line (fig. 10).[20] These seven components formed what became known as the "Aztec art alphabet" and gave shape to the visual language that characterized officially sponsored art and artisan production in the twentieth century. The combination of these elements by an astute student would result in a Mexican flora and fauna populating what would come to be recognized as a quintessential Mexican landscape. In this student drawing, intended as a *recuerdo* (memento), the concerted application of nearly all of the motifs transforms an otherwise laconic scene into a modern, pulsing, even psychedelic representation of a peacock grazing alongside a church (fig. 11). Modern artists considered these pre-Hispanic indigenous visual codes to elicit the spirit of the Mexican race, that is, the "cosmic race" of mestizos imagined by Vasconcelos in his famous essay.[21] Needless to say, Vasconcelos enthusiastically embraced Best Maugard's art theories and found a place for them at the core of his burgeoning educational program: the Best Maugard Method (*Método Best Maugard*).

In 1923 Best Maugard published his guidelines for what he called "new art" based on very old techniques, and art students from primary and secondary school provided all of the illustrations as proof that this method of "Mexicanization" could be taught effectively. By providing meticulous instruction on how to draw everything from the national seal (an eagle perched on a cactus devouring a snake) to a modern electrified trolley car,[22] Best Maugard ensured that the schoolteacher had only to gently guide the student to incorporate elements of self-expression within the guidelines stipulated in his book.[23] The Ministry of Education swiftly mandated the distribution of his book, titled *Método de dibujo: Tradición, resurgimiento y evolución del arte mexicano,* as the official text of the art curriculum program in Mexico City's public schools. The first edition saw an impressive print run of fifteen thousand copies, and the book remained influential enough for a second edition published in 1964 and a third edition with a CD-ROM demonstrating the method in 2002. The illustrations in the book that served as step-by-step instructions for the successful production of a Mexican style of art were produced entirely by children, the first generation of Best Maugard's pupils. Although these child artists operated under his close scrutiny, the publication of their efforts served as the direct models for their peers' education. When time or money to distribute copies of the indispensable

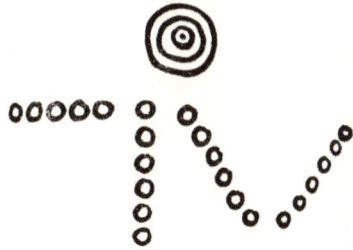

10. Best Maugard's seven
motifs, 1923. Best Maugard,
Método de Dibujo, 26–31.

11. Child's drawing from Best Maugard's *Método de Dibujo*, demonstrating the combination of motifs applied to local themes. Best Maugard, *Método de Dibujo*, n.p.

text came up short, officials expedited condensed pamphlets that outlined Best Maugard's technique.[24]

The Best Maugard Method was taught in public schools under the title "Mexican Drawing," and his publication served as a handbook of artistic nationalism.[25] Within the first year of his book's publication, his method was being applied in 248 primary schools; in total, 71,157 pupils guided by 75 instructors learned his techniques in Mexico City in 1923 alone.[26] Aside from their decorative value, the seven motifs had practical application in popular arts—weaving, artisan work, handcrafts, embroidery—and employed native materials such as hemp, palm leaves, gold, and clay.[27] The integration of Best Maugard's motifs into cottage craft industries for domestic and tourist consumption was one of the most effective means of disseminating the new Mexican look.[28]

The elementary school art education program stated four goals: to cultivate aesthetic sensibility, to teach appreciation of national artistic traditions, to enable students to express their ideas, and to beautify the child's home, school, and community. A successful art program employed a systematic curriculum that both allowed for the individual interests of children and drew inspiration from their local environment. Educators encouraged children's creativity by banishing tracing paper and patterns to avoid copying. From time to time SEP inspectors visited schools to ensure that teachers carried out the art education program according to the established norms.[29] Elementary and secondary schoolchildren could expect a structured half hour of drawing and handicraft instruction three days a week. First graders had drawing class for twenty minutes every day.[30] Older students engaged in practical application of drawing skills; young ladies at the School of Domestic Education produced embroidery, lace, artificial flowers, and decorative paintings all based on the approved drawing techniques.[31] The unifying theme in the drawing and handicrafts curriculum was that all drawing, design, and crafts be distinctly Mexican. And as it turned out, the real Mexico lay beneath its modernizing facade, in the pre-Columbian ruins and ancient peoples that populated its past.

Best Maugard saw children as fundamental to Mexico's visual cultural revolution. While adult art teachers under his tutelage struggled to unlearn the formal training they had learned in the academy, the children exposed to his method seemed unhindered by acquired aesthetic conventions. He believed that his curriculum could unlock the innate expressions of national identity inexplicably locked away inside the youthful subconscious; he conveyed these convictions to a foreign observer by describing children's art as "pure" and "true," as well as "boldly primitive" and "exotic."[32]

Though the Best Maugard Method uprooted the entrenched academy that had relied on antiquated neoclassical standards of drawing, the program suffered significant modifications with the administrative changes that accompanied Vasconcelos's departure from the secretariat of the SEP in 1924. Manuel Rodríguez Lozano assumed the directorship of the Department of Drawing and Handicrafts upon Best Maugard's departure, followed shortly by sculptor Juan Olaguíbel in 1925. The latter shifted the emphasis of the drawing program away from Best Maugard's formulaic approach and toward an emphasis on drawing from nature, in a move that worked to make children's art less methodological and more broadly applicable to the rest of their course work.[33] Despite the technical shift, Best Maugard's pivotal reorientation of the Mexican aesthetic remained. Under Olaguíbel's direction what remained of Best Maugard's instruction were the application of the motifs to decoration and the selection of "nationalist" subject matter. But Olaguíbel believed in liberating students from the schematic confines of the method and sought to make drawing a more appealing and engaging endeavor.[34] Olaguíbel waxed poetic about the transformative power of drawing—like Best Maugard, he recognized its revolutionary potential, but he saw the process of drawing as more viscerally linked to individual psychological well-being and emotional growth.[35] For children, he considered drawing to be the written music with which they could express their most intimate thoughts, the best vehicle for them to interact with the outside world. He saw in the fantastic etchings of children the premonitions of a future reality.[36] In this spirit Olaguíbel created the magazine *Pulgarcito.*

Vasconcelos, Best Maugard, Olaguíbel, and the artist community sought to codify a set of images in ways that would become universally recognizable as Mexican, and to a great extent they succeeded. But the key to their success would be in training future artists, designers, architects, industrial workers, and artisans. A theoretically informed elementary art curriculum that built its instruction systematically upon Best Maugard's method served this purpose. *Pulgarcito* facilitated the broad visibility of this aesthetic shift. The road to creating a nativist aesthetic steeped in official history was not without its potholes, and schoolchildren around the country participated in the process. Somewhere between objects of socialization and agents of constructing history, young artists asserted their will, not necessarily as precocious Mexican citizens but rather as willful children.

Pulgarcito: Forging a Virtual and Real Community of Child Artists

The public school art curriculum, while revolutionary and appealing to its child audience, had a relatively limited scope in its goals to nationalize artistic production. Olaguíbel's creation of a cocurricular children's art magazine allowed for new artistic methods and subject matter to reach a broader public. The Department of Drawing and Handicrafts, with the financial backing of the government and commercial sponsors, published *Pulgarcito* from 1925 to 1932 as a free monthly children's art magazine, distinguished from all other publications of its kind by its entirely child-produced content. Children participated in their own socialization through their contributions to the magazine. *Pulgarcito* is Spanish for "Little Tom Thumb," the seventeenth-century fairy tale by Charles Perrault about a tiny boy who repeatedly saves the lives of his siblings from the jaws of a child-eating ogre through heroic, selfless acts. The moral of the story—never underestimate the worth of the weakest, most diminutive members of society—resonated with the mission of the magazine, which was to provide a forum for the artistic expression of children with national and international circulation. *Pulgarcito* had a ready market.

Pulgarcito first came out in May 1925 as a twenty-page magazine; within a month so many children's contributions flooded the editorial offices that the length grew to thirty-two pages, and by the end of the year the magazine boasted a hefty forty-two pages and increased its circulation, as children and adults alike scrambled to get their hands on a copy. Within the first year of publication SEP officials approved the expansion outside of the Mexico City school districts to the Department of Rural Schools (Escuelas Rurales). At the apex of publication in 1928, ten thousand issues of *Pulgarcito* reached Mexico's primary schoolchildren.[37] Although it organized its artistic instruction around the Best Maugard Method, in particular in the sections devoted to decoration and domestic arts, *Pulgarcito* nearly supplanted *Método de dibujo* as the official text, due to its fresh monthly thematic emphasis, visually appealing format, and child-produced content. The magazine paid homage to Best Maugard's method by continuing to provide artistic instruction based on his motifs, but the overall emphasis tended toward translating guided educational experiences into nationalist image production. Editors characterized the eponymous Pulgarcito as a little boy, scampering across the magazine's pages, announcing new competitions, and reminding young readers of proper hygiene and moral and civic behavior. What began as a recreational supplement to the educational program quickly became a pedagogical must-have, and in 1926 Secretary of Education José Manuel Puig Casauranc praised *Pulgarcito* as the "bible" of the Department of Drawing and Handicrafts.[38]

Children's print press did not come about in Mexico, as such, until around 1870, and even then the genre of children's magazines seemed to target a muddied audience of parents, child specialists, and children themselves. Where magazines did imply an audience of child readers, they almost always exuded positivist overtones of the proper manifestations of socialization and civilization. Otherwise, nineteenth-century publications for children contained fanciful fairy tales directly translated from French and English and promoted the romanticized Victorian childhood ideal.[39] The revolution prioritized literacy as a basic responsibility of the government, and literacy campaigns in the 1920s opened up diverse niche markets for the printed word. As a result, a proliferation of magazines appeared for interest groups across the social spectrum, and children were no exception. Commercial, religious, and governmental presses all churned out literature for children—pamphlets, how-to manuals, puzzles, fairy tales, moralistic tales, cartoon strips, advertisements, and popular histories number among the genres of children's literature available in print beginning in the 1920s. Yet even given the flurry of printed material that found its way into children's hands—and then passed along to other children until it dissolved to tatters—*Pulgarcito*'s interactive format, with drawings and text produced almost exclusively by its audience, remained peerless.[40]

The organization of the magazine, boasting more drawings than text, forced readers to scrutinize the images more closely to draw out meaning, a practice that boosted the visual literacy of the generation. The children who read *Pulgarcito* grew up in an age swirling with new visual stimuli, due to the advances of print technology and mass dissemination (see chapter 3). As cultural receivers they were much more adept at reading visual codes and filtering desired messages from the environment choked with industrial signage, mass-produced commercials, and circulated printed material.[41]

With the exception of the opening article (a drawing lesson often written by Olaguíbel), the occasional civics page, and "Pulgarcito's Mailbox," discussed below, children's essays constituted all of the magazine's text. Children, as in Best Maugard's book, provided all of the illustrations adorning *Pulgarcito*'s pages; once commercial sponsors signed on—Nestlé, Spaulding, a public bathhouse—children illustrated the advertisements too (fig. 12). Finding advertisers for a magazine directed only at children could have posed a serious business challenge, but given the rapid rise of consumer savvy among younger people, creative opportunities for advertising abounded. The trolley company Compañía de Tranvía paid for ads but made its services more relevant to their young readers by also sponsoring a contest in every issue of the magazine, in which the child with the best submission depicting safety rules for trolley riding won a cash prize. In a process described by Joanne Hershfield, the magazine's open attitude toward commercial advertisements coexisted with a state project of marketable nationalism, in a cultural forum that showcased Mexico's increasing engagement with a global culture of modern consumption, all while maintaining strong nationalist content.[42] The new technology gained visibility among young children in the pages of the magazine, and the contest urged them to pay close attention to the mechanics and operation of the trolleys, ensuring a generational shift toward acceptance in a rapidly modernizing urban environment.

The comfort of a magazine as a shared cultural reference helped to unify social groups that otherwise might have had

12. Advertisement for a local public bathhouse drawn for *Pulgarcito* by child contributors, 1926. *Pulgarcito*, December 1926, n.p.

very little in common. *Pulgarcito* was accessible to young children in everything including its titular logo, scrawled in a childish hand and marked with ink blots as if to suggest that no judgments should be made on the natural imperfections of children's work. Upon receiving her shipment of twenty-five copies of *Pulgarcito*, a schoolteacher from Santa Elena in the northern state of Coahuila wrote to the editors to express her gratitude; she enthused that the magazine was the best friend to come visit the children since the construction of their school.[43] As described by Benedict Anderson, children experienced a sense of belonging to a nation through their interaction with a circulated, published literary form.[44] Yet beyond merely imagining themselves as part of the community, the child contributors created the cultural form itself, on their own terms, and without the required tool of literacy—albeit according to guidelines set by adults. Children across the nation were encouraged to send in submissions, as *Pulgarcito* extended the arm of the government out from the country's cultural and intellectual core. Shortly, fortunate schoolchildren who could get their hands on a copy found themselves members of a virtual community of their peers, collaborators, and consumers of *Pulgarcito.*

Among the citizens of an imagined nation of *Pulgarcito* readers, natural hierarchies emerged. The structured nature of collaboration in *Pulgarcito*'s production allowed for certain child contributors to gain greater visibility on the magazine's pages, and therefore among the community of child readers. Contributors gained recognition for their collaboration either through publication or via prizes in the form of money or merchandise from advertisers. In fact, the editors relied upon their readers' competitive spirits and reminded potential contributors that, if published, their drawing would enjoy universal recognition among readers nationwide, all of whom would "express their admiration for that fortunate child."[45] Eventually, the regular contributors became familiar to readers not only through their constantly published artwork but also because editors began placing head shots of the most famous children next to their articles or pictures for more widespread recognition. These precocious artists began to enjoy celebrity among their peers at an early age through this new medium. For example, Mario Aburto, one of *Pulgarcito*'s most consistent prizewinning collaborators, became readily recognizable among readers through his ample exposure (fig. 13). Mario not only entered and won nearly every contest but was even selected to write an homage to *Pulgarcito* on the occasion of the magazine's first anniversary. Needless to say, the article bordered on sycophantic, as the author was indebted to *Pulgarcito* for launching his early starship to fame.[46] Occasionally, the magazine reiterated the personality status of the regular contributors in such spreads as that pictured in figure 14, a photomontage of head shots of some of the most "indefatigable" collaborators. Mario's portrait figures among the constellation of budding artistic stars, and the caption below the two-page spread suggests the degree of their incipient fame, noting that the reader might already recognize some of the faces of these distinguished frequent contributors.

CONCURSO

1º—Todo niño bien educado debe subir al tren sin correr.

2º—El niño bien educado debe subir al tren cuando esté parado, y no subir cuando está en movimiento.

3º—El niño que es educado, al subir al tren, no debe permanecer en el estribo más que el tiempo debido.

4º—Los niños, siempre deben subir correctamente, y sin atropellar a las personas.

5º—Para que un niño tome un tren, no debe estar jugando en el momento de hacerlo.

6º—Manera incorrecta de subir a un tren: el niño que sube al tren cuando está en movimiento, está expuesto a un gran peligro.

7º—El niño que toma a media calle el tren, está a punto de que le pase una desgracia.

8º—Para bajar de un tren, debe uno bajar por la parte delantera, y no por detrás.

13. Mario Aburto's winning contest entry and accompanying photograph, 1926. *Pulgarcito*, February 1926, 21.

Félix de la Portilla was another frequent contributor and prize-winner, sometimes contributing two essays and a drawing in a single issue. Whether children like Mario and Félix were relatives of the editors or children of high-level government functionaries or just exceptionally talented children (a dubious evaluation, as their art does not particularly stand out), they emerged as a privileged social strata. In a way the resulting hierarchy among children, already a marginal social group just edging its way into civic society, paved the way for future political stratification as these children grew up already accustomed to recognizing the favoritism characteristic in the political system—a feature endemic to Mexican politics in the twentieth century.

Pulgarcito was not just a site for positive feedback for its child contributors; the forum also facilitated public shaming among the virtual community. In their anxiety to get the product right,

COLABORADORES DE "PULGARCITO"

He aqui este gru
trabajadores, que,
riño sincero, han
qarcito" sin desma
que "Pulgarcito"
año de vida, abre su
entre estas infantiles

po de infatiqables
llenos de fe y de ca-
laborado en "Pul-
yar un instante. Hoy
cumple su primer
corazón y lo reparte
cabecitas.

DE ENTRE ESTE NUMEROSO GRUPO, MIS QUERIDOS LECTORCITOS, PODRAN
JOSE SANCHEZ, MARIO ABUNTO, MIGUELITO SOTO, JESUS HERNANDEZ, AN

CONOCER A JULIAN ESTEVES, BENJAMIN CASTAÑEDA, MARIO SAN MARTIN,
GEL SHARP, ALEJANDRO DIAZ Y TANTOS OTROS QUE SERIA LARGO ENUMERAR

14. Head shots of outstanding contributors to the magazine. The same issue contains a similar spread featuring the girl contributors, 1926. *Pulgarcito*, May 1926, 36–37.

born perhaps out of their belief in the perfectibility of cultural production, the editors wielded a stick against any nonconformists. "Pulgarcito's Mailbox" ("El Buzón de Pulgarcito") appeared on the last page of every issue with announcements and drawing advice, but more often it featured public reprimands of individual children who had somehow failed in their creative submission. The most reviled crime was that of submitting a copied or traced work of art; in his book on methods Best Maugard berated the nineteenth-century art programs based on copying European models as suffering from a lack of originality, and in the pages of *Pulgarcito* the act amounted to high treason of national ideals. Shaming, though it still constituted public attention, came at a price to the aspiring artists who submitted drawings of questionable integrity; the publishers often announced the transgressors' full names, schools, street addresses, or towns, so that these children were certain to be recognized. For example, the unfortunate student Jorge Domínguez opened his October 1, 1926, issue of *Pulgarcito* to the last page to see his name and street address in bold print, followed by a diatribe by the editors. Employing the formal address of "Ud." to set the tone for the gravity of the matter, the editors accused Jorge of tracing or copying his submission from another source. They expressed indignation at the affront to their sensibilities that his defective, malicious drawing had occasioned and suggested that his lack of originality would permanently damage his sense of self-worth.[47] Another letter to Luz María Castañeda implied that she had had a bit too much adult help with her essay, resulting in an utterly unoriginal, uninfantile piece.[48] Every month several children suffered a similar fate in "Pulgarcito's Mailbox," certain to become the laughingstock of their peers both locally and across the nation. In an economy of social capital the dynamic of "Pulgarcito's Mailbox" allowed certain children to achieve stardom, while others found themselves pushed to the margins of their social cohort. Admittedly, the editors' comments, edited and published in the magazine, neither constitute children's direct voices nor reveal the raw drawings that children submitted; we can only imagine children's responses upon seeing their names published as part of a public admonition. The fact that the editors publicized primarily negative feedback—intended, no doubt, to be constructive and to yield more conscientious submissions—nevertheless underscored individual children's relative feelings of self-worth, as they received the criticism with the full knowledge of its public nature.

Pulgarcito thus offered readers the potential for either social peril or collegial fraternity through its competitive format. Juan Olaguíbel and the other *Pulgarcito* editors converted this virtual community into a tangible reality, through the creation of ample physical spaces of social interaction for the readers of *Pulgarcito*. In the afternoons, the editors of *Pulgarcito* opened the doors of their downtown offices to any children, both from the neighborhood and from outlying states, to come and draw at one of the three huge workshop tables that stood for precisely that purpose.[49] Olaguíbel designed the creative space, available after classes were let out at four in the afternoon, both for didactic purposes (Best Maugard's techniques and exemplary student drawings were always prominently displayed on the walls) and to allow for interaction and exchange of ideas among the potential contributors. The ad hoc drawing sessions became so popular that the editors began publishing guidelines for behavior in the public building, as well as suggested times to arrive, admonishing that it would do no good to skip classes to go draw, since they would not open the doors until four.

While doubtless many children came to hone their drawing skills so that they might be published in the pages of the magazine devoured by their friends and siblings every month, others saw the drawing session as an extension of the playground and went only to socialize. Young Ana Cires suffered humiliation at the hands of "Pulgarcito's Mailbox" for her lackluster appearances at the afternoon sessions; the editor noted that she might have observed, on her frequent and notable visits to the drawing tables, that children are indeed capable of brilliant artistic production. Such children could expect to earn prizes for their diligence. Ana, however, would receive no such prize so long as she continued to be disruptive, unproductive, and disrespectful toward the medium of drawing.[50] Perhaps adults expected all of the children to be as industrious as Mario Aburto and submit page after page of Aztec motif–inspired nationalist sketches, but in reality many children were probably more like Ana Cires, excited about the new social space opened to their ranks but less concerned with the pedagogical goals. The high index of insubordination with the editors' expectations for propriety— both in the virtual and in the real interactions that *Pulgarcito* offered—underscores the fragility of interpreting children's reception of cultural projects intended for their benefit.

In theory the programs that *Pulgarcito* editors conceptualized with the goal of creating safe, healthy sites of sociability for their readers could only be applauded. The magazine hosted parties for children to interact with their peers outside of their homes, classrooms, and neighborhood blocks. *Pulgarcito*'s first birthday allowed for full-scale participation in the event, hosted by the city's Teatro Hidalgo in downtown Mexico City and celebrated by a series of musical and theatrical acts carried out by *Pulgarcito* readers from primary and secondary schools. Children spent weeks designing and painting the sets and backdrops for the theatrical pieces, which included a rendition of the fairy tale of the titular character Little Tom Thumb. A whole issue of the magazine dedicated to the details of the party surely elicited yearning and pouting from children in the outlying states who were unable to attend this reunion of their friends—the editors acknowledged the networks of peer recognition that the magazine had fostered by naming the recognizable ones: Mario Aburto, Félix de la Portilla, and José Castañeda, among others. Much of the May 1926 edition recounted the glorious events of the birthday celebration for the vicarious enjoyment of those children not in attendance.

The Ministry of Education, through its Department of Drawing and Handicrafts, sought to make *Pulgarcito* an agent in constructing a uniform cultural experience for children across the country, to further tighten the imaginary strings that tied the nation together. Yet in practice reunions of this sort strengthened the privilege of Mexico City–based readers within their cohort and contributed to the further alienation of children from the provinces and even urban children from other cities far removed from the locus of the festivities. While the creation of physical spaces for social interaction surely reinforced a sense of membership in this new community of their peers for those fortunate ticket holders, the continued exclusion of the majority of the nation's children served only to underscore the privilege of the core over the periphery in the nationalizing efforts of the education program.[51]

Gendered by Design

Pulgarcito could be lauded for its equitable inclusion of girl and boy collaborators. Page for page, girls numbered almost equally alongside boys as artists, prizewinners, and essayists for the magazine in what appears to be a testament to the SEP's commitment to coeducation. By 1925 the Department of Rural Schools boasted several fully integrated coed student council organizations that included competitions and service activities.[52] Though integrated in most subjects, the revolutionary public education system retained gendered divisions in its curriculum.[53] Civic-based organizations such as the Boy Scouts and Girl Scouts that worked parallel to the schools (and utilized school organizational structures and resource bases) divided protocitizens into activities according to so-called feminine virtues and masculine enterprises, a manifestation of gendered nationalism discussed in greater depth in chapters 5 and 6. One could argue that the drawing curriculum in general and the magazine in particular put forth a modern model for citizenship training that allowed for girls and boys to participate in the construction of a national aesthetic on equal terms. A closer examination of the subject matter of *Pulgarcito* drawings published by girls and boys, and the sections of the magazine in which these appear, reflects more traditional gendered patterns of production that echoed parallel gendered divisions within the classroom. Ultimately, the citizenship-training exercises of the drawing program divided girls and boys into conventional domains of economic production: the private and the public spheres, respectively.

The different drawing methods and subjects in the art curriculum were reflected in different sections of *Pulgarcito*, including decorative, technical, observation (*apuntes del natural*), and historical illustration. The decorative drawing section of *Pulgarcito* most clearly points to the persistent gendered division in the public school curriculum as it filtered into the Department of Drawing and Handicrafts. Decorative drawing, intended to provide templates for embroidery and domestic arts, most closely adhered to Best Maugard's drawing method. It placed a heavy emphasis on modernist floral designs. Not surprisingly, nearly all of the published decorative drawings included in the pages of *Pulgarcito*, when attributed at all, were drawn by girls. On the one hand, decorative drawing enjoyed the privilege of being identified as the "most Mexican"[54] of all drawing styles and became the most readily recognizable stamp of national identity due to its highly stylized and formulaic composition

Pulgarcito

POR QUE DEBEN SER DE ESTILO MEXICANO NUESTROS DIBUJOS

Esperamos que nuestros queridos lectorcitos hayan visto con interés la sección que "PUL-

MARIA LUNA.—14 años.—Escuela 36.

GARCITO" ha titulado "Del Extranjero". En ella figuran los trabajos ejecutados por los niños de las

15. Decorative drawing, often done by girls, was deemed the stamp of "Mexicanness" by the magazine editors, 1928. _Pulgarcito_, March 1928, 5.

(fig. 15). On the other hand, decorative drawing restricted the creativity of the student more so than any other genre, curbing artistic license and imagination. The decorative drawings, and the girl artists who produced them, bore the responsibility of conjuring "local flavor" and of transmitting the architectural aesthetic values of the ancients in their modern compositions.[55]

Meanwhile, the incentives in genres of drawing dominated by boys were more economic than moral. Boys' contributions overwhelmingly predominated the recurring drawing contests titled "Why Children Should Ride Streetcars," featuring cash prizes for the top two winners and honorable mentions for three others in nearly every issue. Winning drawings featured busy street and traffic scenarios, coupled with a safety-related caption that introduced proper streetcar conduct to young prospective passengers, as illustrated in one of Mario Aburto's meritorious entries (see fig. 13). Many children—mostly boys—drew scenes of well-orchestrated urban transportation, taking care to depict the mechanical workings of the streetcar with technical precision. But a favorite subset of this competition's winning entries, with captions like "It is very dangerous to alight a streetcar in midstreet, since a truck could easily pass and run you over" or "A driver's carelessness," featured horrific accidents occasioned by the failure of pedestrians, passengers, or conductors to heed the rules of the road. Boys may well have been naturally drawn to the thematic emphasis of this ongoing contest that emphasized technology and offered the promise of danger and disaster. But the appeal of a monthly cash prize—the only contest in the magazine with this level of economic reward—certainly must have appealed to girls as well.

In a rare exception to this male-dominated *Pulgarcito* category, Vicenta Cordero, a thirteen-year-old girl, earned five pesos for her second-place winning drawing titled "A traffic accident," a subject matter undifferentiated from that of the first-place winner, José Cárdenas: "Collision between a streetcar and a truck" (fig. 16).[56] The singularity of a girl's representation in this monthly contest, and the juxtaposition of her drawing alongside that of her male counterpart, encourages closer scrutiny of her subject matter. Indeed, while she followed the modern conventions of sharp diagonal perspective lines and the anonymity of multiple human subjects depicted with stylized repetition, the crowd of onlookers in her scene is nearly wholly composed of women, recognizable by their dresses, shawls, braids, or even economic activity (one woman carries a basket of goods on her head). José's drawing, by contrast, features one or two women, while men in uniforms occupy the central narrative of his piece, as they rush to action, administer first aid, redirect traffic, and assess damage. Women were more visible in Vicenta's world and thus in her drawing seemed a natural inclusion. Yet one cannot help but notice the passivity of Vicenta's drawing compared to that of José: the lack of catastrophe or physical damage (or even a victim), the voyeuristic inaction of the largely female crowd, and the general stillness of the piece. Whether the gendered differences apparent between these two drawings were endemic or exceptional is impossible to determine, given the lack of representation by girls in this category. This discrepancy might have been an editorial decision, which would suggest that girls' depictions of street scenes, urban architecture, and technology did not often meet their demanding criteria. It might also be explained by more deeply embedded cultural and systemic biases that subtly discouraged girls from traversing domains considered masculine, and so they simply did not submit their drawings. In any case, notwithstanding *Pulgarcito*'s commendable role in normalizing the participation of boys and girls in a modern transmission of cultural nationalism, a closer look at the children's drawings reveals the persistence of more traditional gendered structures that reined girls back in to the private sphere.

Drawing Popocatépetl into the National Imaginary

Olaguíbel saw Mexico's urban and rural landscapes as extensions of *Pulgarcito*'s classrooms; he wanted to mobilize children (particularly those living in Mexico City) out to observe their country's unique physical features, those volcanoes and cornfields currently being documented by the muralists. Diligence and talent in art class brought children opportunities to engage further with their fellow readers in the form of excursions of selected students to important national sites in the capital and its environs. The fortunate excursionists usually hailed from schools in Mexico City's neighborhoods in the greater metropolitan area and had all earned the trip on the merit of their performance

CONCURSO

PRIMER PREMIO $10.00, OTORGADO A JOSE CARDENAS. EDAD 15 AÑOS

Choque entre un tranvía y un camión.

JOSE CARDENAS

VICENTA CORDERO

SEGUNDO PREMIO $5.00, OTORGADO A VICENTA CORDERO. EDAD: 13 AÑOS

16. Comparison of gendered differences in the streetcar-safety drawing contests, featuring a rare winning contribution by a girl, Vicenta Cordero, 1926. *Pulgarcito*, May 1926, 20.

in art class. Once again children transcended the boundaries of peer groups constructed by family, classrooms, and geography as they mingled with other children, perhaps strangers, but sharing the experience of being readers of *Pulgarcito* and thus having a common bond. These outings, often hosted by Olaguíbel himself, were designed to instill in children a pride in Mexico's geographic distinctions or industrial potential. The excursions fell into two categories, with two distinct didactic goals.

The first category of *Pulgarcito* excursions brought children to urban industrial centers. The trips to manufacturing and production sites included the textile factory, the Larín chocolate factory, a match factory, and Talleres Gráficos de la Nación, the national printing press that published *Pulgarcito* (where thirteen-year-old Pedro Rodríguez watched his own drawings pass through the machinery and emerge in mass production).[57] These types of urban excursions featured Mexico's modernity in its national industries, technology, and productive power— not coincidentally, the commercial houses visited advertised frequently in the magazine, often running ads illustrated by children alongside testimonial accounts of their visit to the site. The sponsored excursions afforded children the opportunity to witness their country's modern side firsthand, the advertisements encouraged them to support it through economic nationalism, and through the drawing exercises they performed an engineering ritual, the first step in understanding a technological process. For the vast majority of *Pulgarcito* readers unable to attend the excursions, these instructive drawings served as a proxy, delivered by the hand of another child, for industrial knowledge.

The second category of excursions provided perhaps the most compelling visual vocabulary through visits to pastoral locations outside of the city, such as a colonial hacienda, thought by Olaguíbel to be quintessentially Mexican. Subsidized by the Compañía de Tranvías streetcar company that advertised on the magazine's pages and hosted competitions, entourages of students armed themselves with notebooks and pencils to pictorially document their field trips. These day trips could involve as many as six hours of round-trip train travel, in addition to the several hours spent on site observing, absorbing, and drawing the local culture, food, and vistas. As recounted by student José Víctor Silva in 1926, the trip itself fostered friendships among a group of thirty students who had been strangers to each other when they set foot on the train platform. "At first we didn't know each other," wrote José, "but little by little we began making friends to the point of seeming like longtime classmates" by the time they arrived at the hacienda Miraflores. The fleeting sense of community forged through this day trip enjoyed an extended life, as fellow excursionists saw their drawings from a particular excursion displayed publicly at the SEP building and yet again when *Pulgarcito* published them in a collage in a subsequent issue.[58] The publication of the images generated on this fleeting encounter served as a form of virtual reunion, through which the excursion participants could relive their newly forged and perhaps ephemeral friendships for a time.

As one schoolteacher noted in 1931, the drawing program excursions to the countryside not only taught children an appreciation of nature but also inspired them to love it, to absorb the country's folklore, and to become saturated in the "national environment."[59] In these bucolic surroundings children were urged to pay close attention to the details of nature: the local flora and fauna, the colonial architecture, and the humble residences that marked their countryside and impressed upon their souls. Children documented these sojourns in written reports, published in *Pulgarcito* along with the resulting drawings and photographs of the school groups at the site.

A close look at a student drawing from a *Pulgarcito*-sponsored excursion to the Corralejos Hacienda in 1926 suggests the way that an artistic exercise could serve to foment an appreciation of the national landscape. Third grader Manuel Jiménez earned a centerfold spread in the magazine for his rendition of the hacienda and its vast agricultural tracts, an honorific dedication of precious print space that signaled the approval of the editors (fig. 17).[60] The drawing stands out for its geometric precision and inscrutable attention to detail. Apparently drawing from a vantage point on a nearby hilltop, Manuel situated the walled edifice of the hacienda at a diamond-shaped angle at the center of the page, an uncommon and modernist perspective compared to the expected full-frontal, square angle from which one customarily approaches a building. But most impressive is Manuel's depiction of the surrounding cornfields, orchards, vegetable gardens, outbuildings, and forested hills that proceed outward from the hacienda's administrative center. Manuel meticulously penned thousands of identical stalks of corn in ruler-straight rows in an exercise that must have taken hours. Rather than provide the impression of stonework in the wall surrounding the building, Manuel drew each stone and brick. Manuel's technique and subject matter reveal a combined application of the Best Maugard Method and Olaguíbel's tendency toward experiential and emotional drawing. On the one hand, the texture of the building's walls and farmlands is neatly organized into stylized, undisrupted patterns, with uniform shapes and lines coming together to form a pattern, following Best Maugard's formula. But the commitment to perfecting the rows of corn and the attention to all of the details of the economic workings of what appeared to be a successful hacienda system seemed to have produced a sense of reverence in the young author, who was clearly impressed by the scope and orderliness of rural Mexican agricultural production. Just above the visual center of the drawing, Manuel drew a hill topped with cactus plants, an undeniable place marker that situated this scene in Mexico. The overtones of economic nationalism that emanate from this young drawer's piece, and the plenitude of cornstalks streaming across the page, echo the sweeping landscapes of the muralists, populated as they were by the anonymous masses, the people of the corn.

Not coincidentally, *Pulgarcito* most frequently sponsored drawing trips to the village of Amecameca, where visitors can enjoy what has become an iconic view of the snow-capped volcanoes Popocatépetl and Ixtaccíhuatl. Mexico's mountains, and the twin volcanoes in particular, have long been a source of pride, a metaphor for local identity linked with a geographic sense of place. Affectionately nicknamed "Popo" and "Ixta," the mountains have

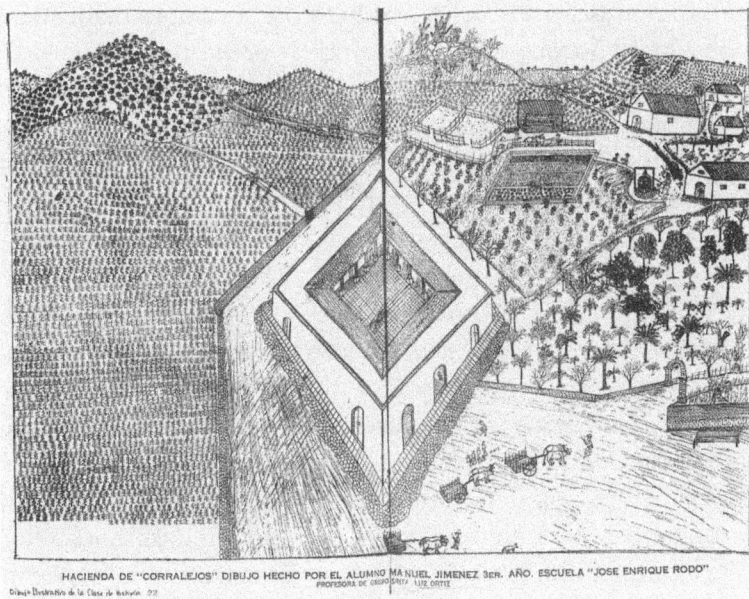

HACIENDA DE "CORRALEJOS" DIBUJO HECHO POR EL ALUMNO MANUEL JIMENEZ 3ER. AÑO. ESCUELA "JOSE ENRIQUE RODO"
PROFESORA DE GEOGRAFIA LUZ ORTIZ

Dibujo Ilustrativo de la Clase de Historia 22

17. Drawing by third grader Manuel Jiménez on an excursion to the Corralejos Hacienda, depicting astute attention to the details of agriculture
that suggests a reverence for the landscape, 1926. *Pulgarcito*, October
1926, 22–23.

presided over the rise and fall of civilizations and empires and
have become important icons for the millions of humans who
have passed through their valleys. The Nahuatl word for "community" is *altepetl*—literally, water-mountain. A stylized mountain glyph symbolized place-names in pre-Hispanic codices, and
the depiction of a stylized mountain representing Popocatépetl
would automatically signal to the Nahua-speaking codex viewer
a reference to a certain location and ethnicity.[61] The twin pyramids that occupied the center of Tenochtitlán before the Spaniards leveled them to create what today is Mexico City's central
plaza were intended to mirror the twin volcanoes on the horizon.
Popo (the active volcano) and Ixta (the dormant one) were considered by the Aztecs to represent a mythological married couple, personified in lore as a virile prince and his sleeping bride.
In the nineteenth century painter José María Velasco always fig-

ured his landscapes in relationship to the volcanoes that ringed the Valley of Mexico; when his paintings were exhibited abroad, he made sure that his signature included the appendix "*mexicano*," strengthening the association between national identity and the geographic features.[62] The association became so entrenched that today, the Metrobus stop named for Velasco on Mexico City's main thoroughfare Insurgentes bears the image of the volcanoes. In the mid-twentieth century calendar kitsch artist Jesús Helguera adopted as a favorite theme the sexualized, noble-savage portrayal of the ancestral duo arranged in various strident poses, juxtaposed against a backdrop of the volcanoes that bear their monikers. Helguera's hyperbolic pairings of the mythic royal couple and the landforms that ensure their immortality have become entrenched in popular culture, especially as requisite décor in international Mexican restaurants and border curio shops.

Around the time of *Pulgarcito*'s first publication, Dr. Atl began painting volcanoes. Dr. Atl, born Gerardo Murillo, adopted an alter Nahuatl identity in an altruistic display of *indigenismo*, expressing entitlement over the indigenous cultural heritage to which all Mexicans (but especially the artistic and intellectual elites) could feel free to lay claim after the revolution.[63] The artist community, famously headed by Diego Rivera, rabidly espoused this brand of *indigenismo*, paying homage to a romanticized indigenous past through their clothing and art subjects, while effectively ignoring the inconvenient reality of an impoverished, marginalized indigenous population that still made up the majority of Mexico's population. Dr. Atl styled the volcanoes, and by extension himself, as metaphors for the Mexican Revolution. He rendered his volcanoes dramatic through the thick application of a paint concoction invented by and named for the artist—Atl color. Atl's smoldering jagged peaks evoked the inherent revolutionary potential spewing forth from beneath Mexico's fertile soil. Even the way he depicted his unkempt curling white beard in self-portraits suggested the billowing ash that boils constantly from Popocatépetl's aperture.

In this cultural environment, in which layers of pride and distance conflated the pyramids and the volcanoes with the

Indians of yesteryear, *Pulgarcito*'s young readers trekked to Amecameca to draw Popo and Ixta. The ancestral majesty of the volcanoes represented the diametrical opposite of the urban factories, and their prominent role in *Pulgarcito*'s excursion program served as a metaphor for the intellectual *indigenista* vogue. Those children deemed to have artistic aptitude witnessed the physical landscapes of both Mexico's modern aspirations and its timeless native past, and they were urged to fuse this dual identity into their drawings. With the encouragement of *Pulgarcito* and inspired from their excursions to Amecameca, schoolchildren included the timeless volcanoes in their history illustration, making a powerful link between the storied indigenous national past and the present. As with the sponsored urban excursions, children on the volcano outings maintained virtual ties to their colleagues through the subsequent publication of their adventures in the magazine. A collage of drawings done from the vantage point of Sacromonte by students on a January 1926 excursion to Amecameca demonstrates the students' different perspectives of the volcanoes. In one drawing a smoking Popocatépetl looms behind the village below it; another artist framed it neatly beneath the arch of the hillside chapel from which he drew; yet another placed the languid Ixtaccíhuatl at the center of his drawing, with Popo's taller peak cut off on the right side of the page.[64] All of these artists, in their own way, paid attention to the particular forms of the volcanoes, the shadows that they cast, and their relationship to the village of Amecameca.

Of course, being children, some of the excursionists failed to take full advantage of the opportunities to enact aesthetic cultural nationalist production offered by Olaguíbel. "Pulgarcito's Mailbox" took a boy named Ricardo to task; he had participated in the latest field trip to Amecameca but had submitted a drawing of Popo that had been copied from an illustrated advertisement featuring the volcano rather than one from his own perspective. The editors noted sternly that he would not be permitted on another sponsored excursion if he did not submit work on par with the originality demonstrated by his peers.[65]

18. Self-portrait of a child engaged in drawing the volcanoes, 1926. *Pulgarcito*, March 1926, 33.

Meanwhile, even among students who did not attend the excursions, the volcanoes often appeared in their history drawings, also published in *Pulgarcito*. It is likely that some of these children had never seen the volcanoes in person but were aware of the signifying power that lent a geographically specific nationalist stamp to their art. One particularly meta-referential drawing by ten-year-old Ramón Moisés Uribe accompanies an essay that he wrote extolling the vocational applications of drawing (and immediately following a student essay about a trip to visit the volcanoes); in this very simple image a person wearing a sombrero sketches the two volcanoes on an easel.[66] Ramón's choice of subject matter on the easel could just as easily have been a cow, vase, or train (objects he mentions in his essay), but he demonstrated an awareness that the act of drawing as a nationalist practice could most succinctly be summarized by doing what his collaborators described: contemplating the country's most iconic landscape features and rendering them one's own (fig. 18). A few months after a series of highly publicized

19. Student illustration of a history lesson, "The Chichimecas' arrival to the Valley of Mexico," with the stylized volcanoes in the background, 1926. *Pulgarcito*, July 1926, 13.

trips to Amecameca, the magazine included in its "History" section a few drawings that included the volcanoes in a depiction of the arrival of the Chichimecas to Tenochtitlán (Mexico City) in the pre-Hispanic era (fig. 19) and the founding of Tenochtitlán. Both of these students, not necessarily excursion participants, depict the volcanoes in the stylized way (as two symmetrical peaks), rather than a realistic study of Popo's jagged peaks and Ixta's softer slopes. This treatment, more squarely in line with Best Maugard's method of reducing observations of local landscape features to a codified set of simple geometric shapes, suggests that the students fused the experiences of their peers—studied on the pages of *Pulgarcito*—with the new formula for producing Mexican nationalist art that infused their classroom curriculum.

The Open-Air Schools and the Indigenous Countryside

As the urban and alpine *Pulgarcito*-sponsored excursions suggest, educational officials situated the revolutionary art curriculum on the shifting grounds between modernity and tradition. Stemming from José Vasconcelos's early advocacy for the "folklorization" of rural culture, the art education program sought ways to make rural life beautiful, relevant, and visible to urban Mexicans.[67] Much as the two field-trip categories had distinct pedagogical purposes, the magazine's format and submission guidelines constructed their audience into two fundamentally different roles. On the one hand, the primary audience (and most frequent contributors) consisted of middle-class, mestizo or white, Mexico City–based children who represented the modern sector. On the other hand, all of the children who lived outside of cities (and really those who lived outside of Mexico City), who were indigenous, who were poor, or who were any combination of these characteristics represented the traditional sector. *Pulgarcito*'s ambivalence to this latter group meant that while editors encouraged and solicited nationwide contributions to the magazine, they carefully scripted the participation of certain children by holding them to an uncomfortable standard as the bearers of national authenticity. In the process editors conflated rural, poor, indigenous, and geographically marginalized identities as one and the same.

One early art initiative of the SEP's Fine Arts Department that set indigenous art education apart from that of nonindigenous children was the Open Air Painting Schools (Escuelas de Pintura al Aire Libre). Originally conceptualized in 1913 by Alfred Ramos Martínez to provide space and resources that would allow indigenous creativity to flow unmitigated by instruction, these schools received state sponsorship in 1920. The popular tenets (if not the methodology) of the Best Maugard Method gave these schools a surge in 1925.[68] The concerted redirection of art education away from the stolid method, marked by Olaguíbel's ascension to the head of the Department of Drawing and Handicrafts and the subsequent publication of *Pulgarcito*, moved away from didacticism and instead sought to leave students to be inspired by the elements.[69] Headed in many cases by leaders of the *indigenista* art vanguard (Dr. Atl was one of the most visible open-air school protagonists), the teachers nevertheless provided little to no technical direction. They were premised on the firm belief, and almost ethnographic fascination, in the power of raw indigenous art inspired by natural settings. Dr. Atl believed that children could make aesthetic contributions to the country's artistic patrimony; when an interviewer asked him about the creative potential of children, he replied that young people ought not to represent the future but insert their creative forces into the present. Not one of the children he instructed, he claimed, had produced a bad piece of art.[70] Enrollments were not required of matriculates, but purity of blood carried enormous value for art educators. Ramos Martínez included his assessment of the ethnic makeup of his four premier open-air schools in outlying Mexico City neighborhoods: he claimed that Xochimilco boasted 100 percent indigenous students, Tlalpam had 70 percent, and Guadalupe Hidalgo and Churubusco had 50 percent. He equated purity of blood with the timeless excellence of their art and suggested that racial mixture verifiably diluted the quality.[71] This biologically determinist approach to art informed the ways that art educators at *Pulgarcito* began to perceive their child readers on unequal terms.

Life outside of Mexico City was subject to romanticized aesthetic treatment, but the *Pulgarcito* readers actually living in the outlying states likely felt alienated from the excursions, parties, and access to the Department of Drawing and Handicrafts' coveted drawing tables enjoyed by their compatriots living in the metropolitan area of the capital. In February 1926 the editors had to establish a "Special Section for the States" to manage the contest entries from outside of Mexico City that arrived late due to distance;[72] while this concession was intended to minimize exclusion, it effectively created a separate office for children from the states and ensured that they would not compete with their peers in the capital, further marginalizing them from *Pulgarcito*'s daily activities.

Under the weight of expectations to produce culturally authentic art, not all contributors from the states inserted their work seamlessly into *Pulgarcito*'s pages. Children hailing from the states considered to be the cultural hubs of the nation (namely, Jalisco, Veracruz, and Oaxaca) bore the burden of representing a brand of cultural authenticity that was just beginning to become fashionable at the time that *Pulgarcito* gained currency.[73] Another victim of "Pulgarcito's Mailbox," Enrique Urena from Guadalajara, made the mistake of submitting a drawing titled *Japan*. The editors wasted little time and no ink in raking Enrique through the coals. First of all, they observed, the drawing had clearly been copied, a criminal act on par with robbery. Second, and most important, the editors expressed shock at the fact that Enrique, *of all children*, hailing from one of the centers of artistic inspiration, should resort to modeling his work on international influences that spoke nothing to the national soul. The editors made a point to extend this admonition to all of the contributors from Guadalajara who were, unfortunately, in large part misguided in their submissions to the magazine.[74] The editors made it clear that Mexico City–based children like Mario Aburto and Félix de la Portilla should handle the drawings of technology; Félix in particular earned a handsome sum through his prizewinning renditions of electric trolley cars and factory mechanics. Meanwhile, one child from Colima received a dressing-down for having submitted drawings of such modern subject matter as airplanes and military men rather than the natural beauty for which the coastal state is renowned.[75] Another more general warning addressed all children from the states, warning them that their submissions lacked originality because they did not represent the local character of the places in which they were produced.[76]

If *Pulgarcito* had lofty expectations of its collaborators from outside of Mexico City, its racialized assumptions about innate artistic ability placed double pressure on indigenous children. A clear example of the ways that *Pulgarcito* editors and competition officials idealized their indigenous child contributors as the messengers of an essentialized Mexico can be gleaned from newspaper reports of the contests. Olaguíbel treated the drawings with an ethnographic eye, considering them "human documents," a metaphor for the nation.[77] Since the Best Maugard system advocated the use of the child's immediate environment as the only inspiration for drawing, contest officials saw children's art as a window into the uncorrupted heart of the Mexican people. In the indigenous children's drawings, they saw detailed evidence of the quotidian life of the proletariat; judges perceived that middle-class children living in Colonia Roma did not employ the raw, vivid colors that came naturally to their more "authentic" rural counterparts.[78] One reporter stated that indigenous children had an innate ability to make art, whereas urban children had already been corrupted by foreign influences in popular culture and were thus unable to render authentically Mexican themes in their art.[79] For example, one of the most celebrated pieces included in a public exhibition of children's art was a narrative illustration done by an indigenous child, patterned in the style of a preconquest codex.

This neatly packaged dichotomous treatment of Mexico's children into categories of modern-urban and indigenous-rural resonated clearly with foreign admirers of the nationalist art program. Emma Reh Stevenson, an American journalist traveling in Mexico in the 1920s and reporting on Mexico's revolutionary educational reforms, wrote an article for members of the American Junior Red Cross, in which she echoed what she had learned from her visits to different art classrooms, excursions, and outdoor workshops across the country: that the best drawings came from the schools outside of Mexico City, where Indian blood is "purer" or "the thickest." In recounting her observations of two students' techniques in particular, Stevenson absorbed and reiterated art officials' discrete expectations of the two categories of children. Furthermore, her gendered descriptions feminize the indigenous-rural art and masculinize the modern-urban styles of production. She identified Matilde Gómez, a thirteen-year-old Indian girl from Xochimilco, as the product of an impossibly idyllic garden paradise who could not conceptualize the logic of drawing a straight line but possessed the "uncanny gift" of capturing humor or pathos in her painted scenes. Matilde contributed visual ethnographies of her humble village life to the Mexican art landscape—flea-bitten dogs, funerary processions, market hustle and bustle. She painted with emotion and used vivid color combinations unimaginable to the Western eye. By contrast, Stevenson described the talents displayed by a fourteen-year-old boy from Mexico City, who documented its "throbbing machinery, fast moving trains, engines and power plants" with strong, lifelike precision. His subject matter, his clean lines, and his interest in technology all situated this boy firmly in the masculine domains of power and control. This young protégé was none other than *Pulgarcito* celebrity Félix de la Portilla. As if struggling to justify the source of Félix's talent, Stevenson appended her celebration of his ability with the observation that, although he lived in the heart of Mexico City, "his skin is as brown as his pictures good."[80] For this foreign observer, as for the art curriculum creators in the 1920s, biology determined artistic ability, and the "cosmic race" had the market cornered on authentic aesthetic production.

The published interactions between *Pulgarcito* editors and the children from outside of Mexico City suggest two trends. First, art educators clearly held children from the states, and those from indigenous backgrounds, to a different standard in terms of the content of their artistic production. The format of the magazine, and the type of feedback that it generated, upheld a social stratification among child artists that privileged those in the city with access to technology and modern ideas. Second, though, the frequency of the editors' remonstrations indicates that children "from the states" persisted in participating in the modern project that their urban peers enjoyed. Despite the negative reinforcement received in "Pulgarcito's Mailbox," children from Jalisco and Michoacán continued to draw the things that compelled them—their subjects of choice continued to be commercial, technological, or foreign items, rather than the mariachi bands and jacarandas that they were supposed to portray. The one-sided declarations of the editors nevertheless imply a much more highly interactive discourse with the child artists, in which a subtle negotiation for cultural authority took place.[81]

The Mexican Race Draws for an International Audience

In the spirit of the Best Maugard Method, Mexican children worked to create the same set of visual cues that would conjure a particular view of Mexico in the foreign ambit. The magazine's editors, regardless of their avowed nationalism, had absolutely no aversion to international content, as long as it was presented in a way that reified the respective nation, such as a Swiss child's contribution featuring winter life in the Alps. Nationalist art from any country had a place in *Pulgarcito*'s "From Abroad" section; it took the form of distilling the represented country to a few readily recognizable visual tropes. So long as Swiss children drew themselves skiing down the vertiginous Alps and Japanese children painted Kakemono and Makemono graphic designs, their etchings could be found among *Pulgarcito*'s pages. The magazine provided a platform for the transnational exchange and surveillance of child-produced visual stamps of national identity. As the Mexican drawing technique gained international attention and acclaim for its originality, Olaguíbel saw *Pulgarcito*'s potential for exporting revolutionary nationalism with a distinctly Mexican flavor. Indigenous children, by virtue of their presumed ancestral proclivity for aesthetic production, had a special role in this mission. Through the magazine specifically and the Department of Drawing and Handicrafts more generally, previously unseen children saw themselves thrust into the international spotlight.

In 1927 *Pulgarcito* editors sent to Geneva the best drawings from their child contributors to a competition to illustrate the Geneva Convention on the Rights of the Child. Illustrations of children's rights themes included the right to be fed, sheltered, cured from illness, assisted in disability, protected from exploitation, and prepared to earn a living.[82] Mexico's participation in this international event signaled to the world its paternalism and protection over its citizens, metaphorically represented by the indigenous children who illustrated the country's submissions. These doubly vulnerable Mexicans—both indigenous *and* minors—made a powerful statement about the revolutionary state and its ability to deliver human rights. The state-sponsored newspaper *El Universal,* along with the national organizing committee of the International Union for Child Assistance (Unión Internacional de Socorros a los Niños), provided the prizes: fifty pesos in cash for first prize, to be deposited in the National School Savings Account and withdrawn along with personal savings by the winner upon completion of his or her primary education;[83] second prize was drawing materials; and third prize was school materials. The competition drew mass participation from the magazine's readership; more than twenty-four thousand children from around the country submitted entries.[84] Those selected to continue on to the international competition earned the honor of posing next to their winning submission for a photograph published in the SEP bulletin (fig. 20).[85] Children from twenty countries participated in this global art forum. According to the results of the contest, the Best Maugard art program paid off; Mexican children came away with more prizes and honorable mentions than representatives from any other country.

Fourteen-year-old Epifanio Flores, an indigenous child from Tlalpan, won second prize with his quintessentially Mexican piece that, according to judges, reflected the ancestral sadness and the traditional pain of the race (*la raza*).[86] By reproducing themes thought to be emblematic of staunch nationalist pride, young Epifanio had gained international renown among thousands of his peers. Normally, a fourteen-year-old indigenous boy would be well over the cusp of adulthood, already subject to social obligations that would poise him to head up a family of his own and bear a man's share of household labor and income. Indeed, in his published portrait in *El Sembrador,* young Epifanio seems to be sprouting the beginnings of a mustache (fig. 21). But by participating in the contest and gaining critical acclaim, Epifanio effectively stretched out his childhood, having been publicly identified in print as a child genius. The category of childhood thus flexed to allow for the inclusion of those who participated in child-centered cultural activities, and public recognition validated inclusion in this social group.

20. Twelve-year-old Juan de Gracia (first place) and fourteen-year-old Dolores García (third place) pose next to their national prizewinning entries that advanced to the international competition held in Geneva, 1927. *Boletín de la SEP* 6, no. 11 (1927): 143–59.

Entre Niños de Veinte Naciones, Triunfaron los Niños Mexicanos

EPIFANIO FLORES

Niño mexicano de 14 años, alumno de la Escuela No. 172 de Tlalpan, D. F., que obtuvo el Segundo Premio en el Concurso Mundial de Dibujos Infantiles que se celebró en Ginebra, Suiza. Epifanio Flores ha honrado a la patria y a la raza con su espléndido triunfo artístico.

Veinte naciones entraron en un concurso de dibujos infantiles, el cual se celebró en la capital de Suiza. De entre esas naciones, los niños mexicanos ocuparon el primer lugar, porque aun cuando no les correspondió el primer premio sino el segundo, obtuvieron mayor cantidad de diplomas y de menciones honoríficas que cualquier otro país.

Para hacer la entrega de estos premios, se celebró el día 22 de junio próximo pasado, una hermosa fiesta en el gran patio del soberbio edificio de la Secretaría de Educación Pública, fiesta presidida por el Secretario del Ramo, señor licenciado Padilla.

El señor profesor don Juan B. Salazar improvisó un bello discurso, del que tomamos los siguientes pasajes:

"A la manera como una fuente de aguas limpias refleja el azul del cielo, la rúbrica del vuelo de una golondrina, el verde follaje del sauz que crece junto a a orilla, así nuestros niños conservan fiel la intuición artísticas de las razas autóctonas que supieron laborar primorosos mosaicos con la pluma de los colibrís y tallar la laca en las jícaras de Uruapan y de Olinalá.

Lo que más llamó la atención de los críticos y de los conocedores de arte fue la bien destacada personalidad del niño mexicano como artista, la pureza y la sinceridad del sentimiento manifestados en la obra de arte. A la tristeza ancestral, al dolor tradicional de la raza manifestado en el espléndido medio mexicano que descubre por el verdor de sus campos, por la luz de sus horizontes y por la esmeralda de sus bosques. Personalidad irreductible y única que ha sabido expresar lo mismo que en la música, en el canto y en el color.

Cuando la Princesa Astrid visitó el Salón de Bruselas, en que se exhibían trabajos de nuestros niños, pidió un asiento para permanecer frente a los cuadros de los artistas mexicanos, y poder así saborear las obras de nuestro arte nacional.

La Secretaría de Educación Pública, por mi conducto, felicita al Departamento de Bellas Artes, al Director de dibujo y trabajos manuales, así como a los profesores de la materia y a los maestros de primaria, en general, que han sabido colaborar en esta obra y llevar a los niños al más franco éxito. Esa labor obscura del maestro de escuela, casi siempre ignorada, hoy, con motivo tan justo, esplende a plena luz y viene a recibir el aplauso de las autoridades escolares, de los padres, de los educandos y del público en general.

Seguid, maestros, trabajando como hasta aquí, sin interrogar la distancia que os separa del propósito final; seguid trabajando sin preocuparos por las escabrosidades propias de la senda que tiene que recorrer el educador. Haced porque vuestra labor logre ser un himno perenne al triunfo.

Para terminar, quiero recordaros un bello pasaje de un escritor ruso: hay algo más bello que las lágrimas de los niños mezcladas con rayos de sol, hay algo más hermoso que la corona de la desposada, que las frentes de los volcanes cubiertas de nieve, y el color de las rosas, y el vuelo de las aves, y el brillo de los astros: ese algo más bello es la libertad; pero más que a libertad es la Patria, y la Patria os da el beso en este día."

2o. Premio Mundial de Dibujo, Medalla dorada "Vermail" obtenida por el niño Epifanio Flores.

21. Fourteen-year-old Epifanio Flores and his international prize, 1929. *El Sembrador*, July 5, 1929, 11.

Through his successful participation in the Geneva competition, Epifanio accessed a social category that might have been denied to him two decades earlier—that of modern childhood. But he owed his celebrity to his indigeneity, another social category only recently redeemed by the revolution. And in the international context, his indigenous identity had more cultural cachet than it did at home, where, as we have seen, ambivalence about the place of indigeneity in forging a modern national identity prevailed. While indigenous children had to carefully navigate the boundaries of their identity in the pages of *Pulgarcito*, they enjoyed privileged participation in the international exhibitions and competitions that the magazine used to promote its nationalist art. In 1927 Luís Martínez, an indigenous boy janitor in the southern Mexico City neighborhood of Coyoacán, won an art prize in Los Angeles, California, that earned him seven hundred dollars, an amount that likely far outstripped his family's annual income.[87] Through the opportunities afforded by the state-funded art curriculum, Luís's talent, bolstered by his ethnicity, gained him international attention and yielded a palpable benefit. The notable absence of the *Pulgarcito* regulars from Mexico City—Félix, Mario, and the like—signaled state officials' preference to highlight the nation's indigenous roots as part of a program to build a profile of mestizo cultural nationalism that could be readily recognizable the world over. On a 1925 visit to Mexico, renowned French psychologist Pierre Janet confirmed the global assessment of the creative aptitude demonstrated by "the Mexican race," detecting in indigenous children's drawings the embryonic potential of the world's finest artists.[88] *Pulgarcito*'s protégés earned accolades abroad, and in very few cases did their ethnicity go unremarked by reviewers.

Newspapers from around the world lauded the magazine for its technical advances, its broad readership, and its success in garnering widespread participation. In the United States the children's drawings garnered considerable attention, to the point of reflecting a panicked concern that Mexican children might be surpassing their northern counterparts in terms of cultural expression. *Pulgarcito* artists even earned favorable comparison to members of the fashionable—and adult—New York art scene.[89] Renowned art historian and art critic Thomas Craven, upon seeing an exposition of their work, declared that Mexican children possessed a "primitive ingenuity," while demonstrating a mastery of composition superior to that even of established members of the New York art scene.[90] A reporter from the United States, upon viewing a *Pulgarcito* exhibition in Stanford, California, mused that the neighbors to the south had outdone the United States, lending national color to their art, while children in the United States still relied on copying European models.[91] Ralph Stackpole, the manager of an art gallery in San Francisco, spent the summer of 1926 in Mexico observing art instruction. He worked together with Diego Rivera to bring a selection of approximately one hundred of those drawings to his gallery, pricing them from between five to twenty-five dollars apiece. *Pulgarcito* published the list of titles on display, along with the names of the students, their schools, and the respective price assigned.[92] The list of titles suggests that the vast majority of selected pieces portrayed nationalist themes rooted in folk culture—a church in Xochimilco, the Festival of San Juan, a piñata, and the volcanoes, among others—all elements emerging to form the official panorama of visual tropes exported abroad.[93]

The talent exhibited by Mexican children made a particular impression upon Europeans. One shipment of drawings, sent to Paris for an exposition and to serve as the basis for an art education class for French children modeled after Mexican techniques, was personally unpacked by Pablo Picasso himself, who had extended his stay in Paris specifically to see the highly praised paintings. The overwhelming success of the pieces in Paris constituted a "triple triumph" in the eyes of renowned French art critic René Jean, for children, foreigners, and Latin America as a whole.[94] One French journalist, marveling at the sophistication of the paintings done by artists between eight and fifteen years old, enthused: "We knew that fruit matured more rapidly in the tropics, but we had no idea that it could be of this quality."[95] Some international critics went so far as to suggest that *Pulgarcito* offered a model in which children substituted for adults as cultural diplomats through their art exchanges.[96] In many ways the editors of the magazine took the suggestion to heart. In 1930 Olaguíbel reported that *Pulgarcito* contributors had seen their work displayed in forty-one expositions as far flung as the United States, Belgium, England, Guatemala, Japan, Spain, Germany, and Switzerland.[97] These international exhibits yielded some exchange between the children of the respective nations; Japanese children exchanged hundreds of drawings with their Mexican counterparts, all to be distributed among *Pulgarcito* readers. A Japanese publicity business took note of the fraternal exchange and published the Mexican drawings in a run of thirty thousand color postcards.[98] Given the mobility of their art, Mexican children's drawings perhaps saw even broader dissemination—in the short term—than the stationary murals of their famous adult contemporaries. Children actively contributed to the worldwide construction of a collective imaginary of Mexico as a place defined by a set of images, icons, and a color palette.

Through the media outlets of international magazines and national radio, Mexican children became aware of the impact that their humble drawings had beyond the borders of their country.[99] The country's tremendous showing in the international competition in Geneva became a source of pride at home, as people flooded the open patios of the SEP building in 1929 to view a homecoming exposition of the prizewinning drawings that had toured Europe a full three years after the Geneva competition. SEP officials, with the support of the Diplomatic Corps and *Pulgarcito*, set up the children's landscapes and portraits in the hallways of the inner courtyard of the SEP's new building in downtown Mexico City, just a few short blocks from Mexico City's main central plaza, the *zócalo*. Significantly, they displayed the children's art on two-sided screens, orthogonally adjacent to Diego Rivera's freshly painted murals that decorated all three stories of the patio's inner walls. The direct juxtaposition of the children's art with that of the muralists symbolizes the combined visual legacy that Mexico exported to the world. The exhibition of twelve hundred primary school drawings—only 10 percent of the number of drawings completed in the first half of 1929—publicly displayed the work of the nation's ingenious young artists that had traveled around the world and come back to native soil. At the *Pulgarcito* offices SEP officials hosted gatherings of the collaborators and distributions of prizes in honor of the young artists' international acclaim. Young artists basked in the spotlight as government officials, dignitaries, and foreign diplomats perused the much-lauded drawings. President Emilio Portes Gil lay claim to the prizewinning contestants, pointing to the international distinctions of "our children" as a barometer of the success of the public school system.[100]

As children perfected their techniques in the decorative, illustrative, and constructive arenas of the art curriculum, they modeled this learned national aesthetic to the upcoming generations. Their demonstrated success in Geneva and elsewhere cemented the *Método Best Maugard* as the official visual expression of *lo mexicano*, and projects moved forward to have children decorate the walls of their own schools accordingly. The guidelines for painting on the classroom walls were rather generous: students needed to operate under the supervision of an art teacher, and their decorations needed to be entirely original (not copied from a printed design).[101] School inspectors representing the Department of Drawing and Handicrafts in 1928 reported substantial progress on adorning the school buildings; the floral decoration of the República Argentina School carried out by fifth grade girls Rebeca Lozano and Ana María Lira in perfect Best Maugard style was even featured in a magazine article about the drawing program. The pupils attending that school would pass that decorated window daily, and it would become a part of their quotidian visual landscape. For the child artists, the creative production of lasting images in a public space constituted the creation of "visual quotes," a document of sorts that attests to children's presence in history where official texts often fall short.[102]

Ironically, even while riding a crest of unprecedented success and widespread acclaim, *Pulgarcito* faced a financial crisis, as administrators in the SEP diverted their attention toward other fiscal priorities. While Olaguíbel labored behind the scenes, churning out memos to his superiors quantifying the magazine's reception and value, he hoped that the power of the magazine among its faithful readers would help to keep it from closing. One of the last issues of *Pulgarcito* features a song (complete with the music) lauding the magazine's success abroad:

Pulgarcito is back,
Satisfied by his tour
He went to Europe, New York
Crossed the sea intact
And now returns, ready
To study with even more dedication . . .[103]

Within a decade after its first introduction in the classroom, the Best Maugard Method had embossed a stamp of nationalism on the artistic production of young Mexicans. At the 1936 Conference of Child Peasants and Workers (part of a spate of child-directed professional-style conferences that promoted class consciousness, discussed more fully in chapter 6), the child delegates from the northern state of Tamaulipas— Consuelo Durán, Herlinda Reyna, and Román Hernández— issued an impassioned, enumerated decree arguing for the right of schoolchildren to exercise agency in executing classroom décor. Having studied and distinguished foreign nationalist art styles from their own, they articulated a strong preference for the "elements that our ancestors used," citing the affection that it inspired in them and the individual creativity that this drawing method offered: "For this reason, we students should intervene in the decoration and layout of our classrooms, to perpetuate *in our style* a part of our nationality, using Mexican motifs." For these child delegates, the Best Maugard Method did not restrict their creativity but rather opened up an officially sanctioned path for creativity and the application of a style that they embraced as meaningful. Student-directed nationalist murals would provide a visual backdrop against which they could, in their own words, "develop our personality in an environment of joy and beauty."[104]

Conclusions

Introduced first in art classes at school and reinforced through the pages of *Pulgarcito*, Mexican children learned the officially endorsed national aesthetic, one that valorized an idealized indigenous past and codified a set of motifs that would readily be recognized by future generations as *lo mexicano*—quintessentially Mexican. Art officials struggled between a belief in the abilities of children to produce something beautiful and valuable when left to their own devices and a desire to control, regulate, guide, market, and Mexicanize those creative expressions. The drawing program helped to expand the community of participating children, allowing them to envision themselves as members of a generation that transcended political and linguistic boundaries. Nevertheless, the parameters of the competitions and exhibits in which they could participate, as set by the editors of *Pulgarcito*, created some restrictions on these children's freedom of expression. Child artists became cultural ambassadors, purveyors of a national identity composed of a set of agreed-upon images, themes, and motifs that were supposed to represent a revolutionary, proletarian nation of mestizos.

Some children embraced the new medium and the new art curriculum, seeing it as a platform for self-promotion and nascent entrepreneurial endeavors. Many behaved as children do and enjoyed the moment, taking advantage of new spaces for recreation and self-expression. Meanwhile, children enjoyed unprecedented access to a community of their peers, both virtually and physically, through the social outlets and opportunities for travel and socialization afforded by *Pulgarcito*. The magazine structured child participation in ways that reinforced social hierarchies across the generation of readers; the physical activities and events hosted in the Department of Drawing and Handicrafts' Mexico City offices made these social divisions more deeply felt by those who remained excluded from the benefits of access to *Pulgarcito*.

Yet indisputably, *Pulgarcito*'s success brought visibility *among* children—by allowing them to see each other through its

22. Children of various social classes gather with art education officials at an exposition of children's art. AGN, Fondo Fotográfico Díaz, Delgado y García, Escultores, Subcaja 31-5.

pages—and also brought visibility *to* the dramatic cross-section of social classes that constituted its diverse readership through the national and international expositions that earned such acclaim. The photograph in figure 22 clearly illustrates the kinds of interactions that the new art program facilitated; it depicts art officials at one of the SEP-sponsored expositions, surrounded by the featured young artists. The children present at the exposition bear ethnic and material markers that reveal their disparate socioeconomic backgrounds. In a society in which the social type of the street boy (*niño callejero*) was broadly associated with bare feet, the honorific presence of a boy matching this description upends conventional expectations.[105] Indigenous, poor, and provincial children no doubt received unequal membership in the club organized around *Pulgarcito*. But it was a level of civic engagement and creative expression, with the full endorsement of high-profile public officials, never before available to children in these social categories. This new sense of membership in a body other than the family or the classroom allowed the youngest generation of revolutionary children to experiment with participation in the civic community.

The Best Maugard Method and the *Pulgarcito* aesthetic had a lasting impact on the visual landscape of Mexican national art in the twentieth century. But not every child who learned to draw the seven motifs and to apply them to local themes in art bought the official art program wholesale. As an adult iconoclastic artist José Luis Cuevas, an outspoken opponent of the muralists' revolutionary social realist style, ranted against the rigidity of art instruction he received as a child in the 1930s. In his "Cactus Curtain" manifesto published in the 1950s, Cuevas berated the art curriculum's narrow emphasis on an "automatic method of drawing, a strict, uniform intensity of line," and the restrictions on idealized, mestizo subject matter. Revolutionary officials appeared so preoccupied with developing a distinctly national style that Mexico remained stagnated as the rest of the international art world progressed.[106] Cuevas's experience demonstrates that even a privileged, white Mexican boy growing up in the capital found the art curriculum to be exclusionist.

CHAPTER THREE

A Community of Invisible Little Friends
Technology and Power in Children's Radio Programs

[We affirm] [t]he exultation of the suggestive themes of machines, blue-collar explosions that shatter the mirrors of subverted days. To live emotionally. To throb with the propeller of time. To march toward the future.

— Second Stridentist Manifesto, Puebla, January 1, 1923

"Troka, powerful Troka!" Anselmo shouts enthusiastically. "Play that extraordinary music again; I want all of my classmates at school to hear it; it is so beautiful! I am sure that they will like it."

— GERMÁN LIST ARZUBIDE, *Troka el Poderoso* (1939)

L egislators passed a law in 1927 that prohibited horse-drawn carts from being driven in Mexico City streets, irrevocably erasing one of the last vestiges of provincial life from the metropolis.[1] Buses and then automobiles rushed in to take their place. Pedestrians accustomed only to side-stepping animal waste in the thoroughfares had to tune their sensibilities—quickly—to the more treacherous hazards posed by the new proximity between man and machine in day-to-day life. But with the advent of the 1930s, scandalized reports of children run over by mechanized transportation began to fade from the city papers' daily headlines. Meanwhile, smoke-stacks and skyscrapers stretched the city's horizon vertiginously upward. Artists and intellectuals documented the mechanization of their country with mixed evaluations, ranging from skeptical *indigenistas* to the enthusiastic, if utopian, Stridentists (*Estridentistas*). In this burgeoning technological milieu, radio emerged as a viable tool for communication, entertainment, and, for the rapidly consolidating revolutionary government, politicization and socialization. In particular, the official SEP station XFX developed radio programming designed specifically for children.[2]

For educational officials, radio posed an important solution to the nagging problem of rural schoolteacher attrition, as it required only the voice of a single teacher before a microphone to reach the ears of thousands of eager learners. The idea to create an educational program specifically for children arose in late 1929 in response to shortages in rural classroom materials and the inability of teachers to cater to the specialized interests of their students. Now, radio hosts boasted, underprivileged parents could no longer justify keeping their children out of public education; they maintained that children's radio programming was comprehensive enough to stand in as a substitute for classroom learning.[3] XFX featured three programs specifically for children in the 1930s, each with a slightly different pedagogical goal and intended audience. *Periódico Infantil* sought to extend the universalizing reach of the public school curriculum into the home and community through essay contests, homework assignments, and research projects regularly assigned to listeners in their free time. *Troka el Poderoso* introduced children to the modernizing benefits of new forms of technology through their personification and animation in adventure tales. Finally, *Antena Campesina* directed its moralizing modernization narrative about technology toward rural, indigenous children.

Radio undoubtedly figured as a tool of revolutionary nation building, as scholars have demonstrated. I argue that through radio, and especially the children's broadcasts designed for XFX, children around the country accessed language and technology shared by their unseen peers on opposite reaches of the airwaves. Because the broadcasters encouraged the listeners to respond to what they heard, many children had the unique opportunity to negotiate the terms of their socialization, sometimes testing the elasticity of their expanding social boundaries. The invisible network that radio facilitated began to tie together a generation in previously inconceivable ways, as children wrote in to the radio stations and listened eagerly for their names and others to echo back to them on the magical airwaves through their shiny radio receivers.[4]

Yet a comparative analysis of the content and reception of these three SEP-sponsored children's radio programs also reveals the uneven expectations that government officials had of children from different social groups as they interacted with and consumed an onslaught of new technologies. Parallel to the patterns that emerged in the pages of *Pulgarcito*, as we have seen in the previous chapter, modern urban children enjoyed social capital, access, and ascendency through their interactions with the new technology, while the experiences of their rural and indigenous peers remained much more ambivalent. On the one hand, the stellar rise of radio as a preferred means of communication, education, and entertainment meant that a new cohort emerged for children to interact with outside of the traditional realms of socialization: the home, the school, and the neighborhood. On the other hand, children's aptitude for adaptation to new technology meant that within a short space of time, radio access drove a dramatic wedge between those children incorporated into the nation's modern culture and those left outside of one of the most immediate forms of cultural connection.

The Cultural Impact of Educational Radio in Mexico

The relationship between governments and radio in the twentieth century has both a sunny and a sullied history. The power of radio to cobble together diverse regional and ethnic identities into nationalism echoed around the world when it was first introduced in the 1920s.[5] In the wrong hands the new medium of radio became a propaganda tool for unsavory political maneuverings around the globe, as it drew the attention of populists of all stripes. Sinister uses of radio as the audio vehicle of totalitarianism and demagoguery can be readily identified, with Hitler's astute application of the technology as the most infamous example. Historians relate the seemingly organic transformation of identity from that of a middle-class, Protestant family to stalwart supporters of Nationalist Socialism through the seemingly innocuous activity of listening to the radio daily over a cup of coffee in the family sitting room.[6] Radio coincided with the rise of the Soviet Union parallel to its introduction in Mexico. In the wake of a bloody revolution and at the cusp of radical social transformation, Soviets saw radio as one of its most valuable tools for retaining the widespread support for their nascent regime among a vast illiterate populace. Children across the Soviet Union listened with equal attention to programs intended specifically for them (and like Mexican children they flooded the radio stations with letters in response) as to the news broadcasts intended for adults. Wartime broadcasts captivated youngsters just as much as the kiddy programs; children's radio programming in the 1930s and 1940s in the United States was mostly characterized by "blood-and-thunder" serials, full of violent crime that remained embedded in children's heads long after bedtime.[7]

Concerns about the wholesale substitution of radio for live education and entertainment merit mention. Radio is often heard in fragments, with important introductory, synthesizing, or moralizing editorial discussion potentially lost on inattentive listeners (the most publicized case, of course, was Orson Welles's 1938 "War of the Worlds" hoax, resulting in three days of mass hysteria in the United States). In Mexico the advent of radio coincided with the comprehensive, ideologically driven, well-funded overhaul of the educational system, and broadcasting was quickly harnessed as a tool of the revolution. The drawbacks of the medium notwithstanding, the power of radio to reach countless ears simultaneously makes it worthwhile to study the ways it was employed, and received, as part of an official effort to construct a citizenry. Furthermore, radio's unrivaled ability to foster conviviality, both through physical and through virtual community, expands the traditionally limited spaces of social interaction available for the historian of childhood to analyze.

Radio sputtered to life in Mexico as the revolutionary fighting died down. The wireless transmission of sound built upon the telegraph technology that escalated communication among factions in the nation's first modern war. Ideologues, entrepreneurs, and visionaries all scrambled to harness the evangelizing power of the radio. Historians disagree over what qualified as the first radio program broadcast in Mexico, but by some accounts it aired from the capital's Teatro Ideal over a commercial, experimental station on September 27, 1921, and featured a singing eleven-year-old girl.[8] Though this broadcast was likely intended for a specific theater audience, the few and fortunate households in the immediate vicinity with radio receivers that tuned in to the program welcomed the dulcet sounds of little María de los Ángeles Gómez Camacho into their homes, and radio in Mexico was born.

As early as 1929 the nation boasted seventeen commercial and two educational stations. The SEP launched CYE (eventually XFX) in 1924 with a transmission of President Plutarco Elías Calles's inauguration from the National Stadium.[9] Among the government and commercial stations that populated the national frequencies in the revolutionary decades, XFX was among the most influential. The station flourished under the directorship of distinguished poet, author, and journalist María Luisa Ross and quickly occupied a central position in the SEP's ambitious rural education program.[10] In its first experimental year on the air, the SEP station broadcast only a little more than a half hour of programming daily; in 1927 it broadcast strategically from 11:00 to 3:00 and from 5:00 to 9:00, capturing mealtime hours at home for the working middle class. By the beginning of the 1930s it ran a full ten hours of programs. By 1945, with television still around the corner, radio was king; music, news, and information from 422 stations wafted invisibly over national soil. Children's programming in commercial radio, primarily the antics and lyrics of Francisco Gabilondo Soler's singing cricket, Cri-Cri, broadcast by superstation XEW— boasted the strongest transmission in the country—from the 1930s until well into the 1960s. If television was the substitute mother of children growing up in the second half of the twentieth century, then radio was the grandmother that reared the previous generation.[11]

Given radio's immediate cultural authority, government officials saw both the possibilities and the dangers of corruptibility that the medium afforded. For that reason, almost at its inception, the government moved swiftly to regulate radio content and transmission radius.[12] In a forward-looking move for the educational future of the nation's citizens, the SEP optimistically employed XFX as an agent in its mission to educate Mexicans far removed from the material resources and curricula.

The obvious question of reception complicates a full understanding of the medium. The presence of a radio receiver in one's home does not guarantee that residents listened to it as intended—or at all. Likewise, the absence of a household radio did not prevent someone from hearing a program at a neighbor's house or at the local schoolhouse. Yet some statistics do provide a glimpse of nationwide trends and suggest the reception that centrally produced radio programs could have enjoyed: by 1940 about one urban home in five had a radio, compared to only one in one hundred in the rural districts. Overall, 91.3 percent of the total radios owned nationwide could be found in cities, raising legitimate questions about the universal education of broadcasts to rural communities purported by XFX protagonists.[13] Nationwide, somewhere between 26,000 and 30,000 radio devices could be found in the country in 1926, leaping to anywhere from 100,000 in 1930 to upwards of 250,000 by 1935. Furthermore, historian Justin Castro notes that simple handmade receivers would have augmented this number.[14] Estimates about the placement of SEP-sponsored radio devices in schools put the total number of apparatuses in the low thousands for the decade 1924–34, peaking in 1930.[15] Historians have noted that interruptions in reception due to frequency problems or electricity inhibited even those SEP radios from having the full intended impact. Nevertheless, the program content—evident from broadcast transcripts and correspondence filtering through the SEP's Office of Cultural Radiotelephony (Oficina Cultural Radiotelefónica)—and letters from listeners reveal the tensions and connections between bureaucrats' intentions and individuals' reception as the nation adapted to the integration of a new transmitter of cultural information.

Radio's cultural influence reached wide, even as individual stations' frequencies often flickered in and out. The new medium of radio transformed the social landscape by creating new shared sounds and information.[16] From the late 1920s, radio reporters appeared alongside those from newspapers at public events, sending descriptions of commemorations and discourses into homes and classrooms across the country. The presence of sound originating somewhere outside of the immediate location had a dramatic impact on the heard world of listeners, eavesdroppers, and passersby. The introduction of new sounds and ideas that gained rapid widespread recognition wrought meaningful cultural changes, signaling a shift from locally produced oral and aural culture to privilege centrally produced music, stories, discourses, and audio culture.[17] As a social phenomenon radio offered opportunities for individuals to join their fellow community members, laborers, or drinkers as they gathered around the apparatus to listen to a program, offering moments of shared experiences and fueling conversations long beyond the scope of transmission or hours of broadcast.[18] Commercial radio transmissions disseminated consumer messages about both products and images that became symbols of national identity (beer and mariachi, for example). More aggressively than newspapers and comic books, radio dictated what the members of the *gran familia mexicana*—Mexico's national "family" imagined and touted by members of the official party—ought to consume; whether or not they actually did is another matter.[19]

Radio was a marvel of abstraction, anonymously translating terms such as *patria* and *mexicano* to countless individuals offering a shred of material evidence. To bolster nationalist content, xfx officials mandated the live broadcast of civic events such as Independence Day commemorations, presidential inaugurations and speeches, and announcements by the secretary of education—events previously situated in Mexico City and available to the rest of the nation only through print journalistic accounts.[20] Some saw the universalizing potential of radio as a liability; as one *El Universal Ilustrado* contributor listlessly editorialized, "[As a result of radio] there will no longer be sad childhoods. They will be happy ones. . . . Everyone will have the same childhood, or more or less similar ones. A happy-sad childhood."[21] Even at its inception, then, radio demonstrated its ability to eradicate social and personal distinctions in a process of national cultural unification. Even as it forged a sense of collective identity among compatriots invisible to each other, radio fostered tangible intimacy, as individuals huddled physically around the substantial bulk of the early radio receivers to hear the latest bulletins and trends together. The high ratio of rural residents to radio receivers, then, may indicate an even tighter unification of community than the statistics suggest. On the other hand, radio also served as a proxy for human interaction, a mechanical intercessor between the government and its citizens, the doctor and his patient, the teacher and her pupil.

Within the national audience, radio had the capability of targeting specialized audiences by creating specific programming—not just for children, as examined here—but also for housewives, farmers, rural schoolteachers, small business owners, and indigenous groups. Certainly, though, the programs did not reach only their intended audience. Children listened in on instructions to their parents on how to properly fertilize a new crop, just as adults hovered around the daily hygiene lesson intended for their children. Evidence of this comes from the June 17, 1930, broadcast of *Periódico Infantil,* in which the announcer addressed his child audience members at the end of a story: "Now we can turn to an educational little discussion. Ah! But first, let me have a quick chat with your mommy. She's right there by your side, isn't she? . . . Pleased to meet you, señora, I am Periódico Infantil xfx, at your service. . . . [P]erhaps on occasion you have listened in on my educational chats while taking a rest from your chores."[22] It is worth noting that parental accompaniment during children's radio hour did not always signal cross-generational collaboration. When Ana María Saldaña sought her father's editorial eye after crafting a response to a broadcast competition, he provided verbal confirmation but would not review her letter. She deflected any potential criticism of her submission (in a passive-aggressive tone perhaps intended for her father in case he had a change of heart) by concluding that her father was unwilling to correct her grammar. He would not even let her use his pen, so she had to write in pencil.[23] Even as radio carved out distinct social and cultural groups through its programming, its boundless nature more democratically promoted cross-generational communication and even united children's culture with that of adults in the mainstream.

Programs designed by government-sponsored radio can be seen as part of a trio of campaigns, along with pediatric medicine and socialist pedagogy, that enabled government officials to join parents—and specifically mothers—and exercise moral authority in raising children. The chorus of adult voices in children's lives expanded in the 1920s and 1930s to include those that the speakers issued forth, an intellectual authority physically embodied by the radio apparatus. Furthermore, specialized programs designed for women and mothers reinforced the dynamic of the new Revolutionary Family. A 1933 program, *Bringing Together the Home and the School* (*Boletín para el Acercamiento entre el Hogar y la Escuela*), reminded adult listeners that every activity in which children engaged had tremendous bearing on their development. The announcer cautioned mothers to be particularly vigilant to ensure continuity between education in the classroom and in the home. One bulletin announced unequivocally that the educational program had achieved perfection, a declaration that insinuated that mothers could corrupt this project through negligence. Instead of occupying children in mundane daily household chores—or worse, leaving their free time to their own devices—such radio bulletins encouraged mothers to engage children in productive, educational activities that would hone their proletarian sensibilities. Radio announcers suggested the restoration of old furniture, toy making, building collections, and the preparation of demonstrations of teacher appreciation as appropriate leisure activities for children under parental direction on weekends and afternoons.[24]

Early radio advocates adjoined to middle-class consumers that mothers would rejoice at the family unification that radio wrought; compelling programs meant that fathers would stay at home to tune in and that children would resist the draw of the street in favor of the family parlor.[25] Certain XFX programs further reinforced the authority of the feminine, domestic sphere. The host of *The Family Doctor* (*Médico Familiar*), with his amenable voice, informed housewives about domestic hygiene and child care through dramatized home visits across the republic and his kindly although paternalistic answers to questions asked by listeners through the mail or telephone. *The Family Doctor* had a segment in which the host addressed the children directly, instructing them on their own health, subtly bypassing the mother's omniscience about all things related to her offspring.[26] The SEP, using the radio, thus entered the domestic sphere, to uphold women's authority as mothers. Even as radio officials educated mothers, they focused the nation's collective attention on that most important purveyor of the revolution's future: the child. The voices emanating from the radio represented additional adult authority figures to the pantheon of adults in children's lives. Yet far from representing yet another set of adult-implemented constraints on children's actions and decisions, the present analysis of children's interactions with radio programs demonstrates that child listeners chose from among the variety of adult influences in their lives and assigned authority to the voices that appeared most relevant to the circumstances or activities at hand.

In order to expand the audience, in 1932 different branches of the Ministry of Public Education delivered seventy-five radio receivers to rural areas within the broadcast range of the station. Public education minister Narciso Bassols used this audience as a laboratory for the future expansion of radio education programs.[27] The SEP manufactured "Titlanti" brand equipment at the cost of thirty-six pesos each, approximately covering the cost of manufacturing, as part of a burgeoning economic nationalist plan to offset the flow of American-made imports.[28] Delivery service included technical information on how to operate the receivers, and the arrival of the receiver resulted in celebrations within the communities. Photographers accompanied the SEP representatives on their arduous journeys on horseback to remote villages to deposit radio equipment, documenting the arrival of the conspicuously modern apparatus placed incongruously in thatched schoolhouses and surrounded by proud barefoot farmers. The arrival of a radio marked a momentous day, as villagers solemnly posed bedecked in their cleanest white clothes alongside the machine, and the presence of a tuba and a drum in one photo showed that the SEP officials rode into town with much fanfare. The officials left the radios in the care of the rural schoolteachers, with painstaking instructions about adhering to the SEP transmission schedule, the logistics of operating the machinery, and recommendations for gathering villagers at appointed times to take advantage of this new educational tool. Once the apparatus of officially produced knowledge had been passed to the schoolteachers, government officials returned only sporadically to inspect the machines for proper usage and upkeep.

The transmission of revolutionary education faced many challenges at its inception. Evidently, radio did not meld seamlessly into the countryside. In the early years, with unreliable batteries and rural electricity that worked in fits and starts, even the successful delivery of a radio did not ensure effective reception. Although the SEP strategically scheduled daily radio programming, many times groups would gather in the school to no avail as the faulty electric current or the weak signal from Mexico City foiled the pedagogical transmission. One inspector visited ten schools in the state of México and reported that he found one radio had a blown fuse, one was broken entirely, one school had no electricity, four schools had not paid the electric bill, and the rest simply were not taking advantage of the educational service for various reasons. Of the ten villagers used only three of the radios as intended by the SEP. None of the villagers reported knowledge of the hours of shows specifically designed for campesinos, teachers, and children. One teacher commented that the schedule did not reflect the realities of village life; a program for campesinos began at six in the evening, but most labored in the fields until at least eight at night.[29] The teacher in charge of each radio received a chart on which to document its condition, the number of hours it was connected to electricity, the times when the signal came through the clearest, the programs that garnered the most interest among villagers, and the average attendance at each program. As evidence that officials wanted to tailor this medium to best fit the seasonal needs of the community, the final section on the questionnaire asked the teacher to note the main crops and climate characteristic of the zone.[30]

Furthermore, the SEP faced competition from other government agencies and commercial radio stations that vied for listeners' precious free time. The consolidation of the official political party, the Partido Nacional Revolucionario (PNR), in 1929 corresponded with increasingly political content diffused through government agencies' radio stations. Educational officials saw radio as an educational blessing but also as a potential curse and in 1933 expressed the hope that XFX through its socialist orientation would combat the antirevolutionary views being propagated by other radio stations.[31] Hoping to corner the market, the SEP delivered radios with the dial fixed to XFX; it did not take long for villagers to break the sealed dial and listen to other stations. SEP radio inspectors visiting several schools in Tlaxcala reported that, despite their precautions, many of the school radio settings had been changed, and villagers could listen to something other than the educational programs emanating from Mexico City. Nearby Puebla represented the greatest competition over the airwaves in this tiny state. Oftentimes, villagers would gather to listen to an appointed SEP broadcast but found the station from Puebla to be clearer—and more entertaining (it proved nearly impossible to pass up a concert by Agustín Lara in favor of an instructional bulletin about proper hand-washing methods). The teachers entrusted with the SEP's mission often participated in tuning the radio to entertainment programs. In many cases, the schoolteachers lived not in the villages but in Mexico City and reported to their schools sporadically, so community members could tinker with the radio.[32]

SEP officials had reason to be concerned about ideological corruption from competing radio stations. One January day in 1935, station XXX, sponsored by conservative daily newspaper *La Prensa*, broadcast the Three Wise Men, who took the microphone to address all children within earshot. They wanted as many children as possible to know they were upset. In stern voices, Melchor, Gaspar, and Baltasar related disappointment over their waning reception by the country's youth on a recent Three Kings' Day. Their annual journey to deliver toys had become increasingly more arduous and dangerous; no longer did children greet them with affection and joy. Instead, children were donning "colored shirts"—a reference to the militarization of children by various political parties, such as the red shirts of the Communist Youth—and picking up weapons instead of toys. The Three Wise Men, now old and tired, lamented the loss of childhood through the politicization of youth.[33] The XXX missive was a response to the anticlerical, secular turn taken by the revolution. In a climate in which the radical Cristero responses to the anticlerical turn sustained by the government (and educational curriculum) of Lázaro Cárdenas still simmered, SEP officials clearly wanted to avoid spreading antirevolutionary propaganda such as this over machines that they worked so hard to install in rural areas.

Despite the initial frustrations of introducing a new technology to the rural population, the persistence of the SEP inspectors and the apparent willingness of the government agency to adapt to initial difficulties eventually yielded a culture in which radio became the predominant source of information, education, and entertainment. In this context XFX implemented the children's radio "magazine" *Periódico Infantil*, hoping to consolidate a uniform base of practical skills, literacy, and technological knowledge across its young audience. Regardless of the concerted effort to conduct the educational campaign over the air, children's correspondence with the editors of the *Periódico Infantil* confirms the trend suggested by the challenges noted above, that urban middle-class children constituted the majority of its audience in the 1930s.

A Radio Magazine for Young Technophiles: *Periódico Infantil*

"This is our homework for today's contest," the radio announcer for the Ministry of Public Education's xfx program *Periódico Infantil* instructed his young audience. "Did you listen carefully, my invisible little friend? Go ahead, grab a pencil and paper and tell me everything, but in writing."[34] Assuming their obedient attention, the announcer went on to applaud the enthusiasm that children had demonstrated in their written answers to questions about short stories broadcast on the program and proceeded to describe the next challenge: an essay contest about the legendary young independence-era hero El Niño Pípila. The escalated task matched the lofty award. The two winning essayists would enjoy the distinctive honor of hearing their stories piped into their homes, schools, or community centers—and bask in the knowledge that unseen children across the nation would be simultaneously doing the same. The subject matter and format of the contest are rich with symbolism. Despite the distinct possibility that the story of El Niño Pípila was apocryphal, by most accounts this figure—credited with facilitating the destruction of the fortress-like Alhóndiga, where Spaniards and royalists holed up during the bloody Hidalgo rebellion— was far from a child. In fact, the Cárdenas-era monument to El Pípila flexes his well-muscled body on a hillside over modern-day Guanajuato in a display of fully blossomed virility. Yet educational officials consciously rescripted the virile war hero as a child, here and elsewhere, to draw children into the official historical narrative.[35] The Alhóndiga represented a bastion of imperialism, tumbled by the morally superior insurgents, personified by the infantilized Niño Pípila.

Children's programming on the sep radio station xfx complemented the agency's project to revise history so as to make it more relevant to children and inspire social action. The astute child contestant, listening to XFX in 1930, may have internalized the underlying message that children wielded the power to enact the revolutionary reforms that would liberate Mexico from imperialist influences and usher in an era of nationalism. Knowing that she was listening and writing alongside a cadre of invisible friends further cemented the young XFX listener's resolve to perform well.

SEP employees of the Department of Primary and Normal Education designed *Periódico Infantil,* an audio children's magazine, to provide radio content that addressed children as a social group with particular interests. *Periódico Infantil* presented simple problems with precise answers and gave clear explanations slowly and with patience, specifically to appeal to young listeners.[36] Alejandro Michel, one of the creators of *Periódico Infantil,* claimed the development of this children's program was the first in the world of its kind.[37] In its first few years officials delivered sixty radios to the states of México, Guanajuato, Hidalgo, Michoacán, Morelos, Puebla, Querétaro, and Tlaxcala. More than half were located in México state.[38]

Periódico Infantil broadcast twice a day, in the morning and in the afternoon, to form a listening habit based on the pedagogical importance of repetition in children's instruction.[39] The regularity of the program reflected educational officials' aspirations for uniformity in public education; children within the scope of the transmission would all be listening to the juvenile gymnastics, spelling quizzes, or story contests at the same moment. The early-morning broadcast took place during school hours so teachers could incorporate it into their lesson plans, causing children to associate the radio with learning. The second broadcast sought a broader audience, including younger children not of school age or those who missed school or did not attend. This schedule, as outlined by educators in the proposal for the *Periódico Infantil,* revealed their assumptions about the audience: to gain optimal results from this programming, young listeners needed to be available twice a day for more than an hour, without any other household or family obligations to distract them from the program.

As could be expected, the plan envisioned by Ross, Michel, and other pedagogues in the radio tower on the Calle del Rélox in downtown Mexico City did not always match the experiences of the intended child audience. Letters from children suggested that many of the classrooms were not equipped with radio or that some teachers did not incorporate *Periódico Infantil* into their curriculum. Student Maria Cristina Carrillo wrote to the station in 1930 to beg pardon for not being able to respond to the morning program, because she had time to listen only in the afternoon.[40] The afternoon broadcast assumed the children had access to a radio outside of their classroom (a rare treat for most villagers in 1930); the broadcasters also assumed rural children would have the free time to sit and listen.

Periódico Infantil relied heavily on listener participation; the radio office maintained correspondence with more than a thousand children over the course of its transmission.[41] Show hosts exhorted children diligently to write daily in response to the contests, quizzes, and questionnaires constituting the show. The reams of letters in the Office of Cultural Radiotelephony provide evidence that many children undertook this task with enthusiasm; it resulted in a community of child listeners, most invisible to each other, yet brought together by the shared experience of listening to *Periódico Infantil*. The interactive format also meant that, increasingly, child listeners became creative agents in the content of a cultural form that would be shared with their peers. Children who sent answers to quizzes, homework assignments, and essay contests considered themselves part of the program's creative production force, signing their letters as "collaborators." Yolanda, one reliable collaborator, wrote on the reverse of a prize notification letter she had received in 1929 from the *Periódico Infantil* to prove that she had been a faithful listener for two years.[42] Radio had become a vehicle for the construction of a social group that had the potential to disregard the social classes, geographic boundaries, and even gendered sectors of childhood. In practice, as we will see, even the seemingly accessible medium of radio did not yield uniform results among its listenership.

The dialectical relationship between *Periódico Infantil* and its listeners resulted in the collaborative construction of a new model of childhood in the modern age. The *Periódico Infantil* broadcasts created an ideal listener and described it to children over the course of more than two years. In turn the program's audience contributed to the construction of this ideal listener through their written collaborations, some of which were broadcast in part and others of which informed the fine-tuning of the program's on-air curriculum. Children's letters offer a glimpse into their everyday lives growing up with radio and relating their daily activities as they revolved around the new presence of radio. The children learned the official standard—promoted over the airwaves—against which they measured their quotidian experiences. Other times they contested this model in subtle ways, asserting themselves as individuals who diverged from the model audience member.

Periódico Infantil instructed its listeners as to what constituted a "*niño educado*" and provided the signposts to become an educated child, one who brushed his or her teeth every morning, for example (lacking toothpaste, one could use a piece of soft charcoal that could be found beneath the *comal* in every rural household).[43] For many children, radio opened a window into the private lives of their invisible peers, and some had the good fortune to be able to modify their own lives to conform to the standards being promoted. In their letters listeners often referred to the gauges by which they now measured their lives: hygiene, education, family life, and listening to the radio. Second grader Conchita Caballero wrote that she listened to the radio every night but expressed insecurity about writing to the program since she did not know all of the answers. She responded to a question about home hygiene, observing that everyone in her family had to wash his or her face and hands (including the kitten) before they could sit down to breakfast. She also offered to send her report card as proof of her diligence in school and offered to bring her drawings directly to the xFX office. She hoped to win a prize for these demonstrations of her hard work. Ten-year-old Gloria Vargas outlined the activities of her day: in the mornings she washed up, brushed and washed her hair, and went to school; in the afternoons she studied piano and did homework, and then she listened to the radio XFX.[44] Both girls expressed their activities with an enthusiasm that revealed confidence in a positive evaluation of how they conducted their lives by the invisible judges, the XFX educators.

A package of notes written, compiled, and submitted by José Pizá Bueno between August 7 and August 22, 1930, reveals the way that children's radio programming had insinuated itself into his life alongside, and oftentimes supplanting, other common childhood activities. Each note reads like a repetitive diary, a compulsive documentation of his stewardship as a loyal listener for the unseen radio officials whom he imagined would keep track of such things. He listened attentively at first to find out if one of his submissions would be accepted or if his name would be announced as a prizewinner. "I had the pleasure of listening to your transmission last night," read most of the entries, while others wax more sentimental: "As greedy children like sweets, I like to listen to you [*Periódico Infantil*]. I listened last night and I liked your transmission even more than candy" and "With the same enthusiasm as when I go out to play, I sat in front of the radio last night to listen to your transmission." Children's radio programming clearly held a powerful sway over its young listeners, rapidly drawing them into a new cultural ambit that was home based and technology oriented. The swift cultural conversion seemed to be complete by José's last entry: "Last night I stayed in to listen to you rather than go out to play with my friends."[45] Certainly, José was not the only child to stay close to home during *Periódico Infantil*'s broadcast, given the guarantee of entertainment and the tantalizing possibility of public recognition.

It did not take long before several children emerged as minor celebrities among the generation coming to define itself by a set of shared cultural activities through radio, much as we have seen in the virtual social networks and hierarchies that emerged in the publication *Pulgarcito*. Medardo Morales Jr. appeared as an exceptional member of the *Periódico Infantil* audience, figuring among the most avid participants in the show's two-year call for letters. He wrote copious and unsolicited letters to the station detailing his ambitious program of self-education spurred by the audio magazine's contests and assignments. Not only did he take full advantage of the educational opportunities presented him by the *Periódico Infantil*, but he also became a minor celebrity within his radio listening cohort, as his contributions frequently merited him on-air praise. Medardo entered nearly every contest and punctually submitted the short-term assignments, but he also flooded the editorial office with unsolicited correspondence documenting his educational development.

Not coincidentally, young Medardo's father was the president of the Mexico City chapter of the Sociedad de Padres de Familia "Pro-Infancia," a parents' organization created by the government to offset the considerable political and cultural power of the Catholic National Parents' Union (Unión Nacional de Padres de Familia), one of the most vocal opposition organizations to revolutionary educational reforms.[46] Medardo's prominence in XFX children's programming likely reflected a political decision by SEP officials to manage the image they wanted to promote of the ideal product of secular, state-run education.

Though exceptional, Medardo's documentation of his intellectual escapades illustrates the possibilities that radio helped to open up to young people who enjoyed free time and the economic and moral support of their parents. Perhaps radio also offered a novel platform for those lacking the social skills to interact productively with the flesh-and-blood playmates and siblings who populated their lives off the airwaves. Medardo represented the ideal audience member for *Periódico Infantil*, an intellectually curious child of some means looking for an alternate outlet to report his explorations of the world that expanded beyond the confines of his home and classroom. In some ways it could be argued that children like Medardo inverted the top-down transmission of information by using the XFX editorial staff as his personal sounding board. Assuming a friend and captive audience in *Periódico Infantil*, Medardo could always be counted on to describe in exhaustive detail educational excursions with his father or grandfather. XFX likely never broadcast these unsolicited reports; they remain in the archives, silent testaments to Medardo's personal evolution, prodded along by radio prompts. A typical letter from Medardo reflected his unusually self-aware and earnest approach: "I promised *Periódico Infantil* that I would persist for the duration of the contest, and even though I am a child, I stand by my word (*tengo palabra*), and I make good on it (*cumplo lo que ofrezco*)." He proceeded to enumerate, as promised, a comprehensive report of all of the paintings and items he saw in a museum exhibit, including transcriptions of the signs that he observed.

Medardo reported that on Sundays his father often rewarded his good behavior during the week with excursions to the countryside, parks, and gardens in the cities or public institutions such as the military barracks, hospitals, jails, insane asylums, and museums. The trips provided the younger Medardo with life lessons along the way, and he reported his sojourns in his letters, keeping radio officials and listeners alike posted on the progress of his intellectual and moral development. On one occasion Medardo Sr. took his son to the hospital to learn about the evils of syphilis firsthand. He reported with horror that he saw bald soldiers with huge ulcers, with black-spotted blisters, without eyebrows or eyelashes, and with lesions on the mouth and tongue. Not only did these letters reveal Medardo's fastidious personality, but they also offer rare documentation of the daily experiences of an urban child from a family that valued learning and viewed leisure time as an opportunity for education.[47]

In a June 1931 story-writing contest, listeners wrote in with votes for their favorite contribution. In this case Medardo did not walk away with the prize, but the letters from his fans recognized him as a standout participant in the radio show. César Augusto Secaldi wrote that Medardo's story "Jorobadito" earned his vote as the funniest and most original of the submissions and added that this boy always seemed to excel in the competitions. One girl, Yolanda Villarreal, who also voted for Medardo, suggested that his was the only original contribution and that the other children had plagiarized stories from published books. She stated that one of the stories submitted as "The Seven Princes" appeared in a book she owned under the title "The Glass Mountain." Though strangers to each other, Medardo had earned Yolanda's vote because of his integrity, in her words, and likely also because of his persistent presence on the prize-winning circuit of *Periódico Infantil* rosters.[48] Medardo came in fourth place with 58 votes (the winner, María de la Luz Amerena, got 248 votes); 737 children voted overall, and prizewinners had to pick up their prizes at the radio station. Whether *Periódico Infantil* officials manipulated Medardo's visibility for political purposes or not, child listeners affirmed his identity as the model participant in the program.

Child listeners got to know each other over the airwaves and occasionally had the chance to meet in person, not unlike the way that the SEP office's drawing sessions in Mexico City forged a tangible community out of its magazine subscribers. The opportunities for physical reunions of *Periódico Infantil* collaborators obviously favored children with means and children from Mexico City (the site of the XFX transmitter), a privilege that was not lost on the young listeners. In August 1930 *Periódico Infantil* sent party invitations through the mail to listeners conscientious enough to write to the station and request their tickets. The party consisted of a meal and prizes for the guests. Concerns that this format benefited only the literate or privileged abounded in children's written responses. Mario Rocha de la Hoz wrote from Coyoacán on behalf of his little brother Luís, who was sick; Mario worried that both his younger brother's age and his infirmity would prevent him from responding in the stipulated fashion and exclude him from the event. Others reported that their siblings did not know how to write but hoped that they could still receive invitations. More letters poured in from disappointed children who had received their invitations too late to attend; dilatory mail service had thwarted their chance to meet their peers. In response, program director José Suárez personally assured each child that there would be another party and that the invitations would arrive in time.[49]

Bringing together children who knew each other only through radio caused anxiety in some young audience members, who feared that stripping away the anonymity of radio would reveal the stark socioeconomic disparity that still marked this generation of revolutionary youth. Gabriel Salazar humbly addressed the organizers of the *Periódico Infantil* party in his capacity as a listener and "collaborator" to the program. "Respectable Sir," read his letter, pocked with grammatical inconsistencies, "I am a poor boy, and if you think it would be convenient for poor boys like myself to attend the party, then I am inclined to accept the invitation that you sent."[50] Gabriel's marked deference in these few simple lines reveals subservience doubtlessly ingrained upon his family over generations through their interactions with other families of means. Gabriel expressed awareness that he was poor and also that other children attending the party might not be. He wanted to make sure that he would not be an imposter, even though he considered himself a creative contributor to *Periódico Infantil*. Despite the radio program's attempt to achieve its goal of creating a uniform educational experience for children across the republic, listeners like Gabriel recognized that socioeconomic disparities were far from eradicated by this technological voice of the revolution.

The terms for participation in *Periódico Infantil*—namely, mailing daily responses—placed economic stress on some listeners, and they piped up to let radio officials know. The announcer of the show requested that the children prepare and submit their clean and well-written answers on a daily basis.[51] This program requirement elicited reactions from listeners that revealed the diverse incomes of their families. In one broadcast young listeners were admonished for not writing in consistently with their answers to the questions, contests, and games. Not surprisingly, Medardo spearheaded expressions of concern and explained with cool rationale the economics of his predicament. In the past, he said, he used to mail his answers daily, but he received only a weekly allowance of 20 cents—daily submissions would cost him $1.62 weekly in postage. He requested that the editors consider accepting packages of answers prepared over the course of a week. Likewise, María Cristina Carrillo sent a package of her answers to the questions over the course of a few days. She included a note at the bottom that she did not have time to send them daily. In a letter that opened firmly with the question "Who do I believe to be worthy of a prize?" Luis Becerril poignantly expressed to the director his awareness of disparities among his peers. He said that he sent three days of answers at a time and that those who sent their answers every day did so because their families had money. Luis noted that although 6 cents might seem an insignificant amount, on some days his mother just could not spare them. He did not think that this fact made him any less worthy of the prize.[52] These children stated their poverty unfiltered by a sense of shame, a demonstration, perhaps, of the emerging pedagogical ideology that idealized the proletarian child. Although intended as a nationalizing and unifying tool for the nation's children, *Periódico Infantil* became a forum for children to publicly acknowledge, and decry, their socioeconomic differences.

There were other ways that *Periódico Infantil* excluded members of its listening audience, however innocuous the program may have appeared. In October 1930 the station sponsored a joint competition with Compañía Comercial "Arva" to encourage young listeners to become as familiar as possible with all aspects of radio's engineering and transmission. Contestants were to learn and describe in writing exactly how a radio worked to help demystify the way stories, games, and songs magically danced across the airwaves and into their homes. Participants were to go to Arva's store in Mexico City, observe the radio on display there, and ask questions of the store clerks. Clearly, this competition privileged the urban children who had access to (and permission to use) local transportation in order to conduct this investigation. The Tlaxcalan children, for example, clustered around their community radio in the remote mountains, would have access neither to the department store radio receiver nor the expertise of the salesman to explain its mechanics to them. The radio would remain a mystery to the rural children, a magical box that had been delivered by city folk on horseback and that transmitted news and sounds emanating from a city they might never visit.

In any case the clerks did not welcome the wave of eager young urban technophiles who flooded their stores in response to the competition. According to an account by the indomitable Medardo, he and a few friends were run out of the store by a surly employee. Discouraged and humiliated, Medardo vowed that he and his friends would not return to ask the rest of their questions, given that Arva employees obviously lacked the goodwill, decency, patience, and care that *Periódico Infantil* had shown them.[53] Ana María Saldaña wrote that, although her family had had several models of radios in their home, she never learned how one worked (due to her age, she noted). After asking her father, she was able to name various parts of the radio receiver and how they were related to each other.[54] *Periódico Infantil* intended the exercise not only to demonstrate the rudimentary mechanical engineering of the radio apparatus but also to bridge a generational gap by encouraging children to interact with adults about the appliance. Clearly, the radio competition sparked enthusiasm about technology in its young listeners, in some cases to the point of exasperation with adults who would not or could not answer their questions. As always, the technological learning curve was considerably steeper for children than for their parents, marking a turning point in which the younger people threaten to make their elders obsolete in a modernizing society.

Periódico Infantil, despite devoted listeners like Medardo and many others, was suspended in 1932. Medardo Sr. proved perhaps as exceptional a parent as his son a radio listener, yet his activities with his son and his participation in the community are indicative of the substantial role radio played for many middle-class families and their children. On March 3, 1931, Medardo Sr. wrote a letter to the SEP on behalf of the Mexico City chapter of the state-sponsored parents' union over which he presided, in which he expressed chagrin at the impending suspension of the program. "Over the past year, we have observed marked advances in the quality of our children's instruction," he penned, "due to the fact that *Periódico Infantil* . . . has come to fill the void left by classroom education, complementing it with manual classes and encyclopedic knowledge. . . . [W]e plead with you in the most attentive and respectful manner that you not suspend this education for our children, considering that it is of great advantage in the progress of our future citizens."[55]

This did not mark the end of children's programming through the SEP radio station; on the contrary, the show was replaced by the *Hora Infantil* program, which carried on the tradition of encouraging children to participate directly and contribute to the daily broadcasts but was directed by a close group of experts on children to make sure that the show remained didactic and educationally sound. Nevertheless, radio officials' stated goal remained to maintain, at all costs, a close relationship between listeners and program directors.[56] The *Hora Infantil* program frequently featured guest hosts from kindergartens and elementary school classes around the republic, as they presented songs, games, and stories to their compatriots. One October 26, 1933, broadcast of the program opened with a performance to the flag sung by the Lauro Aguirre Kindergarten, followed by a recitation by kindergartener Dario Urdapilleta. Additional patriotic pieces followed, all performed on-air by the evening's young guests.[57] This format built upon the tradition, established with *Periódico Infantil*, of privileging children's contributions to on-air production. Now their voices could be heard around the country—literally, not just through a reading of their written submissions. All that remained was to train children across the nation to embrace, and not to fear, the new technologies that would permit this kind of national fellowship to grow and that would usher Mexico into the embrace of modernity.

Radio as Object: Raising a Nation of Young Technophiles

As happens with any technological innovation across cultures and societies, radio captivated the imaginations of the children's lives that it touched. Historians, policy makers, and parents alike have observed children's aptitude for technology, as successive generations approach innovation with intrepid curiosity. Literary and cultural critic Rubén Gallo analyzed a photograph from the 1920s of a young boy, not older than five years, dialing an early radio, noting that the boy looked like he had become fused with the apparatus, an amalgam of human and machine parts as a metaphor for the revolutionary modern child.[58] The boy wore a timeless glazed expression on his face, one reproduced millions of times over on the faces of children as they come into contact with the latest technological advances of their society, from weapons to video games. Radio officials in Mexico sought to harness the natural desire of children, like the boy in the photo, to manipulate technology, while they eradicated any animosity toward technology rooted in superstition. This approach resulted in distinct treatment—evident in programming—of urban middle-class children and rural poor children. Radio programming ostensibly intended for all children to join the technological revolution, but not all children enjoyed access to it.

Government radio programs helped to induct children into the burgeoning world of technology that characterized the 1930s. They learned about other forms of electronics and machinery; saving precious time was a value that children could now develop. Revolutionary officials saw technology as an ally in boosting the nation's productivity and bridging the gap between urban and rural society. José Vasconcelos commissioned public murals that demonstrated how tractors and electric mills increased the country's agricultural bounty.[59] Citing studies of child psychology, SEP officials saw the child as a metaphor for primitive man who demonstrated fear of forces of nature beyond his ability to explain. The simplistic spirits of children and primitive men alike (and, as the discussion of *Antena Campesina* will demonstrate below, SEP officials included contemporary Indians in this category) led them to provide misguided interpretations of inexplicable phenomena. Both children and Indians, then, required directed instruction as to how to harness energy—natural and technological—for the advancement of mankind. Since children viewed both a cloud and a typewriter with the same wonderment, the tabula rasa could be of great advantage to educators who wished to introduce technology.[60]

Juguetes!

Vengan Muchachos!
Vengan!

El Arbol de Navidad de la "CASA DE CONFIANZA" está "CUAJADO" de preciosos juguetes que los Santos Reyes nos ordenan regalar a todos los niños de la Capital que vengan a visitarnos el MIERCOLES 6, en la mañana, hasta la 1. - No es necesario que compren algo, sólo se requiere que vengan acompañados de sus familiares.

"El Puerto de Veracruz" "LA CASA DE CONFIANZA"

Signoret. Allegre y Cia.

23. Three Kings' Day ad for department store Puerto de Veracruz, 1926. *El Universal Gráfico,* January 2, 1926. Courtesy of the Biblioteca Miguel Lerdo de Tejada.

Different media presented technology differently to urban middle-class and rural poor child audiences. At least through the 1930s the presence of the radio apparatus itself, especially at the technology's inception, clearly marked one's home as middle class.[61] In the commercial sector newspaper advertisements had targeted urban middle-class children as a consumer class since the Porfiriato. By the 1920s print ads presented the radio receiver itself as an essential commodity. Store owners knew that children could tug at their parents' purse strings, so they launched an advertising trend that bypassed adults and appealed directly to children through cartoon-like ads and short catchy exclamations in attention-grabbing fonts. Puerta de Veracruz advertised in the pages of the children's magazine *Aladino.* In one example it featured a line of unaccompanied children—notably all light-skinned and fashionably dressed—streaming toward the doors of the four-story department store, in frantic pursuit of the latest Christmas toys (fig. 23).

rca ads from the same magazine appealed both to young readers and to their parents that no playroom could be con-

En el cuarto de juego de sus niños, o en su re-
cámara, no debe faltar un Radio pequeño,
pero de la gran marca

RCA VICTOR

Es un profesor a domicilio, que educa a sus niños, los instruye, los divierte, y un cariñoso
amigo que se los retiene en casa y se los arrulla
a la hora de dormir

Con uno de los pequeños radios

RCA VICTOR

Usted estará tranquila porque sus niños no
saldrán nunca de su casa.

¡Qué más puede usted pedir!

El dinero gastado en adquirir un

RCA VICTOR

está MIL VECES mejor gastado que en los
mejores juguetes

En la soberbia línea RCA VICTOR encontrará el que usted necesita
—— Los hay de 4 y 5 bulbos, a precios sumamente económicos ——
Haga la prueba unos días. Pídalo en demostración a cualquiera Agencia RCA VICTOR Autorizada

AUTOMOTRIZ DE MEXICO, S. A.

DISTRIBUIDORES RCA VICTOR

REFORMA 96   MEXICO, D. F.

24. RCA ad featuring middle-class children, 1934. *Aladino,* January 1934,
n.p. Courtesy of the Hemeroteca Nacional.

sidered complete without a small radio, which would serve as
an in-home teacher as well as provide entertainment. The idea
was that, with the radio, children would never want to leave
the house. In short, the radio assumed the role of both babysit-
ter and playmate (fig. 24).[62] *Aladino* readers learned to identify
with the light-skinned, modernly dressed children in the ads
who lounged about among plenty of toys to occupy the time that
they were not captivated by the radio. A contest conducted by
the magazine established the radio as the most coveted object
among less technologically sophisticated drivable toy cars, scoot-
ers, bicycles, and toy pistols by offering an RCA radio as first prize,
valorizing technology as a desirable commodity.[63] A Christmas
ad in *Aladino* indicated that the radio could be a child-friendly
piece of equipment and suggested that children should have
the liberty to choose their own listening schedule by tuning in
to the station of their choice.[64] The next generation of citizens
would be well versed in technology indeed if all of the nation's
children had access to the shows and the equipment.

Estridentismo for Children: Terror, Technology, and *Troka el Poderoso*

The Industrial Revolution of the previous century had dramatically increased the proximity between man and machine and complicated the relationship between children and technology. Children were at once more vulnerable to the unrelenting dominion of the machine and more deft in their manipulations of it—a characteristic that industrial capitalists eagerly exploited in the years before child labor laws around the world emerged to curb children's presence in factories in the 1920s and 1930s. In the United States the advent of automobiles on New York City streets in the 1920s wrought a flurry of public concern over their encroachment into what had come to be considered "child space." The perceived natural incompatibility between children and technology bore itself out in legal debates and ultimately resulted in the creation of the Playground Association of America and the subsequent retreat of children to protected, domesticated sanctioned spaces free from the dangers of technology.[65] Likewise, at the same time, in Mexico, stories about vehicular accidents involving children appeared commonly in the printed press. Child deaths involving cars and trolleys created general public fear about machines, to which the government responded with the Campaign for the Safety of the Child (Campaña Pro-Seguridad del Niño).[66] But the Mexican government also proactively sought the reconciliation of children and technology, foreseeing the benefits of a nation of young technophiles: children's art magazine *Pulgarcito* featured monthly contests for young collaborators to depict the rules of riding the electrified trolleys supplanting horses and bicycles in the capital's public thoroughfares. Prizewinning children drew the trolleys' mechanical parts in remarkable detail; the contest awarded those who elaborated the workings of these engineering wonders for their peers to see. These exercises quite literally drew some children into a positive yet respectful relationship with technology.

Since the country's first strides toward modernization in the Porfiriato, advocates of technology had to combat technophobia that threatened to keep Mexico mired in the past. The advent of the railroad elicited a rash of praise (and critique) from Porfirian writers and artists grappling with the technology's redemptive possibilities and mitigating its perceived dangers.[67] Architects of the revolution wanted the social benefits of twentieth-century technology and wanted to reduce the dangers associated with its machines. A small sector of the intellectual elite believed that technology would uproot Mexico from its entrenched atavism, provide the impetus for nationalist economic growth, and set the country on equal footing with the rest of the modern world. Artists joined the fray: expatriates Edward Weston and Tina Modotti trained their cameras as tenderly upon toilet bowls and tinfoil as they did on the shiny plaited braid hanging heavily down an indigenous woman's back. Germán List Arzubide was a founding member of the radical technophile avant-garde group that called themselves the Stridentists, and his contributions to children's programming helped to distinguish xfx from other commercial stations. Along with his brother Armando List Arzubide, he worked with xfx in a variety of capacities to render this new technology a useful tool of the revolution. The List Arzubide brothers developed a radio drama that broadcast theatricalized episodes of Mexican history, a cultural labor that gained them distinction as "the constructors of our nationality," by the account of a commentator for *El Maestro Rural*.[68] Germán in particular earned a reputation both for his ardent defense of the proletariat and for his staunch belief in the transformative power of technology.

Based in Xalapa, Veracruz, the Stridentists burst onto the intellectual scene in 1922 and 1923 with the first and second of four manifestos, in which they vocally advocated for the "unconditional surrender to the miracles of modernization" and the "exaltation of the surging theme of machines, of factory explosions that shatter the mirrors of subverted days."[69] Over the decade or so that they were influential in the cultural sphere, Stridentists formed what one scholar has called "a movement focused on agitation strategies through its deep connection to a mechanical aesthetics."[70] Stridentists saw themselves as expelled violently from the womb of the revolution, and their inheritance was one of cultural cacophony, iconoclasm, and disjuncture.

A prolific poet, journalist, and essayist, List Arzibide's literary contributions have been analyzed profoundly by scholars of the avant-garde umbrella and the fragmented movements it nourished. Yet scholars have frequently dismissed the substantial material he produced in collaboration with renowned colleagues in the art and literature worlds as a pastime or an aside to his more serious work. Yet his contributions to children's culture of the 1930s—radio, literature, and puppet shows—constituted the first exposure to multiple forms of media for many Mexican children. Furthermore, the carefully crafted language he incorporated into his children's stories—many of which were broadcast nationally—constitutes a thinly veiled way of reaching an infantilized indigenous or peasant audience that he feared was in danger of missing out on the possibilities of Mexico's modernization.

In 1933 XFX inaugurated a new children's program called *Troka el Poderoso*—Troka the Powerful, or, not quite literally, The Powerful Truck—which aired Sunday mornings at 10:00, in order to reroute children's attentions from fantastic meanderings to practical applications of technology that moved the nation pointedly forward on the path to modernization.[71] Germán List Arzubide himself conceptualized Troka. The titular character was a man-made polymorphous supermachine that embodied trucks, trains, steamships, airplanes, smokestacks, submarines, telescopes, movie projectors—in short, all things mechanical (fig. 25). Troka, probably a Hispanicization of the English word *truck*, had entered common parlance in the United States in the first decade of the twentieth century; it is still used to refer to pickup trucks in parts of Mexico today. Troka embodied the industrious work ethic of all men of all races (in the words of List Arzubide, black men who drained rubber sap from the Amazon, white men who cut lumber in Canada, yellow men who planted rice in China) and was the product of human toil. He boasted an infallible body made of steel, malleable internal organs made of aluminum, joints made of steel ball bearings, a head made of bronze filled with a brain of electromagnetic wires, and a spirit made of electricity.[72] Troka took up residence in the radio station and from there transmitted his tales of travel and the transformation of Mexico from a sleepy rural agricultural country to a modern industrial powerhouse. The narration was put to music by legendary composer Silvestre Revueltas—a clashing, cacophonous soundtrack that evoked images of raw mechanical power. The program saw so much success that List Arzubide published a collection of the weekly episodes as an illustrated short story collection in 1939.[73] Both the radio program and the illustrated children's book that it spawned reveal the tendencies of Mexico's intellectual elite in the 1930s to value mechanized forms of production over traditional, rustic, or nonmechanized labor.

List Arzubide appealed to children's imaginations by masterfully conjuring up vivid futuristic scenarios that featured machines as protagonists. Through Troka's exploits, List Arzubide described Mexico as a country inevitably moving toward a highly industrialized future and threatened that those outside of the technological revolution would remain confined to a dark and superstitious past. Much like the erasure of the countryside enacted by banishing horse-drawn carts in the city, List Arzubide sought to excise the mystical past from his readers' minds, to replace it with a humanistic faith in the power of technology. At the core of List Arzubide's broadcasts (and texts) are discourses of terror: in his stories children (and infantilized campesinos) vacillate between a superstitious fear of natural forces and an ignorant fear of machines. Somewhat ironically, the anthropomorphic man-made machines that List Arzubide touts as saviors in his humanist national paradigm terrorize, bully, and intimidate to convey their righteous message.

Troka el Poderoso helped to facilitate the entry of radio, and its multitude of electronic contemporaries, into the daily activities of children. Troka undertook a humanist mission to present the new man-made technologies of the twentieth century

25. Troka el Poderoso embodied multiple forms of technology. List Arzubide, *Troka el Poderoso*, 14–15.

to children in a nonthreatening way, facilitating their seamless entry into the modern world. The powerful robot, regardless of the technological manifestation that he embodied, overpowered humans in all of the stories. Producers saw the demonstration of machines' power over nature as a necessary tool for uprooting the superstitious tendencies held by the backward masses, a flaw that they believed would seriously impede Mexico's entry into a modern global economy. They argued that the folkloric superstitions learned during childhood had left children ambivalent and weak and employed Troka to awaken in them a modern consciousness that embraced technology as the wave of the future.[74]

One tale, "The Second Appearance of Troka," captured the spirit of the *Periódico Infantil*'s assignment, described above, that sent children scurrying to the nearest department store to learn about the inner workings of the radio. In this story Troka manifests himself as a radio tower, and two curious boys, Anselmo and Raymundo, follow his radio voice to visit him at the station. They climb up the metal stairs that constitute his legs, reaching the beacons of his eyes, as bright as the lighthouse of Veracruz that penetrated the deep maritime darkness of the Gulf. In close contact with Troka-as-radio-tower, Anselmo and Raymundo begin to describe his composition relative to other technologies with which they are more familiar: his eyes made of impressive panes of glass must have been melted in massive ovens and forged in colossal molds; his brain of cables and transmitting wires reminds Raymundo of a visit to the telephone company where he watched information be transmitted invisibly over a mass of cords and wires. The boys then enter Troka's body, where cables from far-flung rural areas such as Necaxa, Tepuxtepec, Tepejí, and Lerma converge in the grand central station of information. Troka reminds Anselmo and Raymundo that, although they might not be so amazed by electricity, those living outside the realm of progress rely on candles to illuminate their nights.[75] Children listening to the program accompanied the boys on their tour of Troka's mechanized body and learned how the radio transmitted the signal into their homes and classrooms. This tale, even transmitted over the airwaves, transformed the magic of radio to a physical scene embodied by human children, a scenario in which imaginative listeners could easily situate themselves. It created a tangible landscape upon which they could envision their invisible community of peers sharing common ground.

Troka sends the fictional boys Anselmo and Raymundo on a romanticized escape from the city as a way to introduce urban children to the countryside, which had untamed features that had to be placed under human control (Troka brags that he commanded the rivers to be obedient to his desires—through hydroelectric energy, irrigation, and potable water). Troka and the two boys take a trip outside of the city, breathing deeply the fresh air and marveling that this afternoon trip would have taken days for the boys' grandfathers to complete, underscoring a reference to the revolutionary road-paving campaign of the 1920s. Nevertheless, they happily return to the city that night and lodge safe and sound in a clean, comfortable, well-lit, and, most important, "hygienic" hotel.[76] This story celebrates infrastructural development in the countryside as a hallmark of revolutionary modernizing campaigns. It places children at the center as protagonists and situates them as the beneficiaries of the physical changes, wrought by machines at the behest of visionary men, to the national landscape.

In one story Troka paints the tireless and efficient typewriter as the protagonist in a world of cumbersome and page-staining pens. The talking typewriter acknowledges that some of his listeners might be too young to use the typewriter but suggests that one day they seek him out for assistance, to complete their work more quickly.[77] At the end of the story, Troka encourages children to seek out and gain familiarity with the typewriter. If children had not yet gained exposure to the typewriter by the time they listened to Troka, SEP officials used radio to ensure the introduction of the time-saving machine into daily home economics. The radio bulletin Bringing Together the Home and the School encouraged mothers to sit their children in front of a typewriter as a way to make school vacations productive, as they could be entertained while learning a life skill. Perhaps more important than the purported physiological benefits of typing (improved vision, eye-hand coordination, and posture), the authors of the radio home bulletin touted the machine as a "symbol of modern progress," and interaction with it would bolster the child's appreciation of a sense of order, cleanliness, and aesthetic appreciation.[78] Typewriters, if properly employed, would facilitate the evolution of a generation of bureaucrats—machine-ready perfectionists with an appreciation for orderliness. Such messages, while available to any xfx listener, certainly resonated most with families with middle-class status or aspirations, ones that envisioned desk jobs for their sons and daughters as the ultimate expression of success.

Even as the typewriter seemed to represent the uncompromising standardization of the written form, it allowed for new creative expressions in mechanical form. Much like the radio, a machine intended to contribute to uniformity, the typewriter's freestyle interactions allowed its user to produce unexpected forms. Rubén Gallo has described the playfulness with which early authors experimented with mechanogenics—physical manipulation of typewritten text on the page that abolished the intended intimacy of the printed letter and suggested instead its revolutionary potential.[79] As if to underscore the individuality that mechanically produced text could represent, when List Arzubide published the broadcast stories of *Troka el Poderoso* in print form in 1939, the opening essay took a mechanogenic form, forcing the reader to break the habit of reading text in linear form. Indeed, the book itself is a work of technology. On the page List Arzubide arranged Troka's words in a schema made possible only by the internal rulers and standardized typeset of the machine. One excerpt, broken up into uneven columns scattered about the page, reads, "Troka is the cinematographer, the spirit of mechanical things, of that which man has invented, has created, with his intelligence, with his effort."[80] The poem suggests human dominion over technological forces, not the other way around. Its arrangement disrupted the natural flow of the reader, forcing him to engage with the typewriter. Through this and other Troka stories, children learned not to be manipulated by yet another structural force in their lives but rather to exercise personal control over the new, modern machines that populated their lives.

Troka's stories pitted modern (new or improved) technologies against their natural counterparts to prove the efficiency of adopting modern means of production. The lightbulb rivaled the moon for providing light, the truck rivaled the river for transporting goods, and telegraph poles rivaled trees as perches for birds—even the smoothly hewn posts that appeared to be at rest bore wires gently humming and ticking with information. As a Stridentist, List Arzubide did not shy away from violence and discord as strategies in framing these encounters, notwithstanding his premature audience. Through the allegorical stories, technology and nature become personified, acquire characteristics laden with ideological value, and engage in competitions that often turn violent. Additionally, List Arzubide often framed the promotion of violence and the ability to incite fear as masculine qualities, and the machines carry out their conquests of their feminized natural counterparts.

The imagery was familiar: Diego Rivera's 1926 mural *The Mechanization of the Countryside* shows an indigenous woman representing Mother Nature seated in a field replete with cornstalks, while around her men till and fertilize the fields with tractors and airplanes. A feminized landscape reached its full potential only with the intervention of masculinized technology, and only through a violent modification of her flesh, a gendered encounter so deeply rooted in Mexican soil that Octavio Paz would lament it decades later as one of the foundational flaws of the Mexican national character.[81] The theme resonates time and again in *Troka el Poderoso*. In one story a shiny new male elevator and a sagging old female staircase compete over passengers in a department store. The elevator cheerfully lifts passengers away from the humdrum and exertion of the staircase. Then it hits a snag when a blackout paralyzes the city, but thanks to the hardworking city maintenance crew, the elevator prevails in the end. The staircase slowly gains an understanding of why the elevator sings joyfully on the way up and on the way down. The people come and go effortlessly from his tiny steel cage without fatigue, free of danger, and happy in the knowledge that electric power has saved them time (fig. 26).[82] Through this short parable, List Arzubide rendered something as commonplace as a staircase cumbersome and therefore obso-

26. The elevator overpowers the staircase. List Arzubide, *Troka el Poderoso*, 69.

lete by being gendered as female and by being placed in opposition to the improved mechanized version, gendered as male.

In perhaps the most violent confrontation between technology and nature, a baby hill and its mother mountain look on as
a male train (*el gusano*, or the caterpillar, as the baby hill calls
it) approaches, intending to bore its way through the stomach
of the mountain to avoid the hassle of having to travel all the
way around her. The train barrels forth jeering, "Choo-choo!
You can't mess with me! Choo-choo, I'm in a rush! Goodbye,
mountain, catch me if you can! Choo-choo!!"[83] The mother
mountain experiences terrible pain at the train's aggressive
penetration, graphically underscoring the gendered conno-
tations of man-made technology dominating Mother Nature.
Intentionally or not, a dose of valorized male attributes accompanied children's introductions to new technological advances
over the radio. This undermined the egalitarianism intended
by radio officials in children's programming.

Rare but valuable evidence exists that some of the children
internalized the violence of the message. Listeners to Troka
on the radio submitted some of their drawings for Troka's (or
the radio officials') approval. A set of pictures drawn in 1930
by a young listener clearly depicts the train before and during
his penetration of the great mountain, evidence that children
heard and absorbed the fearsome message about the power of
technology (fig. 27). In this simple drawing, scrawled over with
captions that summarize the story, the train physically takes
the form of a caterpillar—the only word the baby hill knew to
describe an object as foreign as a locomotive. The child listener
had taken the metaphor literally. In the second panel, the caterpillar's antennae visibly emerge from the wounded hillside.
The artist either had not understood the subtlety of Troka's tale
or was so compelled by the animal metaphor as to render the
technology lesson futile. Yet unlike the woodcut illustration in
the 1939 published story, the child did not personify the mountain with any facial features (fig. 28). The literal, more realistic version drawn by the child suggests a disconnect between
List Arzubide's intended message and the young child's recep-

27. Drawings submitted by a Troka listener, ca. 1930. AHSEP, Dirección de Extensión Educativa por Radio, Subserie "Troka el Poderoso," Reportes de la República Mexicana, Caja 9486, Exp. 49, ca. 1930.

tion—a lesson lost somewhere in the airspace between the Mexico City XFX radio tower and the child's living room.

Like the *Periódico Infantil*, this drawing submitted to the XFX radio offices shows that Troka's exploits elicited written responses from his listeners. María Luisa Sáenz, a fourth grade teacher, praised Troka for awakening enthusiasm for science and the arts in the youth. Ms. Sáenz observed that the apathetic children of yesterday had become active and studious today, thanks to Troka's encouragement.[84] On several occasions Troka asked listeners to send drawings of the technology that they observed in their world. SEP radio officials saw drawing as the best pedagogical way to engage students in the mechanical worlds that Troka described.[85] And once again the format of this brand of interactive learning piqued some children's awareness that they were not on equal socioeconomic footing with their invisible peers. Listener Agustín Ortiz lamented that he could not draw the airplane or the tractor because he was poor and did not have paper. In the same vein eight-year-old Laura Esther Zapata wrote on behalf of a group of students from San Andrés Atenco in México state that their school and their village were poor, "but we have a desire to study and want to take advantage of what we learn from the schoolteacher[.] [W]e heard some of your stories and today we send you some drawings in hopes that they meet your approval and if we are worthy of a mention [on-air] it would lift our spirits."[86] Agustín Yáñez, the head of the

28. Illustration from the published version of Troka el Poderoso's story of the train penetrating the mountain. List Arzubide, *Troka el Poderoso*, 43.

SEP Correspondence Office, wrote back to Laura Esther, thanking her for the drawings, and sent with the letter thirty sketch pads to distribute among her classmates. Laura Esther and her classmates directed themselves to a government official within the framework of their poverty and industrious attitude as a way to garner acknowledgment, inclusion, and a reward, however trivial. In this case the children earned what they sought.

The print version of *Troka el Poderoso* contained engraved woodcut lithographs by Julio Prieto that illustrated each of the moralistic tales in stark social realist style, but since it was published nearly a decade after the program's radio broadcast, the drawings supplied by child listeners could only derive from aural inspiration and that of the mind's eye. The images, far from being mere illustrations of a story, provide a glimpse into children's imaginative life as they applied orally transmitted descriptions into artistic application, drawing from the world around them. The drawings also serve as evidence that some children did indeed listen with attention to the details of the program, providing a rare glimpse into the ephemeral realm of child reception of a cultural phenomenon in the moment that it is transmitted.

Throughout the broadcast and printed version of the Troka stories, List Arzubide espoused a brand of humanism that was deeply rooted in his ideological commitment to the proletariat. He purported to advocate for human dominion over technological forces, not the other way around. He wanted to train his child audience not to be manipulated by yet another structural force in their lives but rather to exercise personal control over the new, modern machines that populated their lives. As clearly stated in his introduction to the text, List Arzubide sought to supplant the superstitious fears about the natural world (the reason for a sudden storm, the mysterious disappearance of the sun every night, the magical germination of plants) with scientific knowledge. The author exploited children's tendencies to ascribe binary positive and negative characteristics to technology and the natural world, respectively. To do so he infused his descriptions of the natural and the technological with value-laden vocabulary: the man-made airplane and elevator "sing joyfully," and the lightbulb "shines splendidly"; meanwhile, the moon "growls" and "screams furiously," marches off violently, pales with anger, and makes a face of profound disgust. Notwithstanding their demonstrated superiority, Troka and his legion of mechanical warriors are undeniably terrifying. They loom and click and glower and threaten their way into children's imaginations. The underlying message of Troka el Poderoso promotes an industrialized version of economic nationalism and the subsequent yielding of proletarian labor and its attendant rustic tools to the power of technological force. The resulting narrative manifests itself as a violent assault upon an unprepared rural population and landscape.

Invisible Children: *Antena Campesina*

Like the *Periódico Infantil,* the *Troka* program elicited letters tinged with jealousy from young listeners who saw themselves on the cusp of an exciting new cultural experience but who felt it just beyond their grasp. When they could they resorted to letters to make their plight known to the radio officials. "I am sending some letters of the lovely stories that you told us," wrote F. de G. Cárdenas Acuña in a scrawling, sloping script. "Are they alright? Mr. Troca [*sic*]: I would like to see your home like those children who will be visiting you on Sunday. S.S.S. [yours truly]." This child had learned of a group of invited children who would be coming to the station and, summoning all of the formalities in his power, had penned a simple petition. His letter included a rudimentary letterhead including the location and date of his letter, the designated recipient (complete with a title: "Señor Troca el Poderoso"), formal salutations, and an address as a postscript: "I await your orders at Mosquito 232 #1."[87] In this case the response seemed to be favorable, as the annotation on his letter says to tell him that he could come by the station to pick up his prize. Fortunately for F. de G., he lived in Mexico City and had access to Troka and his headquarters. As radio's scope projected outward, an increasingly rural audience listened to programs generated in the nation's capital with little hope of interacting directly with the men and women who operated the technology.

Citing studies of child psychology, educational officials saw the child as a metaphor for primitive man who demonstrated fear of forces of nature beyond his ability to explain. The simplistic spirits of children and primitive men alike—a category that List Arzubide extended to include contemporary Indians— led them to provide misguided interpretations of inexplicable phenomena. One of the stated goals of radio transmissions directed toward a campesino audience, according to XFX officials, was to vigorously combat the "absurd beliefs" of the rural population in healers, sorceresses, and conmen.[88] Both children and Indians, then, required directed instruction as to how to harness power—natural and technological—for the advancement of an economically productive nation. By addressing young children, List Arzubide sidestepped a problematic condescension to his indigenous compatriots, but the ample references to children's "primitive" and "magical" minds conflate his audience to include any of those outside of the parameters of modernity. A Lockean view of young people as a blank slate could be of great advantage to educators who wished to introduce technology to a broader audience.[89] In this climate indigenous children received a double measure of condescension from radio officials, in particular through the nature of programming designed specifically for them.

Rural children fortunate enough to have access to radio received a quite different message about technology than their urban compatriots. In fact, SEP radio officials acknowledged the need to modify (or simplify) content for their rural, indigenous audience, whose Spanish vocabulary they claimed was often limited to about a hundred words.[90] Although ostensibly radio was a universalizing medium—any radio capable of receiving the XFX signal would broadcast identical program content—the intended audiences varied for each program. As established above, there is no way to determine who listened to what program. Yet the transcripts and official correspondence about radio education content reveal that XFX officials saw rural children's relationship to technology quite differently from that of urban middle-class children.

Typical programming for a campesino child—distinct from the above programming intended for children in urban centers—emphasized the physical and natural aspects of their growth and development, rather than activities and skills that would prepare them for city life. XFX designated the 10:00 a.m. slot on Fridays for these broadcasts, programming intended primarily to encourage this demographic group to attend, or continue to attend, the rural schools. Program content included songs, a physical education class, story time, biographies, plant and animal life, rural children's hygiene, and a brief general education segment.[91] References to technology for campesino children focused squarely on the domain of agriculture, in an era when major revolutionary programs redistributed rural lands and restored *ejidos* (communal land).[92] On occasion, XFX directed radio messages specifically to campesino youth in a broadcast titled *Antena Campesina*. The announcer encouraged them to work with the maestro of their Escuela Rural to learn the latest agricultural technology that would improve conditions in the countryside.

SEP officials envisioned nationwide broadcasts of their programs, but transmissions still radiated from the nation's cultural and political core. Politics in the 1930s developed along corporatist lines that cemented Mexico City's position as the nucleus of the national political structure.[93] Social events for listeners took place in the capital, where the XFX offices were housed, and established a pattern that privileged children from Mexico City over the rest of the nation with more access to cultural programs. Troka sent invitations to children in the capital for parties where listeners of all backgrounds could rub elbows. Because he could not invite the campesino youth, he called them his *amigos invisibles*. Troka reminded his rural listeners how fortunate they were to have access to the "magic box" of radio. They, of course, could listen to their own dear rural schoolteacher, but with radio they could learn from other schoolteachers from the far-away shining city.

Antena Campesina addressed the rural youth in simplified language that contained an abundance of references to nature, such as radio sound that arrived galloping on horses made of wind.[94] Rural children were not encouraged to run to their local department store to analyze the inner mechanical workings of the radio receiver; rather, *Antena Campesina* still underscored the mysteries of radio technology for its rural audience. This emphasized the sense of magic or spirituality associated with the unseen and unknown that contradicted Troka's expressed desire to eradicate superstition about unexplained forces. SEP radio officials saw radio as the appropriate vehicle for transmitting practical technological information to the countryside, but they did not intend rural children to listen to programs about the scientific progress of the modern generation to which Medardo and his urban middle-class friends belonged.

Conclusions

Educational radio in the 1930s became an important dimension of children's culture, expanding their experiences beyond their immediate interactions within the family, the classroom, and the city block. Through programs such as *Periódico Infantil* and *Troka el Poderoso*, many children joined a community that officials envisioned as national, although the broadcasting range of most stations clearly limited its scope. Educational officials used children's programming to extend the classroom into the home, reversing efforts to separate the family and educational activities developed at the beginning of the nineteenth century.[95]

The Stridentists' faith in the redemptive power of technology informed the SEP officials, who embraced technology and economic modernization in aspects of their curriculum. In particular, the XFX children's program provided the ideal platform for infusing the youngest generations of Mexicans with respect for, and love of, technological possibilities. After all, a child listening to the program over the radio had already taken the first step into the future and was already a young participant in a global modern phenomenon. Radio through daily broadcasts both modeled and served as a portal to new forms of technology rapidly transforming children's environments. Children of means, blessed with free time and resources, were those expected to learn the mechanical workings of the technology that flooded the country in the 1930s; in their adulthood they would be the ones to design, manipulate, and employ these machines as they saw fit for the modernization of the nation. Rural children learned about technology, but the discussion remained enshrouded in mystery and magic, its mechanics explained only in rudimentary terms. The message conveyed through XFX broadcasts indicated that the rural classes ought to possess just enough information about technology to be able to work the land productively. Even as radio facilitated the tightening of an invisible network of little friends through its interactive child programming, some children expressed awareness of their differences as audience members, and still others remained entirely invisible. Their voices did not make it onto the airwaves, their names were not pronounced on the tongues of contest announcers, their letters did not reach the hands of program producers, and their little friends in the cities never knew that they were there, listening silently.

CHAPTER FOUR

Comino vence al Diablo and Other Terrifying Episodes
Teatro Guiñol's Itinerant Puppet Theater

Children's theater will be a powerful medium for propagating doctrine.

—REFUGIO SONI, Mexican delegate to the VII Pan-American Child Congress, 1935

The language is not very appropriate. . . . [T]he boss who commands the *negrito* and Comino with harsh words like "bum," hitting them and threatening them with the figure called the "devil" . . . has left a strong impression on the children. Perhaps the intention is to remove from them the [class-based] fear that has been inculcated in their homes, but for the moment, some of the little ones are frightened [by the puppets].

—GUADALUPE TAVERA, school director, Popotla DF, in a letter to the Children's Theater Department, 1934

Mexican delegates to the VII Pan-American Child Congress felt at home in 1935. As hosts to the hemispheric gathering, they boasted their expertise and innovation in child-centered welfare reform. Featured among the lofty achievements presented to their esteemed colleagues—a newly revised constitutional article making socialist education a national mandate, international renown garnered by the art curriculum, and an unprecedented education budget—delegates boasted about an unlikely tool of the revolution's modernizing auspices: puppets.

The momentum leading up to the transition to the Socialist School had energized the ranks of the SEP. By 1934 the revision of Article 3 infused the curriculum with purpose—and a good measure of dogma. Supporters of the Socialist School saw their cultural programs validated and undertook with more vigor their efforts to elevate class consciousness among the urban workers and peasants filtering into newly built classrooms. The visibility of the proletariat was on the rise in the nation's burgeoning visual culture, and the SEP raced to meet the momentum with a complementary set of ideologically informed extracurricular programs constructed within a "framework of overalls."[1] Puppets—by way of government-sponsored itinerant programs that preached new revolutionary moral and hygienic codes to the masses—served as perfect embodiments of simplified messages, comedic conveyers of thinly veiled social norms. Their appeal among children opened doors to the rest of the community.

Yet as the second opening quote to this chapter suggests, puppetry as the perfect vehicle for the rapid conversion of the countryside met with unexpected challenges. These challenges came from the SEP puppeteers' intended audience, very young working-class and peasant children, and were communicated by schoolteachers, who served as cultural mediators. In the above case a schoolteacher levied a measured but firm critique on one performance in particular that proved too metaphorical for the young children to grasp. The play, titled *Comino Overcomes the Devil* (*Comino vence al Diablo*), formed a staple of the Fine Arts Institute (Departamento de Bellas Artes) of the SEP's itinerant puppet theater repertoire, Teatro Guiñol, in the 1930s.[2] It appeared alone or alongside other proletarian-themed puppet scripts in widely distributed publications of the SEP.[3] Beginning in 1932, and continuing in some versions throughout the 1970s, the Mexican government has employed puppets as ambassadors of modernity to populations perceived as culturally impoverished.[4] For the first decade of this experiment, the period of interest here, the scope of the government project remained limited to the so-called proletarian elementary schools and kindergartens within the greater metropolitan area of Mexico City. By the end of the Cárdenas period (and near the decline of the socialist education program that sustained the puppet shows), the program's popularity had resulted in unofficial offshoots, makeshift theaters, and troupes in remote areas, all inspired by the do-it-yourself manuals published and disseminated in *El Maestro Rural.*

Government-sponsored itinerant puppet shows in the 1930s reflected both the optimism and the bureaucratic stumbling blocks that marked revolutionary nation-building efforts. In the case of Teatro Guiñol government officials and members of the intellectual artistic milieu constructed an aspect of children's culture that they hoped could be universally distributed and uniformly received. To the credit of the SEP, evidence indicates that this process was discursive rather than top-down and that children's disparate and unexpected responses to the plays—mostly informed by their ages and developmental status—resulted in a series of bureaucratic measures to adjust the puppet programs for maximum effectiveness. In the process bureaucratic procedures (an increasingly marked feature of the growing national political party, the PNR) dampened the creative spirits of the artists, musicians, playwrights, and actors involved in Teatro Guiñol, a project they had come to see as a labor of love. An analysis of correspondence (between the puppeteers, the SEP officials, the schoolteachers, and the children), Teatro Guiñol scripts, official statements, drawings, and photographic documents reveals that the children at the center of the itinerant puppet program were actively involved in its development and were not simply passive recipients of revolutionary educational projects.

Puppets as Pedagogy: The Teatro Guiñol of the SEP

Teatro Guiñol provided children with access to another child-centered cultural project in the 1930s. One story, emerging from lore surrounding the origins in Yucatán of the Rationalist School (Escuela Racionalista, one of the secularizing precursors to the national socialist education curriculum), credited an antisocial adolescent named Humberto with beginning the tradition of using puppet theater in the schools in 1917. According to the tale, the reclusive and sickly boy squirreled away in the woods for weeks, pilfering materials needed for costumes and set design, and eventually emerged with a puppet show that was met with tremendous acclaim.[5] This purpose of this origin story is twofold: to credit the structure-free environment of the Rationalist School with fomenting children's creative power and to suggest the innate therapeutic and social value of puppet theater for children.[6] Theater, for adults and children alike, served as one of the most effective ways of fomenting a sense of national identity.[7] Living vicariously through the puppets' capers, children encountered enemies ranging from bacteria to exploitative bosses and learned the appropriate ways to combat social ills. Yet while puppeteers and intellectual engineers constructed the healthy, moralized worlds that the cloth and wooden dolls presented to children, the children often transformed the intended meanings of the performances according to their personal tastes or developmental abilities.

In the early 1930s the Ministry of Education decided to resurrect puppet theater as a didactic tool for the developing socialist educational project, based on the legendary but faded success of the Rosete Aranda brothers' puppet shows that had toured the country since 1832. Puppet theater in the nineteenth century was renowned for its elaborate sets and its performers who bore striking resemblance to the character types made famous by lithographer Claudio Linati in the 1820s. Many audiences were familiar with puppets, the tropes they represented, and the national values they conveyed. Teatro Guiñol put the puppets at the service of the revolution. Officials at the offices of the Fine Arts Institute solicited young playwrights with a clear socialist orientation to ensure that the scripts systematically elevated the working classes.[8]

Yet if puppets were to be employed for more didactic purposes, the theater scenario would have to be scaled down in order to maximize the number of daily performances. First of all, hand puppets replaced the complicated string-operated marionettes; this not only facilitated transportation by eliminating the tangling of strings but also allowed for each puppeteer to operate two puppets at once, one on each hand. Second, the stage became a simplified frame-and-curtain affair that two people could set up in minutes, with minimalist scenery replacing the exquisite pastoral countryside backdrops featured in the Rosete Aranda presentations. Finally, keeping in mind the youthful audience, puppet-show playwrights based the story lines on actions rather than abstract morals that would resonate with the daily activities and icons familiar to children.[9]

What did puppets offer that could not be captured by live theater? A century of popular puppetry expanded by the Rosete Aranda family from Tlaxcala had demonstrated the abilities of puppets to dissimulate the sharply felt political rifts, regional identities, and social injustices of the nineteenth century through inanimate marionettes.[10] But especially after the revolution, puppets lent themselves to the communication of official discourse, closely aligned with an increasingly didactic national curriculum in the 1930s. None other than the brazen Germán List Arzubide, prolific playwright and author of the children's ratio program *Troka el Poderoso* discussed previously and author of the most didactic plays for Teatro Guiñol, declared the Rosete Aranda puppets dead in the introduction to his publication of three puppet plays;[11] those old-fashioned marionettes occupied a world of superstitions and oppression and did not carry their weight to rectify historical injustices. The social archetypes that the simpler hand puppets of Guiñol embodied corresponded to children's simple interpretations of more complex issues and personalities. Lively, comical, and exuberant, puppets offered SEP officials the opportunity to capture the attention of the very youngest children, impressing upon them the moral imperatives, hygienic behavior, and civic responsibilities of the new nation in the process. SEP puppeteers relied on the perceived reduced intellectual capacity of a young—or indigenous—audience and the tendency to conflate reality with fiction. Simplified scenarios filled with physical consequences, they believed, would accelerate the civilization process of the "savage" audiences.[12] The exaggerated features permanently molded into each puppet's face helped the young viewer easily ascribe characteristics of "good" or "evil" to the archetypical character, whether that be the Negrito, the Laborer, the Boss, or the Grandmother. Unlike human actors, who could change their facial expressions to nuance the content of their speech, puppets' static features set the tone for their characters' assigned moral positions. Teatro Guiñol scripts followed through on the visual construction of these revolutionary archetypes.

In a cultural milieu rife with didacticism and moral imperatives, few popular forms of entertainment for children passed muster with revolutionary pedagogues, eugenicists, and administrators. Movie theaters were refuted as centers of vice often maligned as the spaces in which juvenile delinquents acquired and practiced the tricks of their trade. In fact, in 1935 child specialists recommended that minors be prohibited entrance to movies, theaters, bullfights, and wrestling arenas. By contrast Teatro Guiñol, deemed wholesome and educational, changed the pace of life in rural areas isolated from the center. One teacher from a village in Puebla pleaded that they be included in the upcoming tour, claiming that they had no other diversions and that children and adults alike would enjoy the show. She noted that the village council struggled to invent pretexts for festivals.[13] Indeed, photos of puppet shows from the era often feature as many adult audience members as children, men crowding each other's view of the stage with their wide sombreros.

While the resources for Teatro Guiñol provided by the SEP remained limited, the popularity of the puppets ignited nationwide interest and brought puppetry into schools and communities from Chihuahua to Chiapas. Comino and company enjoyed a wide audience; the publication of *Comino vence al Diablo* and other plays in the monthly SEP publication *El Maestro Rural* indicated that not only did educational officials intend for teachers to stage Teatro Guiñol plays on their own but that Comino had access to rural classrooms far beyond the geographical limitations of the puppet troupes in the 1930s.[14] By 1940 Comino and crew had begun taking their antics and messages to rural areas in the states of Michoacán, Tamaulipas, Puebla, Hidalgo, and Tlaxcala. *El Maestro Rural*, edited by the SEP beginning in 1932—the same year as the Teatro Guiñol's inception—saw a circulation of twelve thousand copies in its second year and reflected official recognition of the first successes of educational

29. Children working on the construction and development of a Teatro Guiñol. *El Maestro Rural*, April 1935.

reform, namely, a more literate peasantry.[15] The appearance of
Comino on these pages, which in some cases was rural schoolteachers' only tangible link to the intellectual forces of the SEP
that they represented in the countryside, makes use of the abilities of the literate few in spreading proletarian ideas through
puppetry to children and community members alike.[16] In fact,
El Maestro Rural printed detailed instructions for schoolteachers and their students to construct their own elaborate puppet
stage; one article features the three-week diary of sixth grader
Andrés Rodarte from the Centro Escolar Revolución in Mexico
City, writing his detailed impressions of the process of building
the stage.[17] Schoolchildren also made their own hand puppets
and wrote their own plays, encouraged by teachers to incorporate as much folk knowledge and local vernacular as possible.[18]
Through the literary vehicle *El Maestro Rural*, rural peasants
and their children learned to become self-sufficient in the production of revolutionary knowledge (fig. 29).

In the stated benefits summarized by Mexican delegate Refugio Soni before the VII Pan-American Child Congress, puppets
were a powerful medium for propagating doctrines: the value
of work, the awakening of class consciousness, the benefits of
collectivism, the evils of capitalism, and the power of mechanized agriculture (*maquinismo*).[19] Through the tight regulation
of the production of theater scripts, SEP officials believed that
revolutionary nationalism could be standardized and neatly
packaged into productions of three plays in half-hour performances. Soni outlined the formula for the creation of revolutionary archetypes. Workers and campesinos should always be
portrayed as morally impugned productive actors. Teachers
should be represented as the intellectual guide. Women should
be depicted as "completely modern" and capable, while at the
same time self-abnegating and maternal. And children, in puppet form, should be healthy, strong, playful, disciplined, and
actively engaged in communal life.[20]

Concurrently with Soni's presentation to the conference delegates in 1935, pupils of the socialist educational program saw
puppet theater as an important part of their education. The

March 1935 First Conference of the Proletarian Child attended by child delegates between the ages of ten and thirteen took place in the Colonia Morelos of Mexico City and was organized by students of the Socialist Experimental Schools. Education officials saw it as a forum for children to express frankly their perceptions about their living conditions. The First Congress of the Proletarian Child was a bureaucratized celebration of class consciousness, a highly organized affair featuring calisthenics, choreographed dances, and well-groomed student speakers. Among other demands put forth by selected young orators—including respect for their toys and playtime, parents being persuaded to let them take school field trips, and not being obliged to work in factories—came a plea for children's theater in all of the schools. A photograph accompanying the text of the conference proceedings in *El Maestro Rural* depicted children constructing their own stage and performing their own puppet shows.[21] By 1935 children and adults alike identified puppet theater with the socialist educational project and had learned to employ revolutionary rhetoric to make a case for it to be included in their communities.

Teatro Guiñol represented a brief respite from the ideologically ambiguous archetypes that book-ended the experiment: in the nineteenth century the Rosete Aranda puppet Vale Coyote embodied racial and political disparities, and his mid-twentieth-century heir Cantinflas enacted social critique from the perspective of the *pelado*, or disenfranchised urban poor, with his complicated double- and triple-entendre monologues. Through Teatro Guiñol, under the close watch of a layer of government bureaucrats, the metaphors were simple, and the ideological messages were clear. That, at least, was the hope; as shall be demonstrated, even the most carefully scripted didactic puppet plays left room for interpretation.

The Visionaries: Revolutionary Intellectuals and Idealism in Teatro Guiñol

Teatro Guiñol started off in 1932 as a small enterprise, composed of a tightly knit group of radical intellectuals, artists, writers, and bohemians, most of whom had spent time honing their socialist ideology in Russia and Paris. Mexican diplomats and government functionaries who visited communist Russia experienced disillusionment with the implementation of socialism during the 1920s, and as politicians they turned the revolution in a more conservative direction upon their return home, distancing themselves from the Bolsheviks by breaking diplomatic relations in 1930.[22] Yet the cultural sector did not respond in the same manner to what they saw in Russia. The intellectual architects of the Teatro Guiñol found the inspiration for their educational project through direct observation of the Bolshevik socialist school puppet theater, at its zenith in 1928, promoting ideas about antialcoholism, literacy, and political fervor.[23] Briefly exiled in Russia, Germán List Arzubide enthused that the Russians had hit on the most age-appropriate form of disseminating revolutionary culture and nourished the seedling idea with his compatriots, artists Lola and Germán Cueto, in Paris.[24] They saw the medium as the ideal tool in fomenting a sense of class consciousness through which the youngest generation would come to understand ideas of fighting for equality and against oppression. The proletarian message that the puppets could bring forth would provide the basis for a new morality and combat superstition rampant in the countryside.[25]

In Mexico the puppeteers worked and lived in a community around the corner from Diego Rivera's house, creating the scripts, characters, and scenarios that would convey the official socialist educational program to students in collaboration with like-minded colleagues: playwright Roberto Lago, Russian-born artist Angelina Beloff, painter and writer Dolores Alva de la Canal, artist and writer Elena Huerta Muzquiz, artist Enrique Assad, painter Fermín Revueltas, designer and choreographer Graciela Amador, painter José M. Díaz Núñez, puppeteer Juan Guerrero, artist Julio Castellanos, engraver Leopoldo Méndez, and muralist Ramón Alva de la Canal.[26] As scholars of Mexico's "golden age of puppetry" have noted, this close-knit group of visionaries believed that they were manipulating the strings not only of allegorical dolls but of the nation's socialist future.[27] They poured hours of labor into the details of Guiñol construction, composition, costume, and scheduling. They earned negligible material recompense, and what little fame their efforts garnered was overshadowed by the celebrity of the creatures they manipulated from beneath the stage curtain.

The puppeteers professionalized puppet theater by giving it a name, Teatro Guiñol, and by working as an agency of the Ministry of Education, thus transforming the genre from a form of entertainment to an educational vehicle. Carlos Chávez, then head of the Fine Arts Institute, quickly took the reins of Teatro Guiñol, incorporating it into the subsection Teatro del Niño.[28] The first performance, *El gigante* (featuring an exploitative puppet who grew enormously fat off the food and labor of others), took place in central Mexico City and was attended by dignified functionaries, including Chávez and Secretary of Education Narcisso Bassols, who were seated among neighborhood children. By 1933 the group had developed an ambitious itinerary that took them to nearly four hundred kindergartens in the first six months alone. After little less than one year of operation, Roberto Lago estimated that the troupes had carried out 691 presentations, each with an average audience of 250–300 children—and adults—in attendance.[29]

Shortly, Teatro Guiñol split into two groups with four puppeteers each—Grupo A (Comino) and Grupo B (Rin-Rin)—and eventually others in the following years. Nearly every day each group would present the half-hour show of three plays with a cast of four to six characters, often presenting at more than one school a day. For example, in the second half of 1933 alone, the two groups gave 377 presentations to kindergarteners, an average of four plays each day.[30] Schools had access to eighty-seven fixed and portable theaters, a number that escalated with demand.[31] To broaden access to the puppet theater in the wake of much acclaim, in 1935 puppeteers Ramón Alva de la Canal and Graciela Amador received a government commission to teach puppetry techniques and content to teachers in training at the Escuela Normal Superior.[32] The SEP published instructional pamphlets directing schoolteachers to construct their own stages, and these were reprinted in *El Maestro Rural*, and *El Nacional* ran the scripts of Comino plays in their Sunday magazine insert.[33] The stage itself required little more than a blanket slung over a rope to obscure the puppeteers. The golden age of children's puppet theater lasted until the middle of the 1960s and expanded its activity to the farthest reaches of the republic, as well as international ventures in Cuba, Venezuela, and the United States. The puppets earned international acclaim fairly early on; one letter from a schoolteacher in Madrid requested more information about the *saladísimos muñecos* that had captured the imaginations of Mexican children and sought guidance on how to replicate the experiment in her own primary school classrooms.[34]

Teatro Guiñol's immediate popularity proved a mixed blessing to the puppeteers, as demand far outstripped their available financial and human resources. Letters poured in to the Bellas Artes offices pleading for visits, or at the very least materials for re-creating Teatro Guiñol in their own communities. Sixth grader Josefina Rodríguez, from the Mexico City neighborhood of Anáhuac, penned a letter to the head of Bellas Artes in 1934, expressing her desire for a weekly puppet performance to be given to help raise money for the local school, the construction of which had been halted due to lack of funds.[35] Regardless of the fact that SEP puppeteers never charged for their itinerant performances and were rarely able to repeat performances due to the high demand on their labors, Josefina had demonstrated an astute entrepreneurial application to a relatively new cultural offering. Roberto Oropeza Nájera, a teacher and school inspector from León, Guanajuato, wrote in 1936 requesting a collection of six puppets for the theater annex of a Children's Recreation Center under construction in his town. The head of the theater division responded by denying the request but sent the instructional pamphlet *Introduction, Organization, and Performance of Guiñol Puppet Theater*, as well as the publication *Tres comedias para el Teatro Infantil*, which contained the most popular plays written by List Arzubide. Not content with this material support, Orozpo Nájera insisted in another letter that the expansion of the program should extend outside of the confines of the capital city—he modified his request: just one puppet, this time, so that it could serve as a model in the construction of others. With a detectable tone of indignation, the teacher argued that those in the provinces did not enjoy the benefits of this program, although through the national press they received enthusiastic reports of its reception in the city. His urgency suggests the perceived divide between Mexico City and the provinces, felt more sharply with each new cultural innovation that did not quite reach the national population. As though to add insult to injury, a different government official responded to this second letter: he denied the request but sent him a copy of the same instructional pamphlet.[36]

With their craft in high demand, the puppeteers worked at a feverish pace, driven at first by their revolutionary fervor and then increasingly by pressure from SEP officials to meet the demand that the wildly popular puppets had generated in schools. Letters to Chávez from Grupo Comino and Grupo Rin-Rin reveal some of the daily stressors that compromised the quality of their performances. They requested more consistent access to the single SEP vehicle that each group borrowed every day, arguing that one was often not enough to transport all of the people and equipment required. Often they received the vehicles with no gas and had to pay out of their pockets to fill the tank. This caused them to be late to some of their appointments, and mothers complained that they had to wait at the school when they arrived to pick up their children because the puppet show was running into the afternoon. Furthermore, the road conditions between the pueblos took a toll not only on the SEP vehicle but on the equipment that it carried as well; Germán Cueto of Grupo Rin-Rin requested an upgrade to a 33-rpm record player, since their current 78-rpm machine suffered broken bulbs every time they transported it in the rattletrap car. At the moment, they complained, they could not perform the play *Rin-Rin renacuajo* because the required accompaniment of a Silvestre Revueltas record was damaged beyond audibility.[37]

The puppets emphasized the socialist values and vocational training espoused by the revolution, especially those promulgated by the SEP Cultural Missions sent out to the countryside. The playwrights, many of them members of the Revolutionary Writers and Artists' League (Liga de Escritores y Artistas Revolucionarios, or LEAR) founded by Teatro Guiñol member Elena Huerta, embedded lessons in the scripts that did little to conceal socialist ideology and political didacticism.[38] In so doing they constructed, through the fancy of puppets handcrafted in the image of man (and sometimes rooster or microbe), a utopian version of the citizens they hoped and believed that the revolution would construct through cultural outreach programs such as Teatro Guiñol. In the opinion of one schoolteacher, the puppeteers carried out more revolutionary work with their simple van and rustic stage than the pedantic intellectuals whose theories echoed off the closed walls of conference halls.

Charming puppets proved to be among the champions of the socialist reform accelerated under the Cárdenas administration; one schoolteacher noted that the Teatro Guiñol had promoted more revolutionary works than most contemporary statesmen.[39] Indeed, the plays contained practical representations of some of the most fundamental goals of the revolution. In the play *Comino va a la huelga*, Comino teaches his puppet friends about the provisions for labor reform in the Constitution of 1917: eight-hour days, overtime on weekends, and restrictions on the number of hours that children could work. The puppets exercise their constitutional right to strike. When the boss (*patrón*) wants to continue to force erstwhile laborers like the Negrito to work seventeen-hour days, the exploited puppets chant out their demands while taking recourse to their trademark symbol of resistance—beating the *patrón* with sticks.[40]

In addition to overtly political scenes, the puppet protagonists also found themselves in a series of predicaments that taught lessons about the value of work, the dangers of exploitation, the evils of capitalism, the importance of hygiene, the beauty of collectivism, and the merits of living and working in the countryside. Comino, the protagonist of many of the plays, learned life lessons through interactions with the other characters, often enduring a terrifying episode in the process. In *Illiterate Comino* (*Comino analfabeta*), the stubborn young puppet no sooner declares that he does not want to learn to read than he finds himself in a pit of despair along with an illiterate day laborer and an illiterate woman, both of whom lament their ignorance. Only by invoking the letters of the alphabet does Comino escape. The final scene, the apparition of an illuminated modern building bearing the phrase "The prosperity of a nation is the culture of its children," drives home the moral of the direct link between supporting elementary education and patriotism.[41] Through this simple metaphor, literacy has literally brought redemption.

In another play, *Ignorant Comino* (*Comino ignorante*), Comino gets lost on the spooky Illiteracy Alley because he does not know how to read street signs. Fortunately, he stumbles across one of the government literacy centers, learns to read, and begins to "make justice" by teaching others to do the same;[42] this lesson is lifted directly from the Cultural Missions in which literate children were organized into the Children's Literacy Army (Ejército Infantil), teaching their peers to read in areas where rural schoolteachers were short-staffed.[43] As a reward child literacy soldiers who taught five or more of their peers received certificates proclaiming them a "Good Mexican" and guaranteeing them preferential status for future employment by the Ministry of Education.[44] Comino's experience at the literacy center provided young audience members with a visual example of the satisfaction one could expect to receive from such civil service. Furthermore, the play reinforced government policy during the 1920s and 1930s that children be incorporated actively as agents of revolutionary reforms.

While most plays in the Teatro Guiñol repertoire conveyed a secular, civic morality that corresponded with the new revolutionary ideal, they rarely made explicit political references. One striking exception took place at the pinnacle of revolutionary fervor during the Cárdenas administration: the oil expropriation. Cárdenas's expropriation and nationalization of the oil industry in March 1938 wrested Mexico's natural resources from foreign coffers and signaled the apex of Cárdenas's ideological commitment to implementing the Constitution of 1917. Briefly, Mexicans from across the social strata scurried to deposit their personal cash reserves at the service of the president, to help pay for what they hoped would be a sweeping liberation from economic imperialism. Teatro Guiñol contributed to the nationalist frenzy that ensued. Within a few weeks of the expropriation, List Arzubide had penned a new play, *Oil for the Lamps of Mexico* (*Petroleo para las lámparas de México*), which the puppeteers immediately began to perform. In it Comino and Little Red Riding Hood need to travel through the dark forest to bring medicine and food to Little Riding Hood's ailing grandmother. The Night Watchman keeps ferocious, bloodthirsty animals at bay with his oil lamp. But when the oil begins to run low, the animals convince the Oil Man not to sell his oil to the Night Watchman, so that the lamp will go out and they can devour the children.

TIGER: We can't do anything as long as the Night Watchman's lantern is lit.

OWL: I will put it out with my wings.

WOLF: He will just light it again and he will be able to see us.

HYENA: If only the lantern didn't have oil, it would not light anything up and we could kill Little Red Riding Hood and Comino and devour them.

TIGER: But it will always have oil, the lantern is always burning. What should we do? (*All*) What should we do? (*They all sit thinking.*)

OWL: I know what to do. We will call the person who has the key to the oil, the rich man, and we will tell him not to give any more oil to the Night Watchman.

WOLF: Yes, yes, the rich man has the keys to Mexico's oil and we will tell him that he should let us eat up the children.

HYENA: Yes, and since he also eats children's flesh, he will help us. Let's call him.

ALL SHOUTING: Oil man! Oiiiil maaaaan! Oiiiiiil maaaaan!

The play relies upon familiar tropes of violence to signify the evil forces of greed, corruption, and imperialism: the character of the Oil Man, though never defined explicitly as a foreigner, nevertheless confesses a proclivity for dismembering and eating children. Unlike most other Teatro Guiñol plays, *Oil for the Lamps of Mexico* makes direct reference to Mexico, penetrating the curtain of fantasy and uniting the puppets and the children on the same national terrain.

OIL MAN: I cannot give you more oil, the tanks are locked.

NIGHT WATCHMAN: But the oil is not yours, it belongs to Mexico, to Mexican children. Why won't you give me a little bit to save them? Do you want them to die devoured by ferocious animals?

OIL MAN: I don't care if the animals eat the children. If you give me the eyes of all of the children that are here (*audience*), then I will give you oil.

NIGHT WATCHMAN: You want me to give you the eyes of the children? I'm going to pull out your eyes, if you don't give me oil.

OIL MAN: I won't give it to you . . . I won't give it to you . . . and I will eat the children. (*He cackles and sings.*) I won't give it to you and I will eat the children!

NIGHT WATCHMAN: What will I do? My lantern is going out. The children will arrive and they will be eaten by ferocious animals. (*Shouting*) Oil . . . I need oil to save the children. Oil for the lanterns of Mexico! Won't you give it to me?

(*The lantern begins to go out and in the shadows dance the animals, singing: "He will not give it to you and the children will be eaten . . ."*)

NIGHT WATCHMAN: Oil for the lanterns of Mexico . . .

All Teatro Guiñol plays engaged the children of the audience in some way, asking them questions and drawing them into the theatrical events unfolding onstage. In *Oil for the Lamps of Mexico*, children of all ages are made to feel the consequences of the drama. The younger children would respond to the terrible prospect of having their eyes plucked out, as threatened by the animals and the Oil Man. Older children and adults would respond to the very tangible consequences of having oil withheld and furthermore would feel indignation knowing that the oil rightfully belonged to Mexico. Not surprisingly, the play comes to a resolution when Comino and the Night Watchmen enter wielding sticks and bludgeon the animals and the Oil Man. In the final scene a boy puppet enters—rendered lifelike enough to be representative of the children in the audience—with a piggy bank, pledging to contribute to the country's oil debt. The final verse at curtain call proclaims: "The oil was paid / And the children were saved . . ."[45]

Through this play, List Arzubide and his fellow puppeteers interpreted the crucible of economic nationalism for their child audience as a moral decision between the lives of Mexican children and the greed of rapacious, bestialized entities. The script and its outcome did not leave room for moral ambiguity. In the wake of the oil expropriation, amid heady public acclaim, children across the country flocked to donate their *centavos* to the nationalist cause, just as the puppets in the play urged them to do. That same year, having distinguished himself as a worthy public servant, Comino went to the birthday party of four-year-old Cuauhtémoc Cárdenas, son of the president of the republic.[46]

Yet among his fans Comino's celebrity often trumped the demonstrations of patriotism that he championed. Not long after the nationalization of oil, Lázaro Cárdenas himself attended another of Comino's presentations, this time in the Otomí town of Ixmiquilpan. The children were beside themselves with excitement—at the arrival of their favorite puppet. After the show the president took the stage in typical populist fashion and asked the audience what it was that they most wanted. To his surprise they did not call out for the return of *ejidal* lands, nor did they cry for equal educational opportunities, nor support for labor unions. The unanimous shout that rang out in the crowd was simply, "Bring on Comino!"

The Bureaucrats: The Comisión de Repertorio, Regulation, and Response

Perhaps in part because of the high demand for this innovative pedagogical tool, the plays and playwrights quickly came under the scrutiny of educational authorities, lest the popular form become corrupted in its dissemination. The didactic purpose took precedent over entertainment value as children's puppet theater rapidly became professionalized. As bureaucratic regulation encroached upon the creative license and material realities of the puppeteers, interpersonal tensions began to strain this once utopian cultural enterprise. Concerns about the integrity of the puppet-show content led Fine Arts directors to form the Comisión de Repertorio, a review committee designed to censor and edit the plays and eventually to approve them for performance. In a February 1934 memo Fine Arts head Chávez wrote that observations of some of the productions of Teatro del Niño before smaller audiences and in some of the kindergarten shows revealed that the puppeteers frequently falsified the concepts, words, and even the spirit of the plays through improvisation, and he implored that the plays be learned by memory and properly practiced so that the interpretation would be exact and their educational value would not be compromised.[47] Roberto Lago, Germán and Lola Cueto, Germán List Arzubide, and other leading members of Teatro Guiñol expressed discontent at the increasing restrictions and regulations being imposed upon them from the state, even as they relied on the government offices for their meager recompense and institutional support.

Officials encouraged heavy-handed material such as *Comino at the Strike*, preferring it to anything too artistic.[48] In 1935 Bellas Artes held an open contest for the submission of plays to be added to the puppet theater repertoire. In a statement the department head announced that they sought the participation of young writers with clear socialist affiliations to write plays for all children—but especially for those from the working masses—to see the benefits of a humane and just social organization, teaching them who their class enemy was, how to defend themselves from exploitation, and how to separate themselves from individualist ideas in preference of the collective good. This repertoire must be especially well chosen, because, in his opinion, as well as adhering to proletarian ideology, playwrights should also avoid the use of certain expressions that would result in weepy sentimentalisms in the children that crippled their will to engage in class struggle.[49] Educator Juan Bustillo Oro, in a 1938 contribution to *El Maestro Rural*, expressed the firm position of the SEP regarding the moral and ideological content of the plays taking precedence over their entertainment value. He cited *Comino vence al Diablo* as the premier example of the genre, that its unmitigated stance denouncing labor exploitation—punctuated by Comino's violent blows upon the *patrón*—embodied the type of proletarian message that children's theater was meant to disseminate. He lauded its author, Germán List Arzubide, as being faithful to his revolutionary orientation and applauded him for writing pieces without any artistic pretense. Bustillo Oro enthusiastically proclaimed that such plays served as the "water, mop and broom that would clean the tormented spirits" of the nation's children.[50]

The Comisión de Repertorio exercised its authority to make drastic changes or pull plays from the program. For example, the committee rejected one play written by Elena Huerta titled *Comino, Don Quixote's Squire* (*Comino, escudero de Don Quijote*), a children's adaptation of Cervantes's classic, because they vaguely said it lacked clarity and force. One committee member, Rosaura Zapata, general inspector of kindergartens, contributed her opinions about the play *Firuleque on Vacation* (*Firuleque de vacaciones*), in which the environmental hazards of living in the city contrast with idyllic and hygienic living in the countryside. Zapata recommended a revision of the play, as most children constituting the viewing audience did not have the opportunity to frequent the countryside; furthermore, she feared they would misinterpret the message and mimic the play's details about the wrong ways to cure illness such as keeping rooms closed, not washing the face, and taking too much medicine without the guidance of a doctor. Zapata also argued that instead of being child centered, the play educated only mothers about hygiene and suggested that the play be modified accordingly. In the play *Comino the Itinerant Vendor* (*Comino vendedor ambulante*), about exploitation of child labor, Zapata expressed disappointment that the apples that Comino sold were from California and not San Ángel, a detail she regarded as "depressing." She also suggested changes in some of the language: "I'm going to send you to jail" ought to be softened to "I'm going to punish you."[51]

By 1936 the restrictions of the Comisión de Repertorio created a strain on the creative directorship. In an annual activities report Roberto Lago, one of the group's founders and director of Grupo Rin-Rin, complained that some of the plays his group presented did not achieve their objective because the censoring committee set out to purge, and even mutilate, the best of each play. Lago worried that the strange, random committee remained completely removed from children's perspectives, or the *ambiente infantile*, and thus remained unaware of the issues important to children. Most egregiously, members of the groups had neither a voice nor a vote in the categorical decisions made by the committee that served only to obstruct and impede the logical development of the puppet theater program. In his treatise Lago expressed his hope that the Fine Arts Institute would rectify such problems based on the comments and experience of someone who had been working in this arena for two years.[52] As letters continued pouring in from rural teachers all over the country requesting that the puppet shows be brought to their schools and communities, the intellectuals driving the success of Teatro Guiñol felt mounting demands upon their time. The puppeteers found themselves strained between the surge in popularity from the public schools and the pedagogical urgency placed upon their work from SEP officials. The creative directors found themselves under increasing pressure from the bureaucrats to standardize their performances in the interest of providing a uniform educational service. Visionaries and bureaucrats found themselves at odds about the creative direction that the puppet shows should take. In the midst of these power struggles, another voice emerged that altered the production and performance of Teatro Guiñol. Significantly, the impetus for many of the revisions to the puppet performances came as a direct result of feedback generated by the child audience and conveyed to the SEP officials by schoolteachers.

The Devil Is in the Details: Children's Reception and Response

A hush fell over the gathering of fidgety kindergarteners on a May morning in 1934 in an Ixtapalapa schoolyard, as stage curtains drew apart to reveal an animated stereotypically black hand puppet, the Negro (El Negrito), laboriously hauling firewood back and forth at the behest of his *patrón*. El Negrito complained about his plight, and the children's eyes widened with terror, reflecting the fear demonstrated by the puppet when the *patrón* threatened the arrival of the Devil if he did not keep working. Enter Comino, a cheeky young boy puppet, whose grandmother, accusing him of slothfulness, had brought him to the *patrón* to learn some work ethic. A devil puppet loomed large on the makeshift stage, bellowing out vague threats. Two kindergarteners burst into tears. Not wanting to disturb the rest of the captive audience, the teacher removed the terrified girls and brought them around to the back of the stage so that they could see the puppeteers manipulating the cloth, felt, and wooden dolls. Despite her efforts, the girls remained inconsolable and refused to watch the rest of the show.

Back onstage Comino announced that he was not afraid of the Devil and, roping in an unconvinced Negrito, set out to prove it with violence. The Negrito and Comino spent the remaining acts brandishing sticks, eventually finding the elusive Devil and knocking him senseless. The Devil's mask slipped off to reveal none other than the labor-exploiting *patrón*. The curtain closed on a smug Comino and relieved Negrito looking on as the *patrón* lugged his own firewood across the stage.[53] List Arzubide's *Comino vence al Diablo* was among the best loved, but also most controversial, of the Teatro Guiñol plays. The author's intent, clear to adults and historians, was to demonstrate through physical comedy the process of the proletariat (Comino and El Negrito) gaining class consciousness and overturning oppressive forces. Yet the frightening figure of the Devil and the role of violence often confused rather than enlightened young viewers. The play's widely ambivalent reception by different child audiences, as transmitted by their schoolteachers, suggests the gaps between the layers of intellectual authority (the SEP officials, the Teatro Guiñol puppeteers, and the schoolteachers), as well as the ways that children's responses filtered into those spaces and transformed the end product.

Teatro Guiñol was a unique cultural experiment in that the SEP bureaucrats responsible for its existence appeared to be genuinely vested in the quality of the children's reception. The Fine Arts Institute issued a bulletin to all schoolteachers hosting the puppet troupes asking for their feedback and the reactions of the children to the plays. Teachers began logging their students' responses to the plays, carefully comparing their reactions relative to previous years, and keeping the SEP apprised regarding the changes. The teachers' letters contain rare details about the children's responses to the puppets as well as their own pointed opinions. Schoolteacher Ana Aragón, in Ixtapalapa, reported that her kindergarteners were clearly surprised at the unexpected appearance of the puppets and anxiously watched as the puppeteers constructed the stage. The play that they watched, *Unkempt Comino* (*Comino el desaseado*), shows a dirty Comino plagued by parasites and lice. The lice were so vivid and nasty that they incited fear in the children. For days now, she noted, the children had been obsessed with being lice free as a result of seeing the play.[54] Aragón noted that anticipation for the puppet shows built with each successive year, as previous generations of schoolchildren relayed memories of the plays to their younger peers. Repeated performances enhanced the children's comfort with this novel medium; the first time the puppets came to visit, the children shyly disregarded their inter-active questions to the audience. By the second visit they glee-fully joined in the banter with their wood and cloth friends.[55]

Some letters from schoolteachers arrived to the SEP offices with less detail than Aragón provided. Kindergarten teacher Carmen C. de Rodríguez submitted a succinct note acknowl-edging her students' satisfaction at a recent performance. Car-los González, head of the Fine Arts Theater Department and responsible for sifting through the schoolteachers' documen-tation of the plays, left an annotation on her letter requesting that she please be more explicit and detailed about the chil-dren's reactions in future reports. One particularly concise letter yielded something of a pedagogical rant from González: "The primary goal [of Teatro Guiñol] is not simply that of silly jokes; if there are any scenes that impress upon the children, it means that the plays are achieving their function. Otherwise, they would only be vehicles of entertainment and not of education and instruction." The chided schoolteacher promptly rejoined with a full description of the scenes, characters, costumes, and voices to which her students had responded positively—and negatively.[56] The SEP officials' persistence in soliciting feedback demonstrated their commitment to (and belief in the possibility of) perfecting the art of Teatro Guiñol for optimal reception.

In many cases teachers returned reports that ranged from ambivalent to unfavorable, and it became the duty of the Comis-ión de Repertorio to amend the content accordingly. The Devil proved particularly problematic in ways that List Arzubide almost certainly never foresaw. Luisa Castañeda, kindergarten direc-tor in the Colonia Azcapotzalco, wrote in to the Fine Arts Insti-tute with a list of concerns about her students' responses to the puppet show. The Devil character in *Comino vence al Diablo* had provoked some troublesome questions that she did not quite know how to address, citing her understanding of the school as a strictly secular institution. Students were asking: "Is it true that the devil exists?"; "My mother says that the angels make the devil go away"; "Is it true that the devil can't see God?";

"The patron was only playing devil, but the devil does exist and nobody can hit him except the angels." She maintained that, as a socialist educator, she should not have to address such questions; it would be best if such controversial shows were not brought into the classroom but rather left for popular venues where parents could take their children and answer their queries.[57] Facing responses such as these, the Comisión de Repertorio often replaced the figure of the Devil, always controversial in comments from teachers and children, with another character deemed more appropriate.

Furthermore, Castañeda objected to the grotesque portrayal of the grandmother puppet, which she felt did a disservice to this venerated figure in most children's lives. Her letter, along with scores of other teacher reports documenting children's responses, triggered a flurry of evaluation and analysis in the offices of the Theater Department of the Fine Arts Institute and eventually resulted in some modifications.[58] Regarding the issue of religion, SEP officials' noncommittal response suggested that secular schools should take a neutral position but that teachers should neither attack nor defend religious teachings.[59]

The physical violence characteristic of many of the Teatro Guiñol plays, and featured exuberantly in *Comino vence al Diablo*, yielded mixed results from children, often depending on their age. Not surprisingly, author List Arzubide employed some of the same techniques that marked his radio series turned book, *Troka el Poderoso*, grabbing children's attention through the threat (or, in this case, the direct act) of violence. Hitting, stabbing, and bludgeoning were not unique features to the Mexican puppet theater; the Parisian Guiñol and its Anglo-Saxon counterpart, the Punch and Judy Show, had relied on brutality to engage the audience since the eighteenth century. And with many boisterous juvenile audiences, puppet punches prompted delight. A schoolteacher from the state of San Luís Potosí reported that the "infinite enjoyment" occasioned upon his pupils when watching Comino hit the Devil resonated with them for days and weeks as they recounted those fleeting moments of the performance, suggesting to him that they had absorbed the moral of ideological conquest that this act represented. But he also suggested another, unexpected, outcome of Comino's justified rage: some of his fellow teachers had begun to express alarm that students had internalized a message of violent protest to any authority figure and worried that they might become objects of physical abuse at the hands of emboldened children.[60] Castañeda corroborated this expressed fear and asserted that her students had entirely misunderstood the underlying message of the play and had interpreted Comino's character as a lazy boy who would go to any lengths, even resorting to physical violence, to get out of doing work. Another schoolteacher, Angela Martínez, had herself missed the metaphor, citing its title as *Comino Hits the Devil*.[61]

In many cases the schoolteachers proved themselves to be deft at translating their students' responses to the bureaucrats and intellectuals occupied with the construction of this extracurricular program. Guadalupe Tavera, the school director quoted at this chapter's opening, observed that the two-way violence (the *patrón* beat Comino and El Negrito before they enacted their vengeance on the Devil) muddled the moral imperative intended by the play's author. Her young audience members came away fearful. The poignant revelation at the end of the play, that the Devil was only a disguised *patrón*, utterly bypassed the children. They were afraid. She tactfully suggested that the Teatro Guiñol plays should strive less for physical comedy and more for edification. They should consider, she suggested, eliminating all instances of abuse and fear.[62]

While the schoolteachers' letters provide unique insight into the educational, psychological, and emotional impact of Comino and friends upon their young wards, valuable documentation from some of the children themselves allows for an even closer approximation of how they might have experienced the itinerant puppet show. Evidence of individual children's unique reception of the ideas and images paraded before them for a brief half hour can be found in their artwork. After the stage had been packed off and the puppet troupe moved on to another school, teachers often gave students a time for free expression in the

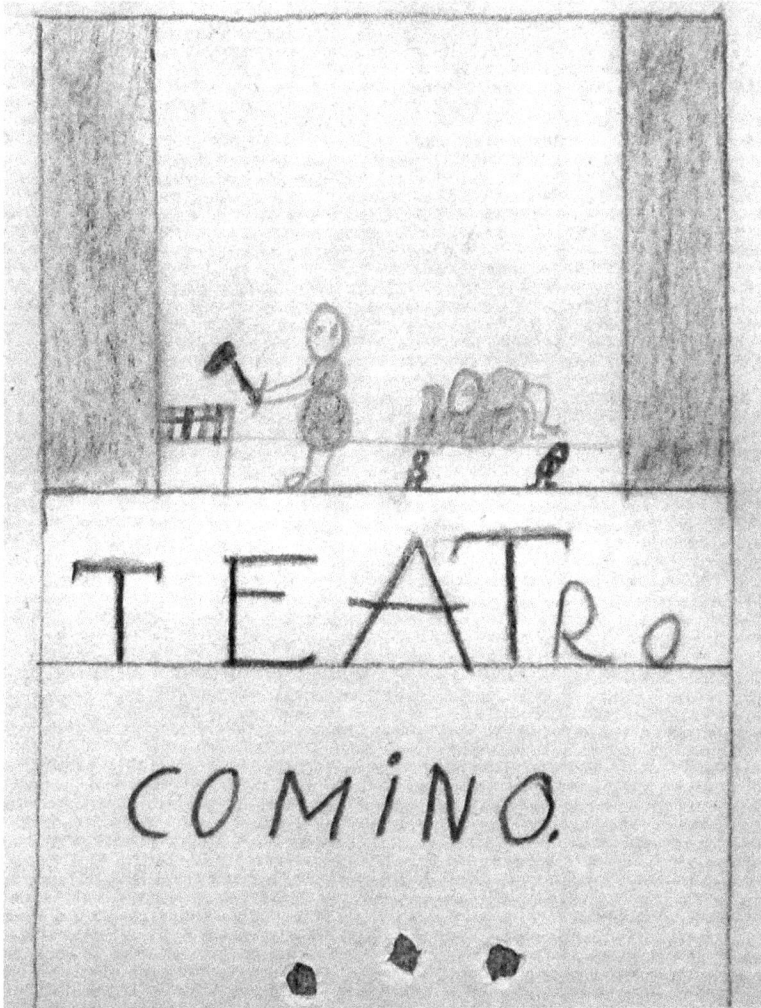

30. A child's drawing of the Teatro Comino presentation of Teatro Guiñol demonstrates an awareness of the performative nature of the show
through the depiction of puppets enclosed in a stage with curtains, 1934.
AHSEP, Departamento de Bellas Artes, Serie Teatro 1932–1936.

form of drawings (fig. 30). These drawings, found in the archives
of the SEP, confirm that the young viewers paid close attention
to the layout of the stage, the clothing and movement of the
puppets, and specific scenes. Given the task at hand—to distill
a sustained, exciting sensory experience to one still image—the

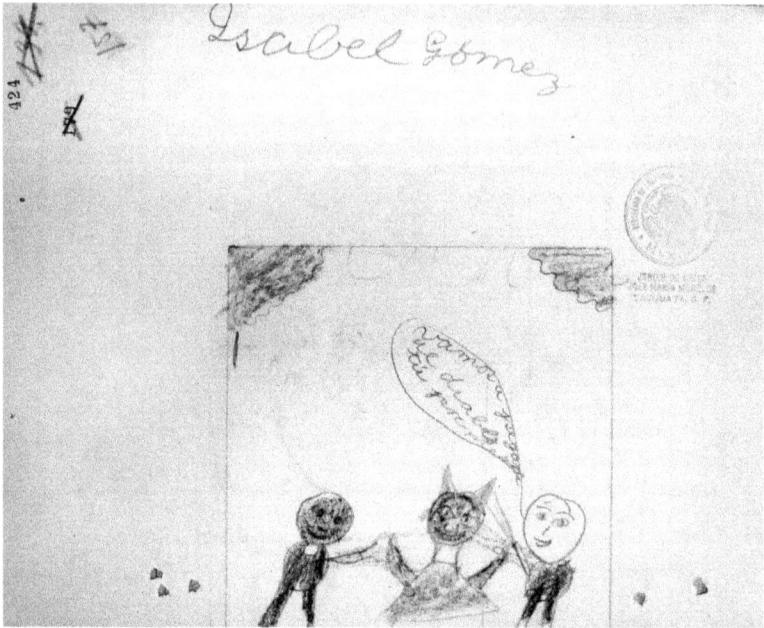

31. A drawing of Comino and El Negrito beating the *patrón*, disguised as the Devil, is one of many appearances of the Devil in children's artistic responses to Teatro Guiñol, 1934. Some children may not have realized that the Devil was a disguised character. AHSEP, Departamento de Bellas Artes, Serie Teatro 1932–1936.

drawings can provide rich insight into the themes, characters, and perspective that made the most memorable impact on the child audience members, many of whom were seeing puppets for the first time. Not surprisingly, after a show that included *Comino vence al Diablo*, the Devil figured prominently in many of the children's drawings, while the *patrón* did not (fig. 31). This corroborates the observations made by the schoolteachers that the message about the exploitation of labor was perhaps lost in the sense of terror and mystery embodied by the Devil puppet and underscored their concerns about this character confusing younger students. Furthermore, violent beatings administered by Comino and El Negrito often appeared in the drawings, occasionally with Comino wielding a sharply pointed stick. Even one of the youngest children, five-year-old

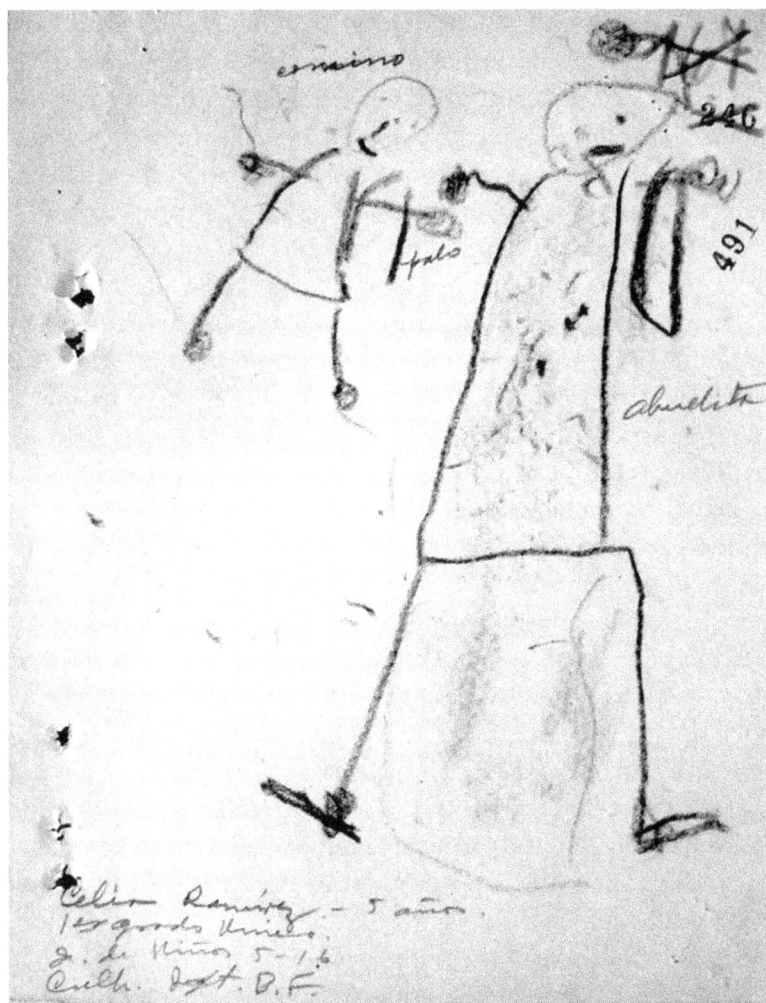

32. An annotated drawing by a five-year-old of Comino and his grand-mother depicts Comino wielding a stick. Violence made an impression on the children, perhaps at the cost of the moral of the play. AHSEP, Departa-mento de Bellas Artes, Serie Teatro 1932–1936.

Celia Ramírez, in a rudimentary sketch of Comino and his grandmother, quite unmistakably depicts a stick figure of Comino clutching a sharp weapon. To clarify the content for SEP officials, the teacher labeled the characters and the weapon: stick (*palo*) (fig. 32). Children's drawings suggested that they retained the message about violence as a solution to social injustice, while the intended message about the evils of labor exploitation did not resonate as clearly. Fine Arts officials reviewed these drawings, made reference to them in their correspondence, and encouraged schoolteachers to continue eliciting such feedback from their students following the performances.

Children often recognized Comino and the other characters—from previous performances, Teatro Guiñol playbills, *El Maestro Rural* articles, *El Nacional* coverage, or simply from the detailed accounts of their peers—and demonstrated their affection for him in letters, poems, and even plays that they wrote based on the shows they had seen. Their familiarity entitled them to frank expressions of dissatisfaction, demonstrations that Comino did not conform to their expectations. The children at the Zaragoza Kindergarten in Colonia Villa G. Madero clearly stated their critiques of the puppets. A spruced-up version of the Comino puppet did not pass muster without hair, they thought, and the gym teacher's appearance struck them as sloppy. The teacher noted that the children presumed the puppets to be living beings. As soon as the curtain lifted, she reported that the kindergarteners turned into little actors in their own right, candidly shouting out responses to the questions posed by Comino's grandmother. For days following the spectacle, even in their simple language, they talked about the puppet shows in animated detail and could not wait for it to return. In another school the children pointedly said that some of the puppets were ugly. Ms. Gomez, their teacher, added that she considered the puppeteers to be talented, and if they took the children's critiques and comments seriously into account, they would be successful in their educational goals.[63] The Comisión de Repertorio, although it had hedged on critiques about the Devil during this sensitive national climate of frayed relations between the church and the state, snapped to action when the orderliness of the puppets came into question. The head of the Theater Department swiftly dispatched instructions to the puppeteers to be diligent about the puppets' appearances, lest their symbolic power as purveyors of modern hygiene be compromised in any way.[64]

Though the Comisión de Repertorio tried to constrain the spontaneity of the artists' interactions with the public, teachers' reports suggested that student interaction with the puppets was one of the most effective aspects of the theater. They responded best to Comino, who had developed into something of a celebrity through press coverage, and were delighted when he played with them by peeking around the curtain or directly greeting them from the stage. Perhaps they identified most with Comino because he was a human boy puppet and not an abstract creature, animal, or monster. One kindergarten teacher noted that she was grateful that the puppets had finally, and more realistically, been furnished with feet, so that the children had a better understanding of how they moved.[65] Standardization of the plays, as requested by the head of the Fine Arts Institute, would reduce student interaction with the puppets, possibly risking the retention of some of the plays' propaganda.

Despite official attempts to perfect the didactic purpose, due to the varying ages and levels of comprehension of the children, misinterpretations of the plays were bound to take place. Perhaps because the young audience responded so immediately to the puppets, some teachers expressed concerns about the kinds of language and messages they would absorb. One teacher took exception to the vulgar language that Comino's grandmother used, not to mention the *patrón*'s physical, verbal, and psychological mistreatment of El Negrito. Furthermore, one teacher interpreted the grandmother's voice as *aguardentosa*, or alcoholic, and demanded that this character be revised. She added that children idealized their schoolteachers and grandmothers and found them to be beautiful and that as a result the puppets representing these characters ought to be treated with more respect by the artists and not be the subjects of a cavalier caricaturist.[66]

A close examination of the drawings remitted to the SEP offices reveals the role that developmental stages as they correspond to biological age affected children's reception of the plays. The drawings indicate different levels of sophistication in the ways different age groups absorbed the play. Kindergar-

33. A younger child's drawing places the stage in the context of the rural, natural setting, 1934. Aside from the stage, the puppets are not distinguished from the live animals that surround it. AHSEP, Departamento de Bellas Artes, Serie Teatro 1932–1936.

teners focused on one single character, taking pains to reproduce the basic form of a character. Often the youngest children's drawings contain no indications that they understood the context or even that they understood that what they had seen was anything other than real. The puppets in the younger children's art live and have adventures in a world that looks very much like the world surrounding the children, with no boundaries between fantasy and reality. For these children, what they had seen onstage was indeed, as List Arzubide had described it, a visual substitute for their own experiences. One drawing from a younger child after viewing a Teatro Guiñol presentation depicts a puppet stage with its characters in the middle of a natural setting (fig. 33). For this child Comino and company perform not before an audience but rather in the midst of the chickens, pigs, and fish that populate the countryside. This young artist did not demonstrate awareness that the pup-

34. An older child's drawing of Teatro Guiñol demonstrates spatial awareness, self-reflective presence as a member of the audience, and difference
between puppets and children, 1934. AHSEP, Departamento de Bellas
Artes, Serie Teatro 1932–1936.

pets in the "box" were any different from the living animals
that populated the village.

By contrast, the drawings of older children indicate that
they fully understood the concept of a dramatic presentation.
They included more physical context, such as chairs and an
audience, and almost always boxed the characters into a stage
and hedged the action with curtains. The most advanced students demonstrated a sense of self-awareness, drawing themselves and their classmates as audience members, an insightful
detail that suggested their awareness of a sense of performance
as well as their role as members of the audience and consumers of a form of education and entertainment. In one example
fourth grade student Alfredo depicted himself and his classmates
carefully arranged in rows, their gaze attentively fixed on the
four puppets acting on the colorfully depicted stage (fig. 34).
The audience takes up an equal amount of space on the page
as the characters on the stage. This awareness of dimension,

35. The drawing by this child demonstrates a degree of spatial awareness and distance from the audience, but the lack of human figures (puppeteers or audience members) and the depiction of the whole suspended bodies of the puppets suggest that the child entered fully into the fantasy realm during the performance. AHSEP, Departamento de Bellas Artes, Serie Teatro 1932–1936.

scale, and space also suggests that older students like Alberto distinguished between the reality of their presence and the fiction of the puppets' experiences. In a similar unsigned drawing, the child pointedly placed the puppets within the stage scenario, complete with curtains and a ladder to separate the physical spaces of the acted drama and the audience (fig. 35). But in this drawing no audience members occupy the bare ground, and the puppet characters float freely in the space of the stage, their full bodies, arms, and legs in clear view. The child included no sign of human beings; neither those manipulating the puppets nor those observing the performance interrupted this child's reverie.

One student, Jorge, drew a scene that evokes his experience as an audience member, perhaps literally. On the colorful stage,

36. A child's drawing suggests the audience conditions at a typical performance. AHSEP, Departamento de Bellas Artes, Serie Teatro 1932–1936.

hoisted above the audience's heads, Jorge drew the recognizable figure of the Negrito, perhaps with Comino and the *patrón*, engaged in the action of the play (fig. 36). On the ground, two audience members strain to see the action: the larger of the two arches achingly backward, almost doubling over in the chair. The second audience member, much smaller than the first, seems to flail behind the craning giant who blocks his view. Jorge's demonstrated awareness of the plight of the audience members—crushed against the stage and desperate to view the performance—provides a glimpse into an ephemeral moment of spectatorship from the perspective of a child. Jorge might have been the larger audience member, placed too close to comfortably view the drama, or, more likely (given the inclusion of the second audience member), he worried about missing some of the spectacle because of the range of size in audience members who often populated these shows.

In addition to the written feedback provided by teachers based on direct observations of their students, SEP officials and the puppeteers themselves took photographs of their young audi-

37. Photograph of audience at a Teatro Guiñol performance, in which children, schoolteachers, parents, and community members alike enjoy the presentation. *El Maestro Rural*, April 1, 1935.

ence, rapt with attention and apparently unaware of the camera. In these images children gape wide-eyed as the dolls come to life on the makeshift stage before which they are crowded. Some are caught in a moment of disbelief, others demonstrate surprise, and nearly all appear to be utterly engrossed. In one photograph of the audience taken at a Teatro Guiñol presentation and subsequently published in a 1935 issue of *El Maestro Rural*, the mixed composition of the audience can be clearly noted, as children of all ages, schoolteachers, parents, and community members alike gaze at the puppets acting beyond the scope of the lens (fig. 37).

Based on observations of their students, teachers recommended finding other ways to stimulate the children that did not rely on instilling fear or resorting to poor treatment of others. In many cases Fine Arts officials sought out such feedback and responded positively, allowing schoolteachers and children themselves to shape this aspect of the cultural educational project. As an example, in 1934 the puppet theater added a third group, Grupo Pirulete, which featured streamlined plays, sets, puppets, and language more appropriate for children under the age of six than the more grotesque puppets of Grupo Comino and Grupo Rin-Rin.[67] In addition, educational officials responded to critiques of certain characters by saying that they were genuinely interested in the children's response and made the point that if the children already idealized the female authority figures in their lives, they therefore would see beyond superficial ugliness. Their only goal, SEP officials claimed, was to make the characters humorous.[68]

In the case of Teatro Guiñol, the interventions that schoolteachers made to the government officials on behalf of their young wards facilitated the inclusion of children's perspectives in the puppet theater's development. In some cases, the observations, protests, and misinterpretations offered by children thwarted the creative efforts and lofty ideals of the revolutionary puppeteers. In other cases their exuberant responses validated the hours of selfless dedication that this small group of visionaries had poured into itinerant puppet pedagogy.

Conclusions

Children's puppet theater in the 1930s demonstrates the extreme lengths to which government administrators and policy makers went to implement an ambitious cultural program to supplement the socialist education project. Mounting layers of bureaucracy, represented by the Comisión de Repertorio, curbed the creativity of revolutionary intellectuals as children's puppet theater became absorbed into the increasingly institutionalized educational system. Evidence suggests that education officials attempted to standardize and perfect the puppet shows in order to close the cultural gap between urban and rural schoolchildren and disseminate revolutionary ideals through an age-appropriate medium. Even so, the revolutionary values played out by Comino and friends (and enemies) did not mold a malleable young generation without contest. Certainly, the allegorical puppet characters' proclamations of thinly veiled propaganda had some effect on budding socialists, as cultural missionaries and socialist educators reinforced the ideology in the community and classroom. Yet rare evidence of children's immediate responses to the plays indicates that reception was not uniform. The child audience members, directly through their drawings and indirectly through their mediators, the school-teachers, interacted with the intellectual authors of the puppet program, frequently enacting modifications of the presentations. A close examination of children's art allows one to peel away yet another layer of adult mediation and interpretation of their experiences. Children's often unintentional participation in their own socialization reveals one example of the uneven process of nation building when viewed from the perspective of the individual beneficiaries of top-down cultural projects.

Clearly, audience reception remained at the forefront of educators' and artists' minds in the production of Teatro Guiñol; the existence of the Comisión de Repertorio, structured to receive feedback on the plays, proves the pivotal role played by the audience, a concept theorized as the "democratization of theater."[69] Theoretical attempts to codify cultural reception often fall flat when applied to children; how does one categorize a child's collapse into screaming terror upon seeing a devil puppet, or her frank observation that the grandmother puppet's voice sounds mean, as "reflective" or "reactive" reception?[70] Children responded to Teatro Guiñol in various ways, sometimes positively and other times with fear or misunderstanding. Many of these responses made their way through the levels of production, and thus transformed how puppet theater was carried out by its authors through official mandates from the SEP. Mixed interpretations of the plays notwithstanding, SEP officials valued children's responses. Teatro Guiñol was not simply a onetime injection of revolutionary consciousness into the empty minds of a new generation; it was a collaborative cultural experiment that provided avenues for participation to its audience. In this way children participated in the cultural dialectic that formed their own childhood experience.

CHAPTER FIVE

Hacer Patria through Peer Education
Literacy, Alcohol, and the Proletarian Child

When *civismo* departs from its core of book learning and the word of
the teacher, when its natural center of activity can be found in the
domestic sphere, its locus of practice in the streets, parks . . . markets,
city centers of government, etc., then we will see less rhetoric that elo-
quently extols civic duties that are never practiced, and we will have
better citizens with civic habits, acquired through school activities.

— JOSÉ VASCONCELOS, cited in *José Vasconcelos*, by Claude Fell

We want our recreation to be more important. We don't want our
teachers to punish our mistakes by taking away recess. We don't want
to be forced to work in factories or workshops. We want our schools
to provide us with spacious fields for recreation and with playground
equipment. We want Children's Theater and a children's library to
become a reality. And we want, somehow, for our parents to be forced
to allow us to attend school-organized excursions.

— MARÍA L. BERNAL, child delegate to the First Conference of the
Proletarian Child, 1935

History often credits José Vasconcelos, minister of education under President Álvaro Obregón from 1921 to
1924, with the widespread diffusion of revolutionary
nationalism through a radically overhauled national education
system. To be sure, Vasconcelos's visionary expansion of the institution allowed for the dissemination of state-produced national
language, symbols, and culture on an unprecedented scale. But
as policy makers recognized in the early years of the revolution,
the key to success of the transformation of a diverse nation into

a cohesive unit lies in its ability to perpetuate itself: the children must be convinced of its worth and able to reproduce it. To that end the labors of Vasconcelos's successors advanced a program of educational reform that tended increasingly toward the forging of a collective identity.[1] In particular Moisés Sáenz (who occupied many important posts in the SEP from 1925 to 1930 and served briefly as minister in 1928), a student of John Dewey, promulgated the idea of the Action School—learning by doing—into the rural areas, a model that proposed a fuller integration of the home, civic, and educational lives of children.[2] The proximity between school and community life reached its apex during the administration of Lázaro Cárdenas with the Socialist School (Escuela Socialista) experiment, a point that marked a substantial ideological turn in the program that lasted until legislators revoked the article reform in 1946.[3] Among other stated pedagogical goals, educational tendencies in the 1920s and especially in the 1930s sought to make the primary school into a laboratory of idealized citizenship practice. The reorientation of the classroom as a microcosm of the nation underscored the value of nationalism in the local application of universal principles; "The school is MEXICAN," proclaimed SEP propaganda explaining the goals of the new Socialist School, "because it tends to unify the diverse social groups that comprise our populace, lending them a cultural, ethnic and linguistic unity."[4]

The Rationalist School of the 1910s, the Action School of the 1920s, and the Socialist School of the 1930s, at least in their ideal fullest implementation, increasingly prepared the child to be a productive member of his or her community, ideologically aligned with revolutionary goals, a champion of the working and agricultural classes, and prepared to carry out the redistribution of wealth promised by the revolution during a time when global capitalism faltered.[5] In a climate in which administrators were charged with carrying out ambitious educational reforms on a pinched budget, children's time became the revolution's greatest asset.

Concerns about children spending their free time unlearning such instruction led to a slew of proactive initiatives to combat ideologically counterproductive activity (or simple sloth) and protect the revolutionary investment. The classroom was intended to be a place of intense activity and creative and economic production for its busy members. As part of the curriculum children engaged in activities that had a social objective: they built school libraries, constructed houses for homeless families, and tended community livestock.[6] As we have seen in chapter 3, the radio show *Program to Unite the Classroom and the Home* sought to make mothers pick up where schoolteachers left off. It devised craft and educational activities to occupy the children's evenings and weekends.[7] And as will be demonstrated here and in chapter 6, education officials intended productivity to carry over into children's structured free time, and they extended this government-sponsored socializing project into the home.

In reality, many of these ideal educational models never saw full or even modest application in much of the country; schoolteachers selectively chose from the national curriculum according to their abilities or preferences, and many rural schools found that material support fell far short of the ambitious program expectations.[8] In parts of the Sierra Norte in Puebla, local reception of revolutionary education spanned a negative range from reticence to outright rejection.[9] Elsie Rockwell's insightful assessment of the application of educational reform in rural Tlaxcala yielded mixed results. On the one hand, the rural Tlaxcalteca classroom did not become the social and spiritual hub of the community as education officials intended, due to complex layers of local political negotiations and existing authority networks. On the other hand, despite its patchy application, the meaning of school culture changed in perceptible ways between 1910 and 1940.[10] And in some communities, though not most, the existing educational infrastructure did undergo a radical transformation, razed and raised anew.[11] When we examine the changing school cultures in the 1920s and 1930s as experienced by children, similar diverse and uneven patterns of reception emerge. As we have begun to see in previous chapters, though the revolution strove to eradicate socioeconomic inequalities in principle, the evolution of children's culture after the revolution tended to produce socially stratified generations—not all that different from the colonial or Porfirian inequalities that the revolution intended to rectify—through rhetorical treatments of indigenous, provincial, and poor children as received by their peers in the city.

Textbooks and teachers introduced a new vocabulary and attendant practices: *patria, civismo, mexicano.* New organizational opportunities arose that allowed children to begin to perform, however unsteadily, the new secular moral code of the nation. As a supplement to their education, children (and often predominantly middle-class children) participated in charity drives and literacy campaigns and political manifestations through which they sought to improve the lives of their less fortunate peers. Children organized into student governments. They assumed positions in a classroom hierarchy, learned low-level bureaucratic procedures, and reiterated snippets of official language learned along the way.

This chapter examines the development of peer-to-peer civic organizations among school-age children that corresponded to main policy points of the respective political administrations. In the early 1920s Álvaro Obregón's administration took on illiteracy and employed the sometimes gimmicky Children's Literacy Army to help the government eradicate ignorance. During the decade of influence exercised by Plutarco Elías Calles known as the Maximato (1924–34), and particularly the latter half of this period, the institutionalization of power purported to unite the Revolutionary Family; during this time student governments emerged parallel to a network of bureaucratic offices from the municipal level to the presidential palace. Culturally, during the Maximato, alcoholism was considered the most trenchant threat to national productivity, and children joined Anti-Alcohol Campaigns in droves to purge the nation of this social ill. Lázaro Cárdenas's demonstrated preference for the poor fostered a class consciousness among the young that tended toward militant defense of the proletariat, expressed most symbolically in the proceedings of the First Conference of the Proletarian Child. Under the careful tutelage of teachers, children developed political personae as child delegates in conferences with national press coverage. The hierarchies that resulted through children's participation in these organizations and civic events trained a generation of aspiring bureaucrats, diplomats, and workers.

Hacer Patria: Performing Patriotism

President Plutarco Elías Calles, at 10:30 a.m. on Independence Day in 1925, commanded the attention of tens of thousands of the capital city's schoolchildren gathered in the modern new National Stadium in the fashionable neighborhood of Colonia Roma. Secretary of Education José Vasconcelos had conceptualized the utopian space as a culmination of Mexican civilization, designed to seat sixty thousand healthy, patriotic mestizo spectators, and Calles was putting it to its intended use.[12] Handing over a flag to a solitary representative of the smartly dressed crowd of children, the president asked them all to pledge their eternal fidelity to the flag as a symbol of honor and to carry the sentiment in all of their scholastic and future activities. A chorus of voices responded with a resounding "Yes, I swear!" that echoed throughout the acoustically perfect horseshoe of the stadium. The chief executive then expressed his most sincere conviction that, as good and loyal Mexicans, the children would comply with their pledge of allegiance in actions required both by the school and by the *patria*.[13]

Six years later in remote Tekax, Yucatán, a group of schoolchildren dressed in traditional white muslin *calzones* and *huipiles* stood in formation along a lye grid on their grassy school patio (fig. 38). They saluted the same flag, with all of the solemnity and bearing of their faraway fellow Mexicans who resided on the spot that its serpent-clutching eagle first alighted. This simple ceremony united, if only for a few minutes daily, a generation that shared little else in common. The presence of this photograph in the SEP's central archives also suggests the propagandistic power of this universally understood gesture of patriotism—that children in the farthest reaches of the nation

38. Boy salutes flag at the Escuela Primaria de Tixcuytún, Tekax, Yucatán, 1931. AHSEP, Fototeca 1930, Sobre 5, September 1931.

held sacrosanct this one civic ritual implied their ability to comply with the rest of the educational revolution.

Patria, a concept weakly translated as "fatherland" or "home country," formed the cornerstone of the educational program, an all-encompassing default term that children learned and repeated. The symbolic power of the flag cannot be overstated. Throughout changes to the organization's moniker, the official party (the PNR, founded in 1929, became the PRM in 1936 and ultimately the PRI in 1946) assumed a monopoly over the flag's red, white, and green in its logo, ensuring a powerful visual synonymy between country and party. Rural schoolteachers learned to emphasize the flag and its colors as the symbolic basis of *la patria* that, once ingrained, would trigger an emotional response in the child identifying with the community and the country.[14] One history and geography textbook, premised on the adventures of two children orphaned by their natural parents but taken in by their fatherland as they journeyed from coast to coast learning the nation's history, addressed its young readers with the unequivocal statement, "Knowledge of the *patria* is the basis of all true civic instruction."[15]

A sense of membership in and duty to the *patria* went hand

in hand with the understanding that one would behave accordingly or, in other words, engage in *civismo*. As the opening lines of a popular civics textbook for primary and secondary schoolchildren said, civic instruction would be formative for their conduct as citizens; when the hour of serving the republic arrived, well-instructed children would respond with the full consciousness of their responsibility.[16] By the 1930s, the increased emphasis on socialist education lent special importance to the instruction of civics; the SEP identified the course designated Civismo as the most crucial site for the construction of "the Mexican that these times demand," one that identified above all with the working classes.[17]

Extracurricular organizations and opportunities arose for children in the years of early revolutionary fervor and led to an expansion of the popular understanding of citizenship. The vast discrepancy, well worth noting, between political and civic engagement in the 1920s (women could not even participate in electoral politics) suggests a sea change in the possibilities in gaining access to the processes of power. The sudden visibility of children in new arenas heralded the downward expansion of political culture to include voices customarily excluded from public life: girls and boys alike. In the examples presented here, children express a collective identity beyond the confines of their family, church, community, or peer groups. They articulate and perform the complex, abstract concepts such as membership in the *patria* (sometimes a notion only loosely cobbled together from symbols such as a snake-clutching eagle, a flag, a Toltec motif, a sombrero). They apply and negotiate sophisticated, ideologically charged terms such as *proletario* and *burgués*. And in the process they learn and perform the mechanics of a government that, reeling from more than a decade of instability, was righting itself through the addition of bureaus, ministries, and agencies. While minors still formed part of a demographic majority that could not formally participate in politics, they emerged in the 1920s and 1930s on the streets, in the newspapers, over the airwaves, in stadiums, and on stages as some of the most vocal *portavoces* of reform. Children's contributions to civic life were validated—when not constructed outright—by their teachers, members of the media, local and national officials, and foreigners alike. These children surely had little doubt that they were citizens of the Mexican nation.

To be certain, adults played a substantial role in the "civilizing process" that transformed dependent children into autonomous beings acting within collectively agreed-upon boundaries of social behavior.[18] In revolutionary Mexico the national school system and its attendant extracurricular programs formed some of the most powerful and all-encompassing agents of child socialization. Evidence suggests that many children growing up during the revolution absorbed the rhetoric and ideals of revolutionary nationalism to widely varying degrees of interpretation. Studies from around the world have indicated this to be true of other revolutionary regimes and modernizing nations as well.[19] But children's participation in the civilizing process, and thus their contribution to refashioning the nation in the modern world, has not been sufficiently studied in Mexico.

Nationalism did not spring spontaneously from the fertile hearts of young Mexicans. The national curriculum systematically introduced the language, the symbols, and the moral imperative upon which these sentiments flourished. A Code of Moral Conduct (Código de Moralidad) circulated among Mexico City public schools in 1925 equated morality with nationalism; ideally, every schoolchild in the capital would begin the day's lessons with a spoken pledge to the flag in which they promised to prove themselves useful and worthy of their country, so that it would grow and prosper. Following this pledge, students recited a daunting list of nearly a dozen moral laws that good Mexicans should observe, such as the Law of Self-Control (good Mexicans know how to control themselves), the Law of Self-Confidence (good Mexicans have positive self-esteem), the Law of Duty (good Mexicans fulfill their obligations), and the Law of Sport (good Mexicans play fairly). The Code of Moral Conduct, ideally the guidepost that marked the beginning of every student's day, recast a religious ethic in secular language, perhaps a gesture to the more traditional

Parents' Associations (Padres de Familia) agitating over Article 3 educational reforms.[20] The Department of Primary and Normal Education (Departamento de Enseñanza Primaria y Normal) issued a monthly report card for students to rate themselves on their moral behavior. For example, to rate her performance regarding the Law of Loyalty, a student would indicate whether she "Always, Almost Always, Usually, Not Often, or Never" expressed loyalty to her parents, school, city, *patria*, and humanity.[21] The checklists and physical and verbal reminders of these basic tenets made the vague practice of *hacer patria* (performing patriotism) appear both quantifiable and attainable to Mexicans in the making.

In 1926 the SEP's Department of Primary and Normal Education began to publish a magazine intended to boost civic engagement in the classroom, to bring about a social revival of sorts that drew upon the energies of the child. Titled *Coopera* (a command, "Cooperate"), the near-monthly magazine provided teachers with suggestions for linking the classroom with the home, the community, and the local economy. Adopting the beliefs of John Dewey, *Coopera* editors strove for the child to see the school as life itself and not a mere preparation for life.[22] The magazine helped to define desirable civic habits and suggested ways that they could be implemented in the classroom. Yet an article contributed from a school director in Sinaloa, and the tone assumed by the magazine in general, indicated the tendency among education officials to identify children's spirits of helpfulness and engagement and to rapidly funnel those through bureaucratic channels, rendering them institutionalized at the end.[23]

By the late 1930s the SEP, through the activities of the Department of Social and Educational Action (Departamento de Acción Cívica y Social), had more thoroughly prescribed the nature and direction of civic behavior. This agency established the language and parameters within which children could interact with their peers and participate in civic life through the creation of extracurricular organizations.[24] Along with a sense of civic responsibility, the activities organized by such agencies imparted a sense of class consciousness meant to be inextricably woven with Mexican national identity. These organizations in many cases mirrored the bureaucratic trappings of the official political structure, both in naming children to offices and in creating social hierarchies among the young participants. Increased opportunities for participation through extracurricular organizations, for those who had access to them, suggest that this generation of children was not simply in *training* to become future citizens. They were *engaging* in civic activity in the moment as children, directly contributing to the revolutionary political climate. That this engagement could be characterized cynically as mimicry, or optimistically as practice, does not diminish one observable phenomenon: new patterns of public service expected of children emerged, and many rose to meet the nation's higher calling with enthusiasm.

Student Councils: Apprentices of Modern Bureaucracy

The national political culture that developed under Plutarco Elías Calles strained between two sometimes contradictory forces: a yet unslaked thirst for popular participation in the processes of power and a concerted effort to channel power upward through the consolidation of an official national party.[25] The resulting National Revolution Party (Partido Nacional de la Revolución, or PNR) provided the auspices of popular democracy through the ample distribution of desks and titles to those who swore allegiance to the Jefé Máximo, Calles himself. The labor sector and campesino organizations were drawn under the PNR umbrella and thus remained under the watchful purview of the state. While the newly branded "nation of laws and institutions" offered a measure of popular participation, its power to restrict and censor the political will was fortified by the sheer magnitude of the bureaucratic machine. In reality, members of the Revolutionary Family did not enjoy domestic parity. The seat of authority remained limited to a tight cluster of the Calles oligarchy, who kept in line the Revolutionary Family's metaphorical children—the labor and campesino groups. Meanwhile, the nation's actual children found that bureaucracy

39. Student council of the Escuela Fronteriza Coahuila, ca. 1936. AHSEP, Fototeca 1930, Sobre 21, 1936–1939.

as a method for organizing productivity extended even as far as their classroom, in the form of school governments.

Children's free time represented national patrimony for education officials. In conceptualizing extracurricular clubs and organizations, officials revealed perspectives of the social role of the child relative to adults, representative of a crucial stage of human development. Student councils, such as the one pictured (fig. 39), allowed boys and girls to perform citizenship by occupying privileged positions in offices (sometimes) elected by their peers. The classroom became a microcosm of the nation, and students filtered into hierarchical positions of leadership and service. Though the roles that children assumed might have been performative, perfunctory, or prescribed, children's offices and duties held value in a modern nation predicated on a culture of service, one that transcended politically motivated mandates.

Education officials took a practical approach to the challenge of elevating a national culture of civic service, applying a developmentalist understanding of children as social beings.

Professor José Teran Tovar of the Department of Agricultural Education, in a missive to rural schoolteachers, emphasized the importance of the "gregarious instinct"—a fundamental characteristic of the human condition that resulted in social behaviors such as seeking out companionship, a desire to please others, and a tendency to assimilate to group activities. This instinct, deemed more acute in children, lent itself to socially productive guidance through the organization of student clubs. According to Professor Teran Tovar, the best way to direct these organizations was to identify natural leaders in this group, the organic intellectuals who would assume responsibility and guide the activities of the rest in an unforced manner.[26] Officials saw clubs and organizations as an opportunity to harness expressions of peer solidarity, another characteristic considered inherent to children. The argument followed that as poor children struggled for self-preservation, children of means would naturally develop compassion for their peers due to their generational bond and would not feel at ease unless they were directly engaged in some sort of civic behavior to eliminate social inequality.[27]

Natural disasters often resulted in classroom charity drives at the national level, yielding modest sums turned out from children's personal savings or through altruistically charged local campaigns. One case in particular lends insight into the way that an innocuous charity drive could serve a dual civic purpose within the context of the new moral code. An earthquake that shook the states of Colima and Jalisco in 1933 wrought devastation on many communities but opened a path for faraway children to *hacer patria* through their charitable contributions. In the process they learned valuable lessons about the fiscal logistics of national charity. From around the nation schoolchildren scrounged together nearly 650 pesos, with a promissory note for the full balance of 1,000 pesos (500 to each state affected), all transmitted through individual schoolteachers and communicated to the intended recipients by Rafael Ramírez, the head of the Department of Rural Schools.[28]

Rather than fold the meager pesos into the general disaster relief budget, Ramírez and his colleagues seized upon the opportunity to publicize a civics lesson in *El Maestro Rural*, ostensibly to be read by schoolteachers to their contributing pupils as an update. The magazine published two letters—one from the director of federal education of Colima, and another from a schoolteacher in Jalisco—directed at "the children of my *patria*." The teachers adopted a language that suggested that their child audience shared a common belief in the universal right to education and housing. The published letters not only expressed their gratitude but also explained the process through which the funds would be specifically earmarked for the reconstruction of campesino children's houses and school buildings. The Jalisco teacher identified the five neediest school zones among which the money would be evenly divided (amounting to a nominal 100 pesos per school) and asserted that the original receipts would be available in the offices of the Department of Rural Schools, for anyone who wished to consult them. Furthermore, he expressed his hope to publish the impressions of the children who directly benefited from their compatriots' charitable contributions once the schools were restored. His articulation of these bureaucratic procedures on a microscopic scale suggests that the schoolteachers, regional directors, and heads of educational departments took quite seriously the enterprise of drawing children into the developing official political culture. From the perspective of children fortunate enough to have their teachers read them these letters published in the pages of *El Maestro Rural*, they would see their sacrifices validated— and could even entertain the fantasy of verifying a physical receipt. Their greatest contribution, though, was more spiritual than material: "[Your contribution] tightens the bonds of the *Patria*; these children no longer feel isolated, they now count on their friends dispersed across the country, to whom they outstretch their caring arms, ready to also extend a hand, like good brothers, whenever necessary."[29]

Most civic education happened in the classroom and the immediate community. Energy expended in the formation of extracurricular clubs and committees rivaled that invested in the building structures themselves. Classroom clubs took charge of

cleaning classrooms, decorating school and grounds, and organizing sports and dance activities. Child officers, democratically elected by their classmates, were to have a demonstrated
aptitude for the committee for which he or she was nominated;
they were to be outstanding, diligent students in terms of schoolwork and conduct; and they were to be healthy, enthusiastic, and
active. Ample opportunities existed for individual children to
find their niche in the civic life of their school. For example, in
1933 rural schools in the state of Durango offered students the
option to participate in the Education Committee, the Health
and Hygiene Committee, the Anti-Alcohol Committee, the Children's Charity Committee, the Reforestation Committee, the
Classroom Materials Committee, the Recreation Committee, the
Communications Committee, the Sports Committee, and the
Agricultural, Industrial, and Commercial Improvement Committee. Student officers worked to enact vigilance over other
children in the community, to act as truancy officers in conjunction with the teachers, to attend home visitations to check conditions of hygiene, to procure a medical kit for the classroom, to
identify orphans and poor children as subjects of charity drives
and school breakfasts, to participate in monthly talks to mothers about infant care, to whitewash the school annually, and to
put on community recreational events such as plays and puppet
shows, just to name a few.[30] Student councils implemented an
institutional hierarchy within the schools that reflected the ver-
tical organization of the nascent ruling PNR. In the classrooms
an umbrella "government club" administered the activities of
the other organizations—making sure that they complied with
their duties, approving their expenses, and administering pun-
ishments such as barring noncompliant club members from
participating in activities or omitting them from printed programs. Children did not govern with complete impunity. These
student government members had to consult with their teachers
before meting out the punishment. Nevertheless, power structures developed out of the student council hierarchy.

Some pedagogues, perhaps optimistically, saw student governments as spaces for the development of a real measure of social

integration. Rather than simple mimicry of political structures, as in the common mock-government exercise called School Republics (Repúblicas Escolares) in which children assumed roles and played at being president and members of the cabinet, progressive pedagogue Gregorio Torres Quintero called for a much more meaningful school community in which children created their own civic culture. Torres Quintero argued that his brand of extracurricular organization would provide children not with fictitious roles but with meaningful duties that would result in a sense of pride and ownership of their school. This would develop, he argued, in parallel attitudes toward their community, village, and city, all of which formed their *patria*.[31] Dr. Alfonso Pruneda, representing the Ministry of Education's Department of Psychopedagogy and Hygiene to the VI Pan-American Conference on the Child in Montevideo, Uruguay, echoed these sentiments before colleagues in 1933. He identified the school as a place where children could re-create a democratic environment, air their grievances, and fortify their relationships without resorting to adult models and losing their status as children.[32]

The Department of Public Welfare (Beneficencia Pública), in a gesture to acknowledge and encourage child leadership in student government, established a Children's Government Day (Dia del Gobierno del Niño) in 1935 among children educated in various government welfare institutions. School administrators designated forty-seven student representatives to attend a daylong conference to discuss the challenges and triumphs of their respective clubs and organizations. Representatives from the Department of Social and Educational Action made sure to record the children's impressions of the conference to make future meetings more productive.[33]

One of the great legacies of the revolution, as described by historians, took form in a literary effervescence from the popular classes directed toward high-level administrators requesting— and expecting—reform at every level of quotidian life.[34] Even as revolutionary presidents struggled to get their house in order, humble individuals penned letters beseeching members of the executive office for a piece of what they, as citizens, believed they deserved to inherit from the revolution. Children, especially those in student government, astutely absorbed this development in political culture. Letters from members of school clubs and student councils indicate that young people felt confident in their grasp of the lower rungs of the political machine. Belén Alegría, president of the Sociedad de Alumnos "Infantil Cultura" of the Escuela Superior Mixta de Huépac, Sonora, wrote directly to President Calles to request that he outfit them with a school library, since their group strove to protect the collective interests and progress of their "beloved *Patria*." *Presidenta* to president, she even suggested a resolution to the foreseeable difficulties in transporting the requested books to such a rural area: an express train should deliver the books to Cananea, where the students would go and pick them up.

The content and format of the students' letter bore the markings of nascent political savvy. In an offhand way they plumbed Calles's regional identity (one of the pillars of *caudillismo*): they asked the president to forgive their frank, sincere manner but added, as he should know, that that was the Sonoran way. They employed the rhetorical flourishes common in formal bureaucratic petitions ("atenta y respetuosamente suplicamos"), as well as revolutionary linguistic conventions ("la colectividad y progreso de nuestra querida Patria"). Finally, and not insignificantly, the petition bore the signatures of Belén Alegría and dozens of members of the organization, the visible stamp of their collective will. For unknown reasons, the presidential reply was no.[35] While Belén likely penned the letter at the urging of a teacher—we cannot pretend to know the impetus behind its actual execution—she and her peers engaged in an official transaction and left behind documentation of their conscientious exercise in employing bureaucratic and patriotic language to obtain a material good to which they felt entitled.

Student council organizations may have assumed characteristics of adult political culture, but they engaged in activities for the improvement of their immediate infantile environments. "En Marcha," the umbrella organization based in Mexico City that supported revolutionary youth organizations in outlying states, provided official letterhead to the school groups for their correspondence.[36] Third and fourth grade student members from the Centro Escolar Benito Juárez in Tetecala, Morelos, submitted the minutes of their most recent meeting, noting that the presence of adults was a legal stipulation of En Marcha and that the voting for election of officers to the various committees, entirely under the charge of students, encouraged their members to engage in the improvement of their school, home, and community life.[37] The children took care to replicate the bureaucratic procedures that would lend credence to their actions. The narrative report of the electoral process reveals tremendous respect for order and protocol; the document's authors related in formal language the process by which the candidates for each position presented themselves before a committee upon nomination, and upon sealing their victory the incumbents immediately applied themselves to officially recording the course of events for posterity ("procediéndose inmediatamente a levantar la presente acta para darle a conocer a las Autoridades y Organizaciones correspondientes"). They submitted the minutes in sextuplicate, and their shaky but elaborate signatures at the bottom of the letter indicate an awareness of the visible and textual trappings of their offices and the gravity of the positions to which they had been elected (fig. 40).[38] Students signed each copy of the typed report, and the handwritten replication of each laboriously stylized signature, complete with looping flourishes, can be traced across the individual sheets, allowing the viewer to witness the development of these children's self-styled public personae through this small instance of political performance. The signature stood as a rudimentary imprint of each student's identity, situated physically among a collective whole and massified through technological reproduction. Through these mechanisms, individual children formed part of the army of what Carmen Nava designates "we, the undersigned" that sought to insert themselves into the national exchange of ideas and resources.[39]

Opportunities to engage in civic action and defend the *patria* were not confined to children within the nation's political bor-

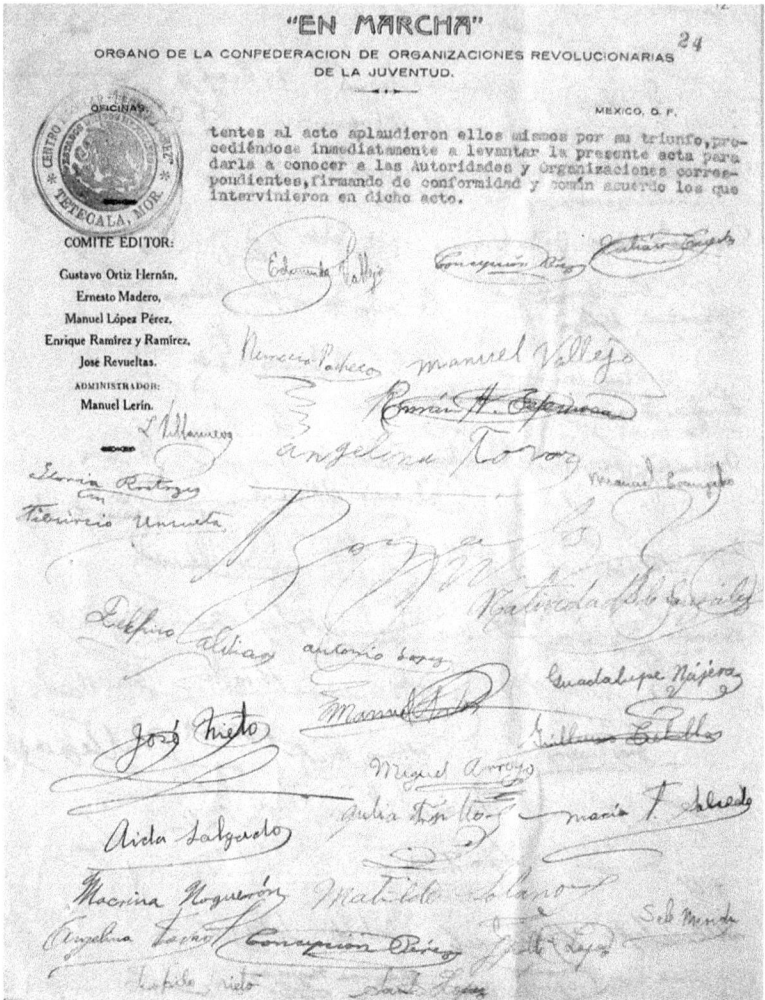

40. Student officers' signatures for school committees demonstrate intentional stylized flourishes, Morelos, 1937. AHSEP, Subsecretaría de Educación Pública, Caja 18, Exp. 14, 1937.

ders. An expanded definition of *patria* transcended geographical boundaries, evidenced by the Department of Civic and Social Action's preoccupation with the civic instruction of Mexican children living abroad, particularly in the southern United States. Children of the Mexican diaspora benefited from the infusion of resources to promote civic duties. Mexican consuls in Texas, Arizona, and California all wrote in to the Ministry of Foreign Relations relating, for example, the activities of Patriotic Committees that taught their peers the importance of the Cinco de Mayo holiday. One group of Mexican and Mexican American children ages eight to twelve from Beaumont, Texas, requested support from the Mexican government in the form of drums, bugles, sheet music, and cadet uniforms so that they could learn the marching band songs played by the Mexican army. The children wrote that they wanted to serve as a representation to the local community of what it meant to honor and love the Mexican flag.[40] These requests served as a testament to the power of *patria* as an organizing principle. Education officials acknowledged the importance of providing as much access as possible to Mexico's history, geography, culture, and revolutionary values to young members of the *patria* living abroad as essential in conserving their patriotic spirit.[41] At home and abroad, the Department of Civic and Social Action intended for children to become entirely self-governing within these institutions, learn organizational structure, and thus learn how to work collaboratively and be productive in society at large through collective action.[42]

School administrators encouraged extracurricular organizations that promoted unity and communication among children, but on occasion these programs spiraled out of the control of adults. Children sometimes thwarted adult participation in their civic instruction. An inspector of educational activities at the public welfare institutions Casa del Niño and the many Casas Amiga de la Obrera reported that the organized campaigns for hygiene, punctuality, and cooperation met widespread student dissent. The children had developed a sense of collective identity, and they had developed their own peculiar dialect that instructors could not understand. Children used this improvised language to communicate with each other and to sabotage the civic instruction activities of assemblies, class, and ceremonies. They transmitted this language through reading correspondence that was passed between institutions, allowing the dialect to flourish among members of the different schools.[43] This example of unexpected and uncontrollable levels of students' independence in the classroom demonstrates that adults saw limits to the desirability of child autonomy. The students' development of a secret language, while not uncommon among children, nevertheless threatened the educators' sense of order and upset the utopian perception (from a welfare institution perspective) of children as malleable and easily socialized. The fact that such a seemingly innocuous development should incite fear and anxiety among adult authorities suggests a disjunction between the official idealized vision of child-directed government and the unpredictable reality of the nature of youth culture.

The practice of citizenship was under way—citizenship as both a top-down process of "civilizing" the population through education and a bottom-up process of constantly negotiating the relationship between the people and structures of authority (the classroom, the municipal government, the district, the state, or the national government).[44] Regardless of their inability to vote in national electoral politics, children in student government enacted a broader definition of citizenship, beyond simply being endowed with voting rights and entrusted with budgets. Whether they were assuming roles of authority over their peers or finding ways to maneuver around such authority, children found the classroom an elastic space to experiment with agency and autonomy. This experimentation, sometimes structured and sometimes spontaneous, allowed children to interact with each other in ways that presaged their eventual emergence as full political beings and members of a national collectivity. Children learned to understand citizenship as a widely cast set of behaviors, values, exchanges, and collaborations that would serve to uplift the nation. Ironically, the very political culture that created the structures within which they could practice new and modern forms of citizenship—that governed by the PNR-cum-PRI—took such an authoritarian turn over the course of the twentieth century that the political voices of children growing up in the 1920s and 1930s were effectively silenced in their adulthood. In the end, barring the real ability to *hacer patria* at the ballot box, the broader civic behaviors learned through student government, welfare, and charity drives provided the more lasting lessons about *civismo*.

Fifth grade girls from Group C of the Abraham Castellanos School no. 32 in the capital formed an organization in 1929 and called it the Asociación Femenina Infantil Para Reformar a México (AFIPRAM). This particularly ambitious group recruited members from neighboring schools, becoming a local nucleus of civic action. Inspired, they claimed, by Portes Gil's antialcohol campaign, they undertook that and other social reform issues as part of their extracurricular labors. Their ultimate goal, to spread (*contagiar*) the spirit of redemption to the masses, met favor with the president, who forwarded their signed memo to the national press for widespread publication and dissemination. The AFIPRAM girls were busy. They fought for public recognition of excellent academic performance, in the form of free trolley and movie passes during holidays. They initiated a Latin American correspondence exchange, to draw together members of a generation from across the hemisphere. They embarked on hygiene campaigns in their neighborhoods, conducting unsolicited "inspections" of the construction and conditions of their classmates' homes. They planted fruit-bearing trees, kept public squares and gardens clean, publicly scorned alcohol and cigarettes, encouraged their families to purchase nationally produced consumer goods, and taught indigenous children to read. Overall, they sought to awaken in others their demonstrated enthusiasm to *hacer patria*, or perform the duties that constituted the most generous definition of citizenship. In their words, the performance of citizenship took the form of "stirring with every living force the vehement desire, the intense fever, to bring about a tremendous national reconstruction."[45] These girls might have been exceptional. They likely benefited from leisure time, supportive family networks, and access to information about the status of educational priorities through their schoolteachers. Yet evidence suggests that, while the AFIPRAM girls certainly assumed more than their share of civic responsibility, children from across the country saw participation in one or more of the activities they describe as viable ways to spend their time once they closed their textbooks.

Children's Literacy Army

In the 1948 feature film *Rio Escondido*, set in the 1920s during the expansion of the Cultural Missions (Misiones Culturales) program, a demure schoolteacher played by María Félix takes on the daunting task of educating and civilizing rural indigenous Mexico. In the background of her melodramatic tribulations, poor brown children appear as the passive recipients of the government's national transformation project. The movie's glorification of the Cultural Missions program, one of the Ministry of Education's first large-scale initiatives after its creation in 1921, has long since been nuanced and even excoriated by revisionists, who recognize the urban imperialism that the program wrought in some parts of the countryside.[46] José Vasconcelos modeled this secular educational outreach program on the "great civilizing mission" that the Spanish Catholics implemented in the centuries after the conquest.[47] Vasconcelos's secular missionary mentality—that of realizing the revolution in the form of practical and useful knowledge produced by new revolutionary agencies—pervaded educational culture both in the cities and in the countryside.

Twentieth-century cultural missionaries, young urban schoolteachers transplanted to far-flung villages of the republic, physically embodied the government's overhauled educational system as beacons of national culture and progress in the countryside. Rural schoolteachers, guided by the indispensable monthly magazine *El Maestro Rural*, imparted such hygienic and educational information to indigenous villagers as brushing teeth, confining chickens to a pen, and establishing community theater and folkloric dance. Cultural Missions also targeted the disadvantaged, uneducated population (many of them rural migrants) in the city with the goal of providing them with access to the mainstream values and activities practiced by the so-called cultured classes. The success of the Cultural Missions—generally panned by historians[48]—relied on the idealistic energy of young teachers, a spirit of self-abnegation, and unpaid or underpaid labor, all resources subject to rapid dissipation. The creation in 1921 of a voluntary Children's Literacy Army (Ejército Infantil en la Campaña contra el Analfabetismo) served to bolster these scarce resources, a creative example of the state's use of free labor to carry out reforms and generate numbers that pointed toward the modernization of the masses. Instead of monetary or material compensation, the corps of child volunteers could enjoy "moral rewards" and the satisfaction of having helped to forge citizens of themselves and their newly literate pupils.

In the early years of the SEP, literacy statistics mattered, however broadly literacy was to be interpreted. On paper, values assigned to Mexicans who could read and write, or the number of libraries, provided a metric by which to measure revolutionary progress. Educational officials saw the estimated 11 million illiterate Mexicans—considered the legacy of thirty years of failed education in the Porfirian years followed by another quarter century of civil war—as a social pariah and a serious detriment to the country's modernizing advances.[49] Just months after the creation of the SEP in 1921, President Obregón announced the creation of 334 literacy centers—informal, rustic, and often ad hoc spaces designated for the voluntary community instruction of the basic tenets of literacy as emergency placeholder measures for the eventual construction of full-scale schools.[50] In his assessment of the first eight months of the Calles administration, Minister of Education José Manuel Puig Casauranc pointedly compared the government's distribution of 13,000 school benches and 94,432 textbooks with those proclaimed by Porfirio Díaz in 1904 to be praiseworthy (a paltry 1,053 benches and 13,176 textbooks).[51] By 1940 illiteracy numbers had budged down to just over 7 million nationwide; while this number still represented more than half of the population, it was the legacy of intensive efforts to transform the countryside.[52] Yet as shall be demonstrated, literacy statistics from the time, especially those generated through rushed literacy campaigns that relied on volunteer children for their success, must be taken with a grain of salt, as they do not necessarily represent fully literate individuals by most standards. Furthermore, although intended to unite the diverse ethnic and cultural groups into what Calles termed, somewhat inelegantly, "a more homogeneous and harmonious mass,"[53] the resulting literacy campaigns objectified the poor indigenous population. Educators believed they possessed the cultural capital that they poured into the empty receptacles, identified as poor campesinos. Children were not just recipients of this massive project, but some became active agents of it as well. Children in the public school system learned to identify their uncultured neighbors and bring them the gifts of the revolution, as part of civil service for the betterment of the *patria*.[54]

The government literacy campaign, facing a paucity of trained adult educators, relied on the community as a whole to eradicate illiteracy and the associated social ills (workplace accidents, labor exploitation, and endemic poverty). Obregón deployed child "soldiers" to the mission, using their spare time to teach their illiterate peers to read through the Children's Literacy Army.[55] Through the Children's Literacy Army, fourth, fifth, and sixth graders gave the gift of reading and writing to their underprivileged compatriots. Inscription in the national program required interested schoolchildren to organize a committee with an elected leader for every ten "literacy soldiers," whose responsibility it was to report to the supervising teacher.[56] The Ministry of Education provided the necessary materials—notebooks, writing utensils, basic texts—and distributed them to confirmed literacy army units, although demand far outstripped the government's ability to supply them all.[57] The Children's Literacy Army was completely informal in nature; no real mechanism existed to register the volunteers, and children submitted literacy claims entirely on their own initiative. The experiment fully embodied the pedagogical trend of the moment, John Dewey's "active child" model, in which adults provided little more than passive guidance to the engaged, inquisitive pupils in their charge.[58] As a result, a quantitative assessment of the scope of this initiative remains out of grasp. But some earnest children took seriously the official mandate issued by Obregón, and he included the statistics that the children generated in the numbers of literate Mexicans without a hint of condescension. Within a year of its inception a reported 5,000 students taught reading and writing skills to 8,947 of their illiterate peers, with outstanding performances noted from the states of Coahuila, Chihuahua, and Jalisco.[59] In 1923 the Children's Literacy Army's second year, a reported 5,445 people had attained "first-level literacy" (familiarity with the alphabet), and 3,534 claimed full literacy, a total of 8,979 individuals exposed to literacy by child volunteers.[60] Though the Children's Literacy Army contributions dropped out of government literacy statistics after the Obregón administration, it enjoyed ongoing informal status and occasional resurgence in the national spotlight; by 1938 the students registered as members of the army nationwide numbered 81,140.[61]

A broadening generational gap characterized the transformation of children's social roles, as members of the Children's Literacy Army grew and the numbers of literate children surpassed the number of parents who could read. The militarization in its title, a feature common to children's organizations of the time around the world, reflected both the bureaucratic structure of the literacy campaign and the gravitas that education officials wanted to lend the program.[62] Furthermore, the militarization suggested a social space for children that shifted away from the family unit toward membership in another institution, underscoring General Calles's pronouncement in the famed Grito de Guadalajara that the child belonged not solely to the family but rather to the community as a whole, the subject of socialization guided by the abstract agent "the Revolution."[63] In another example of militarization of children's role, the Department of Transportation launched an educational campaign in 1936 that featured a Children's Police (Policía Infantil), led by Lieutenant Coronal Rafael M. Pedrajo. Members of the Children's Police, brandishing police-issue badges, enforced local automotive traffic laws and reported the license plates of any violators. Another group of Mexico City children started up a Children's Radio Patrol as a voluntary, auxiliary branch of the Police Department that earned recognition and prizes for reporting any disruptions of the peace in their neighborhoods.[64] These little armies, formed as subsidiaries to government agencies, contributed to the militarization of children's organized civic engagement. The Children's Literacy Army built upon this tradition. The child literacy soldiers across the nation learned the "Literacy Anthem" ("Himno Alfabetizante"), the lyrics to which were published by the national press and Ministry of Education circulars; the anthem unified the members and became a staple at Pan-American Day celebrations and fund-raising occasions for the program.[65]

The Children's Literacy Army drew upon children's preexisting social networks; child "soldiers" were encouraged to scour their homes, markets, neighborhoods, and workplaces for friends and acquaintances who did not know how to read, write, or do basic arithmetic. Once charged with this government-sanctioned duty, children saw their daily surroundings transformed overnight; the unkempt boy who accompanied his mother selling beans in the market suddenly became visible to them as a target for civilization; adding him to their list of literate conquests made him a notch on their gun. Teaching at least five children the basic tenets of literacy earned these budding civil servants a diploma certifying them as a "Good Mexican," the only tangible incentive for participation. Also, successful child educators allegedly received preferential treatment when seeking admission into institutions of higher education or employment within the Ministry of Education.[66] Children learned to take seriously their role as young educators; fifth and sixth graders from the José María Morelos School in Michoacán, upon establishing their first committee, swore a solemn oath to fight *as youth* for the culture of the Mexican people and the eradication of illiteracy.[67]

Members of the Children's Literacy Army enjoyed a highly visible profile in their school communities as well as the satisfaction of participating in the government's literacy campaign as equal partners with adult educators. The social benefits of the position—the government-issued notebooks, the certificate of citizenship, knowledge of the lyrics to the anthem, and even

41. Child handing out reading material to his peers, 1935. *El Maestro Rural*, December 1, 1935, 5.

recognition in newspapers and *Ministry of Education Bulletins*—all set the young soldiers apart from their illiterate peers. One photograph printed in *El Maestro Rural* depicts a boy distributing literary material to children his own age from the back of a van; images such as this contributed to a visual culture in which children performed civic acts as agents of the state (fig. 41). As a historical document we can recognize the propagandistic construction of the photograph: no adult appears in the shot, emphasizing the young literary soldier's autonomy, resolve, and diligence. Yet at the very least, an adult would have been on hand to drive the distribution van, and likely quite a few adults were involved in orchestrating the event and its publicity. But printed in the state-produced magazine alongside an article about the Children's Literacy Army, this photograph strengthened the rhetorical claims that motivated children were forging citizens nationwide through their membership in this organization.

Bureaucratization naturally yielded a social hierarchy among members of the Children's Literacy Army based on degrees of public recognition. Membership required only rudimentary literacy and therefore came easily enough to most schoolchildren who chose to participate. Members reported to elected unit leaders, who reported to schoolteachers, who in turn reported to the Ministry of Education. In each unit, select students identified as the smartest and most dedicated, along with the schoolteacher, conducted evaluations of their classmates. Upon satisfactory evaluation, unit leaders drafted certificates of completion for each newly literate member, which were passed up the chain of command to the Ministry of Education offices. The loose guidelines for literacy required only that learners prove that they understood rudimentary reading, writing, and math skills, and even if their writing proved slow and shaky, they had only to demonstrate mental capacity for understanding the skills.[68] This system, admittedly implemented in the face of a dire lack of trained professional educators, bestowed an enormous measure of power on the child literacy soldiers. They identified, from among their peers and siblings, who was in need of their services. They determined the degree of literacy deemed satisfactory. Effectively, they policed their equals with the backing of the state.

Some individual young educators gained special recognition for their participation in the system. The first member of the Children's Literacy Army, Luz Ramos of Mexico City, earned her photograph in the *Ministry of Education Bulletin* for teaching a group of her peers the alphabet in just a few short hours.[69] The youngest member to be recognized, Honorary Professor Lolita Driscoll, was only eight and a half years old when she embarked on her mission.[70] By having her photograph featured in the literacy campaign propaganda, Lolita served as a model soldier in the Children's Literacy Army: her light skin, school uniform, diploma of good citizenship, and modern haircut literally made her the poster child for the SEP. Lolita embodied the spirit of revolutionary civilizing missions that drew on indigenist ideology that saw the rural masses as potential productive citizens, but only after they were transformed according to urban middle-class standards of education and lifestyle. Illiteracy was considered an ethnic marker to be shed in order to become *mestizo*, and therefore a revolutionary nationalist citizen.

Given the informal and voluntary nature of the Children's Literacy Army, its cultural value seems to be more heavily weighted in favor of the child teachers than those who might have learned the basic tenets of literacy from them. The official recognition and civic membership that the program promised for ambitious young educators probably far outstripped any sustained shift in literacy trends in the countryside. Furthermore, while intended as a unifying campaign, the racialized nature of the program cannot be ignored. Generally, middle-class children with the resources and time available to serve as members of the Children's Literacy Army gained social privilege over the poor indigenous children who remained their persistent target for their literacy. As in many revolutionary programs, the organizers of the literacy campaign believed that the indigenous population remained at risk of potential vice and backwardness if their ignorance was not rectified in their early years. Another way that children attacked what government judged as vice in their communities was through their activities in the Anti-Alcohol Campaign.

National Anti-Alcohol Campaign

Antialcohol propaganda as a mechanism for social control became a government concern as early as the presidency of

Francisco I. Madero and accelerated in earnest in 1920. President Emilio Portes Gil's creation of the Anti-Alcohol Bureau (Dirección Antialcohólica, or DAA) in 1929 triggered an eleven-year National Anti-Alcohol Campaign, for which reformers found it easy to use children's plight as a justification, citing all of the social ills that would befall the next generation if the country's men, indigenous people, and working classes succumbed to drink. Government propaganda encouraged individuals to believe that adult alcohol consumption would result in sickly, physically abnormal, or mentally below-average children. In the heyday of the campaign, the front pages of the papers proclaimed that a full 60 percent of documented juvenile delinquents came from alcoholic homes.[71] The campaign brought children into public view not only as victims of alcohol but also as agents in the war being waged against it. In her well-documented study of the campaign, Gretchen Pierce demonstrates that women and children collaborated in the efforts to stem the consumption of alcohol in their communities and families.[72] The campaign preyed on the guilty sensibilities of husbands and fathers and ceded the voice of moral reason to the youngest members of society; children marching in an anti-alcohol parade dealt a formidable jolt to the conscience of a drinking dad. Clearly, through this campaign, the government conscripted children and their mothers into cultural warfare, and to that end they served as pawns in a program of social engineering. But through the admittedly structured avenues of engagement with the government campaign, child alcohol warriors found new ways to vent their energies. Both in the school and in the community, the antialcohol movement provided ample opportunities for children to practice activism, organize, and socialize. It also allowed for directed creative expression in various outlets: theater, music, art, composition, public speaking, and political action. And because of the centrality of this campaign to revolutionary propaganda, children's voices emitted in this arena were heard.

Children were exposed to a good deal of moralizing in regard to alcohol during this campaign. One of the most commonly used national geography textbooks, *Una vuelta a la República Mexicana por dos niños,* inserted lengthy, non sequitur conversations about alcohol between the two child protagonists and the adults with whom they came into contact on their adventures.[73] Daily newspapers contained antialcohol articles, anecdotes, verses, and cartoons alongside the puzzles and fairy tales in full-page spreads for children (*Página Infantil*) that youngsters must have struggled to wrest from their parents' grasp. Countless religious publications, many specifically for children, dedicated entire issues to educating youth about the evils that alcohol brought to the less than vigilant child, with stories titled "Long Live Water! Death to Alcohol!" and "A Family's Disgrace." In one such text, a question-and-answer section about wine reminded young readers that although God made the grape, man was responsible for making the wine.[74] As the antialcohol culture pervaded the country, children created an increasing amount of the supporting propaganda, in the form of drawings, clubs, essays, and theater performances.[75]

As these and many other forms of children's media indicate, antialcohol sentiments saturated popular, educational, and religious cultural outlets. Yet children did not merely absorb and reiterate this message; they quickly became its most powerful and visible champions. Whether they took the message to heart and upheld their naive, impassioned promises never to touch a bottle or not, in the excitement of the moment their expressions were earnest.

Nowhere were young people more effective in mobilizing their parents' belief in the campaign than through mass appearances in the streets. Portes Gil announced a nationwide antialcohol day on November 20, 1929, to coincide with the national holiday celebrating the advent of the Mexican Revolution. Children poured into the streets of towns and villages across the country, brandishing homemade posters, banners, and sashes emblazoned with antialcohol sentiments. Photographs of the day's festivities filtered in to the president's office from all of the states, and children figured prominently among the celebrants. At the Escuela Rural Federal Amozoc in the state of

Puebla, students put on a play for the community: an image of the production shows a dying child at center stage who had fallen under the evil influences of some loose women lingering nearby, and an empty bottle on the bedside table appeared to be the culprit. In Guadalajara hundreds turned out for a protest along the city's main thoroughfare; children from various schools carried a banner that declared: "Children protest the whip of alcoholism."[76] Photographs from various schools in Chiapas showed children gathered in their school yards, festooned with antialcohol banners, flags, sombreros, and other symbolic trappings of the nation. Despite their distance from the capital, residents of this southernmost state were not to be excluded from the national initiative. The disproportionate number of children populating the photographs suggested that the youth responded with enthusiasm.[77] Marching afforded children an opportunity to perform a visible declaration of civic engagement in a public space, enacting political agency in the eyes of onlookers regardless of how deeply held their personal convictions might have been. Collective manifestations of identity thus bound participants to the state and formed an important component in the performance of citizenship.[78]

Many of the creative expressions about alcohol came in the form of writing. Students of the Escuela Carlos Carrillo in Hermosillo composed an antialcohol corrido to the tune of "El Venadito."[79] Another Hermosillo school, the Escuela Federal Tipo Narciso Mendoza, sponsored a statewide contest for fifth graders to submit an original, uncorrected essay about the negative physical and social effects of alcohol. The winner, Bernardo Petet of the Escuela Superior para Niños, outlined some of the worst symptoms in his essay, "The Detriments of Alcohol on the Body." Bernardo seemed to have had occasion to witness some of these effects: loss of reason, unwarranted boisterous behavior, laziness, distance from society, fighting, crime, and abuse of wives and children.[80] In Colima the banner of the monthly publication produced by children of the Escuela Cooperación Educativa, *La Voz del Niño*, bore antialcohol slogans coined by sixth graders Consuelo G. Macías and Gustavo Pérez.[81]

Twelve-year-old Manuel Flores A.'s illustrated composition spoke to an even broader audience. Published as a pamphlet by the Ministry of Education with nationwide circulation, Manuel's essay addressed the indirect effects of alcohol on children, including the popularly observed "monkey man" phenomenon, most likely fetal alcohol syndrome, resulting from parental drinking to excess (fig. 42). Manuel's evaluation of physical and mental deviance, depicted as exaggeratedly abnormal by his childish hand, speaks to a rare shift in who authorizes what is socially normal; in this case Manuel identifies and stigmatizes his own peers, children of alcoholics. The young boy's use of the "science" of classification (pictorial and textual definitions of the terms *idiota* and *imbecile*, for example) makes this pamphlet— published with the official stamp of the SEP editorial press, the DAPP—an exercise in neopositivist application, resurrected for the purposes of a revolutionary-era social campaign. Minister of Education Ezequiel Padilla published Manuel's pamphlet in its unaltered state, just as the original drawings and text had been submitted, as proof that children both internalized and served as powerful allies in the antialcohol campaign.[82] Through this publication, Padilla sent the message that children's contributions to the war on alcohol had equal value as those of adults.

As the images in Manuel's pamphlet attest, visual imagery carried substantial weight in this campaign that largely targeted a poor population assumed to be illiterate.[83] Images of uncorrupted children in dangerous proximity to alcoholic beverages had a powerful visual impact not lost on propaganda artists for the campaign. Photographs of children posed in their Sunday best pouring barrels of liquor into drainage ditches provided the best evidence of a successful antialcohol campaign.[84] As demonstrated in chapter 2, the official art curriculum constructed a national aesthetic and aspired to artistic uniformity for children across the country as they learned and reproduced a set of images that defined what it meant to be Mexican. The Ministry of Education's Department of Drawing and Handicrafts (Sección de Dibujo y Trabajos Manuales) joined forces with the Anti-Alcohol Campaign in 1929 in a widely publicized initia-

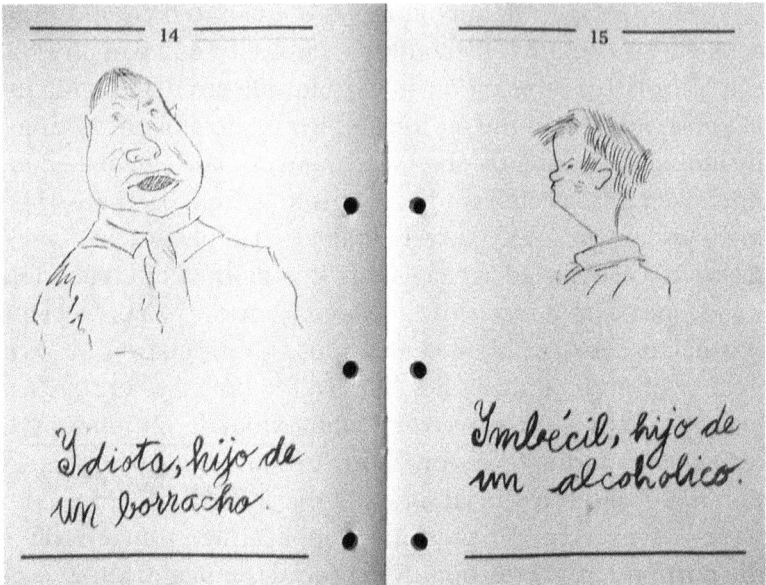

42. Pages from *Alcoholismo*, pamphlet published by twelve-year-old Manuel Flores A. (Mexico City: DAPP, n.d.).

tive touted by President Portes Gil himself, who stated that anti-alcohol drawings done by children would have special appeal to the public. A mere two months into the program, primary school children had submitted more than two thousand drawings representing the two themes: "The Child of an Alcoholic" and "The Destroyed Home."[85]

Public displays of the drawings formed a critical component of the campaign, cementing the association between child-induced guilt and patriotic abstention. Schoolchildren from Sonora paraded their drawings through the streets. One depicted a father holding a bottle of alcohol in one hand, with the other grasping his genetically deformed son, who also held a bottle.[86] An open-air exposition of student drawings in Mexico City's Garden of the Student (formerly the Jardín del Carmen) featured eight hundred drawings on easels lining the park's walkways, free and open to the public for their perusal. High-profile visitors to the exposition included the president and his entourage of government functionaries. Radio broadcasters publicized the event with an audio report of the government campaign and its success through the children's visual contributions.[87] The use of a public space to exhibit child-produced visual propaganda underscored the new power that children wielded in the DAA campaign. Casual passersby and purposeful visitors alike consumed the visual messages on display.

Even free of government sponsorship and promotion, individual groups of children saw the antialcohol campaign as an opportunity to leverage other social aspirations. By the Cárdenas period, DAA activities were in full swing nationwide and offered officially sanctioned spaces for social organization. In 1937 a student band from Valle del Bravo in the state of México, emboldened from a recent trip to the capital in which they had met the president, wrote a letter to Cárdenas asking to be given an official commission to be antialcohol proponents in their community. In exchange for their services promoting the message (through loudspeaker announcements and musical compositions performed on Sundays in theirs and neighboring communities' public squares), they asked for a small stipend, new instruments, and official recognition from the chief executive himself.[88] This petition speaks both to children's perceptions of the accessibility of the upper levels of government administration and to their demonstrated confidence that they could make a valuable, even vital, contribution to a nationwide campaign.

In Mexico City the most enthusiastic young adherents to the Anti-Alcohol Campaign, which officials rhetorically militarized into a children's "army" much like the literacy campaign, attended Children's Anti-Alcohol Assemblies in 1936 and 1940. The structure of the conference, comprised entirely of child delegates, mirrored highly bureaucratized adult professional gatherings, without infantilizing the proceedings or the guidelines in the least. It provided a space for children to hone their civic behavior in a civilized, modern, and public forum, all while training the young delegates to become professional advocates for a political cause. The official trappings of the event constructed professional identities for the children participating in it. A pamphlet delineating the guidelines for the First Children's Anti-Alcohol Assembly—a six-day conference sponsored by the SEP, the Ministry of Public Health, and the Office of Civic Action and held at the elegant Palace of Fine Arts in the heart of the city. The organizers called for the participation of children aged eight to fifteen from all primary schools in the federal district. Child delegates were chosen from among the winners of essay and drawing contest submissions. Conference organizers categorized participants into sections based on grade level; a democratic selection process ensured that an equal number of delegates represented all zones of the city. An inspection committee verified each delegate's personal information so that their identifying credentials would be in order for the published conference proceedings. Both assemblies boasted official letterhead. At the sessions a secretary took minutes in the *Children's White Book* (*Libro blanco de la niñez*), documenting the official ceremonies, the plenary sessions open to all members, and the smaller panels organized by age group. Child delegates read their papers aloud in the panels, followed by moderated discussions and votes for the best presentations, all led entirely by children. At the closing ceremonies, winning essay and drawing submissions received cash prizes, medals, and diplomas of honor. In a gesture of respect for the work carried out by the children, on the inaugural day of the conference, all alcohol distributors in the city closed for business.[89]

The first assembly garnered critical acclaim from international observers, who in turn hosted similar children's conferences. Child delegates from the Cuban antialcohol convention sent their best wishes to their Mexican peers, and messages of solidarity poured in from China, Peru, and Nicaragua. Basking in the success of this now global children's forum, organizers of the second assembly sought the participation of the utmost symbol of Mexican children's dedication to temperance—none other than six-year-old Cuauhtémoc Cárdenas, the only son of President Lázaro Cárdenas. He signed the honorific first line in the *White Book*, followed by the signatures of his codelegates. Radio stations XEFO and XEDP broadcast live transmissions of the speeches in the opening ceremony.

The proceedings of the First Children's Anti-Alcohol Assembly reveal an impressive degree of productivity. The delegates compiled a list of 125 recommendations to government officials and community leaders. Their numerous recommendations suggested that the delegates felt optimism in the political power they exercised as children within the system. They asked the police to take seriously the reports from children of alcohol abuse; they requested the Ministry of Education to publish a newsletter for children active in the campaign; they recommended an obligatory tax on all centers of vice (bars, gambling halls, and brothels) for the pain inflicted upon children by the use of alcohol, which would be used to fund orphans' homes; and they proposed a Youth Anti-Alcohol Day, complete with white flags for people and businesses that supported the cause.[90]

The conference provided the forum for one of the goals of the Anti-Alcohol Campaign: to create public intellectuals from a young age, by allowing them to practice formal composition, creative expression, and, most important, public speaking.[91] Vast coverage from the national media and the large audience of child delegates offered young orators access to a broader audience than they could muster in their classrooms and communities. The formality of the conference and its bureaucratic trappings lent an air of sophistication to the recommendations of these child delegates, something that they might not have enjoyed in a more casual forum. Moreover, the participants in this conference gained political prowess through direct experience and were afforded the opportunity to convert policy into action. Certainly, adults operated behind the scenes, offered logistical and schematic guidance, and lent organizational support. Undoubtedly, some children, including young Cuauhtémoc, were too young to fully grasp the social impact or symbolic power that their presence had on a politicized social reform campaign. But the funneling of children's energies into the DAA campaign planted the seed of political action into the hearts of some. Nowhere was this brand of child activism more politicized than in the Conference of the Proletarian Child.

The Conference of the Proletarian Child

Vicente Zavala, a student at the Escuela Estado de Sonora in Mexico City, took seriously his responsibilities as the general secretary at the First Conference of the Proletarian Child (Primer Congreso del Niño Proletario). Surrounded by a flurry of reporters from the national press, he took advantage of the spotlight to voice the concerns of his constituents, the "little proletarians" who had long suffered hunger and oppression: "Now that [Minister of Education Ignacio] García Téllez has taken poor children into consideration, it's time for the voice of the little proletarian to be heard." They wanted to see their parents' conditions improved, he stated. They wanted books and better homes—ones with bathrooms and ventilation. The basic necessities identified, Vicente waxed philosophical: "We want liberty, we want to see the definitive end of the bourgeois dictatorship."[92] His statements echoed those of hundreds of other children, identified as "proletarian," who participated in multiple sessions of the 1935 conference. Along with his fellow child delegates, Vicente's ideological statements placed the proletarian child at the forefront of the public's mind over the space of two weeks in March 1935, just six months after the constitutional implementation of the socialist educational curriculum. The proletarian child was quickly becoming a nationalist archetype, and the children selected to participate in this conference served as its spokespeople. The conference heralded the shift toward socialist education and helped to showcase the new vogue of class-conscious rhetoric.

Its intellectual architects, SEP officials and organizers of the VII Pan-American Children's Conference, also timed the event exquisitely to coincide with the convergence of the hemisphere's leading experts on childhood on Mexico City. The conference proceedings unfolded in a fishbowl, the national press captivated by the spectacle of children behaving as political beings in an environment seemingly free of adult influence. A careful analysis of the content of the conference and the reported actions of the child delegates reveals more puppetry than spontaneous expressions of class consciousness by the children. Nevertheless, the structural forces at play in 1935, following more than a decade of established official recognition of children's civic engagement in state-sponsored organizations, heightened the gravitas with which the Conference of the Proletarian Child was received at the moment, among children and adult spectators. The student councils, Children's Literacy Army, and Anti-Alcohol Campaigns all bolstered national citizenship as a form of belonging, of social inclusion in a nation based on a commonly held set of secular, moral values. In fact, the union of children and politics did not always sit well with education officials. In a 1927 memo to schoolteachers across Mexico, Subsecretary of Education Moisés Sáenz warned of the dangers of placing children at the service of political parties as agents of propaganda and prohibited teachers from canceling classes to bring students to local political marches and rallies.[93] Clearly, he was concerned about the unbalanced inculcation of radical ideas. But by 1935 the official position had nearly reversed, and children took center stage in the nation's political theatrics. By comparison the Conference of the Proletarian Child presented a new model of national citizenship for children as political actors—not future citizens but contemporary agents of decision and change. While a good measure of this performance was illusory and highly constructed, it nevertheless rippled outward, generating more conferences and bringing more children's demands into the national discourse.

As scholars have shown, love of *patria* was neither spontaneous nor unanimous but rather emerged out of a protective sense of loyalty in opposition to a perceived threat.[94] In the 1910s the old regime proved the perfect foil. At moments foreign imperialist overtures fueled nationalist fires. And as the revolution evolved, revolutionary and conservative politicians alike evoked *patria* to signal their respective visions of citizenship. But the global economic crisis of 1929 proved the fallibility of capitalism, and the official position of the Mexican as proletarian gained currency. The Cárdenas administration in particular encouraged this ideological bent in the educational system, riding into power on the momentum of the newly reformed Article 3 and implementing the Socialist School in 1935. While this designation lasted only until 1945, was always hazily defined, and elicited strong negative reactions almost from its inception, the choice of terminology signaled Cárdenas's ideological position toward the nation's youth. Over the course of the *sexenio*, students learned to define *patria* in classist terms, to elevate proletarian identity, and to employ the language of class consciousness.

The 1935 meeting of the VII Pan-American Conference on the Child in Mexico City, discussed in chapter 1, showcased Mexico's advances in socialist education and the professional child-related fields of pediatrics, pedagogy, and child psychology. With the protection and promotion of childhood on the forefront of so many national agendas, Mexico seized the spotlight. Partly in preparation for the significant international event slated for October 1935 and partly as a vehicle to promote elevated class consciousness in children as a goal of the socialist educational program, education officials held the First Conference of the Proletarian Child during the first two weeks of March 1935 (fig. 43). The children's conference prefaced the VII Pan-American Conference on the Child by design, and spawned regional and similarly themed children's conferences throughout the year (and throughout the 1930s) across the country in an apparent inclusionary sweep of youth politics: among these the Conference of Proletarian Children of the Republic (Congreso de Niños Proletarios de la República) (with representation by children from eighteen states), the Children's Conference (Congreso Infantil) in San Luis Potosí, the Conference of Peasant Children (Congreso de Niños Campesinos), and the Worker-Peasant Children's Conference (Congreso Infantil Obrero-Campesino) drew substantial participation and national attention. The goals of the conference, as stated by García Téllez, were to both learn from and instruct the proletarian child and to provide a space for him to voice the changes that he envisioned in his school.[95] The young delegates organized their sessions around the following four issues: the eco-

43. Poster from the First Conference of the Proletarian Child, March 1935. *El Maestro Rural*, April 1, 1935, 3.

nomic problem, the social problem, the educational problem, and "what we expect from the government and from society."[96]

The First Conference of the Proletarian Child reified the image of an idealized proletarian child as a new national archetype. After the revolution, but particularly during the Cárdenas era, reformers quickly turned their sights to the "proletarian child," a trope that filtered into textbooks, theater productions, dance performances, and literature.[97] They elevated a politicized product of generations of class warfare that, because of his condition as a child, felt even more acutely his parents' social marginalization.[98] Schoolteacher J. J. de la Rosa P. saw children as the last voiceless social group and considered them to be the last vestiges of slavery in an exploitative capitalist system. He saw the Conference of the Proletarian Child as the first opportunity that this group would have to voice their grievances, especially regarding their place in the economic order. Long gone were the days when children's only perceived desires were to eat candies and chocolates; the conference provided them the opportunity to prove that they were political beings, aware of their place in society, and capable of expressing opinions and instigating change. A newspaper article published a few weeks before the opening ceremony invited adults to observe and absorb their childlike souls; the journalist encouraged adults to scrutinize the proletarian children's actions, thoughts, dreams, visions, and attempts to resolve adult problems. In so doing, he maintained, adults would begin to see children as friends and collaborators in social action.[99] Perhaps fearful of the erosion of ideological fervor, Cardenistas believed that the emergence of a generation of proletarian children—ideologically pure and morally justified in their demands for social justice—could galvanize an increasingly fragmented population. As symbols, the proletarian children were irresistible: to the press, to their parents, and to the international community of child specialists descending upon Mexico for the conference.

From the children's perspective the national attention they received from the conference and the official trappings that characterized its sessions allowed them to accelerate their professional identities in the public limelight. Children participated in every level as in the antialcohol conference discussed above, and the democratic procedures for selecting representatives appeared above reproach. Once selected, child delegates were issued official identification badges. To all appearances these self-governing proletarian children behaved autonomously, enacting public discussion of their social conditions spontaneously yet in an orderly fashion. Indeed, the children sometimes rejected the intermediating presence of adults in their sessions; in a much-publicized episode to underscore their commitment, in one session, young delegates proclaimed that teachers would be afforded neither voice nor vote in the proceedings and relegated them to the observation seats at the edges of the auditorium.[100]

The carefully scripted event was a militant bid to rectify social hierarchy, but in the process it set up the patterns of organizational strata that came to characterize other institutions, like national politics and unions. Ironically, considering the theme of the conference, representation among child delegates was uneven and closely monitored by education officials behind the scenes. Only children from the capital attended the First Conference of the Proletarian Child. The careful selection of attendees according to their ideological formation and the strategic location of the conference suggested that the purpose was to model ideal proletarian behavior to children rather than simply to provide a snapshot of a cross-section of working-class childhood. The Ministry of Education wanted children from across the nation to see and hear the pure expressions of class consciousness and social organizations modeled by their more authentic peers in the city.[101] Conference organizers made concerted efforts to broadcast the proceedings across the nation. They produced soundie newsreels of the event, radio broadcasts by the child delegates to their compatriots, and summaries in the national press. Yet in some instances the conference allowed participants to acknowledge the gap between children in Mexico City and those in the countryside. One session realized in the Santa Anita Farm School brought urban working-class children in contact with children of campesinos in a discussion of their respective conditions and mutual problems and ended with both groups of children signing a "socialist pact."[102]

The strategic choice of venues for the First Conference of the Proletarian Child allowed Mexico to showcase its best and bright-

est in the overhauled Socialist School system. The highly publicized opening festivities of the conference, and many of the
sessions, took place at the Francisco I. Madero Model School.
Founded in 1921 as a laboratory for the Active School initiative,
it figured among a handful of model schools (sixteen model
schools in state capitals in 1935)[103] that enjoyed almost unlimited
government funding to experiment with the ideal implementation of pedagogues' visions of social action. Established in the
rough, working-class Mexico City neighborhood of Colonia de
la Bolsa, the school enrolled students familiar with class struggle. Contemporary scholar Frank Tannenbaum referred to it as
"the miracle school," and educator John Dewey, on his 1926 visit
to collaborate with educators, praised the Francisco I. Madero
School as one of the standout schools of its kind in the world.[104]
Under the guidance of a limited staff of twelve teachers, the
pupils lovingly cultivated the earth and attended classes in the
fresh air, putting in practice the labor and organizational systems of the most modern countries. A student-produced school
publication edited by student director Miguel Angel Escobar and
administrator Reinalda Avila, *Escuela Francisco I. Madero*, scrupu-
lously cataloged children's achievements. The Madero School
originally intended to promulgate among its students a version
of economic nationalism compatible with capitalist models of
industrial competition but cloaked in the revolutionary rhetoric
of solidarity, collectivism, and social utility.[105] By 1935 it offered
the perfect Petri dish for the cultivation of proletarian identity
and rhetoric from a select group of students.

Besides the Madero School, conference organizers painstak-
ingly chose the seven other schools around the city that would
host the multiple sessions of the event based on the supposed
proletarian character of the site and the pupils. For example,
students at the Estado de Guerrero School, the site of one of the
plenary sessions, reportedly built the school themselves over a
period of years, from whatever materials they could scrounge,
whether a brick or a peso.[106] The choice of the Madero School
as one of the locations for the First Conference of the Proletarian Child, then, came as little surprise. Yet the child dele-

gates hailing from the selected schools seemed to sense the potential for resentment from their compatriots. Only children from these schools had a voice and a vote in the proceedings, although the general assembly sessions were open to spectators from the public. In a conference's inaugural speech, child delegates from the Madero School addressed their comrades through the national press. They recognized their elevated status as a beacon for future conferences and claimed that due to the experimental nature of an all-children's conference, its initial radius needed to be reduced.[107] Madero School children thus acknowledged the sphere of privilege in which they found themselves and drafted this statement to justify their position of leadership. It could be argued, furthermore, that they were already implementing some of the tactics for justifying the limits of democratic participation.

Child delegates used their newfound platform to open the discussion on children's role in society and how children could participate effectively in class struggle. One minor disturbance in the conference proceedings suggested the degree to which children both understood and defended their ideological position; at one session a boy and a girl representative from the Red Pioneers, the communist youth organization, infiltrated the panel presentation. At first conference attendees cordially welcomed the pair and allowed them to participate in the discussion. Shortly, though, the young crashers asserted control over the democratic discussion, taking the reins of the conversation and steering it in the direction of their group's agenda. The child delegates spontaneously cried out in protest and ousted the infiltrators, who attempted to indoctrinate the members present.[108] The Red Pioneers incident reveals that children negotiated some terms of their ideological orientation; they accepted the socialist platform of the conference, but they recognized the ideology of the Red Pioneers as going beyond their group's collective vision of the best direction for the revolutionary generation. By expelling the communist youth, the young proletarians demonstrated their ability to differentiate between degrees of leftist orientation and socialization.

Through the formal structure of the conference, child participants gained awareness of themselves as political beings. In fact, the feature of peer evaluation at the conference heightened this awareness; in one of the various contests and competitions that occupied the delegates, children kept track of each other's grammatical errors, effective directorship of panels, and presentation style. They also evaluated the content of the conference on the whole, made suggestions for improvement, and supported the implementation of ideas that arose over the course of the event.[109] Some delegates came more politicized than others; in some cases, budding orators at the early sessions intimidated their peers into silence. Yet the fact that those spouting political rhetoric were children quickly infused enthusiasm into the event, and as the conference progressed, the precocious leaders charged the atmosphere with a sense of collective identity. One of these leaders, conference president Enrique Romero, assumed the stage at the opening ceremony dressed in a suit. Children surrounding the stage raised their fists in solidarity, as he expounded on the need to take social action and to provide an international model. Enrique then led the crowd in a pledge to fulfill the duties bestowed upon them by all voting members of the representative schools.[110] For an instant, Enrique embodied leadership and encouraged action.

Even as they learned adult oratory skills, conference procedures, and governance protocol, delegates expressed an awareness of themselves as children, with a special set of rights as stipulated by the 1924 Declaration of the Rights of the Child out of Geneva. In this way child delegates distinguished themselves from adult politicians, as they reiterated their condition as children. María L. Bernal from the Escuela Estado de Sonora pronounced the importance of recreation when she stated that for children, play was an indispensable thing, as necessary as air for birds and water for fish. She called for adults to respect the importance of their playthings, for teachers not to exercise punishment by depriving them of recreation, for schools to provide playgrounds and equipment, for children's theaters and libraries to be placed in the schools, and for parents to be obliged to allow them to attend school-sponsored excursions.[111] These demands seem like reasonable, common requests of the average child; when spoken in a political event by a child designated a professional role in an official proceeding, these words gain power.

The presence of girls in prominent offices at the conference presented the vision of progressive politics that surpassed the advances made by adult counterparts. The conference invitation stipulated that half of the delegates be girls.[112] Student Julieta Peralta served as president of the Fourth Regulated Session, hosted by the Worker-Farmer Fraternity School in the village of Santa Anita. Reporters lauded Julieta as an intelligent delegate and enthusiastic fighter in defense of the socialist cause.[113] She assumed the responsibility of sending a telegram to invite none less than President Lázaro Cárdenas to the following day's conference proceedings, signing off as general secretary on behalf of all of the conference delegates. Cárdenas respectfully declined but dignified the girl's request with an immediate response from his secretary.[114]

Significantly, gendered treatment of the conference participants originated only from the adult onlookers and not from the children themselves; another girl also named Julieta had her speech about minimum wage featured in a press review of the conference, which reported that she grew emotional due to her passion for the topic.[115] The photographic representations of the conference published in *El Maestro Rural* captured conference president Enrique Romero midspeech in an active pose, highlighting his impassioned locution and his modern professional suit, and provided a caption that identified him by name (fig. 44). By contrast the only published close-up of a girl delegate remained anonymous; the girl at the podium not only went unidentified by a caption but was also photographed from behind, her face obscured by her braids—a significant visual commentary that conflated gender and ethnicity as aesthetic categories and negated her political voice and public identity (fig. 45). Neither the girls nor the boys discussed gender issues. Numbers from student council elections reflect the

44. Child delegate and conference president Enrique Romero, speaking at the First Conference of the Proletarian Child. *El Maestro Rural*, April 1, 1935, 11.

gender equality apparent in politically oriented youth groups; students from the En Marcha youth organization in Tetecala, Morelos, elected five girls and six boys to posts in the student government.[116] Speeches about socioeconomic inequality and prejudice based on age trumped gender as conference topics. Perhaps the adult conference organizers behind the scenes of these children's performances de-emphasized issues of gender to suggest that in the socialist ideal, class-based issues of egalitarian treatment were more important. Or perhaps their silence on this issue, combined with the high index of girl participants, indicates that children assumed gender equality in their generation to be a given.

For those fortunate enough to participate, the conference was transformative. A reporter from *El Nacional* compiled the opinions of several delegates about their experiences. José Joaquín Girón, a fifth grader from the Estado de Sonora School,

45. Anonymous child delegate, with emphasis on the girl's ethnicity. *El Maestro Rural*, April 1, 1935.

remained convinced of the power of the Socialist School system and spouted boldly against its detractors who, in the "service of capitalism," sought to derail the "*niños proletarios*" from their path. Clearly, José Joaquín had learned to use rhetoric to express a determined ideological position and to launch a classist critique of the conditions suffered by his community. His words represent the first level of socialization: imitation of authorities. Yet not all of the child delegates were mere small embodiments of their revolutionary elders. Luís Rodríguez H., José Joaquín's classmate, demonstrated a quite nuanced attitude toward the new pedagogical approaches he experienced; his vocabulary and observations revealed his understanding of the cultural mission shared by schoolteacher and pupil that socialist educators strove to perpetuate: "If this conference achieves its goals, our parents' conditions will improve, and subsequently our own. If our parents remain unconvinced of the benefits of socialist education," Luís remarked, "they can come to our classes and see for themselves how we are being guided by our teachers." Luís situated himself in a mediating position between the parents (vestiges of an intransigent past) and the teachers (messiahs of a progressive, modern present). His words, published in a daily newspaper and viewed across the republic, reveal a sophisticated blend of the pedagogical tenets upholding the Socialist School and simple and practical ways that daily classroom life could be improved from the perspective of a child.[117]

While undoubtedly teachers and sep administrators guided the actions and words of the child delegates, the experiences lived by these children during their participation in the conference accompanied them back to their classrooms, where they enjoyed a measure of fame and prestige. Not only had they savored the public validation of their ideas and actions, but they acquired hero status among their peers as recognized official ambassadors of working-class children in a national institution. In the words of delegate María Ortiz, from the Domingo Sarmiento School, the conference "left in me and my *compañeros* magnificent teachings and experiences, and for that reason we hope that another conference convenes soon, with delegations from all of the schools across the capital, that the contingent be greater and that the enthusiasm awakened among all be more powerful, and that the voice of humble children be heard more widely."[118] Children like José Joaquín, Luís, and

María became models for their classmates. Though we recognize that adult influence mitigated, to varying degrees, the content of their performances, the public recognition of these child delegates' speeches signaled to their cohort that children could—and should—have a political voice.

The socialist curriculum and its extracurricular offerings, especially the overt politicization evident in children's conferences, drew sharp critiques from some sectors disenchanted with the secularization of education. Parents interested in retaining Catholic beliefs rankled against the tenor of the Socialist School's curriculum. Across the country bishops decided on a case-by-case basis whether local schools had crossed a line, indicating when parishioners could no longer send their children to school in good conscience, for fear of mortal repercussions.[119] For some parents, even those who would have fallen into the "proletarian" designation of the time, the behavior of child delegates at the conference represented the worst imagined outcome of educational reform: not only did the state wrest their children's labor from the family plot, but it had also occupied their minds and energies with its moralizing campaigns.[120] Still others viewed the young politicians in training not as making a contribution to the future development of the nation but rather as evidence of the robbery of the innocence of childhood. The same religious organizations that spoke out against Calles's Grito de Guadalajara, decrying his statements as trampling parents' rights, contended that children in the socialist school had assumed too many responsibilities. Detractors argued that these young people, rather than acquiring valuable tools for self-government, were suffering the loss of childhood.[121]

But one photograph taken of a session of the First Conference of the Proletarian Child, whether staged or candid, provides a visual synopsis of this event's significance for those children present. A child delegate, which contextual cues suggest to be Enrique Romero, dressed in a light-colored suit, stands on a small outdoor platform encircled by his fellow conference attendees. The photograph captures the children from behind and at a distance, removing the presumably adult photographer from the nucleus of the activity. In fact, no adults can be discerned from among the crowd. The orator has just said something that evoked a reaction from his peers, many of whom raise their fists in solidarity. In the outer ring of participants, some children remain observant and contemplative, their attention fixed on the spectacle. The child leader in the center, at the moment he is photographed, occupies a position both physically and politically superior to his peers, and he has commanded the respect of some of them and the attention of them all. This moment may well have been a fleeting snapshot of an observed social dynamic. Nevertheless, the image crystallizes a complex mixture of experiences and emotions during the brief space of the First Conference of the Proletarian Child. Solidarities forged among children along the lines of age, social class, and political identity. At the same time, hierarchies emerged, and the development of public personas in some children edged others to the sidelines.

Conclusions

In June 1929 the newspaper *El Universal* sponsored a nationwide oratory competition among high school students. The participants, ranging from thirteen-year-old boys to young men in their early twenties, delivered polished discourses that they might have practiced as younger children over years as student council representatives. Each state across the republic pitted their most talented young speakers against each other, and the respective victors competed for the national title. The runoff for the Mexico City representative was particularly heated, as rivaling schools heckled the orators from the opposition with schoolboy taunts. Those who surmounted the rabble with poise and dignity and managed to deliver a rousing speech were rewarded. One young man, aged nineteen, convinced the judges of his merit with a sweeping discussion of the global moral crisis that followed World War I and the literary and cultural figures that contemporary youth ought to look to for inspiration. The young man's colleagues hoisted to their shoulders the winner of the Mexico City title of the competition.[122] Public speaking skills proved good building blocks for populism. Nearly two decades later that young man would rise to the nation's presidency; the young celebrated orator was none other than Adolfo López Mateos (1958–64).

Children's entree into civic life in the 1920s and 1930s took on a highly structured, formal appearance that in many ways mirrored the bureaucratization of the revolutionary government. The literacy, antialcohol, and proletarian children's campaigns all expanded democratic access to new organizations for children. Some children took on leadership roles, learning responsibility and enjoying newfound social capital. Other children participated as observers, invigorated by the new political climate and opportunities for social action and interacting with an expanded group of peers. For perhaps the first time, children were not just future citizens; they were acting on their rights and responsibilities as active citizens on par with their adult contemporaries, and adults were beginning to recognize the organizing potential of their ranks. Perhaps even more significantly, the performances of citizenship enacted by children in public spaces attracted the attention of their peers, who saw children's voices validated by adults, institutions, and media outlets.

Much like the growing PNR political machine, and eventually the PRI that Adolfo López Mateos would preside over in his adult years, hierarchies emerged within these organizations that created limitations. To counter the noted social stratification, the term *proletarian* became a unifying identity with cachet, a valued commodity on the political market that extended to children's organizations and popular culture. Schools, conferences, and organizations bearing the stamp of the Socialist School drew national attention, as well as resources and acclaim. Despite the socialist rhetoric, class boundaries often became solidified and strengthened, as children sought out their poor compatriots as targets for their civilizing mission. These organizations, among others of their kind, made inroads to the wide participatory scope promised by the revolution, drawing a new social group into the sphere of political action.

CHAPTER SIX

Hermanitos de la Raza

Civic Organizations and International Diplomacy

If you could save a million children from suffering and thousands from death . . . would you not welcome the opportunity? [In Mexico] [t]he teachers are splendidly trained in practical helpfulness but the schools are inadequately equipped and the villagers dreadfully poor.

— Mexico Child Welfare Bureau pamphlet, Los Angeles, California, 1932

Now I address you, little cubs of the old Spanish lion; as of today you will stay under cover of the wings of the Aztec eagle.

— ERNESTO HIDALGO, minister of foreign relations, to exiled children of
the Spanish civil war upon their arrival in Veracruz, June 7, 1937

In the early 1930s the Mexico Child Welfare Bureau, headed by the well-intentioned Dr. Lincoln Wirt in the United States and with the tacit permission of Mexico's Ministry of Education, organized the collection and delivery of Friendship Health Chests, or *botiquines*, made up of medical supplies, children's clothing, and playground equipment from schools in the United States to needy children in rural Mexico. First Lady Josefina de Ortiz Rubio, whose husband presided from 1930 to 1932, offered a lukewarm endorsement of the charity initiative that asserted Mexico as a bilateral partner, citing that the contributions symbolized a closer knitting of the bonds of friendship between the children of Mexico and the United States.[1] Dr. Wirt sent the health chests to Mexico with the intention of creating bonds of friendship, but the propaganda that accompanied the good-faith gesture reinforced racialized Good Neighbor–era policies that established the United States as the cultural imperialist power, a father figure extending health and well-being down to an infantilized nascent democracy. Official correspondence regarding the *botiquines* suggests uneven expectations in the degree of mutual fraternal sentiment that the program would foster. Schools sending health chests, mostly from California, expressed disappointment when they did not receive messages of gratitude for their generosity. Dr. Wirt sent several notes about the security precautions that they employed, encircling the chests in metal wire to avoid thievery en route, revealing his ideas about the savage, bandit-ridden areas to which their gifts were destined. In one letter Dr. Wirt condescendingly makes reference to the high quality of the contents, including an outfit originally intended for a California baby, toys, clothing, a volleyball, an air pump, a net, and two baseballs.[2] Likely, Mexico's less than enthusiastic reception of Wirt's overtures could be explained by increasing efforts in the 1930s to project an image of Mexico as modern, healthy, and capable of caring for its own citizens. Fawning gratitude to their wealthier North American counterpart would undercut this national image on the global stage.

A few short years later, in 1937, Mexico received five hundred child exiles from the Spanish Civil War to euphoric national acclaim.[3] A whirlwind of national media coverage inverted Mexico's international reputation as a recipient of charity. With a perceptible measure of smug satisfaction, government officials responsible for hosting the Spanish orphans indicated the irony of a former colony providing refuge for the victims of the war-torn motherland. In the immediate wake of the Spanish children's prolonged stay in Mexico (many, in fact, never returned to Spain), Cárdenas officials handily pointed to them as beneficiaries of Mexico's successful recovery from the revolution. For several years the Spanish children served as symbols of the kinds of services that the modern, prosperous, and politically stable nation could provide to the global community. In reality Mexico in the 1930s was far from meeting the material needs of all of its citizens, but opportunities to showcase some of the advances in education and child welfare reform could not be passed over, and thus the case of the Spanish exile children became one of the celebrated national rallying points of the era. These two instances of child-oriented charity in the 1930s—destined from the United States to Mexico and from Mexico to Spain—provide examples of the complex set of international discourses of modernity taking place that situated children at the center.

As previous chapters have demonstrated, children and youth in revolutionary Mexico were folded into a more participatory political culture; they became visible agents of civic action, political mobilization, and national and international charity as never before in the country's history. The young people of Mexico were at the forefront of a country reinventing itself as a nation of literate, productive, modern citizens. Even as Mexico underwent radically modern restructuring, American popular youth literature—including the *Junior Red Cross News*, Boy Scout publications, and short adventure novels—persisted in their portrayal of a rural, Aztec Mexico. Meanwhile, comparable Mexican youth publications—*Tihui*, *El Scout*, and the *Manual del Explorador*—reinforced the ways that membership in extracurricular organizations heralded the emergence of a strong nation based on the healthy, active, moral bodies of its youth. The tension between these two visions of Mexico forms the core of this chapter, and the Mexican youth are the protagonists, situated at the crossroads between their experiences growing up in a modernizing nation and the rest of the world's old-fashioned vision of Mexicans as a static people.

Individually and collectively, as part of a growing self-awareness as members of a transnational community of their peers, Mexican youth sought membership in organizations such as the Junior Red Cross, the Boy Scouts, and, to an extent, the Girl Scouts, beginning in the 1920s and 1930s. Although the norms, codes, and aesthetics of these organizations were imported from abroad—namely, Great Britain and the United States—the Mexican national chapters quickly subverted much of the foreign content and adopted distinctly local characteristics. As recognized international members, the youth were then able to use these organizations as platforms to export their particular brand of nationalism, in part on their own terms. Many of the organizations and initiatives presented here, while not necessarily state-sponsored programs, enjoyed the support and occasional collaboration of government agencies, in particular the SEP, especially when they espoused the SEP's culture of education and civic engagement.

Gender, Age, and Race in Modern Articulations of National Identity

Three features of this emerging discourse of national identity in the transnational sphere form the analysis of internationally oriented organizations: gendered expressions of nationalism, the fluidity of categories of childhood and youth, and the troubled inclusion of the indigenous past. First, it bears mentioning that boys and girls alike enjoyed membership in Scouts and the Junior Red Cross (along with the international prestige lent by the official trappings of the organizations), yet boys and girls learned to express revolutionary nationalism according to the respective gender norms that these transnational organizations upheld and reaffirmed. Everything from the names of the subcommittees (Explorers versus Big Sisters) to the day-to-day activities (international conferences versus domestic service) belied the distinct social spheres in which boys and girls were expected to carry out service to the *patria*.[4] Mexico aspired to a standard of modernity accelerated in 1920s Germany, for example, which branded civilization and progress on the gendered bodies of its youth on display.[5] In what I call expressions of gendered nationalism, the Boy Scouts focused on the construction of a self-controlled masculinity, with an emphasis on strengthening the body, conquering the national terrain, exercising dominion over local flora and fauna, and ultimately becoming the master of one's physical environment. Meanwhile, the Junior Red Cross, and in particular the service-oriented Big Sister Committee, emphasized domestic service, charity, and compassion toward the less fortunate as expressions of feminine nationalism. Nevertheless, despite the powerful gender-normative civilizing forces of the Boy Scouts and Junior Red Cross, members of these organizations gained social value *as child citizens* upon expressing their civic identities in the international arena.

Second, the Mexican political culture of the 1920s and 1930s valorized childhood and youth above other categories as part of a national metaphor for the country's moral renewal. This allowed for all from very young children to young adults in their early twenties to claim membership in the same social space. As Steven Mintz has argued, the relatively recent deployment of age as a category of analysis has proved social perceptions of age to be more mutable, and thus more widely applicable, than other categories such as gender.[6] Historians have effectively demonstrated fluidity between childhood, adolescence, and adulthood, as these are defined by the historical moment, the cultural context, and the assumptions of contemporary intellectuals as historical producers of knowledge in each instant.[7] Most "children" that appear in the documents, photos, and articles of Boy Scout and Junior Red Cross popular media outlets fall between the ages of seven and eighteen. In many cases, the terms *child, boy/girl,* and *youth* are used interchangeably without making biological distinctions regarding the subjects in question. Especially in the case of the Boy Scouts, young men upwards of their early twenties often formed the ranks of the "boys," especially in international appearances. On the other hand, the literal translation of the Cruz Roja de la Juventud (referred to here by its standardized name in English, Junior Red Cross) would be Red Cross Youth, yet the organization garnered the bulk of its membership from elementary school children much younger than the adolescents suggested by its title. For older youth, whose day-to-day lives otherwise might have been indistinguishable from those of adults, the opportunity to participate in a *children's* organization allowed them the possibility of a new social identity. Furthermore, the modern-day concept of "adolescence" did not gain currency in Mexico until the middle of the twentieth century.[8] In the 1920s and 1930s the social identity of minors can be understood only on a case-by-case basis. Notwithstanding the slippage along the lower rungs of the chronological ladder, the overwhelming surge in civic participation among young people in revolutionary Mexico suggests that "childhood" and "youth" both emerged as viable categories for social identity beyond the traditional family sphere. Children and youth began to enact citizenship in ways that were recognized by their social and political seniors and saw these actions reinforced in an international climate of youth movements.

Third, citizens of both Mexico and the United States relied on the myth of an idealized Aztec past in the construction of respective visions of Mexico, but each construed that past in different ways. U.S. cultural sources conflated a mythic past with a stagnant present, while the Mexican counterparts sought to relegate indigeneity to the past and project a whiter version of Mexico as the modern present. Both approaches can be indicted for their oversight, to the point of neglect, of the real and living native population of Mexico. Mexican Boy Scouts passed over indigenous neighbors, and even members of their ranks, in favor of the noble-savage trope from which they extracted symbolic power and aesthetic tokens. And despite the modernizing overtures projected by Mexican youth, Americans persisted in seeing their counterparts south of the border as bronzed vestiges of a pre-Colombian storybook civilization, fixed in a rural and romantic past. The stark disjuncture between symbolic and real native Mexicans manifests itself clearly in the mission and actions of these transnational organizations and takes on a different hue whether viewed through a Mexican or an American lens.[9]

These three categories—gender, age, and race—thread in and out of the broader discussion of Mexican cultural nationalism as it was learned, expressed, exported, and received by members of transnational youth organizations in the 1920s and 1930s. Before delving into the national chapters of the Boy Scouts and Junior Red Cross as case studies, I turn briefly to a discussion of the backdrop of Pan-Americanism and internationalism against which selected national tropes emerged.

Activating Mexico's Youth

As explored in previous chapters, discussions of the corrupting potential of free time on children formed one of the main preoccupations of child specialists attending the 1935 Pan-American Child Congress. The remedy, officials believed, was to direct children's activities through reputable, morally grounded organizations and structured activities. The Department of Psychopedagogy and Hygiene formed programs through "active education" schools based on the model established by North American pedagogue John Dewey and eventually experimented with a more dogmatic expression in the Socialist School begun in 1934. In addition to the state-sponsored antialcohol campaigns, healthy child contests, gymnastics, student council, charity drives, and environmental clubs, schoolchildren in the 1920s and 1930s turned to the government-sanctioned national chapters of the Junior Red Cross and the Tribus de Exploradores (subsumed in the Boy Scouts) to fill their after-school hours. To be clear, the unprecedented access to extracurricular activities and private organizations with national and international missions was often limited to middle-class urban children, despite much rhetoric to the contrary.

To maximize children's productivity and exposure to revolutionary ideology, education officials saturated their environment with images, sounds, and didactic material. To this end under the Socialist School initiative, in 1937 the government of Lázaro Cárdenas founded the Office of Social Action as an agency of the Ministry of Public Education. According to the director, Carlos Uribarri Kast, it met "the urgent necessity to socialize children within a child-oriented environment, one that ran parallel to modern life and, in accordance with the educational ideology of the moment, intervene[d] in extracurricular activities, organizing the free time of minors, and providing them with instructive recreation and work to distract them, drawing them away from harmful activities and bad company." Organizations for youth, argued Uribarri Kast, provided the child with "a better interpretation of revolutionary nationalism and initiation in true citizenship."[10]

In the context of this revolutionary rhetoric and attention to the activities and potentials of the nation's youth, both the Boy Scouts and the Junior Red Cross saw burgeoning membership among Mexican youth. With their origins hailing from international headquarters and with religious bases as their foundations, the national chapters of the Junior Red Cross and the Boy Scouts were imagined as moralizing institutions for the nation's youth. In Mexico the religious expressions of the Boy Scouts were both present and coexisted uncontested alongside a starkly socialist national curriculum. In a political arena in which a deeply Catholic populace sputtered up against a staunchly secular government (expressed over the 1920s and 1930s by the extremely violent Cristero wars), children learned to practice diplomatic citizenship from an early age. In fact, the rhetorical shift from the late nineteenth century, when children were referred to as "future citizens," to the early twentieth century, when they became "little citizens," demonstrates the degree of confidence in children's agency and voice in forging national peace, solidarity, and modernity. Once that was achieved to satisfaction, the young members of both the Boy Scouts and the Junior Red Cross were poised to project this identity abroad.

Mexico in the Eyes of the U.S. Media

A fund-raising pamphlet distributed by the Mexico Child Welfare Bureau in the United States provides a striking illustration of attitudes about rural children south of the border. Two images purport to represent five indigenous boys before and after benefiting from the health chests (fig. 46). The first photograph, subtitled "The Raw Material: Native youths from the hills seeking admission to the government school in Mexico City," depicts the boys in a stilted pose reminiscent of National Geographic ethnographic photography, exaggeratedly bedecked in the indigenous clothes of sombreros, serapes, and huaraches that appear to be fresh out of the boxes. Their expressions are hostile; they embody the "savages" that such health kits sought to reform. The second photograph, captioned "The Same Boys Five Months Later: There are many such boys and girls in Mex-

THE RAW MATERIAL

Native youths from the hills seeking admission to the government school in Mexico City

THE SAME BOYS FIVE MONTHS LATER

There are many such boys and girls in Mexico eager for an education

46. Mexico Child Welfare Bureau propaganda pamphlet. Departamento de Escuelas Rurales, Dirección General, Caja 26, Exp. 24, 1932.

ico eager for an education," shows five young men in civil servant uniforms, their cropped hair combed back with pomade, holding their caps military style to their chest, their wild expressions transformed into ones of steely determination. They stand on the steps of an official building, and the angle of the shot lengthens them. Tall, authoritative men shed their ethnicity—and their childhood—thanks to the help of the Mexico Child Welfare Bureau. These two photographs confirm Mexico as an infantile Indian land requiring U.S. charity to transform its savage residents into productive citizens.[11]

International exchange—including correspondence and membership in global organizations such as the Junior Red Cross and the Boy Scouts—purportedly allowed middle-class children the opportunity to gain equal footing with their counterparts in Europe, Australia, Asia, and the United States. Despite advances in fraternal understanding, international objectification of Mexican poverty displayed in foreign media such as this persisted. The characterization of Mexican children in U.S. popular and political cultures, while well intentioned, was often paternalistic and condescending. Children became the object of New Deal–era charity from the north; perceptions of abject poverty and disenfranchisement of rural indigenous children eclipsed the great modernizing strides being made by and for children in the cities.

Officially endorsed racialized depictions of Mexico's young population echoed in U.S. popular culture as well. Children's literature from the early twentieth century reduced the country's diversity to descriptions of encounters with renegade border types like Pancho Villa and the Mexican Rangers. One such novel, *The Boy Scouts under Fire in Mexico*, published in 1914, depicts American Boy Scouts Rob and Tubby, who find themselves in Mexico during the revolution. Excited by the possibility of participating in the crossfire, the young characters express the hope that they will even come across some real-live "Indian" insurgents.[12] In such novels Mexico appears barbaric, uncivilized, and lawless: a place for adventuresome American Scouts to try out their survival skills before escaping back across the border to the order of the modern world. Popular youth literature authors in the United States relegated Mexico to a caricature, an easy trope of poverty and savagery against which to promote their own version of modern nationalism and performance of citizenship for youth.[13]

The *Junior Red Cross News*, published from 1919 into the 1940s,[14] not only reported news from member countries with national chapters of the organization but also ran country-based pieces intended to capture the culture and lifestyle of children around the world. Mexico appeared frequently in the magazine, in fictional or journalistic stories told through the eyes of "typical" Mexican children. More often than not, the magazine's stories took place in the countryside or humble neighborhoods and featured children identified either as poor, indigenous, or both, as protagonists instructing the English-speaking world about an aspect of their culture. Pastoral tropes contextualized these children's lives. One American observer described travels in Mexico to his Junior Red Cross audience: "These people are still close to the soil, and live by the work of their hands. . . . They have leisure and sensitivity to beauty. They do not know about bathtubs; they bathe in the river. An airplane flew over one village, and the people all insisted that it was Jesus Christ."[15] A series of stories place eight-year-old Pepita, a wealthy Mexico City girl with a North American father and a Spanish mother, in adventures alongside Pancho, a humble eleven-year-old peasant boy, whom she respected "because he knew that there was magic in all common things."[16] Mexican children in Junior Red Cross publications lived in a world cloaked in superstition and myth.

Yet some *Junior Red Cross News* correspondents grappled with Mexico's emerging modernity. While the authors lauded the creativity with which Mexican educational officials expanded the rural educational curriculum—lending equal importance to crop planning and literacy, for example—they consistently framed the educational advances in the language of retention of ancient lifeways. American observers expressed optimism that despite the incorporation of rural villages into Mexican national life, they would be able to "salvage those ways of life which are beautiful and conducive to their happiness";[17] at the same time, they noted that Mexico's rural school system offered "the only road to nationhood."[18] Their narratives charged indigenous children with the task of carrying ancestral qualities into the modern age. Speaking of the mystical ruins that would be disturbed to allow the Pan-American highway to bisect Mexico and connect the two continents, Anna Milo Upjohn wrote of a young boy in the rural school system: "Manuel's hands may some day grasp pick and shovel to unearth those ruins. But may those slim, dark fingers never lose the magic touch of the past through modern tools."[19]

Some of the nationalist material culture consciously produced by Mexican children suggested an awareness of the pervasiveness of this premodern profile that they had in the international sphere. On a fall day in 1928 the middle school children of the Stevens Practice School at the Philadelphia Normal School delighted at the arrival of a package from Tampico, Mexico. It was a school correspondence album, arranged through the international exchange program of the American Junior Red Cross. The pictures, letters, dolls, and miniature objects that accompanied the album spoke of a rural, romantic Aztec Mexico; the young correspondents privileged a precolonial past and highlighted moments of imperial splendor, as they introduced Mexico to the young American recipients. In their narratives ancient Aztecs hurled their beautiful princesses bedecked in the storied gold of the New World from towering pyramids to appease the "idols" that they worshipped, and modern-day society ladies harked back to Spain in their Old World costumes of mantillas, earrings, combs, and shawls. The dolls that accompanied the album—by request of the Junior Red Cross to depict the most "typical" costume worn by Mexicans—featured the male and female "types" quickly becoming the country's national emblem: the *charro* and the *china poblana*. This Hispanophile pair, a construction of the nation's revolutionary cultural nationalism, had only recently entered into Mexico's purview but underwent rapid acceptance, commodification, and international dissemination.[20] Other cultural artifacts included in the album further underscored a romantic image of a rural society based on subsistence agriculture and artisanry: a decorated sombrero, a woven rug bearing a vaguely indigenous motif, a flat mortar for grinding corn, a wooden whisk for whipping hot chocolate, a clay grill and a fan to keep the embers alive, and a clay pot for storing water.[21] Overall, the Mexico received by this group of American youngsters bore no distinct features of modern democratic society but rather perpetuated a caricature long established in American lore of a barbaric, romantic, ancient land south of the border. In a twist, curiously enough, the school responsible for submitting that album was none other than the American School at Tampico, attended largely by children of expatriates relocated to the region to manage U.S.-owned oil companies and living in an enclave. While some of these children might even have been born in Mexico and held Mexican citizenship, they regarded the country with a degree of distance and bestowed upon it the quaint rural characteristics largely promoted by the United States.

The school correspondence album introduced or reiterated the *charro* and the *china poblana* as the typical Mexican costume, emblazoning in American children's imaginations a single image of the racial type, social class, and disposition of the Mexican child. American children living abroad contributed most prolifically to the consolidation of these national types in children's media. In the *Junior Red Cross* magazines, accompanying illustrations unfailingly depicted Mexican boys in sombreros with a bright, stylized *sarape* popularized in the northern weaving city of Saltillo draped over one shoulder and girls in lush dark braids with flowery skirts and a woven shawl, both often in the company of animals in their care. The magazine published one set of letters of American children living in a mining camp in San Luis Potosí, which described in detail the *charro* and *china poblana* costumes and included photographs of the young correspondents wearing the costumes.[22]

As children learned about their peers in other countries— their different schedules, the different setup of their classrooms, what they ate, what they did with their free time—they also had to think about how to present themselves. The group preparation of an album or even a letter required a measure of self-reflection with potentially profound implications for the shaping of their identities.[23] What did it mean to be Mexican? What is different about Mexican life? What assumptions do other children make about Mexico? Children identified themselves to their peers with descriptions of their toys, excursions, pets, and altruistic activities. Furthermore, they had to think about how to present their country as a unit; letters reveal that children identified their country by its holidays, industry, urban centers, typical clothing, national heroes, and patriotic holidays. Unfailingly, children turned to the emerging national types of the *charro* and the *china poblana* as depoliticized (not to mention whitened) versions of themselves. Their projections contributed to the barrage of images of this genre portraying a dancing, sanitized Mexico that children abroad consumed in popular culture.

A Junior Red Cross wartime pamphlet illustration provides a glimpse of the context in which American children consumed some of these staid cultural representations of Mexico. In it a classroom of American boys and girls unpacks the contents of a school correspondence album from Mexico. On the chalkboard behind the children, someone had drawn the by then typical stamp of the sombrero-wearing Mexican sleeping beneath a tree and surrounded by cactuses. The students interact with the components of the international correspondence: the Mexican flag, a drum, a *sarape*, the *china* and *charro* doll pair, and other artisanal trinkets. The items have been laid out as though in a museum exhibition, and the children's respectful interactions with them set a tone of reverie for an ancient and different culture.

The pervasiveness of this monolithic visual treatment of Mexican children caused American children to replicate it as the only authentic representation of their southern neighbor. In a May 1938 celebration of "Junior Red Cross around the World," a classroom of California children dressed as repre-

47. American children dressed in "typical" Mexican costume. *Junior Red Cross News* (April 1941): 218–19. National Archives and Records Administration.

sentatives of many nations; prominently featured in the front row, a young blond boy donned a sombrero and a carefully slung *sarape* over his shoulder, next to his braided girl counterpart, perhaps the most readily identifiable national types in the group.[24] (Just a few years later Walt Disney's Mexican-based rooster Panchito Pistoles would instruct all American children that "snappy serapes" formed a requisite element of Mexican costume.)[25] In another event schoolchildren from Grand Rapids, Michigan, staged a mock "international convention" of Red Cross member nations and dressed as delegates; the photograph accompanying the news brief pictures two pairs of identically dressed boys and girls, bedecked in the expected costumes (though notably, their versions of the costumes appear to be particularly tourist oriented, as the *sarapes* are imprinted with the word *Mexico* and the hats have decorative fringe on them) (fig. 47).[26] Interestingly, this particular pair of tropes—the *charro* and the *china poblana*—was probably the whitest available stereotype of Mexicans reproduced in most cultural outlets at the time. Even in its commodified exported manifestation, Mexican national identity underplayed the real indigenous roots.

Pan-American Dreams

A telephone rang in Mexico's National Autonomous University one spring day in 1931. Fifth grader Rafael del Paso picked up the receiver and answered in English. On the other end of the line, a boy in Washington DC spoke a greeting. Rafael delivered his prepared statement into the mouthpiece, as university officials and newspaper reporters stood by. "The Mexican children send a cordial salutation to the children of the United States, whom we respect and love with all of our hearts," Rafael proclaimed. "We hope that as adults we Mexicans will contribute to the world's progress, teaching a better appreciation of natural beauty and of the art that characterizes everyday life in our villages." He went on to express sentiments of generational solidarity and spoke to the peaceful future he hoped they would share as adults, yet maintained references to sources of nationalist pride: ancient Aztec heritage, an iconic indigenous president, and the integrity of village life.[27] This singular episode, clearly an exceptional one judging from the documented high-profile press and academic presence, nevertheless serves as a metaphor for the nature of Pan-American cultural exchanges between Latin American nations and the United States. On the one hand, there is the predominance of Anglophile structures such as the choice of language (English, despite being the official language of only one of more than a dozen member nations at the time). On the other hand, the monolithic characterization of Mexico that young Rafael proffered over the telephone echoed the new cultural tropes gaining currency at the time, both at home and abroad, as unifying symbols of national identity.

The internationalism that arose out of the First World War opened avenues for participation in civic life to children across the globe. In the Americas the Pan-American Union formed in 1890 primarily as an organization to foster economic cooperation among countries in the hemisphere, but it quickly expanded to include cultural exchanges intended to create and deepen fraternal ties. The decline of oligarchic and military regimes at the turn of the twentieth century accompanied a rise in democratization across Latin America, characterized by fervent expressions of nationalism. The early decades of the twentieth century saw the rise of Pan-American unity in the hemisphere; themes of international cooperation marked Latin American political and cultural diplomatic efforts even as the world order shifted. Pan-Americanism harked back to the nativist independence movements of the previous century that emphasized both the region of the Americas—as distinct from European colonial powers—and emerging individual nations. In the twentieth century hemispheric solidarity not only drew upon cultural commonalities such as language, religion, and colonial heritage but also drew upon the strongly nationalist campaigns gaining momentum in countries such as Mexico and Brazil in the first third of the century.

In an era of crisis adults turned to children to amend their broken world. The implication that adults had failed in peacetime relations relied on a linear understanding of human biological age, resting on the assumption that once lost, children's innocence could not be regained. A 1925 spread in the *World's Health* magazine cited the potential power of uniting this generation through correspondence; it stated that the children of the world, guided by their teachers and aided by their Red Cross Societies, by means of their pens and pencils, their scissors and needles, their paste and paintbrushes, would approach one another across borders, mountains, rivers, and oceans, in a new camaraderie.[28] In fact, officials sought to reduce adult mediation in the correspondence; a memo from the Intellectual Cooperation Section of the Pan-American Union recommended that Red Cross correspondence organizers maintain the integrity of children's creative submissions and not try to standardize correspondence or lend it too much official char-

acter. The adults should provide only the necessary administrative service to facilitate the free and spontaneous flow of
correspondence between children.[29]

Children, then, featured prominently in international and
Pan-American exchanges, as the most newly visible participants
in rising democracies the world over. As demonstrated in chapter 1, concern for the welfare and education of children brought
together professionals from across the hemisphere in one of the
most influential and lasting series of regional collaborations:
the Pan-American Child Congresses (1916 to the present). In
1931 the renowned Pan-American peace advocate and Chilean
poet and teacher Gabriela Mistral reminded students in the
Americas of the privileges and responsibilities that came with
being continental citizens.[30] Over the 1920s and 1930s in Mexico, children shifted from being the objects of Pan-American
concern to being agents of Pan-American unity, as both their
real and their symbolic visibility in civic life gained more official attention. While intellectuals and experts produced the
widely disseminated rhetoric about children, charitable organizations, church youth groups, and international agencies continued their projects in the cultural domain, working actively to
get children directly involved in forging ties with their international peers. Events such as this symbolic telephone exchange
between young boys of two American countries launched children into diplomatic roles during peacetime bridge building.
Not traditionally seen as political actors, the children of the
revolution enjoyed unprecedented attention as cultural diplomats during these decades.

Among Latin American countries Mexico assumed leadership in the exchange of music, mass media, and art and became
the regional heavyweight in the Pan-American cultural arena
around the time that it hosted the Pan-American Child Congress of 1935. Agustín Lara became a household name across the
continent as the strains of his ballads transcended the nation's
boundaries. International magazines printed color spreads of
the muralists' bold social realist stylings. Renowned educators
such as Gabriela Mistral and John Dewey traveled to Mexico

to absorb enthusiasm surrounding the incipient socialist curriculum in Mexico's heavily funded model proletarian schools. In step with the torrid pace of the country's cultural revolution, Mexico's children emerged as the vanguard of young Latin American letter writers. Emboldened by the warm reception of their country's cultural renaissance, Mexican children assumed a confident—even haughty—tone in their exchanges with peers in the region. The invention of civic holidays such as Pan-American Day and the Día de la Raza provided them with the opportunity and voice to express nationalist pride with a secular evangelistic fervor.

Pan-American Day, or Day of the Americas, celebrated on April 14, was an occasion for intellectuals from the "three Americas"—South, Central, and North—to address hemispheric youth. In official ceremonies children participated as well, albeit under the direction of adult organizers. At a 1939 Pan-American Round Table Association meeting in Mexico, child delegate Raúl Vargas addressed the gathering. He told them that even though they were children, they had already grasped the idea that the nations of Washington, Hidalgo, Bolívar, Martí, and other American patriots should unite to bring about social and economic equality.[31] Much of children's political activity in the international arena took the form of creating a young cadre of peace ambassadors. In a missive directed to the Pan-American Union, a representative from a residential ranch for orphan children in Santa Clara, Cuba, requested all of the countries on the continent to engage in a symbolic day of peace by pointing all cannons toward the ground on behalf of the colony's one hundred residents who initiated the plea.[32]

The Pan-American Union had its headquarters in Washington DC, but the unifying principle of a common mestizo heritage found expression in Pan-Hispanic exchanges, escalating the "cosmic race" into the realm of superlatives.[33] Many international celebrations and exchanges usually clustered around the Día de la Raza, celebrated on October 12. The holiday celebrated the discovery of the Americas and rehabilitated Christopher Columbus as a unifying symbol for the hemisphere.[34]

Schools dedicated the day to civic ceremonies, festivals, and discourses on mestizo racial unity in the Americas. For example, in Morelia, Michoacán, a group of three hundred schoolchildren performed a concert in honor of the holiday featuring songs typical of different regions and recitations proclaiming the glories of the Latin American race.[35] In 1933 the Seventh International American Conference in Montevideo, Uruguay, came up with the template for a flag, the Bandera de la Raza—a white background (symbolizing peace) with three purple crosses (a reference to shared Catholic heritage) and a sun (representing the indigenous people) rising behind the center cross.[36] The flag and a related anthem engendered peace, understanding, and love among the "*raza indoespañola*." Mexico adopted the flag as the official banner of the Día de la Raza, to be raised at all official buildings on October 12 in a solemn ceremony, and at the behest of First Lady Aida Rodríguez schoolchildren initiated a campaign for their hemispheric brothers and sisters to do likewise.[37] Students of Escuela Municipal no. 4 in the state of Durango wrote to children in El Salvador encouraging them to adopt the flag. The Central American country's secretary of education responded favorably to the children's "beautiful and vibrant invitation."[38] Similar letters found their way to Puerto Rico, Ecuador, Cuba, and Peru through the Mexican children's initiative, and their letters often triggered longer-term correspondence between the children. Most correspondence elicited an immediate, enthusiastic response.

One invitation to adopt the flag directed to fifth grader Susana Elejalde in Lima received a positive response; not coincidentally, the Peruvian girl attended the Escuela República de México.[39] In order to foster a more concrete sense of brotherhood, many schools adopted the name of another American republic. Children walking through the door of a building emblazoned with the moniker "Escuela República de Brasil" were reminded daily of their South American counterparts. The sister-school pairings tilted the axis of identity formation for pupils. Exchanges involving Mexican children suggest a conceited awareness of the cultural advances that their country had made as perceived by the rest of Latin America. In 1922 a school in Argentina adopted the name Escuela República de México; Mexican schoolchildren quickly drafted a letter, expressing the hope that their South American counterparts would be able to make the rapid moral, cultural, and scientific advances that they had achieved.[40]

A letter from schoolchildren in Colima de Tobás, Costa Rica, addressed "the future men of the great Aztec nation." Their letter recognized Mexican presence at the forefront of international child correspondence and thanked them for being such good representatives for the smaller Latin American republics in the hemisphere. The Costa Rican children reminded their Mexican brothers and sisters that they held the future of their *patria* in their hands and looked forward to the day that they emerged as noble, intelligent leaders.[41]

Schoolteachers organized their young wards to send off cultural albums to the children from a school that bore their country's name or vice versa. Chapter offices of the Junior Red Cross organized and distributed albums and portfolios locally, taking charge of any translation that needed to be done. At the Escuela República Argentina, in step with the socialist educational program that taught children to be self-sufficient and take initiative, fifth and sixth grade members of the school's Junior Red Cross spent a portion of every day revising their portfolio materials, alongside countless other student-directed civic activities in which they were engaged.[42] Teachers in the United States commented that the preparation of these portfolios often triggered a greater interest in the region from which their new pen pals hailed, fulfilling the Junior Red Cross mission to expand the child's point of view and breathe life into his schoolwork.[43] As a result, geography, history, art, current events, home economics, industrial arts, and language classes became infused with international references supplemented by tangible primary source material from the portfolios. A typical album contained the lyrics to the national anthem or other patriotic songs; biographies of national heroes; descriptions or photographs of historic sites and monuments; discussions of the local landscape, customs, and food; and other cultural memorabilia. Fourth grade Chilean schoolteacher Juana Guglielmi Urzúa reported that the album received from children of the Mexican school República de Chile encouraged her students to spark further correspondence with children from their sister country.[44]

The children exchanged national flags, always received with great pomp and ceremony, and learned each other's national anthems. Yet evidence that children responded to Mexican exports beyond elements of officially sponsored culture can be seen in one episode: in 1937 a Mexican class sent the national flag to chapter members of the Junior Red Cross in Peru during Red Cross Week festivities; upon receipt of the flag the band of six hundred cadets spontaneously burst not into the *himno nacional* but rather into a rendition of the popular Mexican song "Allá en el rancho grande."[45] Other times the correspondence reflected children's understanding that distilled symbols of national culture would help to readily identify their respective countries; in 1933 a group of Brazilian orphan girls sent a letter to Mexican girls in the public welfare institutions and promptly received a gift of four little sombreros and a handwoven satchel manufactured by the girls in their home economics workshops.[46]

The Pan-American Union promoted pen-pal programs between schoolchildren at the primary and secondary levels as a viable way to foment cultural diplomacy and supported programs such as the National Bureau of Educational Correspondence at George Peabody College in Nashville, Tennessee, founded in 1919. The Spanish-language exchange program began in 1920, matching six thousand correspondents in Latin America and Spain with their U.S. counterparts in its first five years.[47] Organization officials believed that children who corresponded with their international counterparts would develop into higher-quality adults with an appreciation of the value of other cultures, rather than a shortsighted vision of only what his or her own country had to offer. In addition, the officials hoped international pen pals would learn practical skills from one another and develop shared interests that transcended geographical boundaries. At the outset the letters would be written in the mother tongue of the author, but if the correspondence was to be sustained over a longer time, the students would develop foreign-language skills through this exercise alongside what they learned in their classes. Over time many of the pairings yielded lasting international friendships, as correspondents exchanged photos and anecdotes of their private lives.[48] The organizing officials took great care to match students up with writing partners of the same sex, assuming that their interests would be closer together. Moreover, the pen-pal correspondence was not intended to develop into romantic interest between correspondents.[49]

The Junior Red Cross international school correspondence initiative, also endorsed by the Pan-American Union, was more concerned with fostering international ties that spanned the ocean, boasting participation between thirty thousand classrooms around the world by 1927. By 1929 the Junior Red Cross counted eleven million members in its ranks, with headquarters in fifty-five countries. At that year's Junior Red Cross Conference in Geneva, they stated their goal to engage all of those children in school correspondence. The vast majority of Junior Red Cross correspondence tied together children from the United States and Western Europe. But Latin American countries participated in the exchange as well. Junior Red Cross organizers expressed their hope that relationships forged through the letters would diminish international friction simply by raising the level of the interwar generation's global awareness.[50] The Mexican division of the Junior Red Cross, established in 1928, summarized its mission neither as an arbitrating, individualizing charity nor as a recreational institution but rather as a socializing one based on service and education. A special subcommittee within the Junior Red Cross, the Committee of Foreign Children (El Comité de Niños Extranjeros)—sometimes called the Committee of Universal Fraternity (El Comité de Fraternidad Universal)—took charge of promoting knowledge about children outside of Mexico and organizing the correspondence program.[51]

For those not fortunate enough to belong to an organized letter-exchange program, other avenues provided access to the international children's community. Free publications such as *El Maestro Rural* and the SEP bulletins often included foreign greetings and messages of solidarity addressed to "the children of Mexico." A 1930 letter from Australian schoolchildren in New South Wales published in *El Maestro Rural* briefly outlined the Pacific nation's history—a reference to forging a new, free, and productive race from enslaved and outcast ancestors resonated with the mestizo paradigm that Mexican children were now being taught.[52] Accompanying the letter a map of the American and Australian continents drew a direct line from Sidney to Mexico City, a unifying gesture linking the hearts of the two nations, while reducing all of the interfering geography to blank space.

In 1935 one group of fifth grade Mexican students from a small village in Chihuahua corresponded with their counterparts in Havana, Cuba. A response, penned by Cuban student Victor San Emeterio, came to the attention of Mexico's Ministry of Foreign Relations and was promptly published in *El Maestro Rural*, a widely circulated biweekly magazine for rural schoolteachers from the Ministry of Education. Victor relayed his compatriots' most sincere greetings to their peers, acknowledging "the love and pain of the race (*la raza*)" and empathizing with the "noble yet justified pain that our race provokes."[53] As evidence of solidarity the Cuban students evoked the names of independence heroes from both countries: Hidalgo, Morelos, Maceo, and Martí. Historical references to Mexico's Grito de Hidalgo demonstrated that the Cuban students understood the links between Latin American independence movements, rather than individual, unrelated nationalist expressions. They acknowledged shared cultural traditions; radio broadcasts of music from both countries soothed souls on both sides of the Gulf of Mexico. Sixth grade Cuban student Antonio Guzmán Upierre proposed four activities that would further unify the two groups: expositions of each other's drawings, essay competitions, programs to raise money for the exchange of national flags and the Bandera de la Raza, and the request that a famous Mexican poet write the lyrics to the "Anthem of the Race" ("Himno de la Raza") and a famous Cuban poet compose the music.[54]

Children's toys, and especially dolls, became commodities symbolic of international friendship, as museums and exhibition halls around the world displayed them as emblems of humanity. Early-twentieth-century modern toys bore a false simplicity, as Walter Benjamin noted, that undercut the technical achievements in toy making perfected in Germany in the nineteenth century. Rather than produce items that reflected technological advances, many preferred to develop a relationship with the primitive in a time of industrial development.[55] As symbols of play dolls represented innocence and infantile cooperation and collaboration, characteristics that lay at the core of international peace.[56] Dolls also allowed for the perfect embodiment of stereotypical national types: paired male and female dolls that typified a country provided the perfect package for the creation of a single national phenotype as well as a gendered ideal. Not surprisingly, by the mid-1920s the *charro* and the *china poblana* became the favored version of Mexico to be exported abroad, as seen in the exchange between the children of Tampico and Philadelphia.

Other countries looked to Mexico to provide models of the incorporation of folkloric toys and games for their children's instruction. Requests came from Spain for traditionally dressed dolls from Mexico, for both children's education and to foment international friendship as part of a display in an annual fair. The Ministry of Foreign Relations (Secretaría de Relaciones Exteriores [SRE]) responded simply with a directive to its bureaucrats to send two dolls with "indigenous characteristics." Spanish officials countered that they wanted more varied representation from twelve different regions of the country, and the SRE complied. This representation of ethnic regionalism reflected the power that children's playthings had in constructing nationalist images. Swaddled in the stereotypical material trappings of their nation of origin, each doll literally embodied the national ideal, codifying a set of ideas about different regions while ostensibly promoting the idea of peace.[57] In another instance, a teacher from Jefferson School in Shawnee, Oklahoma, wrote to the Ministry of Education that her students had fashioned two six-inch dolls, representative of a typical elementary-aged American boy and girl, that they would like to exchange for similar dolls from Mexico.[58] It would be left to the children themselves to determine what constituted "typical" Mexico for international export.

A quite elaborate request for international doll exchanges made its way to President Calles's office from the Church of Christ headquarters in New York. As a labor of their Committee of World Friendship among Children, the church organized a Festival of Dolls, in which dolls representing their countries of origin traveled around the world bearing messages of goodwill, accompanied by passports documenting their ports of entry and length of stay. Young volunteers in New York assembled and dressed the dolls according to the specifications of each country, all based on the new American doll prototype, made of washable materials, fifteen inches high, with articulated arms and legs, moving eyes with eyelashes, a sewed wig, a cotton stuffed body, and a "mama voice."[59] Evidence has not been located of Mexican participation in the Festival of Dolls; nevertheless, children's playthings commonly served diplomatic and educational purposes abroad at World's Fairs and expositions.

The SRE considered an international charity toy drive hosted by the Sunshine Letters Club at "one of the finest hotels" in Detroit to be a good form of publicity for the country and sent along a doll dressed in typical *china poblana* fashion.[60] The doll represented the nation's children as conflated with their playthings. When the doll was donated to a poor child, Mexico's growing toy industry received favorable press in Detroit papers.[61] Doll diplomacy and other examples of nationalist children's culture served a purpose in international affairs. Even in the throes of nationalist fervor, upper- and middle-class children across the globe were forging a spirit of international camaraderie through shared cultural references and experiences.

While the exchange of letters, albums, and dolls served to strengthen nationalist sentiments for both the sender and the recipient, it also expanded the transnational brotherhood among Latin American children by providing them with common cultural experiences, music, language, and symbols.

Exploradores at Home and Abroad:
Straddling Modernity and Tradition

The *Washington Post* reported, in a smattering of articles in 1927 and 1928, on the curious phenomenon of Mexican Boy Scouts making pilgrimages on foot between their nation's capital and that of the United States. In May 1927 two young men named José and Gregorio (their last names were not provided) arrived in Washington DC, en route to New York, ostensibly with the sole mission of extending fraternal greetings to their brothers, the American Boy Scouts.[62] The following year eighteen-year-old Robert Domínguez, another Mexican Boy Scout, followed in their footsteps and earned national attention by collecting autographs of local governmental authorities along the way, culminating in meeting First Lady Grace Coolidge at the White House, after waiting several days as a guest of the Mexican Embassy. In his photograph in the *Post* Robert was the picture of the modern Boy Scout: his uniform appeared pressed, his hair neatly combed, his face tanned from the long journey, and his smile amicable and confident. He wore the trademark kerchief of the Boy Scouts in a knot tied neatly at his throat.[63] Like his predecessors, Robert continued on to New York, impressing the nation with his stamina, charm, and goodwill, as he exported a vision of Mexican youth that competed with that of a nation of savage atavists. These young men acted as ambassadors of modernity, in their capacity as members of an internationally recognized organization. Their presence in the U.S. press complicated the vision of ancient Mexico for American readers and served as a cultural symbol of international solidarity in peacetime years. Nevertheless, they fought an uphill battle, as a view of the barbaric Mexico remained firmly entrenched in the international collective imaginary.

The Boy Scouts, founded in England by General Robert Baden-Powell in 1899, became a global phenomenon by 1908 with the publication of the manual *Scouting for Boys*.[64] The Mexican Boy Scouts, inaugurated in 1917 as the Corps of Mexican Explorers and later the Tribes of Mexican Explorers (Tribus de Exploradores Mexicanos), grew under the direction of German-born Mexican citizen Federico Clarck.[65] Clarck had dedicated years to the observation of Boy Scout organizations in eighteen countries around the world. He modeled his vision directly on the international Boy Scout organization, but it quickly adopted a distinctly nationalist hue. Clarck published a four-volume manual titled *El Explorador Mexicano*, versions and excerpts of which appeared in related popular children's magazines published by the Boy Scouts, *Tihui* and *El Scout*. These publications, based heavily on the U.S. magazine *Boys' Life*, were nevertheless edited to include references to national history, geography, and heroes. The combination of foreign elements and national symbols lent a gravitas to the patriotism that these publications inspired in their boy readers, all of which reflected Baden-Powell's philosophy that nationalism and internationalism ought not to be mutually exclusive categories. Organized Scout activity began in earnest in the calendar year of 1928; in September of that year the First National Congress of the Tribes of Mexican Explorers met to assess their labors nationwide. At this meeting, sponsored in part by the Ministry of Education, 122 Scout delegates representing forty-eight institutions nationwide convened under the direction of José U. Escobar, national director of the Explorers.[66]

Mexican boys responded overwhelmingly to the new social option. At the 1928 meeting, a scant year after the formalization of Explorer activities, Mexico City alone boasted twenty "tribes" of Explorers that served 700 members, with another 150 in San Luis Potosí, 90 in Puebla, and 120 in Chihuahua. Representatives from many other states in the republic had written to the national headquarters either expressing interest in forming a nationally recognized chapter or announcing that Scout mobilization had already taken place.[67] Between 1921 and 1938 the number of Mexican Boy Scouts had gone from 876 to 11,724 members across the republic, not including the uncounted numbers of affiliated and unofficial groups.[68] Escobar enthused that the only limitation on Scout membership was the availability of qualified directors, since boys everywhere were anxious to join. To that end the Ministry of Education founded an Academy for Scout Leaders as part of the National Preparatory School, which by 1928 had enrolled 90 young men in training to lead future troops.[69]

The Mexican Boy Scout program was not officially integrated into the national educational curriculum, but the SEP did support the organization by sponsoring its publications (including the monthly magazine *Tihui*) and encouraging teachers to promote membership among their students. In 1928 the SEP hosted the First National Explorers' Conference, a four-day affair presided over by Minister of Education José M. Puig Casauranc. Moisés Sáenz served as the SEP liaison to the organization, and under his advisement the Boy Scouts' curricular material remained aligned to the national curricular goals. Members could fulfill the training requirements for leadership positions within the National School of Physical Education, a dependency of the SEP. Boy Scout troops tended to form around the social nucleus created by the classroom, although not exclusively.[70] The Mexican Boy Scouts approximated the moral, nationalist behavior that revolutionary officials at the SEP imagined in molding the ideal citizen of the nation's youth. Its close relationship with the SEP notwithstanding, the Boy Scouts retained status as a private organization, a status that allowed it to enjoy the support of other nongovernmental organizations, such as the Asociación Cristiana de Jóvenes and the Asociación Cristiana Femenina (the national branches of the YMCA and YWCA [Young Women's Christian Association]), that otherwise would not have worked comfortably under staunchly secular state auspices.

Only the Mexican military rivaled the Boy Scouts in its methodical construction of a homosocial space and articulations of traditional gender conducts, couched in the language of revolutionary nationalism. Above all, the organization helped to foment the incipient masculinity of its young members. According to the organization's guidelines, officially admitted members needed to be at least twelve years old, on the cusp of manhood.[71] Recruiters assumed that the young men would respond to their articulation of a masculine ideal: a desire to be exemplary citizens, soldiers, and men. The magazine *Tihui* reminded its readers of the importance of masculine values:

> To be a man is to put aside egoism, engage in selfless acts. To be a man is to climb great spiritual heights, so high (higher than the steepest mountains). . . . To be a man is to be simple, to be formal, to be a gentleman, to be friendly, to be generous. If you want to follow this sacrificial path of self-discipline and education, of self-control, come and join the Explorers, who will receive you with open arms, as a new brother. . . . [O]nce you are convinced of your ability to meet these requirements, resolve yourself to join our ranks, to work with enthusiasm for the grandeur of our *Patria*, and for the good of humanity.[72]

As if to underscore the affirmations of masculinity mentioned above, photos of Scout excursions published in *Tihui* accentuate the physical quality of the young bodies and their dominant position over nature. The boys always appear atop of a feminized natural form, whether mountains, hills, trees, or rocks, with their arms jauntily akimbo. The relationship between nascent masculinity and a nation newly articulated by a succession of revolutionary administrations took the form of exploring, experiencing, and conquering the national terrain. The expeditions of the Scouts served to familiarize youth with the Mexican countryside and to prepare them for future military campaigns through hikes, equestrianism, and camping trips. Even the name of the organization, "Explorers," evoked its principal purpose: to explore the country and learn its geography in order to foment an understanding of what it meant to be Mexican based on the physical experiences of the group members. Through their apprenticeships and excursions, the youngsters learned to emulate national military heroes, learned the names and properties of native plants and animals, and became familiar with the geographical features of the national landscape.

They took hiking trips to the iconic volcanoes Popocatépetl and Orizaba and other sites around the republic. In this sense the Explorers, or Scouts, reaffirmed the geopolitical boundaries of the nation through their explorations of its limits.

One of the stated goals of the Boy Scouts was to awaken a sympathy and appreciation for military life. The Boy Scouts were also considered a way to morally cleanse the military, allowing it to serve as a feeder organization for the national military over the course of a generation. In a memo Clarck once articulated to the secretary of war and marines that he hoped to create a reserve for the nation, with the "possibility of plucking from the young Explorers, true and good Officials so that [military men] may all be cultured and educated."[73]

Such preoccupation with the establishment of societal norms manifested itself in the public arena as a nearly obsessive concern for the gender socialization of children. Not surprisingly, the Boy Scouts' link to the military attracted the attention of a few demagogues. In a moment in which Mexico was undergoing a crisis of masculinity—the country had not yet recovered from the death of a generation of virile revolutionaries—some citizens feared that the Boy Scouts were insufficiently masculine and aggressive to defend the nation in the event of an armed conflict. In both the press and official papers, a small flurry of correspondence from individuals reveals a hypermasculine, militarized countercurrent to reform the Boy Scouts. In 1925 private citizen José Antonio Del Río sent President Plutarco Elías Calles a manifesto about the crisis of young masculinity and the urgent need to address the issue on a national level. Making reference to Calles as the patriarch of the "greater Mexican family," Del Río called attention to his responsibility as head of the nation to intercede "with a strong and virile hand" in the socialization of the youth, "to cement a strong and vigorous nationalism."[74] According to Del Río, only a strong state could control the civilizing process to establish the behavioral patterns of its citizens. He argued that the best approach would be to "organize the youth; put them in the first instance on the track to order, bringing to completion a true readjustment in the discipline of the people . . . forge the national spirit through an education based on practical teachings of civics and organization, and with this we will have given shape to a nationalism that is truly vigorous and forceful."[75] Clearly a product of a generation unsettled by a decade of violence, mayhem, and fragmented government, Del Río expressed the commonly held belief that the survival of the nation depended upon the socialization of a generation of young men under the careful direction of father figures, educators, and especially strong presidents like Calles.

By another token Professor Alfred Sánchez O., proponent of a more radical branch of the Boy Scouts that he would have designated the Mexican Legionnaires, expressed the necessity to defend the *patria* and argued that the strengthening of masculinity could not reach its potential through the Boy Scouts. According to Sánchez, the "regrettable but inevitable" need to kill the enemy should take precedence over natural history in the Scouts' training. As part of a weeklong series of editorials that Sánchez ran in the newspaper, he exclaimed, "But are we going to try to suffocate our bellicose instinct? . . . What child has not gleaned pleasure from military arrogance, martial expressions, the marching of the troops?"[76] The proposed Legionnaires never came to fruition; nevertheless, the hyperbolic discourse evoked by both Sánchez and Del Río in the national press over young masculinity captivated the public imaginary.

Notwithstanding the foreign inspiration that led to the foundation of the Mexican Boy Scouts, Clarck and the other coordinators moved rapidly to infuse the corps with identifiably national content. At the 1928 national meeting the executive committee and members voted overwhelmingly that the Explorers would be a nationalist organization and not simply a Mexican mimicry of a foreign institution.[77] To that end delegates proposed incorporating Boy Scout activities more seamlessly into the primary and secondary educational curriculum. As *Tihui* announced, "The Tribes of Mexican Explorers are inspired by the best teachings of Baden-Powell, and recognizes as brothers all of the members of the Great International Brotherhood of Explorers; but our institution possesses a unique program, adapted to our needs, that has not been copied from other foreign organizations, and that has as a base the heritage of the great founders of our country."[78]

Through survival techniques learned in the open air, physical challenges to strengthen the body, and practical exercises in the natural sciences, the boys learned a brand of civics that converted the rather abstract revolutionary nationalism into a set of basic, tangible techniques that became the indispensable tool kit for initiation into citizenry. One of the highlights was "Boy Scout Week" (Semana del Explorador), a reunion of Scouts from around the country in the nation's capital during the month of November (to coincide with the celebration commemorating the start of the Mexican Revolution). In 1929 the activities that constituted the event consisted of an antialcohol parade (the favored cause of then president Emilio Portes Gil); an open house at the national headquarters to showcase their activity space to family and friends; a *vivac* (campfire activity with dramatic presentations) in Chapultepec Park; a pet exhibition and contest; assembly of troops and ceremony awarding honorary degrees and diplomas; an excursion to a nursery on the outskirts of the city; a night of theater with presentations by various Boy Scouts; a day of visitations to prisons, hospitals, and correctional schools; and a vigil in honor of the heroes of independence.[79] For Scouts from outside of Mexico City this week of activities forged in them a sense of community with their compatriots, and coming to the capital city gave them an idea of the grandeur of the country that they represented and protected through membership in the organization.[80] But the presence of so many uniformed Scouts all over the city also served to make them more visible to the rest of the nation, a source of pride and honor, cloaked in modern uniforms based on European models. The Boy Scouts thus underscored *mexicanidad*, or Mexicanness, even as they emblematized the international youth movement.

Yet even as events such as these brought together far-flung branches of the Boy Scouts, the organization grappled with a troubled relationship with its regional—primarily indigenous—

membership. Scout officials took ambivalent approaches to the symbolic and real treatment of indigenous representation in the organization. At the suggestion of the Ministry of Education, Explorer culture projected nativism through many elements that reinforced the unifying myth that all Mexicans boast an Aztec heritage.[81] The youth adorned their uniforms with an eight-point badge in a motif inspired by the Aztec calendar stone. Corporate structure divided the members along hierarchal groups denominated "tribes," as if to underscore the ancestral nature of groupings of young men to learn about nature, survival, and warfare. Hierarchical titles all derived from Nahuatl, the language of the Aztec empire, and corresponded to levels of the pre-Columbian government. The individual members of each tribe were called *tequihua* ("explorer" in Nahuatl); the leaders of the troops at different levels all had corresponding Nahua names: *tepushtlato, tecuhtli, tlacatecuhtli,* and *tacatecatecuhtli,* in order of rank.[82] The indigenous names of the various groups had no relationship to the ethnicity of the membership; to the contrary indigenous people served as more of a mascot to the organization than as a meaningful cultural representation.

The cases of the Girl Guides in England, Canada, and India during the same decades prove instructive; in these organizations the noted underrepresentation of local ethnic and indigenous groups among Guide membership signaled a "tension between the ideal of inclusiveness and the reality of exclusiveness."[83] In Mexico, despite the fact that many Scouts hailed from white middle-class backgrounds—a trend reflected in the photos published in the manual and in *Tihui*—Scout culture fostered a brand of national pride based on an idealized indigenous past. The phenomenon of nativism in nature-based organizations characterized the Boy Scouts and Girl Scouts in the United States as well; titles and camps named after tribes were more symbolic than anything and reflected no measure of educational or cultural content. In the Northeast of the United States during the first decades of the twentieth century, the Camp Fire Girls promoted a nativist aesthetic in the girls' uniforms (a simple vest adorned with colored beads that corresponded to the different "honors" or duties that the girls completed). The girls also received ceremonial names derived from indigenous languages.[84]

The relationship between the Mexican Scouts and their supposed ancestors manifested itself in much the same way. Rhetorically, the Scouts celebrated "the virtues of audacity, fortitude, bravery, ingenuity, knowledge of the secrets of natural life," characteristics ascribed to the ancient native tribes; they aspired to embody these virtues that "abounded in those men." For Scouts, the pre-Columbian "bronzed race" was the fountain of their appreciation of nature. Regardless, Scout officials made it quite clear that, despite having derived from ancient civilizations "the most noble and fertile elements," the organization did not intend for the youth to regress to savagery. In reality, living native groups still bore the stigma of atavism in relationship to the modern world.[85] Scout culture relegated indigenous groups so far to the distant past that it overlooked their rich potential to contribute to the Scouts' natural science education in life. Rather than acknowledge the millions of living native people who populated the country, the editors of *Tihui* encouraged their young readers to "love that which sleeps in the silence of death, to comprehend that which palpitates in the throngs of life."[86]

Scouts learned, then, that indigenous culture was best understood as a historical echo, rather than a vibrant source from which to learn modern-day lessons. Notwithstanding the copious references to an idealized past within the Scout program, little evidence exists to suggest that the Scouts fought to rectify the miserable political, social, and economic conditions suffered by the actual indigenous people of revolutionary Mexico. To be sure, in some cases, Scouts made an effort to improve the lives of their indigenous countrymen, albeit with a measure of condescension. There exists a reference in a document from the 1927 IV Congress of Students, in which the tribes of Explorers assumed the "lofty social mission in favor of the redemption of our Indians," but no further details emerge.[87] Ignacio Acosta, one of the "Distinguished Boys" of the Scouting group named "the Maya Tribe," carried out social projects in the states of

Tlaxcala and Morelos and claimed that his personal mission was to "civilize the Indians,"[88] further evidence that he and his peers likely did not consider them to be on par with the expectations of modernity espoused by the organization.

In addition to the indisputable national content, the Mexican Scout organization remained faithful to European and U.S. models. The international visibility of the Mexican members broadcast to the world the message that Mexico had completed its civilizing mission among the revolutionary generation and boasted a modern young population. Postrevolutionary historiography has not traditionally characterized Mexico as an exporter of culture but rather as a country that absorbed and modified international modes and norms within a nationalist framework. Historian Joanne Hershfield suggests that postrevolutionary Mexico was characterized by a version of modernity that combined and confused foreign influences with newly constructed forms of nationalist expression, thus allowing traditional and modern hallmarks of culture to coexist.[89] The case of the Boy Scouts in the international arena demonstrates that Mexico not only projected global modernity outward through its participation in international youth organizations, but it did so by making explicit references to a recently articulated set of distinctly national cultural symbols.

One of the much-publicized advantages of being a Scout was membership in a brotherhood, the ability to identify each other through a mutual understanding of commonly shared signs, codes, symbols, and basic techniques that were hallmarks of Baden-Powell's founding organization. Scout brothers were to sacrifice themselves for each other and with open arms receive each other in any corner of the globe.[90] Allegedly, or ideally, Scouts learned Esperanto as a universal language to be able to communicate with their brothers abroad. All Scouts used the international slogan "Be Prepared" (Siempre Listos).[91] But above all the uniform stood out as the most conspicuous stamp of international Scout culture.

The modernity aspired to by the meticulously dressed Scout came at a cost: the abandonment of Code 6 in the *Manual del*

Explorador, which read: "The Explorer is a friend to all and considers all other Explorers to be his brother, without class distinction."[92] Technically, the manual stipulated the uniform as a requirement, a measure designed both to avoid "disorder" as well as to maintain "the respect that our Institution deserves."[93] Ostensibly, the uniform also served to erase class differences, and therefore to allow the boys to focus on forging brotherly bonds based on character. Scout officials made an effort—at least in the manual—to maintain democracy among the organization's membership. Any corps of Explorers that wanted to make the uniform obligatory had to first ensure that no prospective member would be excluded due to lack of resources. Clarck did his best to disabuse boys of the apparently conventional wisdom that the most "basic" kit for the Scout ought to include "at least one gendarme suit, traffic police gaiters, a canteen imported from Boston or Saint Louis, an American camp tent, and an assortment of other things that would allow only the most well-off boys, those capable of spending seventy or eight pesos in vanities, to become Explorers."[94] Clarck's declaration, reiterated in *Tihui,* suggested that many boys still perceived exclusivity among the ranks of the Explorers and that lack of access to a uniform still kept some boys away.

Yet this equalizing rhetoric did not match the commercial flurry in which Boy Scouts often found themselves caught up; children's magazines, daily newspapers, and pamphlets featured advertisements for Boy Scout paraphernalia that suggested that, in addition to demonstrating their service to the nation, the boy Explorers were expected to support the national economy as well, through the purchase of their uniforms, accessories, and related goods in Mexican stores, approved official outlets of Boy Scout accessories (fig. 48). A template of the ideal Explorer's accoutrements printed in the manual demonstrates that a boy would need to be well accommodated in order to fulfill expectations.[95] From an early age, then, Mexican boys learned the value of economic nationalism and its physical manifestation proved through the standardization of uniforms. The uniform was a symbol of modernity and economic prosperity, a luxury

48. Advertisement in *Tihui* for Explorer supplies, 1927. *Tihui*, no. 2 (January 1927): 37. Courtesy of the Hemeroteca Nacional.

out of the reach of many boys, and one that attested globally that Mexico was capable of participating on an international level in Scout culture. The child defender of the *patria*, then, was a middle-class boy, one who stood apart from the average boy (a glaring contrast to the proletarian model upheld by educational officials in other realms).[96]

Individual Scouts' physical appearances and details of their uniforms received special attention in the Scout cultural media outlets, earning praise when they conformed to the standards set by their international peers. Authenticity mattered. In 1921 Clarck petitioned the Calles government to fund a shopping trip to New York, so that he could purchase one hundred official Boy Scout uniforms and accessories (hunting jersey, riding pants, silk kerchiefs, tents, cots, hatchets, and first-aid kits). Clarck procured gymnastic equipment from Hamburg, in his native country, so that the boys' exercise and routine could be structured and yield the same results as on young German boys.[97] Presumably, the correct official trappings would help to ensure that Mexicans be perceived as authentic members of global Scouting culture.

Clearly, the average Mexican boy struggled to keep up with the aesthetic standard. One photograph of the Telpatl Tribe, a recently founded corps in the state of Veracruz, depicts its humble members with straw sombreros making an excursion by foot from their school, because they did not have the money to pay for the train fare. Only the kerchiefs tied at their necks identify them as Explorers.[98] In another photograph of the same "tribe," the small country boys can be seen on the peak of a local hill, near where they live. They are wearing the same sombreros and white tunics customary among indigenous people, and they carry woven satchels instead of the manufactured backpacks advertised for sale at official Scout stores.[99] Official Scout publications, sponsored by the Association of Mexican Scouts (Asociación de Exploradores Mexicanos), tried to promote Scout membership as within reach of all Mexican boys. Nevertheless, the uniform and its accessories distinguished a first-rate Scout from his peers.[100]

Tihui published articles and photos of exemplary Scouts, praising them in all aspects from the cleanliness of their uniforms to their acts of charity in a section of the magazine titled "Distinguished Boys." Not surprisingly, none of the humble *tequihuas* in the photograph from Veracruz received special mention in this section; the poorer troops only appeared depicted in groups. The distinguished boys—a quick overview of their photographs indicates that they were overwhelmingly light skinned, and at least one boy, Shafick Kaim, was foreign born—enjoyed a featured profile in the magazine that instructed their fellow Scouts and readers on exemplary Scout behavior. Readers learned, for example, that young Nicolás Carmona was fastidious in the care of his uniform, so much so that he chose to wear white pants on rural excursions to demonstrate his dedication to cleanliness; Janet del Castillo liked to wear his boots in the style of the Three Musketeers, and both boys earned an official Scout kerchief for their charity work.[101] These personal details underscore the observation that the ideal child defender of the *patria* was also a child of means.

The introduction of the Boy Scouts to Mexico met with resistance from various individuals. Some expressed aversion to the military nature of the corps. Others viewed Boy Scouts with animosity because of an automatic association with U.S. or British culture. The Mexican consul in Texas reported that first-generation Mexican American families' greatest fear of impending cultural decay was to see the son dressed in a Boy Scout uniform, saluting the American flag.[102] Professor Alfredo Sánchez O., the aforementioned proponent of the nationalist military corps of Legionnaires and the most vocal critic of the organization, warned that even if children could afford the uniforms and accessories—including the twenty-cent monthly *Tihui*—the brown-skinned little Explorers would never blend with the blond-haired, blue-eyed Scouts abroad.[103] Yet it was the middle-class version of Mexican youth, armed with a readily identifiable uniform and a confident affability, that Mexico exported to the world. The Mexican Boy Scouts formed part of the international Boy Scout organization and thus signaled Mexico's arrival on the modern stage, with a growing middle class and a strong, healthy, and patriotic youth. They approached Scout activities eager to participate on an equal level alongside their international peers. Yet the American collective imaginary, as we have seen, was already saturated with a monolithic version of Mexico and its inhabitants.

Young cultural ambassadors such as the long-distance-walking Scouts José, Gregorio, and Robert literally transported an alternate vision of their country into the United States. Their presence in the U.S. press helped to counter, however moderately, antiquated notions of Mexico. Mexican Scouts quickly gained footing in the international arena and in the process found that they had to negotiate the difference between their modern version of *mexicanidad* and that imposed from abroad. Whereas at home Mexican Scouts learned to eschew indigenous identity in all but symbolic realms, when abroad they found idealized nativism to be imbued with positive characteristics. Some evidence suggests that, through their engagement with transnational organizations, Mexican youth more openly adopted ethnic cultural markers, thus subverting the cultural imperialism built into the Scout organization.

In 1937 at an international Boy Scout conference held in Washington DC, the Mexican delegation called the attention of the press by setting up camp directly beneath the Washington Monument. They proudly raised the Mexican flag over their camp and, lest there be any doubt as to their provenance, wore brightly colored woven *sarapes* from Saltillo, the "Mexican blanket" that adorned nearly every popular depiction of Mexicans in American culture. The boys hailed from Monterrey, Mexico City, Torreón, and Puebla (among the country's most modern cities) and camped between peers from Lithuania and the Netherlands.[104] In Mexico the ideal Scout would avoid such glaring accoutrements that associated him with the popular classes and would opt instead for the European-style militarized uniform. But in the United States, and under an international spotlight, Mexican Scouts faced the quandary of distinguishing themselves as distinctly Mexican; they turned to the imagery codified in American popular culture and embraced it as their own.

As if to demonstrate their deft ability to navigate the muddy waters of exported national identity, after the conference "los boys mexicanos" (as the Mexican national press dubbed them, Anglicized by virtue of their presence in Gringolandia) went to New York City to tour the Empire State Building and the offices of the upcoming World's Fair (where technological, architectural, and scientific feats would be showcased as accomplishments of distinct nations). There, retired marine chief of the U.S. military William H. Standley received the young men and remarked that they were the most virile and distinguished group of Boy Scouts he had ever met. The photo that accompanied the article affirmed that Mexico had sent its most masculine youth on the international tour; some of the "boys" competed with Standley in height, and a few showed the furtive signs of mustaches (fig. 49). In this encounter the attention received by

49. Mexican Boy Scouts in New York, during a visit to the World's Fair headquarters. *Hoy*, August 7, 1937, 63.

the Explorers in the Mexican national press affirmed the relationship between Scouting and militarized masculinity, as well as their role as cultural ambassadors finessing the line between nationalism and internationalism.

The Mexican Junior Red Cross and the Big Sister Committee

The Red Cross movement had nineteenth-century European origins but gained momentum in the 1880s with its foundation in the United States by Clara Barton. At the behest of President Woodrow Wilson in 1917, the Junior Red Cross formed and organized youth for relief and aid during the First World War. The Mexican Red Cross immediately incorporated a youth section upon the official establishment of its national chapter in 1926. Each issue of the organization's monthly magazine, *La Cruz Roja Mexicana*, dedicated several pages to youth activity.[105] In April 1928 the first national chapter of the Mexican Junior Red Cross was formed officially, through which children (and especially girls) across the country began to enact the modern principles of international fraternity and patriotic service.

The international Junior Red Cross, and all of its member national chapters, assumed as a primary goal "training for citizenship"; Red Cross officials broadly defined citizenship as becoming a serviceable member of society, rather than carrying out political rights and responsibilities.[106] Young members understood citizenship to be both national and global, as Junior Red Cross organizations swelled in numbers in the peacetime era. By 1931 Mexico figured among forty-eight countries with a nationally recognized chapter, and regional organizations such as the Pan-American Union formed to maintain fraternity among the distinct national groups.[107] International exchanges, primarily through school correspondence, kept the young members in touch with one another and, along with official magazines, provided the primary means by which they learned about the lives of people their age in other countries. These avenues of communication had a dual impact: On the one hand, children learned and expressed a national sense of self relative to their international peers, as internationalism crested. On the other hand, the unprecedented flow of information among and between member nations necessitated a distillation of diverse cultures into a codified set of national "types," readily identifiable by essentialized costumes, ethnic features, and iconic geographies. The Junior Red Cross international exchanges allowed for children to project recently acquired national identity (in the words of the American Red Cross national director, no longer "my country—*against* the world" but "my country—*for* the world"),[108] an important shift that marked the 1930s, and poignantly so in Mexico. Mexico participated through its own chapter of the Junior Red Cross, which translated patriotic service to a reflection of international values of brotherhood and charity.

As implied by their name, the tribes of Mexican Explorers ranged the physical terrain of their *patria* and the globe, conquering mountain peaks and embodying modernity. By contrast, despite a relative spike in possibilities for children's civic engagement in the 1920s and 1930s, schoolgirls learned to love the *patria* from the safety of their homes and neighborhoods.

Girl Scouts existed in Mexico as early as 1925, although on a much smaller scale than the Explorers. Like their male counterparts, the Girl Scouts engaged in excursions to experience physical, moral, and personal development as individuals. Nevertheless, the majority of their activities fell within the traditional gendered sphere for women in the household.[109] At the First National Congress of Explorers in 1926, a presentation by delegate Celia Tovar marked the difference between the expectations of youth organizations for men and for women: "If humanity urgently needs the perfection of man, no less urgent is that of woman, the irreplaceable base upon which the home, society, and Patria are formed."[110] The editors of *Tihui* carefully justified the physical excursions of female Explorer groups in the context of a modernized domesticity, framing the girl explorer in her future role as "the wife of tomorrow, the strong woman, the clean woman, the mother of our future sons, greater than her present state, since these roles have not yet been realized."[111] Relative to their male classmates, young women's citizenship exercises were seen more as training than as immediate action.

Most commonly, middle-class girls blessed with spare time put their civic duties to practice through the Junior Red Cross. While open to boys and girls alike, the Junior Red Cross came to be one of the most popular and socially accepted domains in which girls could develop a civic identity. In fact, Junior Red Cross membership gained a reputation as an exemplary activity precisely because of its dual emphasis on confraternity and gendered performances of service. Evidence of this can be observed in a staged photograph, taken in 1931 or 1932, of students from a school in Tamaulipas enacting a first-aid rescue (fig. 50). The content and circumstances of the photograph allow for its interpretation. The activities and uniforms displayed by the students pantomime the gendered roles that the international organization encouraged. The spheres of the image are divided down the middle: boys stand to the left, and girls stand to the right. The girls wear the starched white nurse frocks and headdresses typical of Red Cross volunteers that suggest their angelic, virginal, and hygienic presence. The

50. Students at a school in Tamaulipas enact a first-aid rescue, ca. 1932.
Archivo Histórico de la Secretaría de Relaciones Exteriores.

boys wear Western garb, collared shirts and ties, and one even
wears a suit. They project a visage of transnational modernity,
scientific knowledge, and moral authority. All of the students signal their affiliation by wearing the red cross on their armband
or headdresses. One of the boys straddles the victim, rendered
unconscious by an unknown cause, administering direct medical attention (and thus, presumably, the cure and solution to
the problem). Meanwhile, one of the girls cradles the victim's
head in her lap, resting a soothing maternal hand on his fore-
head while she solemnly regards the camera. Regardless of the
drama of this emergency rescue, it is not the visual focus of the
photograph. At the center of the image, framed both by the
arch of the school building and by a banner that proclaims the
school as an "Escuela Tipo" (or model school), stands the young
man in the suit, perhaps representing a Red Cross administrator. Of the dozen figures, he bears the authority, sanctioning
the rescue and embodying a version of modern, civic-minded
childhood upheld as the ideal. The boys engage in more active

and authoritative roles, whereas the girls appear more passive and symbolic. The photograph, housed in the archives of the Ministry of Foreign Relations, appears to have been collected as part of an international propaganda effort by the Mexican government to demonstrate the intellectual, economic, and social productivity of children in the nation's schools.[112]

The organization had several subcommittees, but the only one that limited its membership exclusively to girls was the Big Sister Committee (Comité de la Hermana Mayor). The subcommittee name makes a doubly gendered reference to both the traditional domestic role of girls (the big sister as mother's little helper) and the historically religious origins of the Red Cross (nuns or "sisters" carrying out much of the charity work). According to the bylaws of the committee, the Big Sister represented the private sphere of the home while she was at school, and she was the ambassador of modern education within the home. At school the Big Sister collected clothing for donation to the poor, doled out snacks to the other children, read stories to the younger students, protected the younger students on the playground during recess, accompanied younger students home after school, and took care of them during school field trips. At home the Big Sister took care of sick parents, cooked and sewed, applied modern scientific puericulture techniques learned at school to the rearing of younger siblings, and organized simple social receptions, contests, and exhibitions of their domestic talents.[113]

Far from revolutionary in its treatment of feminine childhood, the Big Sister Committee upheld the traditional role of girls as agents of domestic harmony.[114] Yet in the creation and naming of a Junior Red Cross Committee, the language used in the manual gave revolutionary value to the civic and domestic responsibilities and chores that, frankly, composed the schedules of many girls' lives anyway, where previously they would not have been given any recognition. These activities all trained the young girls to be little mothers but with the added responsibility—framed in nationalist discourse—to raise future citizens of their own according to the dictates of health and science that were being transmitted through the Red Cross.

Classist assumptions informed the creation of this elite subgroup of girls. National Red Cross officials justified the creation of the Big Sister Committee based on a study that alleged that girls from impoverished homes had more than twenty-four counted domestic chores, many of which they carried out inefficiently. The language employed by Red Cross officials betrayed a misunderstanding of the root causes and daily experiences of poverty and suggested that the poor simply did not possess the knowledge to clean their homes according to modern hygienic standards.[115] By contrast the same officials characterized girls from middle-class homes with a tendency to spend their spare time reading novels, potentially introducing morally corrosive forces for female youth.[116] The Big Sister Committee would bridge this gap, ostensibly by optimizing the free time of middle-class girls and putting it to work at the service of their less educated, and by implication less capable, lower-class peers. Condescension followed as a nearly inevitable by-product of juxtaposing the two social groups. The young members of the Big Sister Committee from the Galación Gómez Elementary School in the nation's capital took the charge to heart; they re-created a miniature "humble" home as a teaching model to demonstrate efficiencies and organizational tools that would instruct impoverished women on hygienic home economics that characterized the modern "cultured person."[117]

The Western auspices of the Red Cross in Mexico drove an uneasy wedge in race relations, as members struggled to showcase their nationalism while also demonstrating their transnational modernity. Nowhere was this disjuncture more poignantly displayed than in the Red Cross iconography. The February 1928 cover of the magazine *La Cruz Roja Mexicana* displays a scene following a devastating flood. A pair of tattered campesinos, infantilized by their diminutive stature, sag wearily into the embrace of a looming white Red Cross nurse, as their humble house lies in ruins in the waterlogged landscape behind the trio. The Red Cross represents their salvation, but while they represent the typical picturesque rural ideal (complete with sombrero and colorful serape), the nurse bears no visible mark of

Mexican national identity. Whether lighter-skinned girls participated more substantially in national chapters of the organization or not, the imagery published in venues such as this magazine and in official publications gave the impression that national charity was the white woman's burden.

But for those girls who did participate, they saw the shape of their daily lives transformed by the new sense of purpose offered through the Junior Red Cross. A published chart of the organizational structure of the Junior Red Cross provides a visualization of the intended scope and scale that the ideal Junior Red Cross chapter could span in the community. The case of one particularly active chapter of the Junior Red Cross—that of the República Argentina girls' school, founded in 1928—suggests the power that membership in a transnational organization could have in the transformation of everyday women's work into a source of patriotic pride. For the girls at this Mexico City school, committee work formed the central activities of their daily lives; each day they reviewed the ongoing projects of each committee and dedicated innumerable after-school hours to the preparation of first-aid kits, flea-eradication campaigns, construction of national albums, political propaganda, and more. Junior Red Cross girls from the Escuela República Argentina scurried tirelessly beneath starched white nurse caps to assemble care packages for earthquake victims in the western states of Jalisco and Colima and sent hundreds of dollars in clothes and toys to homeless children in Japan. Their charitable acts also furthered Mexico's reputation as making enormous advances in education and technology.[118] Under their own initiative they obtained potable water for their school, participated in a polio vaccine drive, repaired and redistributed used clothing to poor children, and established international correspondence exchanges with Spain and other countries in the Americas.[119] The girls understood the organization's local charity emphasis, as recast in the language of the Junior Red Cross manual, as part of an international effort to improve the human condition.

This particularly engaged group garnered national approval for their efforts alongside the Society of Mothers, coming to the aid of the victims of deadly earthquakes that struck the states of Jalisco and Colima in 1921, by holding a drive that allowed them to send seeds, clothing, shoes, and other basic necessities. Their national profile gained an even greater boost when they sent assistance to the victims of a flood in the central village of Actopan. National Red Cross officials praised the República Argentina schoolgirls: "It is no exaggeration to say that our Junior Red Cross is always present, constantly attentive to situations in which their cooperation might be of use, and, within the realm of possibility, can be counted upon to come to the assistance of those in need."[120]

At first glance the Big Sister Committee perpetuated the traditional role of women from girlhood, without advancing the condition of the revolutionary woman or expanding her political or social participation. Yet the official stamp imprinted by the Red Cross as an established organization gave these girls' everyday work international importance. The girls understood their contributions to be part of a global peacetime effort, approved by the Geneva Convention, and thus transcending neighborly charity.[121] From time to time the Big Sisters' efforts flashed upon the international stage; one school's Big Sister Committee wrote and staged allegorical theater presentations titled *The Charity Fairy, I Am the Big Sister, The Junior Red Cross,* and *Day of the Americas* that gained so much attention that not only did the young organizers win prizes, but their original scenes were adapted and reproduced by the Pan-American Union in Washington to promote their adoption by other schools around the world.[122]

The international profile of the Big Sister transformed the unglamorous position of the Big Sister into that of a cultural ambassador, a link between the ancient knowledge of the home and the modern world. Through the Junior Red Cross, Mexican girls could extend their domestic responsibilities to their school life and feel themselves part of an international modernization project, despite the traditional nature of their labors. As the headmistress of the República Argentina school indicated, "We are convinced that the Junior Red Cross is the best civics teacher; we believe that through this organization, the girls provide valuable services to others and we are certain that they are efficiently preparing themselves to fulfill, down the road, the social mission incumbent of women in this day and age."[123] Above all, through their civic action, girls learned to be independent and to protect themselves and, in turn, other children. In this way they participated in the growing state project to protect children. Significantly, though, the process of civic engagement through the Big Sister Committee forced the girls to effectively stop being children. Like the Boy Scouts, through the process of gender-normative socialization, little by little the girls left their childhood identities behind.

Conclusions

The Boy Scouts, the Junior Red Cross, and the formal and informal international exchanges discussed in this chapter indicate the range and variety of ways that Mexican children in the 1920s and 1930s were exposed to, and enacted, prevailing models of nationalism on an international stage. Given the profile of those children and youth that participated most fully—urban, middle class, educated—the transnational model resonated more through these organizations than the locally produced proletarian model discussed in the previous chapter. And while the children who participated in the First Conference of the Proletarian Child gained unprecedented national attention, the international trekkers who donned universally recognizable uniforms performed upon a larger stage. Internationally inspired youth organizations interacted closely with homegrown nationalist models, sometimes seamlessly, and other times in competition for young hearts and minds. What emerges in the panorama of Mexican childhood in the 1920s and 1930s is a landscape populated with multiple opportunities for civic engagement. The options available to and the choices made by each child varied by region, aptitude, preferences, and socioeconomic status.

The history of youth organizations demonstrates that through membership, boys and girls did not depart far from the gendered parameters of civic action that governed Mexican society before the revolution. The Big Sisters of the Junior Red Cross manifested a servile, domestic culture in their daily activities, whereas the Explorers strengthened their muscles and cultivated outward physical signs that corresponded to the national—and international—ideal. A cursory overview would suggest that the work being carried out by the socialist school to combat gender and ethnic inequalities, a recently studied topic that has gained much currency in scholarship of postrevolutionary Mexico, was simply not taken up by organizations like the Boy Scouts and the Junior Red Cross with international bases.[124] The experiences of the Explorers reflect the scholarship on the respective missions, activities, and customs of the Boy Scouts and Girl Guides in the United States, which demonstrates that the official definition of citizenship saw gendered differences when put into practice by boys and girls.[125]

Despite the tendency to separate boys and girls regarding their civic duties, the activities in which these children engaged acquired revolutionary value and international import given the political and historical context in which they were carried out. If an institution designated a specific function and title to the volunteer work conducted by a girl during her free time, that girl saw herself as a useful part of a national project, or a representative of her country in an international effort. The generation of children described here also learned to export nationalism—that abstract love that one comes to feel for one's *patria*—to countries abroad, due to the growth and popularity of internationally recognized organizations such as the Red Cross and the Boy Scouts in Mexico. They learned to be citizens of the Mexican republic and at the same time to transcend the geopolitical boundaries that justified nationalist sentiments in the first place. They saw and consumed media coverage of activities being carried out by their counterparts around the world and began to imagine themselves as members of a modern global community of children.

National identity is a concept that is constantly in flux, but each expression of it can be linked to an official project. In this case the intersections between the state's educational program and institutionalized internationalism reflected in the daily activities of a generation of children. Media reports of these activities helped to define the ideal of what it meant to be Mexican, not only for the participants but also for their peers who observed the actions of "distinguished" young citizens through the press. The "invention" of the Mexican national tableau—in the creative and imaginative sense described by Ricardo Pérez Montfort—saw increased diffusion in the representations of national identity enacted by children.[126] Nevertheless, the majority of lower-class and indigenous children did not contribute with equal weight in the production of cultural nationalism; if anything, they served primarily as symbols and targets of these projects. Although children from humble origins did form their own *tribus* with the greatest enthusiasm, they did not enjoy the same visibility, nor did they possess the economic resources to travel abroad dressed in the Scout uniform. The transnational nature of the organizations examined here served to elevate the importance that children lent to their daily activities and placed Mexico in the international eye as a modern country exporting its own version of nationalism, albeit a constructed and superficial version of the country's real population and social situation. Children's expressions of nationalism reflected in the documents from the 1920s and 1930s, then, suggest at once a heightened civic presence and the construction of a "democratic" state that continued excluding the majority of its citizens.

Conclusion
Exceptional and Everyday Citizens

The capital city bustled on March 19, 1938. The night before, President Lázaro Cárdenas had taken to the airwaves and stridently announced the nationalization of the oil industry. At the Bellas Artes palace, in the heart of the city, citizens surged forth to donate their personal savings and in-kind valuables to offset the considerable expense that this revolutionary measure would exact from the national budget. Swept up in the emotional current alongside their parents, children offered the contents of their piggy banks (*alcancías*) to their president. Reporters' cameras flashed as the crowd opened to make way for a small heavily jowled boy just shy of four years old bearing a clay piggy bank nearly half his size. Little Cuauhtémoc Cárdenas's face expressed a blend of duty and disorientation. If the president's announcement was the culminating political event of the revolution, the appearance of his young son, Cuauhtémoc, at the impromptu fund drive epitomized the ideal civic role of the revolution's heirs. The poignant moment captured on film summarized the official myth analogizing children to revolutionary action in 1938: those who bore arms for a righteous cause in the revolution saw its material yield benefit their children, the next generation. In turn, due to the secular moral code imparted through a concerted state-sponsored educational program, these children learned to return these proceeds back to the revolution. Even the boy's nickname, "*Cuate*"—buddy, or pal—situated the most high-profile heir of the revolution as an "everyboy," the nation's son. Yet this highly symbolic and staged event was an exceptional circumstance, and Cuauhtémoc represented the minority. Even Cuauhtémoc cited his hazy memory of that day as special, exciting, confusing, out of the ordinary—he does not recall responding to an ideological nationalist calling.[1]

Pedagogical idealism diminished precipitously following the euphoria of the oil expropriation, dragging government funding for education down with it. Rural schoolteachers saw the moral and financial support for the more radical aspects of socialist education run dry. The international news media helped to introduce more international education and socialization techniques for children. In the 1930s Mexicans began to look increasingly beyond their geopolitical borders for a more transnational model of childhood and shifted away from the state-sponsored revolutionary nationalism typified by the *niño proletario*.

Nevertheless, the foundation for the next revolutionary generation had been laid. Official efforts to forge a common national identity from the fragments of the revolution were first realized through programs, missions, projects, and campaigns targeting children. Evidence suggests that the general population quickly mastered the government's agenda and began to reiterate official rhetoric about the revolutionary role of children in their petitions to the government. Moreover, children's increased access to commercial, cultural, and civic activities transformed their role from one relegated to the family to one as a member of a broader community. Children of the era enjoyed new media that increased their knowledge of others on the local, national, and international levels. Beginning in the 1920s the children's letters and drawings sent to radio, publications, and community organizations allowed their voices to be heard in unprecedented ways.

Many children growing up in the 1920s and 1930s benefited from the revolutionary attention they received in the family and the classroom—thanks to radio programs and public health centers that instructed mothers and the tireless efforts of rural schoolteachers who followed the guidelines set in *El Maestro Rural*. Those fortunate enough to have time to tune in to the radio formed a bond with children listening to the same tale of *Troka el Poderoso* or the *Periódico Infantil*. Children able get their hands on a tattered copy of *Pulgarcito* thumbed through pages bearing the same Aztec-inspired motifs and pastoral themes that they learned how to draw in their art classes. On the radio, in the newspaper, and in the streets and plazas, children witnessed youngsters their own age taking part in civic life through parades, political rallies, fund-raisers, art shows, theater. Many, in their free time, became members of the local chapter of the Junior Red Cross, the Boy Scouts, or the student council. They learned to write letters, make speeches, ask for assistance, and claim their basic human rights. They experienced government administration at the grassroots level, grew along with it as it flourished into a fully institutionalized bureaucracy, and honed the skills to maneuver within the system.

Most important, their voices were heard by adults. Their letters were read aloud over the air, they were invited to march before dignitaries in civic celebrations, their opinions were transcribed in the daily news, and their artwork was flown around the world to the delight of international connoisseurs. Children contributed poignantly and enthusiastically to the construction of a Mexican national aesthetic that became readily recognizable by the 1930s, not just by their compatriots but also by the rest of the modern world into which Mexico rapidly began to integrate.

Culturally, this generation experienced the popular revolutionary nationalism envisioned by ideologues such as Vasconcelos, Obregón, Calles, Cárdenas, and List Arzubide. Children learned and performed behavior presented to them in puppet shows and theater presentations, they drew the concentric circles and zigzag designs that made up the new revolutionary aesthetic, they dressed and performed as *chinas poblanas* and *charros* in festivals, and they perpetuated these nationalistic practices into the second half of the twentieth century. Adults constructed ideas about national identity based on the revolution's romance, filled with valiant men and women, folkloric indigenous peoples, and hardworking campesinos, all of whom formed communities. Children growing up in the span of two decades learned the revolutionary imaginary until they considered its themes timeless and authentic. In short, children helped to unfold the cultural panorama recognized as "*lo mexicano.*"

Politically, these children grew up as part of the PNR/PRM/PRI generation. They participated in the party machine according to their experiences growing up. Exceptional middle-class urban children such as Medardo Morales or Mario Aburto had the time and resources to take advantage of the networks available during their childhood to become prominent in the PRI. Everyday children in the countryside who may have had scant access to spotty radio shows and had never been to a SEP-sponsored party for listeners grew up as clients to the urban-based patronage system of the PRI. Challengers to the political system, in many cases, may have emerged from children who had been excluded from the revolutionary benefits as they grew up.[2]

The modern nationalist childhood experienced by many children during the 1920s and 1930s did not extend equally to everyone within the age group. The divide between urban and rural proved the greatest obstacle to the construction of a uniform childhood. Although the SEP strengthened its efforts in the countryside following national road-building efforts and using communication technology, many rural children remained at the margins of the childhood lived by youth in the city. Poverty also proved a nearly insurmountable barrier in bringing young people into the fold of the Revolutionary Family. The Department of Public Welfare extended many of the SEP initiatives into welfare institutions for disadvantaged children, but it could not reach the thousands more children who still roamed the streets, illiterate and uncared for. While many street children found, stole, and earned money for childish pursuits like candy and the movies, they did not benefit from the pedagogical initiatives developed in the classrooms. Biologically speaking, young people in the countryside and in the city streets may have been children, but by the cultural definition of childhood these young people were not children. Those who did not engage in the leisure activities, play on the modern apparatuses in public playgrounds, or understand the proletarian rhetoric that saturated public school puppet shows did not obtain the cultural capital that formed the inheritance of the revolutionary generation.

The second half of the twentieth century saw the institutionalization of the Mexican Revolution as successive administrations attempted to fulfill the promises delivered in the Constitution of 1917. By the 1940s, and particularly under the administration of Miguel Alemán (1946–52), the Institutional Revolution took a turn away from protectionist nationalism and took a business-oriented tack. As a result a deluge of popular culture from the North influenced children's lives, and the floodgates would remain ever open. Ideologically oriented, government-produced children's culture could not often withstand the stiff competition offered by Donald Duck (whose own imperialist ideology ought not to go unnoted). Cri-Cri, the singing cricket who made his radio debut in 1934, initially struggled for survival on the airwaves due to heavy SEP criticisms that his scenarios lacked educational and moral value. Throughout the Cárdenas era the SEP prohibited Cri-Cri songs from being played in the schools. Yet the cheeky little cricket far outlived his government-created counterparts, Troka and Comino, and went on to dominate children's radio culture for much of the remainder of the twentieth century, enjoying sponsorship from the likes of Coca-Cola.[3] Cri-Cri's success runs parallel to the ideological shift away from cultural nationalism and toward entertainment and commercial value that can be noted in children's popular culture from the 1940s onward. As historian Susana Sosenski has suggested in her analysis of print advertisement for children's goods in the 1950s, changes in consumption patterns signaled a paradigm shift in the modern model of childhood in Mexico. The child consumer of the Mexican Miracle eclipsed the proletarian child of the Cárdenas era as the embodiment of ideal citizenship practice.[4] The spaces of citizen formation shifted from schoolyard patios to department store window displays. Children assumed their new preferred place in the *patria*: in front of the cash register. This model of the mid-twentieth-century modern child citizen as an economic actor nearly severed the already strained ties that linked rural poor children to their nation.

While children's cultural milieu became watered down—or enriched, depending on the perspective—by transnational forces, other legacies of these two child-centered decades remained. The insertion of the child as a powerful cultural signifier was an indelible visual contribution, but the signified had shifted. Nowhere was this more pointedly employed than in Luis Buñuel's globally acclaimed 1951 feature film *Los Olvidados* (The forgotten ones). In it the recognizable archetype of the proletarian child had lost his redemptive power and instead fell victim to the ravages of urbanization, poverty, migration, and human cruelty. Buñuel's children retained their metaphorical power, but revolutionary reform was stricken from the scene. Meanwhile, in the classroom the SEP revised the textbooks. Teachers learned to retreat from the socialist mission and to embrace the more modern, transnational models of childhood that generically emphasized good citizenship without resorting to anticapitalist actions.

By the start of the second half of the twentieth century, the children's revolution of the 1920s and 1930s had been folded into the Institutional Revolution. Many welcomed this shift for its modernizing auspices, even as others lamented the passing of an era. The U.S. lifestyle magazine *Look* ran a trite retrospective in 1961 on the legacy of "the children of the revolution," now grown up. The featured Mexicans ran the gamut of ideological perspectives, but all appeared upwardly mobile, economically successful, and modern. Among them, characterized as an "angry young man," author Carlos Fuentes excoriated the fossilized state of his country's revolutionary culture and pointed to Cuba's recent developments as a source of inspiration. Iconoclast artist José Luís Cuevas's "Cactus Curtain" manifesto earned him a profile alongside the famed author. In 1956 he had published a rant that revealed his thinly veiled distaste for the forced program of social realism taught to him as a child in this scathing critique of the muralist chokehold on national identity. Born in 1934, Cuevas spent his formative years immersed in the glorification of the "grandeur and purity of the Mexican race," an official position embraced with such fervor as to border on xenophobia. Cuevas's controversial call for a break from *indigenismo* and *mestizaje* as national narratives stemmed from his observations, on Mexico City's streets, of the growing throngs of impoverished *indígenas* and *mestizos* who did not appear to benefit from the watery diet of rhetoric that they were served by the revolution.[5] The juxtaposition of these two members of the revolutionary generation in one article reveals that, while they looked to different sources (Cuba and Paris), both had grown weary of the asphyxiating nationalism that had marked their upbringings. This assessment came even as the young oratory champion Adolfo López Mateos, who rose to fame in the 1920s as a precocious talent, sat in Mexico's presidential chair. In a remarkable twist of fate, Cuevas and Fuentes met in a chance encounter in a U.S. airport returning to Mexico, both carrying the edition of *Look* in which their profiles had been published. The coincidence sparked a conversation, and the two men forged a lifelong friendship over the course of their return flight.[6] Not unlike the pages of *Pulgarcito* from their childhood, celebrity generated in the print media still held the power to create generational bonds, ones that sometimes translated into real, meaningful interpersonal exchanges.

The incomplete profile of childhood sketched in these pages has suggested an expanded and complex interpretation of citizenship in Mexico during the space of two decades. For children, as for anyone, "citizenship" is only as meaningful a concept as "nation" or "Mexico," or whatever geopolitical body within which one has membership. The exceptional children featured here and the everyday children whom they either represent or obfuscate all saw themselves drawn into a relationship with cultural nationalism as propagated by a state that saw children as its most valuable assets. Some performed according to the guidelines stipulated by adults and by state officials; though their actions might ring hollow to historians, for many of their contemporaries the impact of children engaged in productive activities resonated as a meaningful revolutionary reform. For others, listening to their children provide lip service to the revolution did little to mitigate the continuity of colonial or Porfirian structures of oppression.

The overall ideal of childhood transformed in the wake of the Mexican Revolution, resulting from new technologies, professional knowledge, nationalist expressions, and global influences that all contributed to the milieu in which children learned to be citizens. Beyond simple mimicry of adult behaviors, children participated in nation building in meaningful ways, and these actions were often validated by the state in an era of increasingly child-centered political policies and cultures. This book builds on the personal experiences as documented in archives, memoirs, and transcribed interviews of children who grew up in these decades. In no way does it represent the experience of every Mexican child growing up in the decades following the revolution, nor does it even attempt to characterize the experiences of most. But it suggests new ways of thinking about nation building that go beyond the traditional political actors and see citizenship as a more dynamic practice than just exercising political or economic rights. It goes a degree beyond the studies that have looked at the spaces of negotiation between levels of state, municipal, and local authorities and the everyday citizens that legislation and cultural policies affect. Children were at the forefront of much of the revolution's rhetoric—any revolution, in fact—and many scholars are quick to see through this rhetorical device as a political ruse, a populist strategy, or an emotional appeal. Less prolific, though, are the historical efforts that attempt to delve into that last level of negotiation: that between the historically mute children and the adult agents attempting to shape their lives.

The challenges associated with working with child-produced sources have been duly noted.[7] Some critics of this preference suggest that a fuller picture could be painted through the inclusion of oral histories, in which adults put their childhoods into the perspective of the rest of their lives and what they know about the history that has transpired since. A useful supplement to this account would be an oral history– and memoir-based assessment of childhood, as related by leaders and citizens of this generation in their adulthood. Conversations with individuals who grew up during the heyday of Mexico's cultural revolution would reveal many more firsthand experiences, though they may be clouded by time and aggregated to the power of collective memory. Perhaps then answers to the nagging questions will be revealed: Did Mario Aburto and Félix de la Portilla become community political leaders as presaged by their precocious childhoods? Did Medardo Morales assume a midlevel administration job in the PRI, rewarded with a modest pension for his lifelong conscientious attention to structures of authority? The addition of firsthand interviews to this story would add another dimension to the writing of the history of childhood. Children's voices can be heard in the historical record with remarkable consistency for the 1920s and 1930s, and the inclusion of these same voices aged by wisdom, cynicism, travails, and success adds another dimension to the examination of their childhood.

Former president Plutarco Elías Calles, in 1934, delivered his Grito de Guadalajara, in which he urged immediate attention to the question of the nation's youth who would determine the course of the revolution in the future. His emphatic exhortation validated and accelerated the rash of institutions, agencies, and campaigns under way that allowed the government to shape childhood and to educate children as revolutionaries. The changes wrought during these decades expressed the way that the revolutionary officials viewed and treated the nation's future citizens. This became the world of those children's experiences in which they played, dressed, and learned the part of being Mexican in a revolutionary era.

NOTES

Introduction

1. Enrique's story is included in an anthology of Guanajuato primary schoolchildren's descriptions of their lives, *Voces Nuevas,* edited by Francisco Hernández y Hernández, excerpted in *El Universal Gráfico,* June 5, 1937.

2. Beezley, *Mexican National Identity.*

3. James and James, *Constructing Childhood,* 14–15.

4. Sosenski and Albarrán, *Nuevas miradas a la historia de la infancia en América Latina.*

5. This sentiment is echoed in Blum, *Domestic Economies,* 179.

6. Zepeda, *Enseñar la nación.*

7. Alcubierre Moya, *Ciudadanos del futuro,* 14; Galván Lafarga, "Del ocio a la instrucción."

8. Schell, "Nationalizing Children through Schools and Hygiene."

9. Bazant, *Historia de la educación durante el Porfiriato,* 59–60.

10. Martínez Moctezuma, "Lecturas recreativas."

11. Wilkie broke down educational statistics by presidential term in *Mexican Revolution,* 160–61. Only the López Mateos administration of the 1960s, with more money available, spent more on education.

12. Weber, *Peasants into Frenchmen.*

13. Puig Casauranc, "El privilegio de tratar con niños," in *De nuestro México,* 141–42.

14. Pérez Montfort, "Los estereotipos nacionales y la educación posrevolucionaria (1920–1930)," in *Avatares del nacionalismo cultural,* 35–67.

15. Rockwell, *Hacer escuela, hacer estado,* 322–25.

16. Lerner, *Historia de la Revolución Mexicana,* 18–19.

17. Cárdenas repealed the antireligious aspect of socialist education in 1936 due to the violent reactions that it incited from the Cristeros; nevertheless, opposition to socialist education persisted throughout his administration, and it faded away quietly after 1939. Vaughan, "Educational Project of the Mexican Revolution," 109.

18. Vaughan, "Educational Project of the Mexican Revolution"; Vaughan, *Cultural Politics in Revolution*; Rockwell, *Hacer escuela, hacer estado*.

19. López, *Crafting Mexico*, 4.

20. See especially Bazant, *Historia de la educación durante el Porfiriato*; Vaughan, *State, Education, and Social Class*; Vaughan, *Cultural Politics in Revolution*; Schell, *Church and State Education*; Palacios, *La Pluma y el Arado*; and Rockwell, "Schools of the Revolution."

21. Lomnitz, "Final Reflections."

22. One of the greatest strengths of the Liberals—staunch commitment to freedom of instruction—proved also to undermine their influence, as Conservatives (and, by definition, the church) persisted in promoting their version of national sovereignty in private schools. See Zepeda, *Enseñar la nación*, 42–82.

23. Eineigel, "Distinction, Culture, and Politics," 103–5; Schell, *Church and State Education*.

24. Butler, *Popular Piety and Political Identity*, 84.

25. "La escuela socialista es la escuela de la traición," *La Defensa del Hogar: Salvemos a la Patria Salvando a la Niñez* (Puebla), no. 2 (March 22, 1936): 1.

26. Agustín Iturbide ushered in independence in 1821 on a Conservative platform and ruled briefly as emperor. One of his "three guarantees" upon which he founded the nation was the sacrosanct position of Catholicism as the only official religion of Mexico. *La Vanguardia: El Periódico de los Niños* 1, no. 18 (1921): 6; *La Vanguardia: El Periódico de los Niños* 1, no. 46 (1922): 2.

27. *La Cruzada Eucarística*, no. 7 (July 1923): 23.

28. *La Cruzada Eucarística*, no. 9 (September 1923): 23–24.

29. Wright-Ríos, "Revolution in Local Catholicism?"

30. *Patria potestad* is the legally recognized set of rights and obligations of parents regarding minors.

31. "Acotaciones del Momento: El Sindicato de Niños," *El Universal Gráfico*, November 8, 1924, 3.

32. Peter Stearns, in *Childhood in World History*, observed global changes to childhood roughly from the eighteenth to the twentieth centuries, noting that these changes were of course not universal. He saw hallmarks of "a modern model of childhood" as the transition of the child from a unit of labor to student and consumer.

33. Ariès, *Centuries of Childhood*.

34. Heywood, "*Centuries of Childhood*"; Fass, *Children of a New World*; Stearns, *Childhood in World History*.

35. Mintz, "Teaching the History of Childhood," n.p.

36. Another important work that lays the foundation for the long history of institutionalization of nationalism through education is Vásquez, *Nacionalismo y educación*. See also Zepeda, *Enseñar la nación*, 13–20.

37. For Latin American comparisons, see Nava, "Forging Future Citizens"; and Plotkin, "Education and Politics: The Political Socialization of Youth," in *Mañana es San Perón*, 83–134.

38. A recent and useful collection of social histories of childhood in Mexico is Herrera Feria, *Estudios sociales sobre*.

39. Only recently has the history of childhood gained currency as a field of study distinct from family or gender history. See the first periodical in the field, *Journal of the History of Childhood and Youth* 1, no. 1 (2008).

40. Piccato, "De la ciudadanía a los ciudadanos," 327–28.

41. Wakild, *Unexpected Environment*; Sluis, *City of Spectacles*; Vinson and Restall, *Black Mexico*; Zolov, *Refried Elvis*; Bliss and Blum, "Dangerous Driving"; Lear, *Workers, Neighbors, and Citizens*; Vaughan and Lewis, *Eagle and the Virgin*.

42. For an overview, see Albarrán, "Century of Childhood."

43. *Boletín de la* SEP 4, no. 7 (1925): 103–8.

44. James and James, *Constructing Childhood*; Coles, *Political Life of Children*.

45. Halbwachs, *On Collective Memory*, 54.

46. Baxter, *Children in Action*, 5–6.

47. Baxter, *Archaeology of Childhood*, 27–32; Bergerson, "Listening to the Radio"; Elias, *Civilizing Process*.

48. Cordero Reiman, "Modern Mexican Art."

1. Constructing Citizens

1. Blum, *Domestic Economies*.

2. See statement by Beatriz Alcubierre, historian of Mexican children's literature in the nineteenth and twentieth centuries: "La única forma de [estudiar al niño] es a través de los discursos, de las imágenes, y de las estrategias que los adultos han empleado para introducirlo en su mundo y que anteceden a toda práctica social relacionada con la infancia: los cuales, por supuesto, están determinados en todo momento por el contexto material en que se formulan," in del Castillo Troncoso, "La invención de un concepto moderno," 101. Notable exceptions that strive to recover children's voices and establish them as agents in history include Kelly, "'Thank You for the Wonderful Book'"; and Sánchez-Eppler, *Dependent States* and "Practicing for Print."

3. Ann Blum describes the developing tensions and overlap between the categories of "protected and working childhoods" and the ways that these distinctions were implicated in a vast network of policy, domestic labor, and child circulation practices. Blum, *Domestic Economies*, xx.

4. Marten, *Childhood and Child Welfare*.

5. Tenorio Trillo, "Stereophonic Scientific Modernisms."

6. The hygiene, eugenics, and puericulture movements emphasized reworking the role of the woman and the family in broader society. See Blum, *Domestic Economies*; Stepan, *"Hour of Eugenics"*; Applebaum, Macpherson, and Rosemblatt, *Race and Nation in Modern Latin America*; Olcott, Vaughan, and Cano, *Sex in Revolution*; and Bliss, *Compromised Positions*. See all of the contributors here, but especially Vaughan, "Modernizing Patriarchy"; and Pierce, "Fighting Bacteria."

7. Staples, "Primeros pasos de la higiene escolar decimonónica"; Chaoul Pereyra, "Escuelas de primera, segunda y tercera clase"; and Aréchiga, "'Un niño sano no puede ser un niño malo'"; Agostoni, *Curar, sanar, y educar*. For the continuities between Porfirian and revolutionary methods of measuring children, see Stern, "Responsible Mothers and Normal Children," 383.

8. Blum, *Domestic Economies*, 159–62. A personal account of the development of modern pediatrics can be found in the oral history PHO/8/31, Entrevista realizada al Dr. Jesús Lozoya Solís, realizada por Beatriz Arroyo, el día 8 de diciembre de 1977 en los laboratorios INFAN de la Ciudad de México, Archivo de la Palabra, el Instituto de Investigaciones Dr. José María Luis Mora. For the instruction of home hygiene inspectors, in which they are trained to inspect medical conditions, cleanliness, moral environment, space for recreation, use of beds ("lucha por el uso de la cama"), and more, see *Boletín de la SEP* 4, nos. 9–10 (1925): 210–12. One hygiene inspector in Villa Victoria, Michoacán, in 1936 reported that, of 115 "proletarian homes" visited, 96 percent demonstrated acceptable living conditions—91 percent had kitchens, 36 percent had sinks, but only 16 percent had toilets. Archivo Histórico de la Secretaría de Educación Pública (AHSEP), Dirección General de Educación Primaria en los Estados y Territorios, Dirección de Educación Federal, Caja 129, Exp. 13, Folios 46–47, 1936. See also Agostoni, "Las mensajeras de la salud." For a 1933 radio bulletin that encouraged mothers to carry on the educational efforts of the schoolhouse, see AHSEP, Dirección Extensión Educativa por Radio, Boletines de Acercamiento entre el Hogar y la Escuela, Caja 9488, Exp. 49, 1933; and Caja 9485, Exp. 49, 1933.

9. For the transformation of eugenics discourse from European prototypes to something particularly Mexican, see Stern, "Responsible Mothers and Normal Children." Continuity in scientific knowledge from the nineteenth century was common to other Latin American countries. In Brazil medical intellectuals adapted Jean-Jacques Rousseau's Enlightenment ideas about the perfectibility of man to the broader questions of national identity and citizenship. See Schwarcz, *Spectacle of the Races*. Educators in Brazil's early national school system strove to leave behind nineteenth-century racialized ideas in favor of a progressive "new" race, but policy and practice indicated a softer brand of Lamarckian explanations of social deficiencies that did not stray far from their nineteenth-century predecessors. See Dávila, *Diploma of Whiteness*.

10. For the Geneva Convention agreement in Mexican circulars, see *Boletín de la SEP* 4, nos. 9–10 (1925): 217–22. According to the proceedings,

officials should recognize the vital forces influencing the child's physical and moral development that came through organized recreation, the home, the school, and religious institutions.

11. Felix Palavicini had a career-long interest in education and family reform. He attended the constitutional congress in Querétero in 1917 as a member of President Venustiano Carranza's education cabinet; though he supported women's rights and suffrage, he also took issue with the secularization of the education program. See Stern, "Responsible Mothers and Normal Children," 373–74.

12. "Primer Congreso Mexicano del Niño," *El Universal,* January 19, 1921.

13. *Memoria del Primer Congreso Mexicano del Niño.*

14. See nearly daily coverage in *El Universal,* January–April 1920.

15. Dr. Rafael Santamarina, "Conocimiento Actual del Niño Mexicano desde el Punto de Vista Médico-Pedagógico," in *Memoria del Primer Congreso Mexicano del Niño,* 264–65.

16. The leading influence promoting stages of cognitive development was Swiss child expert Jean Piaget; as an example of his publications, see *Child's Conception of the World.*

17. Archivo Histórico de la Secretaría de Salubridad (AHSSA), Salubridad Pública, Higiene Escolar, Caja 3, Exp. 19, 1922; Beltrán, "La mediación de la inteligencia de los mexicanos."

18. AHSSA, Salubridad Pública, Higiene Escolar, Caja 3, Exp. 11, 1922. See also *Contribución del Departamento de Psicopedagogía e Higiene,* 7.

19. Blum, *Domestic Economies,* 154–55.

20. *Utopia—No Utopia,* 25–33, 56–57.

21. Pan-American Child Congresses took place in the following locations: Buenos Aires, Argentina (1916); Montevideo, Uruguay (1919); Rio de Janeiro, Brazil (1922); Santiago, Chile (1924); Havana, Cuba (1927); Lima, Peru (1930); Mexico City, Mexico (1935); Washington DC, United States (1942); and Caracas, Venezuela (1948).

22. *Memoria del VII Congreso Panamericano del Niño,* 2:5.

23. As we now know, this narrative of state-sponsored orphans was actually a fiction that scripted over a bustling child-circulation system that involved mothers, domestic workers, and state officials. See Blum, *Domestic Economies.*

24. *Memoria del VII Congreso Panamericano,* 607–32.

25. Professor Rosaura Zapata, one of the exceptional educators of the era and general inspector of kindergartens for the SEP, was the only woman on the Mexican organizing committee in the section of education. She received special recognition for her outstanding participation in the conference. Women were instrumental in the foundation of the institution, first started by Argentine feminists in 1916, and men soon joined. See Guy, "Pan-American Child Congresses," 272.

26. Jackson, "Order in the Nursery"; Buck, "Meaning of the Women's Vote in Mexico," 14.

27. Blum, "Public Welfare and Child Circulation."

28. A concise treatment of Habermas's theory of the public sphere as it relates to recent studies of citizenship can be found in Piccato, "De la ciudadanía a los ciudadanos," 326–27.

29. Expressed by Calles in 1934 and discussed in Blum, *Domestic Economies*, 130.

30. Gutman and Coninck-Smith, *Designing Modern Childhoods.*

31. Notably, the actions of the 1926 Tribunal de Menores and the 1931 Ley Federal del Trabajo sought to define and regulate child labor and in fact justified it despite the restrictions stipulated by Article 123 of the constitution by claiming that it was a constructive way to curb dangerous tendencies. See Sosenski, *Niños en acción,* 59, 73, 265–84.

32. "Lo que el niño necesita para tener salud," *El Niño,* January 1929, 29.

33. Kozlovsky, "Adventure Playgrounds and Postwar Reconstruction," 187.

34. *Boletín Municipal* 8, nos. 9–13 (1922): 193–96. For related debates and issues regarding children's space in the Alameda Park, see a discussion about the appropriateness of putting a library kiosk in the children's park (the argument against it was that children go to the Alameda to play and rest and essentially to do everything but read) in *Boletín Municipal* 8, nos. 18–21 (1922); and a plea to keep the merry-go-round, which was deemed the "only moral diversion" that children had in the park, in *Boletín Municipal* 9, no. 9 (1923): 111–12.

35. "¿Son para los grandes los juegos de los parques infantiles?" *El Universal Gráfico,* February 9, 1926. Another debate about the morality of children's recreational space occurred with the surge in popularity enjoyed by the YMCA in Mexico in the 1920s and 1930s. Especially during the cultural wars that defined the Cristero Rebellion, Catholic publications for children lashed out against the YMCA as being a representative of all possible evils: the devil, Protestantism, foreign imperialism, and antinationalism. Catholics argued that the only way to combat these invasive cultural influences was through the construction of Catholic children's recreational centers. See "Debemos establecer lugares de recreo y centros culturales para los niños," *La Defensa del Hogar: Salvemos a la Patria Salvando a la Niñez,* no. 60 (July 17, 1938); "La YMCA es una sociedad netamente extranjera, Protestante, y antisocial," *La Vanguardia: El Periódico de los Niños* 1, no. 14 (1921); "Centros de embrutecimiento," *La Vanguardia: El Periódico de los Niños* 1, no. 22 (1921); *La Vanguardia: El Periódico de los Niños* 1, no. 9 (1921).

36. Children's parks were established around the country as spaces for the healthy distraction of neighborhood youth. For just a sampling, see "Será renovado el parque infantil de Veracruz," *El Universal,* August 5, 1931; "Proyecto para construir el gran parque infantil 'Presidente L. Cárdenas,'" *El Nacional,* April 16, 1935; "Un parque infantil en la ciudad de Saltillo,"

Exelsior, July 7, 1935; "Parque infantil en Córdoba, Veracruz," *El Nacional,* July 31, 1937; and "Los trabajos de construcción de un parque infantil en la población de Tlalixcoyan, Veracruz," *El Nacional,* January 21, 1939.

37. Archivo General de la Nación (AGN), Fondo Obregón-Calles (O-C) 803-R-9, 1921.

38. *El Universal Gráfico,* December 5, 1924.

39. Rockwell, "Schools of the Revolution"; Vaughan, "Educational Project of the Mexican Revolution" and *Cultural Politics in Revolution.*

40. Sosenski, *Niños en acción,* 210; Loyo B., "En el aula y la parcela."

41. Waters, "Revolutionizing Childhood" and "Remapping Identities."

42. "La niñez proletaria tiene ya plena confianza en el mañana," *El Nacional,* March 12, 1935.

43. AHSEP, Departamento de Enseñanza Primaria y Normal, Caja 4654, Exp. 18, 1926, found in *Utopia—No Utopia,* 19, 58.

44. Emma Reh Stevenson, "Mexico's Story in Color," *High School Service* (American National Red Cross) 5, no. 1 (1928): n.p. See also *La Voz del Niño* (Órgano de los niños de la Escuela Cooperación "Educativa," Colima) 3, no. 5 (1930), found in AHSEP, Departamento de Bibliotecas, Caja 997, Exp. 122, 1930.

45. Archivo Histórico "Genaro Estrada" de la Secretaría de Relaciones Exteriores (AHSRE), L-E 213, 1932–1933.

46. Kozlovsky, "Adventure Playgrounds and Postwar Reconstruction," 171.

47. "Los juegos de los niños: Consejos a los papás," *El Universal Gráfico,* October 17, 1925.

48. *Memoria del VII Congreso Panamericano del Niño,* 2:214.

49. "Aparatos de Recreo y Gimnasia: Catálogo G47" (New York: J. J. Vellvé, n.d.), in AHSEP, Departamento de Escuelas Rurales, Dirección General, Caja 25, Exp. 31, 1932.

50. AHSEP, Departamento de Escuelas Rurales, Dirección General, Caja 25, Exp. 31, 1932.

51. AHSRE, L-E 213.

52. For a discussion of the history of child welfare in Mexico, see Blum, "Children without Parents"; Velasco Ceballos, *El niño mexicano ante la caridad y el Estado*; and Rómulo Velasco Ceballos, "La salud del niño, preocupación fundamental del Estado," *Revista Mexicana de Pediatría* 31, no. 3 (1926). After the Constitution of 1917, public welfare was no longer seen as an aspect of Christian charity or philanthropy but rather the obligation of the state to care for its citizens. For a brief institutional history of Mexico's welfare system through the Beneficencia Pública, see Gutiérrez del Olmo, "Introducción."

53. Olguín Alvarado and Tena Villeda, "Los niños en el Manicomio General de México," 6–7.

54. Between 1911 and 1925, 346 minors were registered at La Castañeda. Olguín Alvarado and Tena Villeda, "Los niños en el Manicomio General de México," 9.

55. When children of employees were discovered to be living among the patients, administrators took swift action and demanded that "normal" children not mix with the sick ones and that they should be kept instead in the day-care center that was annexed to the children's ward. Likely, this separation of normal and abnormal children proved difficult to enforce. See AHSSA, Fondo Manicomio General, Serie Administración, Caja 31, Exp. 10, 1937.

56. AHSSA, Fondo Manicomio General, Sección Administración, Caja 15, Exp. 10, 1933.

57. Olguín Alvarado and Tena Villeda, "Los niños en el Manicomio General de México," 15–16. For a list of songs that children learned and to which they choreographed their calisthenics, see AHSSA, Fondo Manicomio General, Serie Administración, Caja 9, Exp. 29, 1936.

58. AHSSA, Fondo Manicomio General, Serie Administración, Caja 4, Exp. 9, 1935; AHSSA, Fondo Beneficencia Pública, Sección Asistencia, Serie Departamento de Acción Educativa y Social, Caja 9, Exp. 8, 1935.

59. Dr. Alfonso Millán and Dra. Matilde Rodríguez Cabo, "Nota sobre el funcionamiento del Departamento de Psiquiatria Infantil del Manicomio General de México," in *Memoria del VII Congreso Panamericano*, 1013–22.

60. For a sample daily schedule of children's activities in the ward, see AHSSA, Fondo Manicomio General, Serie Administración, Caja 4, Exp. 9, 1941.

61. "Informe de Labores, Oficina de Acción Educativa y Social," AHSSA, Fondo Beneficencia Pública, Sección Asistencia, Serie Departamento de Acción Educativa y Social, Legajo 2, Exp. 12, 1921–1936.

62. Nava Nava, *Los abajo firmantes*.

63. AGN, O-C 121-E-D-12, 1923.

64. Blum, *Domestic Economies*.

65. AHSSA, Fondo Beneficencia Pública, Sección Establecimientos Asistenciales, Serie Casa de los Niños Expósitos, Caja 25, Exp. 14, 1924.

66. Blum, "Making and Breaking Families."

67. AHSSA, Fondo Beneficencia Pública, Sección Establecimientos Asistenciales, Serie Casa de Niños Expósitos, Caja 26, Exp. 2, 1926.

68. AGN, Rodríguez 330/165, 1932.

69. AGN, Rodríguez 330/165, 1932.

70. No reply was recorded. AGN, Rodríguez 330/165, 1932. For a similar letter from Jalisco, see AGN, Fondo Archivo Particular Emilio Portes Gil (EPG) 363/204, 1929.

71. AGN, O-C 805-H-161, 1927.

72. AGN, EPG 363/204, 1929.

73. Blum, *Domestic Economies*, xxvi.

74. This most frequently cited line from the July 1934 Grito de Guadalajara sums up Calles's position: "Youth and childhood do and should belong to the Revolution," reproduced in *El Maestro Rural*, August 1, 1934.

75. The experiences of Calles's children diverged in many ways from that of the Mexican child—read as the proletarian child. For many documents on his younger children's lives, especially Plutarcito (Caco) and Leonardo (Nanis), see correspondence between the children and their father, in Fideicomiso Archivos Plutarco Elias Calles y Fernando Torreblanca, Archivo Plutarco Elías Calles (APEC), Expediente 3, Elias Calles Llorente, Plutarco José y Leonardo Gilberto, Legajo 1, Folios 16–36, Inventario 1732. See also Buchenau, *Plutarco Elías Calles.*

76. A discussion of changes in photographic and lithographic technology as it relates to child portraiture can be found in del Castillo Troncoso, "La invención de un concepto moderno," 108.

77. Blum, "Picture of Health"; Blum, *Domestic Economies,* 140–53; del Castillo Troncoso, *Conceptos, imágenes y representaciones.* Images of children during the revolution can be found in Alcubierre Moya and Carreño, *Los niños villistas.* For the conflation of war and play, see Albarrán, "Guerrilla Warplay."

78. León Díaz Cárdenas, "El niño indígena y el niño proletario," and Felipe Ferrer Baynon, "El cultivo integral del niño proletario," in *Memoria del VII Congreso Panamericano del Niño,* 2:423–24, 412.

79. Sansón Flores, *El niño proletario: Poemas clasistas,* 8.

80. *Características biológicas de los escolares proletarios.*

81. "Concurso del niño robusto," *El Nacional,* August 22, 1935; "Concurso del niño sano," *El Nacional,* April 22, 1935; "Concurso del niño sano en la Capital del E. de Coahuila," *Excelsior,* April 28, 1931; "Concurso del niño proletario sano, Bellas Artes," *El Nacional,* November 25, 1936.

82. Velázquez Andrade, *Fermin Lee.* See Diego Rivera, "Children's Drawing in Present Day Mexico," *Mexican Folkways* 2, no. 5 (1926).

83. "Los niños mexicanos pintados por Diego Rivera," *Artes de México* 5, no. 27 (1959); *Los niños mexicanos de Diego Rivera.* Even today, children continue to learn their patriotic history through examination of Rivera's murals; third and fourth graders have an entire curriculum based on the murals: *Programa de visitas "Los niños a la SEP."* The only comparable inclusion of children in Mexican art is the late eighteenth-century casta paintings. See Katzew, *Casta Painting;* and Cline, "Century of Childhood." For a comparative Latin American example, see Dean, "Sketches of Childhood."

84. Ricardo Pérez Montfort, "Nacionalismo, niños y Diego Rivera," in *Los niños mexicanos de Diego Rivera,* 66.

2. *Pulgarcito* and Popocatépetl

1. Coffey, *How Revolutionary Art Became Official Culture,* 186.

2. CONACULTA was founded in 1988 to preserve and promote artistic and cultural creation.

3. "La Historia Patria hay que enseñarla, pudiéramos decir, emotivamente, citando los ejemplos de nuestros héroes y de nuestros grandes hombres, de

tal manera, que emocionen al niño, que vayan más al corazón que al cerebro; debe ser una ciencia más bien educativa que instructiva, que más que enseñe, eduque y sirva para orientar su criterio y fortificar su carácter." *Diario de los Debates* (de la Cámara de Diputados de los Estados Unidos Mexicanos) 1, no. 68 (1920): 18–25.

4. For a discussion of Vasconcelos's literary project, see Alcubierre Moya and Bazán Bonfil, "*Lecturas clásicas para niños.*"

5. A nuanced differentiation of the political projects of the three muralists and their respective relationships with the state can be found in Craven, *Art and Revolution in Latin America*, chap. 1. For a more thorough discussion of the political clout wielded by artists, and particularly the three muralists, in the 1920s and 1930s, see Rochfort, "Sickle, Serpent, and Soil."

6. Kaplan, *"The Art That Is Life."* For more on the intellectual and artistic development of a generation of artists in Mexico, see Azuela de la Cueva, *Arte y poder.*

7. Glusker, *Avant-Garde Art & Artists in Mexico.*

8. Though he supported the art program, Rivera took issue with Best Maugard's method, saying, "If the roses, little baskets, kiosks, and young deer of Best were preferable to the stamps of Julien and the chromos of flowers of la Kleinn which the children obliged by their teachers were copying in the schools, then they changed 'samples' of abominable taste for those of excellent taste, but not because of this had the exterior and tyrannical pressure upon the child's spirit ceased." Rivera, "Children's Drawing in Present Day Mexico," 5–6.

9. José Clemente Orozco distinguishes himself among the muralists as being more readily critical of the official history of the revolution, frequently drawing attention to the facile corruptibility of humankind regardless of ideological position. See Craven, *Art and Revolution in Latin America*, 46–50.

10. Naive art is a genre in which artists appear to have little or no training, although they might actually be highly trained. See Coffey, *How Revolutionary Art Became Official Culture*, 187. For a discussion of the history of infantilization of Indians in Mexican art, see Curiel et al., *Pintura y vida cotidiana en Mexico*, 135–37.

11. Gamio, *Forjando Patria.*

12. Cordero Reiman, "Best Maugard Drawing Method," 51–53.

13. López, "Noche Mexicana," 23–24; Gonzáles, "Imagining Mexico in 1921."

14. The Sección de Dibujo y Trabajos Manuales later became the Sección Técnica de Dibujo, specializing only in drawing and leaving the handicrafts aside.

15. Cordero Reiman, "Best Maugard Drawing Method," 61.

16. Best Pontones, "El método 'Best Maugard.'"

17. *Boletín de la SEP* 3, no. 10 (1925): 78–79.

18. Hobsbawm, *The Invention of Tradition.*

19. López, *Crafting Mexico*.

20. Best Maugard, *Método de dibujo*, 28–31. See also Azuela de la Cueva, *Arte y poder*, 104–9.

21. José Vasconcelos published the original work in 1925, and since then it has seen many translations and editions. Vasconcelos, *La raza cósmica*.

22. Best Maugard, *Método de dibujo*, 80, 92.

23. Best Maugard allows the schoolteacher a small degree of leeway in art instruction, noting that schoolteachers should feel free to depart from his recommendations wherever they wished, as long as they "follow another procedure found in our popular arts." Best Maugard, *Método de dibujo*, 93.

24. *Boletín de la* SEP 1, no. 2 (1922): 201.

25. Best Maugard, *Método de dibujo*, 132–33; Azuela de la Cueva, *Arte y poder*, 53–55, 104–9.

26. Fell, *José Vasconcelos*, 444.

27. Best Maugard noted that a preliminary pitfall of teaching his method was that children, upon learning the seven motifs, would become overly enthusiastic and saturate their drawings with them, not knowing how to be selective. He advises, though, that with patience and age, children will learn to choose when and where it is appropriate to include them. Best Maugard, *Método de dibujo*, 15, 94.

28. *Boletín de la* SEP 3, no. 10 (1925): 78–79.

29. "Dictámenes sobre Enseñanza de Dibujo," AHSEP, Departamento de Bellas Artes, Serie Dibujo 1923–1933, Caja 23, Exp. 1, 1931.

30. *Boletín Municipal* 5, no. 11 (1920).

31. *Boletín de la* SEP 1, no. 3 (1922): 236–38.

32. Alma Reed, "Mexico Delves in Past to Create National Art," *New York Times*, May 20, 1923, x6.

33. Cordero Reiman, "Best Maugard Drawing Method," 44–45. Juan Olaguíbel, also a famous sculptor, created such iconographic statues as the *Diana Cazadora* on Avenida de la Reforma, and Guanajuato's *Pípila*.

34. Azuela de la Cueva, *Arte y poder*, 55; Diego Rivera, "El sentido estético como receptor de las aspiraciones de los pueblos," *El Niño*, May 1929, 23–24.

35. Best Maugard and his protégé and successor, Manuel Rodríguez Lozano, believed firmly that children's drawing was not art but rather a technique that allowed them to develop other faculties. Their goal was not to create a generation of child artists but to furnish children with a graphic language, one that would help them to understand their world and to succeed at their vocations. See the statement written by Rodríguez Lozano, "Dictamenes sobre Enseñanza de Dibujo," AHSEP, Departamento de Bellas Artes, Serie Dibujo 1923–1933, Caja 24, Exp. 1, 1931.

36. *Boletín de la* SEP 3, no. 10 (1925): 78–79.

37. Distribution went from two thousand in 1925 to five thousand in 1926 to ten thousand in 1928, demonstrating a steady increase in demand for

the publication. Over the entire run sixty-five thousand copies of *Pulgarcito* were published. Corona Berkin and Santiago Gómez, *Para la infancia*, 20.

38. *Pulgarcito*, May 1, 1926, 5–9.

39. Alcubierre Moya, *Ciudadanos del futuro*, 141–71.

40. An Argentine children's magazine by the same name—*Pulgarcito*— was published in 1904 but did not feature child-produced content, nor was it distributed for free. It did include a section of letters to the editor, as well as other entertainment and instructional content. See Szir, *Infancia y cultura visual.*

41. Szir, *Infancia y cultura visual*, 17–18.

42. Hershfield, *Imagining "la Chica Moderna,"* 8–9.

43. *Pulgarcito*, May 1, 1926, 14.

44. Anderson, *Imagined Communities.* Scholars have recently adapted Anderson's useful theory to the Latin American case, expanding the argument about print media to include other cultural forms such as images and ceremonies as symbols around which Latin Americans forge identities. See especially Chasteen, "Introduction: Beyond Imagined Communities"; and Guerra, "Forms of Communication, Political Spaces, and Cultural Identities."

45. *Pulgarcito*, February 1926, 38.

46. *Pulgarcito*, May 1, 1926, 38–39.

47. "El Buzón de Pulgarcito," *Pulgarcito*, October 1, 1926, 41.

48. *Pulgarcito*, October 1, 1926, 41.

49. *Pulgarcito*, August 1, 1926, 41.

50. *Pulgarcito*, August 1, 1926, 41.

51. For a thorough example of the uneven application of the education program due to specific local experience and demands, see Vaughan, *Cultural Politics in Revolution.*

52. *Boletín de la Secretaría de Educación Pública* 4, no. 10 (1925): 213–14.

53. The proposed organization of the school day for Mexico City elementary schools, as distributed by the school inspectors' committee in 1920, provided for gendered division in the classroom as early as the second grade, in which girls undertook "feminine labors," while boys took arithmetic. By the third grade and onward, girls continued in "feminine labors," while boys engaged in military exercises. *Boletín Municipal* 5, no. 2 (1920), circular no. 42.

54. "Por qué deben ser de estilo mexicano nuestros dibujos," *Pulgarcito*, March 1928, 5–11.

55. "Por qué deben ser de estilo mexicano," 7, 10.

56. *Pulgarcito*, May 1926, 20.

57. *Pulgarcito*, May 1926, 31–32.

58. *Pulgarcito*, October 1926, 25–26.

59. *Pulgarcito*, March 1931, 15.

60. *Pulgarcito*, October 1926, 22–23.

61. M. Miller and Taube, *Gods and Symbols of Ancient Mexico and the Maya*, 120.

62. Fernández, *El arte del siglo XIX en México*, 89–90; Ades, *Art in Latin America*, 101–9.

63. Rubenstein, "Nahui Olín."

64. *Pulgarcito*, February 1926, 30.

65. *Pulgarcito*, February 1926, 40.

66. *Pulgarcito*, March 1926, 33.

67. Beezley, "Creating a Revolutionary Culture," 424.

68. Azuela de la Cueva, *Arte y poder*, 123. Academia de San Carlos director Alfredo Ramos Martínez began the open-air schools in 1920, and there were eight of them in Mexico City by 1928. Education officials also created Centers of Popular Art Instruction (Centros de Enseñanza Artística Popular) as part of the experiments to expand access to artistic production and instruction. Lear, "La brocha y el martillo."

69. Caplow, *Leopoldo Méndez*, 12–13, 17–20.

70. *Boletín de la Universidad*, IV Época, 3, no. 6 (1921): 74.

71. *Monografía de las escuelas de pintura al aire libre*, 9.

72. *Pulgarcito*, February 1, 1926, 18.

73. See especially Pérez Montfort, "Una región inventada desde el centro: La consolidación del cuadro estereotípico nacional, 1921–1937," in *Estampas de nacionalismo popular mexicano*, 121–48.

74. *Pulgarcito*, June 1, 1926, 42.

75. *Pulgarcito*, March 1928, 41.

76. *Pulgarcito*, July 1, 1926, 40.

77. *El Universal*, October 14, 1927.

78. *El Universal*, October 14, 1927.

79. *El Universal*, October 26, 1927.

80. Stevenson, "Mexico's Story in Color," 16–18.

81. Baxter, *Archaeology of Childhood*, 2005.

82. *Boletín de la* SEP 6, no. 4 (1927): 279–80.

83. The Caja Nacional de Ahorros Escolares was a savings program implemented among primary schoolchildren to encourage thrift and savings and to foment a culture based on a capitalist, cash economy. Children deposited earnings into a personal account and sometimes into a collective account.

84. *El Universal*, October 28, 1927.

85. *Boletín de la* SEP 6, no. 11 (1927): 143–59.

86. "Entre niños de veinte naciones, triunfaron los niños mexicanos," *El Sembrador*, July 5, 1929, 11.

87. Frances Toor, "The Children Artists in the Mexican Revolution/Los Pequeños Artistas y la Revolución de la Pintura," *Mexican Folkways* 4, no. 1 (1928): 26–28.

88. *Monografía de las escuelas de pintura al aire libre*, 7.

89. Best Maugard, *Método de dibujo*, 132.

90. Best Maugard, *Método de dibujo*, 132.

91. *Pulgarcito*, March 1931, 22–23. American artist Walter Inglis Anderson, a contemporary of Best Maugard and likewise an enthusiast of children's art, studied Best Maugard's seven motifs and techniques and adapted versions of it to American art, with moderate success.

92. *Pulgarcito*, October 1926, 16–17.

93. Ricardo Pérez Montfort identifies the historical roots and popularization of some of these cultural stereotypes in his collection of essays *Estampas de nacionalismo popular mexicano*.

94. The drawing workshop for French children was sponsored by the Asociación Paris-América Latina. One fan and curator of international art exhibits wrote to the sep director in Paris that the work of Mexican children on display in France paralleled that of the great modern masters of the day. He then offered to pay for the inclusion and installment of these pieces alongside that of contemporaries from the United States and Europe, "under equal conditions." René Jean waxed poetic over the technical perfection evident in the Mexican children's work, noting their mastery of the subtlety of line and gradations of tone to the effect of sophistication well beyond their years. *Boletín de la sep* 5, no. 10 (1926): 77, 79–81.

95. *Boletín de la sep* 5, no. 10 (1926): 85.

96. *Boletín de la sep* 6, no. 12 (1927): 255–60.

97. AHSEP, Oficina Cultural Radiotelefónica (OCR), Conferencia y Boletines, Caja 9474, Exp. 12, Folios 19–24, 1929.

98. Famed Japanese painter Fujita bemused the precocity of these young artists, noting that perhaps their aesthetic maturity should not be so surprising, considering that in Mexico girls commonly wed at twelve and were mothers at sixteen. *Boletín de la sep* 5, no. 10 (1926): 82.

99. Olaguíbel frequently provided radio bulletins for the official sep radio station, announcing the successes of Mexican children's drawings in international exhibitions. For a discussion of the role of radio in consolidating a generation of young listeners into a peer group, see chapter 3 on radio. AHSEP, OCR, Conferencia y Boletines, Caja 9474, Exp. 12, Folios 19–24, 1929.

100. "Sección de Dibujo y Trabajos Manuales de la sep," *El Niño*, January 1929, 49–51, 53, 56; "Exposición de dibujos," *El Sembrador*, August 20, 1929, 7; "Exposición de Dibujos Escolar de 1929," *El Niño*, August 1929, 27–29; "Éxito de nuestros niños en el mundo," *El Sembrador*, September 5, 1929, 22.

101. *Boletín de la sep* 7, no. 6 (June 1928): 231–33.

102. F. F. [*sic*] Olaguíbel, "La Enseñanza del Dibujo en las Escuelas," *El Niño*, March 1928, 17. Andrea N. Walsh uses the term *visual quotes* to refer to indigenous children's drawings in British Columbia as documents that persist from the era in which the artists were children as distinctly different documents than oral histories that allow only for people to recapture their childhood through the filter of adult memory. See Walsh, "Healthy Bodies, Strong Citizens," 300.

103. *Pulgarcito*, March 1931, 31.

104. "Ponencias al Congreso de Niños Campesinos y Obreros," *El Nacional*, October 18, 1936 (emphasis added).

105. Sosenski, *Niños en acción*, 157.

106. Cuevas, "The Cactus Curtain."

3. A Community of Invisible Little Friends

1. Ortíz Monasterio, *Mexico*, 96.

2. The SEP station first launched with the call letters CYE and changed them shortly thereafter to CZE. In 1928, following a convention in Washington DC to standardize international radio, the SEP station obtained the call letters XFX. I owe sincere thanks to Justin Castro for his comments and collegial exchanges, which have substantially improved this chapter.

3. *Memoria de la SEP* 1 (1932): 538–39; AHSEP, Obra de Extensión Educativa por Radio, Caja 9475, Exp. 10, Folio 35, 1930.

4. Most recently, see the excellent comprehensive study of the long rise of radio technologies in Mexico in Castro, "Wireless."

5. T. Lewis, "'A Godlike Presence,'" 28.

6. Bergerson, "Listening to the Radio," 100–101; Gombrich, *Myth and Reality*. For contemporary editorials, see Kunzer, "'Education' under Hitler"; and Siepmann, "Can Radio Educate?"

7. Kelly, *Children's World*, 479–81; Boemer, *Children's Hour*.

8. Ornelas Herrera, "Radio y cotidianidad en México," 145.

9. *Una historia hecha de sonidos*, 119. For a description of this event, see Castro, "Wireless," chap. 7.

10. Hayes, "National Imaginings on the Air," 248.

11. *Una historia hecha de sonidos*, 126; Pérez Montfort, *Avatares del nacionalismo cultural*, 99–100; Gallo, *Mexican Modernity*; Granados, "Quién es el que anda allí? Cri-Cri en XEW y otros programas infantiles," in *XEW*; Pérez Montfort, *Avatares del nacionalismo cultural*, 114–15.

12. Hayes, "National Imaginings on the Air."

13. Whetten, *Rural Mexico*, 300–301.

14. Hayes, *Radio Nation*, 33; Castro, "Wireless," chap. 8.

15. Castro, "Wireless," chap. 7.

16. Gallo, *Mexican Modernity*, chap. 2. For a discussion of the phenomenology of soundscapes, see B. R. Smith, *Acoustic World of Early Modern England*; and Schafer, *Tuning of the World*.

17. Hayes, *Radio Nation*, 12, 31.

18. For descriptions of the new social spaces that radio forged, see Castro, "Wireless," chap. 8.

19. Pérez Montfort, "'Esa no, porque me hiere,' Semblanza superficial de treinta años de radio en México, 1925–1955," in *Avatares del nacionalismo cultural*, 91–115.

20. AHSEP, Obra de Extensión Educativa por Radio, Caja 9475, Exp. 10, Folio 11, "Programa de Acción de la Obra de Extensión Educativa por Radio de la Secretaría de Educación Pública," 1930.

21. "El radio dueño del mundo," *El Universal Ilustrado*, July 20, 1922, 35, in Ornelas Herrera, "Radio y cotidianidad en México," 151.

22. AHSEP, Dirección de Extensión Educativa por Radio, Caja 9775, Exp. 10, Folio 35, "Periódico Infantil, Anexo N. 2," 1930.

23. AHSEP, OCR, Caja 9476, Exp. 45, Folio 525, "Concurso Periódico Infantil," 1930.

24. AHSEP, OCR, Boletines de Acercamiento entre el Hogar y la Escuela, Caja 9485, Exp. 49, 1933.

25. Ornelas Herrera, "Radio y cotidianidad en México," 161.

26. *Memoria de la SEP* 2 (1933): 877–80.

27. AHSEP, OCR, Caja 9472, Exp. 18, Folios 7–9, "Acuerdos (C. Secretario): Dotación de Aparatos de Radio," 1932.

28. AHSEP, Departamento de Enseñanza Técnica, Escuelas Técnicas, Sección Técnica de Radio, Caja 13, Exp. 2, Folio 1, 1928. See also Castro, "Wireless," 240.

29. AHSEP, Departamento de Escuelas Rurales, Dirección General, Caja 21, Exp. 8, 1933.

30. AHSEP, Departamento de Escuelas Rurales, Dirección General, Caja 21, Exp. 5, 1932–1933.

31. *Memoria de la SEP* 2 (1933): 875.

32. AHSEP, Departamento de Escuelas Rurales, Dirección General, Caja 21, Exp. 8, 1933.

33. "Los santos reyes ante el micrófono," *La Prensa*, January 8, 1935.

34. "Periódico Infantil," AHSEP, Obra de Extensión Educativa por Radio, Caja 9479, Exp. 27, Folio 26, 1930.

35. Historians still debate whether the Niños Héroes de Chapultepec, if they existed at all, were actually children. These military cadets were credited with leaping to their deaths cloaked in the Mexican flag rather than surrendering to the invading U.S. forces in 1847. El Pípila was probably a young man named Juan José de los Reyes Martínez. Henderson, *Mexican Wars for Independence*.

36. *Una historia hecha de sonidos*, 56.

37. AHSEP, Obra de Extensión Educativa por Radio, Caja 9475, Exp. 10, Folios 1–36, "Programa de Acción de la Obra Extensión Educativa por Radio de la Secretaría de Educación Pública," 1930; AHSEP, Departamento de Escuelas Rurales, Dirección General, Caja 22, Exp. 34, 1934.

38. AHSEP, Departamento de Escuelas Rurales, Dirección General, Caja 22, Exp. 34, 1934.

39. See also Hayes, *Radio Nation*, 7–8.

40. AHSEP, OCR, Caja 9475, Exp. 14, Folio 32, "Reportes de Periódico Infantil," 1930.

41. AHSEP, OCR, Caja 9475, Exp. 9, Folios 82–86, "Informes de Obra de Extensión Educativa por Radio," 1929–1930.

42. AHSEP, OCR, Caja 9480, Exp. 25, Folio 10, "Concurso de Cuentos," 1931.

43. AHSEP, OCR, Caja 9475, Exp. 10, Folio 26, 1930.

44. AHSEP, OCR, Caja 9476, Exp. 45, Folio 247, "Concurso Periódico Infantil," 1930; Folio 258.

45. AHSEP, OCR, Caja 9475, Exp. 14, Folios 34–53, "Periódico Infantil, Reportes del," 1930.

46. Two years later, in 1933, the SEP created the nationwide Association of Parents of the Mexican Republic (Asociación de Padres de Familia de la República Mexicana) in response to the increasingly powerful Catholic opposition union of parents. Furthermore, also in 1933, the government allowed only SEP-sponsored parents' unions to participate in the administration of schools. See Eineigel, "Distinction, Culture, and Politics," 167–75.

47. Eineigel, "Distinction, Culture, and Politics," 167–75; Folios 20, 538–39. For example, Mary Kay Vaughan described the rich panorama of artist Pepe Zúñiga's childhood experiences in her biography of his life. See Vaughan, "Pepe and Nico in the Vecindades" and "Cri-Cri."

48. AHSEP, OCR, Caja 9480, Exp. 25, Folio 10, "Concurso de Cuentos," 1931; Folio 4.

49. AHSEP, OCR, Caja 9475, Exp. 14, Folio 31, "Reportes de Periódico Infantil," 1930; Folios 95–119, "Reportes de Periódico Infantil," 1930.

50. AHSEP, OCR, Caja 9475, Exp. 14, Folios 4–15, "Reportes de Periódico Infantil," 1930.

51. AHSEP, OCR, Caja 9479, Exp. 27, Folios 17–29, "Periódico Infantil," 1930.

52. AHSEP, OCR, Caja 9475, Exp. 14, Folio 29, "Reportes de Periódico Infantil," 1930; Caja 9476, Exp. 45, Folio 468, "Concurso Periódico Infantil," 1930.

53. AHSEP, OCR, Caja 9476, Exp. 45, Folio 467, "Concurso Periódico Infantil," 1930.

54. AHSEP, OCR, Caja 9476, Exp. 45, Folio 525, "Concurso Periódico Infantil," 1930.

55. AHSEP, OCR, Caja 9478, Exp. 2, "Sociedad de Padres de Familia 'Pro-Infancia,'" March 3, 1931.

56. AHSEP, OCR, Caja 9472, Exp. 21, Folio 1, "Proyecto de Ampliaciones y Modificaciones para XFX," 1932.

57. "Programas (Conciertos), Obra Educativa por Radio," AHSEP, OCR, Caja 9484, Exp. 1, 1933.

58. Gallo, Mexican Modernity, 118.

59. Rochfort, "Sickle, Serpent, and Soil," 48.

60. List Arzubide, Troka el Poderoso, 7–11.

61. Ornelas Herrera, "Radio y cotidianidad en México," 156, 164. See also Castro, "Wireless."

62. *Aladino: La Revista de los Niños,* January 1934. The magazine was in circulation from 1933 to 1935.

63. *Aladino,* February 1934.

64. *Aladino,* December 1934, back cover.

65. Zelizer, *Pricing the Priceless Child,* 33–34.

66. "Campaña pro-seguridad del niño," *Boletín de la* SEP 6, no. 7 (1927): 43. For a sampling of these reports, see "Una niña atropellada por un auto," *Excelsior,* March 2, 1920; "Niño atropellado por un tren eléctrico," *Excelsior,* April 9, 1920; "Por no ser atropellado, un chiquillo se lastimó," *El Universal Gráfico,* November 12, 1924; "Querían linchar a un chófer que atropelló a un niño," *El Universal Gráfico,* November 21, 1924; "Fue atropellado un niño," *El Universal Gráfico,* November 28, 1924; and "Niño atropellado en Atzcapotzalco," *El Nacional,* August 9, 1929.

67. Matthews, *"De Viaje."*

68. Mauricio Magdeleno, "Radio," *El Maestro Rural,* November 1, 1934, 29.

69. Primer Manifiesto Estridentista, 1922, Veracruz, Segundo Manifiesto Estridentista, 1923, Puebla. See Rashkin, *Stridentist Movement in Mexico.*

70. Francsico Reyes Palma, Documents of 20th Century Latin American and Latino Art, International Center for the Arts of the Americas at the Museum of Fine Arts, Houston TX, Record ID 737586.

71. AHSEP, OCR, Caja 9484, Exp. 7, "Campaña de Propaganda de la Oficina Cultural Radiotelefónica," 1933. *Troka el Poderoso* also aired on some commercial stations.

72. List Arzubide, *Troka el Poderoso,* 17–19.

73. *Una historia hecha de sonidos,* 63–64; List Arzubide, *Troka el Poderoso.*

74. AHSEP, OCR, Caja 9484, Exp. 7, "Campaña de Propaganda de la Oficina Cultural Radiotelefónica," 1933. See also Morales Muñoz, "Troka el Poderoso."

75. List Arzubide, "Segunda Aparición de Troka el Poderoso," in *Troka el Poderoso,* 23–27.

76. List Arzubide, *Troka el Poderoso,* 145; Waters, "Revolutionizing Childhood"; List Arzubide, *Troka el Poderoso,* 151–55.

77. Germán List Arzubide, "La Máquina de Escribir," in *Literatura Revolucionaria para Niños,* edited by Díaz Cárdenas, 123–24. Though initially reviled as a symbol of Porfirian modernity by revolutionaries such as novelist Mariano Azuela, who had a typewriter smashed in his 1915 *Los de abajo,* Stridentist Manuel Maples Arce rehabilitated the typewriter in 1921 as part of his "Manifesto de Estridentismo," praising its futuristic qualities. As the revolution became increasingly institutionalized, the typewriter became the bureaucrat's greatest ally, allowing him to churn out reports in triplicate. Gallo, *Mexican Modernity,* 69–70, 77, 91.

78. AHSEP, OCR, Sección Dirección Extensión Educativa por Radio, Caja 9488, Exp. 49, "Mensaje de Acercamiento entre el Hogar y la Escuela," 1933.

79. Gallo, *Mexican Modernity,* 95–96.

80. List Arzubide, *Troka el Poderoso*, 14.

81. Rochfort, "Sickle, Serpent, and Soil," 48; Paz, "Sons of La Malinche."

82. List Arzubide, "Las Escaleras y el Elevador," *Troka el Poderoso*, 125–27.

83. List Arzubide, "La Montaña y el Ferrocarril," *Troka el Poderoso*, 99.

84. AHSEP, OCR, Caja 9486, Exp. 49, Folio 3, "'Troka el Poderoso' Reportes de la República Mexicana," 1933.

85. *Memoria de la SEP* 2 (1933): 886–87.

86. AHSEP, OCR, Caja 9568, Exp. 49, Folios 5–6, "'Troka el Poderoso' Reportes de la República Mexicana," 1933.

87. AHSEP, OCR, Caja 9486, Troka el Poderoso, Reportes de la República Mexicana, 1933.

88. XFX *Programa de Trabajo para el Bimestre de Mayo y Junio de 1933*, 15, Rodolfo Usigli Collection, Box 23, Folder 6.

89. List Arzubide, *Troka el Poderoso*, 7–11.

90. AHSEP, Departamento de Escuelas Rurales, Dirección General, Caja 21, Exp. 8, 1933.

91. AHSEP, Departamento de Escuelas Rurales, Dirección General, Caja 22, Exp. 34, 1934; *Memoria de la SEP* 1 (1932): 538.

92. *Memorias de la SEP* 2 (1933): 885–86.

93. Davis, *Urban Leviathan*.

94. AHSEP, OCR, Caja 9484, Expediente 1, "Programas (Conciertos), Obra Educativa por Radio," 1933.

95. I thank participants in the Semanario de la Historia de Higiene e Educación at the Instituto de Investigaciones Históricas at Universidad Nacional Autónoma de México, headed by Claudia Agostoni, for insight into the changing relationship between the home and the classroom over the course of the nineteenth and twentieth centuries.

4. Comino vence al Diablo

1. José Muñoz Cota, "Introducción," 4.

2. Also sometimes written as Teatro Guignol. The name Guiñol comes from a prodigious Italian puppeteer in the early nineteenth century, named either Guignol or Chignol, reportedly responsible for the popularity of puppet theater expressly for children throughout Europe. The makeshift stage itself soon became known as *teatro guignol*. Lago, *Teatro Guignol Mexicano*, 15.

3. *Comino vence al Diablo* appears first in an anthology of three plays by List Arzubide, *Tres comedias infantiles*. The play also appears in *El Maestro Rural*, October 1938, 20–21, 25.

4. An excellent article that traces the experiences of National Indigenist Institute "cultural promoters" and their puppets in the Maya highlands displays stark continuity between that program and the Teatro Guiñol that predated it by thirty years is S. Lewis, "Modernizing Message, Mystical Messenger: The Teatro Petul."

5. De la Luz Mena, *Escuela Racionalista*, 153–56.

6. The author, José de la Luz Mena, was a champion of the Rationalist School and compiled a series of testimonies from the school that situated the origin of some of the most lauded aspects of children's culture (art programs and children's magazines, among others) in the early days of this pedagogical experiment in Yucatán. His rather shortsighted and nationalist version speaks to his faith in the power of the Rationalist School but disregards some of the broader, transnational contexts in which puppet theater and other socially productive forms of modern children's culture originated.

7. An example of the conscious use of theater to promote national identity comes from Spain in the short-lived Second Republic from 1931 to 1936. See Holguín, *Creating Spaniards*, chap. 3.

8. "Memoria de la Secretaria," AHSEP, Departamento de Bellas Artes, Sección Teatros, Caja 3969, Exp. 18, 1935. For more about the development of nineteenth-century Mexican national identity through stories from the Rosete Aranda puppet troupes, see Beezley, *Mexican National Identity* and "Cómo fue que El Negrito salvó a México de los franceses."

9. List Arzubide, *Tres comedias infantiles*, 5–19.

10. Miranda Silva and Beezley, "Rosete Aranda Puppets," 336–37.

11. List Arzubide, *Tres comedias infantiles*, 7.

12. Germán List Arzubide equated children to "savages," in line with the infantilizing tendencies that characterized much of the educational missions in the revolutionary period in "El Teatro Infantil," in *Memoria del VII Congreso Panamericano del Niño*, 2:252–54.

13. Sosenski, "Diversiones malsanas"; Abelardo González Garza, "Proyecto de reglamento para la asistencia de menores de edad a los espectáculos públicos," in *Memoria del VII Congreso Panamericano del Niño*, 1:191; AHSEP, Departamento de Bellas Artes, Serie Publicaciones, Caja 64, Exp. 41, 1935. Religious publications spoke out against the movies and their negative influence on children, especially *La Vanguardia: El Periódico de los Niños* (1921–22).

14. "Literatura para niños: *Comino vence al Diablo*," *El Maestro Rural*, October 1938, 20–21, 25.

15. The magazine was intended to link the SEP to both rural schoolteachers and newly literate campesinos. *El Maestro Rural* was also circulated among Mexican schoolteachers working in the United States and throughout South America and the Caribbean. In 1936 Cardenas changed the goals of the magazine so that it targeted primarily an audience of rural schoolteachers. Palacios, "Postrevolutionary Intellectuals."

16. For examples of the impact that *El Maestro Rural* bore on the morale and sense of integration of rural schoolteachers, see their letters to the editor in *El Maestro Rural*, January 1935, 38–39.

17. "Trabajos de Teatro Infantil," *El Maestro Rural*, September 1936, 38–39; "La construcción del teatro infantil y de títeres," *El Maestro Rural*, June 1934, 31.

18. Rafael M. Saavedra, "Instrucciones para Orientar y Facilitar la Creación de la Obra de Teatro," *El Maestro Rural*, August 1934, 25–27.

19. Soni, "El Teatro Infantil," *Memoria del VII Congreso Panamericano*, 239, 243.

20. Soni, "El Teatro Infantil," *Memoria del VII Congreso Panamericano*, 240.

21. See chapter 5. *Memoria de la* SEP 1 (1935): 35; "Aspiraciones Infantiles," *El Maestro Rural*, April 1935, 15–17, 28; *El Maestro Rural*, April 1935, 17.

22. Spenser, "Encounter of Two Revolutions."

23. "El Teatro del Muñeco," *El Maestro Rural*, April 1935, 36–37.

24. List Arzubide's brief exile resulted from his vocal anti-imperialist demonstrations, causing an outcry when he denounced U.S. intervention in Nicaragua by representing the U.S. flag being trampled by Sandinistas. His exile bolstered his credentials as a bona fide revolutionary nationalist. Carmen Carrara, "Presentación," in List Arzubide, *Teatro guiñol*, vi.

25. AHSEP, Department of Bellas Artes, Serie Teatro, Caja 4949, 1934.

26. *Época de oro del Teatro Guiñol de Bellas Artes.*

27. Giménez Cacho et al., *El Teatro Guiñol de Bellas Artes*, 18, 32.

28. Lago, *Teatro Guignol Mexicano*, 20.

29. AHSEP, Departamento de Bellas Artes, Serie Teatro 1932–1936, Caja 71, Exp. "Teatro del Niño," 1934.

30. AHSEP, Departamento de Bellas Artes, Serie Teatro 1932–1936, Caja 71, Exp. 43, 1934.

31. *Memoria de la* SEP 1 (1933): 121.

32. *Época de oro*, 2005.

33. *El Maestro Rural*, April 1, 1936, 23.

34. AHSEP, Departamento de Bellas Artes, Serie Teatro, Caja 72, Exp. 56, 1934.

35. AHSEP, Departamento de Bellas Artes, Serie Teatro, Caja 72, Exp. 56, 1934.

36. AHSEP, Departamento de Bellas Artes, Serie Teatro, Caja 4949, Exp. 126, 1936.

37. AHSEP, Departamento de Bellas Artes, Serie Teatro 1932–1936, Caja 71, Exp. 43. Music was an important part of the plays; every play started off with a musical prelude, often recognizable as folkloric, popular pieces such as "La bamba," "El jarabe tapatío," and "La bicicleta." Silvestre Revueltas, who at the inception of Teatro Guiñol was the director of the National Conservatory, composed some original pieces, such as "El renacuajo paseador," specifically for the puppet shows. *Época de oro.*

38. Sosenski, "Niños limpios y trabajadores."

39. León Cárdenas, "Letters to the Maestro Rural: How to Make a Teatro Guiñol," in *Época de oro*.

40. List Arzubide, "Comino va a la huelga," in *Tres comedias infantiles*, 47–58.

41. "La prosperidad de la patria es la cultura de sus hijos," in María de los Dolores Alva de la Canal (Para la Campaña de Alfabetización), "Comino Analfabeta," in *Época de oro*.

42. Jorge Contreras Sánces (Para el grupo Comino), "Comino Ignorante," in *Época de oro*.

43. As early as 1922, scarcely a year after the institutionalization of the SEP, an estimated 5,000 children were signed up for the Ejército Infantil and had taught 8,947 of their peers the basic tenets of reading and writing, an initiative discussed further in chapter 5. *Boletín de la Secretaría de Educación Pública* (SEP) 1, no. 3 (1922): 468–69.

44. *Boletín de la SEP* 1, no. 4 (1923): 83–85.

45. List Arzubide, "Petroleo para las Lámparas de México."

46. Cárdenas, *Época de oro*, 2005.

47. AHSEP, Departamento de Bellas Artes, Serie Teatro 1932–1936, Caja 71, Exp. "Teatro del Niño," 1934.

48. AHSEP, Departamento de Bellas Artes, Serie Teatro, Caja 3969, Exp. 18, 1935.

49. AHSEP, Departamento de Bellas Artes, Sección de Teatro, Activities 1935, Caja 3969, Exp. 18, 1935.

50. Juan Bustillo Oro, "La Moral en el Teatro Infantil," *El Maestro Rural*, November–December 1938, 37.

51. AHSEP, Departamento de Bellas Artes, Serie Teatro, Caja 73, Exp. 11, 1934.

52. AHSEP, Departamento de Bellas Artes, Serie Teatro, Caja 73, Exp. 57, 1936.

53. AHSEP, Departamento de Bellas Artes, Serie Teatro 1932–1936, Caja 71, Exp. "Teatro del Niño," 1934.

54. AHSEP, Departamento de Bellas Artes, Serie Teatro, Caja 71, Exp. "Teatro del Niño," 1934 and Exp. "Teatro del Niño," 1936.

55. AHSEP, Departamento de Bellas Artes, Serie Teatro, Caja 71, Exp. 43, 1934.

56. Such annotations by Carlos González can be found on several letters submitted by teachers that were not considered to provide enough useful details. AHSEP, Departamento de Bellas Artes, Serie Teatro 1933–1936, Caja 71, Exp. 44, 1934.

57. AHSEP, Departamento de Bellas Artes, Serie Teatro 1932–1936, Caja 71, Exp. "Teatro del Niño," 1934.

58. AHSEP, Departamento de Bellas Artes, Serie Teatro 1932–1936, Caja 71, Exp. "Teatro del Niño," 1934.

59. AHSEP, Departamento de Bellas Artes, Serie Teatro, Caja 4949, 1934.

60. "Cartas a los Maestros Rurales," *El Maestro Rural*, March 1, 1936, 23–24.

61. AHSEP, Departamento de Bellas Artes, Serie Teatro 1932–1936, Caja 71, Exp. 43.

62. AHSEP, Departamento de Bellas Artes, Serie Teatro, Caja 73, Exp. 11, 1934.

63. AHSEP, Departamento de Bellas Artes, Serie Teatro 1932–1936, Caja 71, Exp. "Teatro del Niño," 1934.

64. AHSEP, Departamento de Bellas Artes, Serie Teatro 1932–1936, Caja 71, Exp. "Teatro del Niño," 1934.

65. AHSEP, Departamento de Bellas Artes, Serie Teatro, Caja 4949, 1934.

66. AHSEP, Departamento de Bellas Artes, Serie Teatro, Caja 4949, 1934.

67. "Grupo Periquillo" and "Grupo Nahual" were added before the Teatro Guiñol expanded to unofficial and local presentations, all based on the work of the two original groups. AHSEP, Departamento de Bellas Artes, Serie Teatro, Caja 71, Exp. "Teatro del Niño," 1934.

68. AHSEP, Departamento de Bellas Artes, Serie Teatro, Caja 4949, 1934.

69. Bennett, *Theatre Audiences*, 128.

70. For a discussion of cultural reception of Soviet films in these terms, see Tsivian, *Early Cinema in Russia*, 1–12.

5. *Hacer Patria* through Peer Education

1. For a discussion of the real and mythologized contributions of Vasconcelos to the spread of cultural nationalism, see Beezley, "Creating a Revolutionary Culture." The ministers of education following Vasconcelos were José Manuel Puig Casauranc (1924–28 and 1931), Ezequiel Padilla (1928–30), Narcisso Bassols (1931–34), and Gonzalo Vázquez Vela (1935–40).

2. Not coincidentally, John Dewey spent a good deal of time in Mexico observing its educational innovations and wrote about it in his text that compares educational systems internationally. See Dewey, *Impressions of Soviet Russia*.

3. See Meneses Morales, *Tendencias educativas oficiales en México*.

4. *El Maestro Rural*, July 15, 1935, back cover.

5. Arce Gurza, "En busca de una educación revolucionaria."

6. Booth, "Socialist Secondary Education in Mexico." Programs to promote the active child sprouted in the 1920s and flourished in the 1930s. Vaughan, *Cultural Politics in Revolution*, 43–44.

7. See the *Mensaje de acercamiento entre el hogar y la escuela* in AHSEP, Dirección Extensión Educativa por Radio, Subsección Boletines para el Acercamiento entre el Hogar y la Escuela, Caja 9488, Exp. 49, 1933.

8. Vaughan, *State, Education, and Social Class*, chap. 7.

9. Acevedo Rodrigo, "Struggles for Citizenship?"

10. Rockwell, *Hacer escuela, hacer estado*, 335.

11. Rockwell, *Hacer escuela, hacer estado*, 17.

12. Regarding stadiums, see Gallo, *Mexican Modernity*, chap. 5.

13. *Boletín de la SEP* 4, no. 7 (October 1925): 100.

14. Prof. Adolfo Velasco, "Las primeras experiencias sociales que deben procurarse a los niños," *El Maestro Rural*, April 1, 1932, 6.

15. "El conocimiento de la patria es la base de toda instrucción cívica verdadera." García, *Una vuelta a la República Mexicana*. García modeled the format of his book, which follows two children on their adventures throughout the country, as they encounter individuals who instruct them about the country's rich history, regional geography, and natural history, on a French version by Mrs. Fouillée, under the pseudonym G. Bruno. To maintain what he considered the unique character of Mrs. Fouillée's original version, many of the chapters were openly plagiarized, swapping out French heroes and regions for Mexican ones. To assure the reader that this was not the result of an inferiority complex or cultural imperialism, García emphasizes in his preface that the substitutions, such as the caves of Cacahuamilpa and the waterfalls of Necaxa, are equally as iconic and perhaps unrivaled in the world.

16. Monroy Padilla, *Civismo*.

17. *Memoria de la SEP, de septiembre de 1936 a agosto de 1937* 2 (Mexico City: DAPP, 1937), 749.

18. Norbert Elias describes the "civilizing process" as a social conditioning conducted in the public realm, by parents primarily and by the larger community secondarily. Elias, *Civilizing Process*, 158–59. For a comparison between Elias's and Foucault's theories of socialization, see D. Smith, "*The Civilizing Process* and *The History of Sexuality*."

19. The seminal work in this category is Weber, *Peasants into Frenchmen*. For an exploration of the way organizations shaped girls in the United States, see S. Miller, *Growing Girls*. For a quite Foucauldian discussion of policy and institutions of discipline designed to control wayward children in the United States, see Sealander, *Failed Century of the Child*. For the role of education in socializing youth and cobbling a sense of Russian identity prior to the Russian Revolution, see Eklof, *Russian Peasant Schools*; and Dowler, *Classroom and Empire*. For China's Cultural Revolution, see Zang, *Children of the Cultural Revolution*; and Kwong, *Cultural Revolution in China's Schools*.

20. Susana Sosenski argues that the *Código de Moralidad* also infused students with a particularly class-based work ethic and served to justify the perpetuation of child labor in both the formal and the informal sectors, despite legislation and rhetoric to the contrary. See Sosenski, *Niños en acción*, chap. 4.

21. The complete list of moral laws is as follows: Ley del Dominio sobre Si Mismo, Ley de la Buena Salud, Ley de la Bondad, Ley del Deporte, Ley de la Confianza en Si Mismo, Ley del Deber, Ley de la Confianza, Ley de la Veracidad, Ley del Trabajo Bien Ejecutado, Ley de la Cooperación, and Ley de la Lealtad. "Código de Moralidad," *Boletín de la SEP* 4, no. 7 (1925): 103, 3–4.

22. *Coopera* 1, no. 1 (March 15, 1926).

23. Francisco Manriquez, "Una categoría de hábitos cívicos que la escuela debe cultivar," *Coopera* 2, no. 1 (March 1927): 15.

24. It later became the Office of Social Action (Oficina de Acción Social) under the Cárdenas administration in 1937. Parallel departments to promote civic education and activities were created in other government agencies, such as the Department of Educational and Social Action (Departamento de Acción Educativa y Social) created by the Secretaría de Salubridad Pública in 1929. These agencies linked their activities to a network providing civic instruction across a broad spectrum of society. AHSEP, Subsecretaría de Educación Pública, Caja 22, Exp. 2, 1938. See also *Guía de la Sección Asistencia*, iv.

25. For a critical discussion of the classic scholarship on the institutionalization of revolutionary political culture in the twentieth century, see T. Benjamin, "Leviathan on the Zócalo."

26. Prof. José Teran Tovar, "El instinto gregario y los clubes infantiles," *El Maestro Rural*, July 15, 1934, 6.

27. "La solidaridad en el niño," *El Maestro Rural*, March 15, 1935, 3–4.

28. "La cooperación infantil en la vida nacional," *El Maestro Rural*, July 15, 1933, 24–25.

29. "La cooperación infantil en la vida nacional," *El Maestro Rural*, July 15, 1933, 25.

30. AHSEP, Departamento de Escuelas Rurales, Clubes Escolares y Comités de Acción Social-Escuelas Rurales, Caja 5, Exp. 3, 1933. The Junior Red Cross also provided several similar committees for community action.

31. Gregorio Torres Quintero, "No a la República Escolar, sino la Comunidad Escolar," *Boletín de la SEP* 4, no. 10 (1925): 217–18.

32. *Informe de la Secretaría de Educación Pública*, 34.

33. AHSSA, Beneficencia Pública, Subsección Asistencia, Serie Departamento de Acción Educativa y Social, Caja 9, Exp. 8, 1935.

34. Written petitions to governing authorities, of course, extended back to the colonial period. The revolutionary period, especially during the presidency of Lázaro Cárdenas, saw a remarkable influx of letters, due in part to increased (though varied) levels of literacy and in part to a collective belief in the nearly magical powers of the presidential office in an era of redistribution. See MacGregor, *México de su puño y letra*; and Nava Nava, *Los abajo firmantes*.

35. AGN, O-C 805-H-101.

36. "En Marcha," Órgano de la Confederación de Organizaciones Revolucionarias de la Juventud.

37. Committees included Protection of Plants and Animals, Works and Materials, Recreational Studies and Publicity, Health and Hygiene, Executive Committee, Coordination of Cooperatives, Protection of Children, Civil and Social Action, Home Economics, and Order and Justice.

38. AHSEP, Subsecretaría de Educación Pública, Caja 18, Exp. 14, 1937.

39. Nava Nava, *Los abajo firmantes*, 7–13.

40. "Labor Nacionalista-Despertando sentimientos patrios a niños mexicanos en el extranjero," AHSRE, III-220-10, 1933; "Guardia de honor por niños mexicanos," AHSRE, IV-276-28, 1930.

41. *Memoria de la SEP* 1 (1937–38): 473–90. For correspondence between Mexican government officials and schools in the United States with Mexican and Mexican American students, see AHSRE, III-220-10 (1933); for the mariachi instrument request, see AHSRE, IV-276-28 (1930).

42. See the guidelines for student council organizations, or Sociedades de Alumnos, in AHSSA, Fondo Beneficencia Pública, Sección Asistencia, Serie Departamento de Acción Educativa y Social, Caja 1, Exp. 10, 1930.

43. AHSSA, Beneficencia Pública, Subsección Asistencia, Serie Departamento de Acción Educativa y Social, Caja 1, Exp. 10, 1930.

44. For a discussion of citizenship in Latin America as both manifestations of belonging and political agency, see Taylor and Wilson, "Messiness of Everyday Life."

45. "Asociación Femenina Infantil Para Reformar a México," AGN, EPG 363/204, 1929.

46. For a discussion of national identity based on racial ideologies of the day as they are played out in this movie, see Hershfield, "Race and Ethnicity in Classical Cinema."

47. "Misiones Culturales," in vol. 12 of *Los mejores de la SEP*. See also Palacios, "Postrevolutionary Intellectuals." For a discussion of the religious models upon which Vasconcelos premised his pedagogical theory, see Alcubierre Moya and Bazán Bonfil, "*Lecturas clásicas para niños*"; and "Misiones Culturales," in vol. 12 of *Los mejores de la SEP*. See also Palacios, "Postrevolutionary Intellectuals."

48. Vaughan, *State, Education, and Social Class*, 181–84.

49. Rafael A. Romo, "La guerra al analfabetismo," *El Maestro Rural*, December 1, 1935, 5.

50. Puig Casauranc, *La educación pública*, 221.

51. Puig Casauranc, *La educación pública*, xiii.

52. Results from the 1940 census estimate that a total of 7,198,756 Mexicans—51.6 percent of the population—remained illiterate, the lowest percentage on record since 1900. Whetten, *Rural Mexico*, 420.

53. Puig Casauranc, *La educación pública*, xvii.

54. For a description of the uneven process of acculturation undertaken by cultural missionaries in Estado de México, see Civera Cerecedo, "Del calzón de manta al overol."

55. After 1937 it was reorganized and renamed Ejército Infantil de la Cultura, with the same goals but with even added emphasis on the roles and responsibilities of children, youth, women, workers, military officers, and so on in contributing to the eradication of illiteracy in the country. *Memoria de la SEP* 2 (1938–39): 306.

56. *Boletín de la* SEP 1, no. 4 (1923): 83–85.

57. The schoolteacher served as liaison between the Children's Literacy Army and the SEP, informing the agency when their classroom had registered enough members, elected the required officials, and identified illiterate children. *Boletín de la* SEP 1, no. 3 (1922): 468–69.

58. Vaughan, "Cambio ideológico en la política educativa de la SEP," 83.

59. *Boletín de la* SEP 1, no. 3 (1922): 468–69.

60. Fell, *José Vasconcelos*, 47.

61. *Memoria de la* SEP 1 (1937–38): 459–67. Some 826 children from Mexico City participated.

62. Militarization of children's organizations was a common feature, especially in the Boy Scouts and other boy-oriented programs. After World War I males were discovered to be weaker than the ideal, and increasing energy went into the construction and display of masculinity among boys, through marches and public displays of calisthenics. The Mexican Revolution served as a point of reference that paralleled the experience of World War I for other countries. Intellectual architects of programs to build masculinity stressed that a military aesthetic and organization should stress the positive aspects of the military—honor, obedience, order, and respect—rather than transmit bellicosity. Militarization would also ensure control over children outside of the context of the classroom structure. See the plans to organize a Mexican Children's League, by Professor Alfredo Sánchez O., described in chapter 6.

63. From an excerpt of the 1932 Grito de Guadalajara given by Calles in the town of the same name, declaring the centrality of the child in the revolutionary project, in "La Revolución se apoderará de la juventud por medio de la escuela," *El Maestro Rural*, August 1, 1934, 2.

64. "Quedará constituida la Policía Infantil en el Distrito Federal," *El Nacional*, March 30, 1936; "Imposición de placas ayer a la Radio-Patrulla Infantil," *El Nacional*, June 7, 1942.

65. *Memoria de la* SEP 2 (1938–39): 307.

66. A schoolteacher who could claim twenty members of the Literacy Army also received a diploma of good citizenship. *Boletín de la* SEP 1, no. 4 (1923): 83–85. See the case of the young Angelina Sólis of Nuevo León, who taught her peers and contributed to the school magazine *Zoolmecatl* as a child in the early 1920s and went on to become a *maestra rural* and continued to work for literary publications, in Ramos Escobar, "Niños redactores e ilustradores."

67. AHSEP, Subsecretaría de Educación Pública, Subserie Comité Nacional de la Campaña Pro-Educación Popular, Caja 22, Exp. 38, Folio 136, 1938.

68. Evaluations were conducted by "el profesor acompañado por otros dos de sus alumnos designados entre los más aplicados." *Boletín de la* SEP 1, no. 4 (1923): 83–85.

69. *Boletín de la* SEP 1, no. 2 (1922).

70. *Boletín de la Universidad*, IV Época, 2, no. 4 (1921).

71. "El 60% de los niños delincuentes son hijos de alcohólicos," *El Nacional*, August 7, 1929.

72. See Pierce, "Sobering the Revolution" and "Fighting Bacteria."

73. García, *Una vuelta a la República Mexicana*, 333–34.

74. J. Díaz G. and Manuel V. Flores, "La desgracia de una familia" and "¡Viva el Agua! ¡Muera el Alcohol!" *Comino: El Periódico de los Niños* 2, no. 8 (1936): 3, 12. This issue has an article that claims that the fall of the Toltec empire came with the discovery of *pulque*. "Preguntas y respuestas sobre el vino," *El Heraldo de los Niños: Periódico Espiritual para los Niños*, no. 8 (October 1, 1939): 8.

75. "Festival Antialcoholico Infantil" (1935), Centro Nacional de las Artes, Fondo Reservado, Programas de mano, GP-MF00895.

76. "La niñez protesta el látigo del alcoholismo."

77. Descriptions are from images in albums commemorating the antialcohol rallies in various states, in AGN, EPG, Caja 23, Inv. 982/2276; AGN, EPG, Caja 31, Exp. 80/28. See also Pierce, "Fighting Bacteria," 512.

78. See Taylor and Wilson, "Messiness of Everyday Life," 162.

79. AGN, EPG, Caja 34, Exp. 80/54.

80. AGN, EPG, Caja 33, Exp. 80/53.

81. *La Voz del Niño*, 1930 in AHSEP, Departamento de Bibliotecas, Caja 997, Exp. 122, 1930.

82. See the preface written by Padilla circa 1928–30 in Flores A., *Alcoholismo*.

83. See Pierce, "Sobering the Revolution," chap. 3.

84. AGN, LCR 553/11.

85. AHSEP, OCR, Subserie Conferencia y Boletines, Caja 9474, Exp. 12, Folios 270–72, 1929.

86. AGN, EPG, Caja 34, Exp. 80/54.

87. AHSEP, OCR, Subserie Conferencia y Boletines, Caja 9474, Exp. 12, Folios 270–72, 1929.

88. Nava Nava, *Los abajo firmantes*, 54.

89. "Convocatoria para la Celebración de la Primera Asamblea Infantil Antialcohólica," September 28–October 3, 1936, AGN, LCR 553/11.

90. AGN, EPG 553/11.

91. Program for Anti-Alcohol Education in rural schools in AHSEP, Departamento de Psicopedagogía e Higiene, Subserie Propaganda Antialcoholica Esc. Rural Federal, Caja 5123 (146), Exp. 79, Folios 12–24, 1930.

92. "México da una muestra de adelanto en pedagogía," *El Nacional*, March 6, 1935.

93. *Coopera* 2, nos. 5–6 (July–August 1927): 18.

94. Snodgrass, "'We Are All Mexicans Here.'"

95. "También Habrá Congreso de 'Niños Proletarios,'" *Excelsior,* February 5, 1935.

96. *Memoria de la* SEP 2 (1935): 73.

97. Lerner, *Historia de la Revolución Mexicana,* 97–98.

98. León Díaz Cárdenas, "El niño indígena y el niño proletario," and Felipe Ferrer Baynon, "El cultivo integral del niño proletario," in *Memoria del VII Congreso Panamericano del Niño,* 2:423–24, 412.

99. J. J. de la Rosa P., "El Congreso del Niño Proletario," *El Nacional,* February 14, 1935.

100. "Interesantes asuntos tratados en el Congreso de Niños Proletarios," *El Universal,* October 16, 1935.

101. "Solemne Inauguración del Primer Congreso del Niño Proletario," *El Nacional,* March 1, 1935.

102. "El sentido clasista del niño proletario," *El Nacional,* March 7, 1935.

103. Sánchez, *Mexico,* 111–12.

104. *Boletín Municipal* 14, no. 23 (December 31, 1926): 28–29. John Dewey had a firm basis for comparison, having traveled around the world to visit revolutionary school systems and develop a comparative pedagogy of social action. For his reflections on Mexico vis-à-vis international counterparts, see Dewey, *Impressions of Soviet Russia.* See also Tannenbaum, "The Miracle School."

105. "Escuela Industrial Modelo 'Francisco I. Madero,'" *Boletín Municipal* 14, no. 12 (January 13, 1926): 32–37; *Boletín de la* SEP, 1923 and 1924, in Sosenski, *Niños en acción,* 236.

106. "La niñez proletaria tiene ya plena confianza en el mañana," *El Nacional,* March 12, 1935. The list of participating primary schools in Mexico City is: Francisco I. Madero, Domingo F. Sarmiento, Quetzalcoatl, Escuela Granja de Santa Anita, David G. Berlanga, Estado de Guerrero, Francisco Días Covarrubias, and Estado de Sonora. *Memoria de la* SEP 2 (1935): 72.

107. "Solemne inauguración del Primer Congreso del Niño Proletario," *El Nacional,* March 1, 1935.

108. "Expulsan del Congreso a los 'Pioneros Rojos,'" *Excelsior,* March 15, 1935.

109. "Interés por el concurso," *El Nacional,* March 23, 1935.

110. "Congreso del Niño Proletario," *El Maestro Rural,* April 1, 1935, 8–11, 30.

111. "Es a nuestra edad el juego una cosa indispensible, y tan necesario como a las aves el espacio y el agua al pez." "Aspiraciones infantiles," *El Maestro Rural,* April 1, 1935, 17, 28.

112. *Memoria de la* SEP 2 (1935): 73.

113. "Un original concurso se presentó en el Congreso del Niño Proletario, ayer," *El Nacional,* March 8, 1935.

114. AGN, LCR, Caja 0101, 135.2/44, Folios 77–78, 1935.

115. "México da una muestra de adelanto en pedagogía," *El Nacional,* March 6, 1935.

116. AHSEP, Sección Subsecretaría de Educación Pública, Caja 18, Exp. 14, 1937.

117. "Lo que dicen los niños," *El Nacional,* March 18, 1935.

118. "Lo que dicen los niños," *El Nacional,* March 18, 1935.

119. Lerner, *Historia de la Revolución Mexicana,* 35–36.

120. See individual community responses to state intervention in the family, and in particular in children's labor patterns, in Acevedo Rodrigo, "Struggles for Citizenship?" 187–93.

121. Catalina d'Erzell, "Ya no habrá niños en México, digo yo como mujer," *La Defensa del Hogar: Salvemos a la Patria Salvando a la Niñez,* no. 19 (November 22, 1936): 1–2.

122. Adolfo López Mateos went on to the national finals held in the Teatro Hidalgo but did not win the national competition. The national champion was the Oaxacan delegate, Roberto Ortiz Gris, who, in the spirit of Benito Juárez, "pertenece a los de abajo." "Quienes triunfaron ayer en la gran prueba oratoria," *El Universal,* June 9, 1929, 1, 7, 11; "Brillante prueba del torneo de oratoria," *El Universal,* June 9, 1929, 2nd section, p. 4; "El Jurado y algunos de los campeones," *El Universal,* June 15, 1929. Ortiz Gris went on to the international competition in Washington DC and later became a visible supporter of the Cárdenas administration. But although he did not win the highest honor in the oratory competition, López Mateos was already clearly possessed of the talents that would allow him eventually to rise to the highest political position. See B. T. Smith, *Pistoleros and Popular Movements,* 99.

6. *Hermanitos de la Raza*

1. AHSEP, Departamento de Escuelas Rurales, Dirección General, Caja 26, Exp. 24, 1932.

2. AHSEP, Departamento de Escuelas Rurales, Dirección General, Caja 26, Exp. 24, 1932.

3. As I discuss in depth elsewhere, some of these exiles were neither "children" nor "orphans," nor in some cases even "Republican," as they were often described in the national press celebrating their arrival. The state sponsorship of these children was highly symbolic and in many cases devolved into instances of neglect, due to their strategic and propagandistic role in promoting a particular brand of nationalism during the later years of the Cárdenas administration.

4. *Patria* can be roughly translated as "mother country" or "fatherland." Revolutionaries evoked the term to incite a sense of loyalty to an abstract entity that was in the process of being redefined.

5. Jensen, *Body by Weimar.* Recently, scholars have focused on the ways in which international children's organizations articulated distinct defini-

tions of masculine and feminine identity, as well as established the mindset for a generation about the relative socioeconomic position of countries around the world during the first decades of the twentieth century. Among others, see Block and Proctor, *Scouting Frontiers*; Mechling, *On My Honor*; and Parsons, *Race, Resistance, and the Boy Scout Movement*. For an analysis of internationalist imperialism between the Girl Guides of England, Canada, and India, see Alexander, "Girl Guide Movement."

6. Mintz, "Reflections on Age."

7. Paris, "Through the Looking Glass."

8. Bliss and Blum, "Dangerous Driving," 165–66.

9. A similar process, the tension between "play" and "real" Indians in the United States is addressed in Deloria, *Playing Indian*.

10. "Oficina de Acción Social, Plan de Trabajo," *Memoria de la Secretaría de Educación Pública* (Mexico City) 1 (1936–38): 487.

11. Ironically, many *botiquines* experienced long delays in delivery due to strict customs laws at the Mexican border designed to protect the economy from an influx of foreign goods. Secretary of Foreign Relations Eduardo Hay had to override customs officers' decisions to allow the chests to enter the country. This was evidence of a highly organized administration that enforced laws to protect its economic sovereignty. See correspondence in AHSEP, Departamento de Escuelas Rurales, Dirección General, Caja 21, Exp. 7, 1932–33.

12. Payson, *Boy Scouts under Fire*, 91. See also Deering, *Border Boys with the Mexican Rangers*.

13. Another example of this genre is Richards and Landazuri, *Children of Mexico*.

14. The American Red Cross published junior publications under the titles *High School Service, Junior Red Cross Journal*, and *Junior Red Cross News*.

15. Carleton Beals, "Those Mexicans," *Junior Red Cross Journal* 8, no. 4 (1931): 76.

16. Constance Lindsay Skinner, "Two Terrible Bandits," *Junior Red Cross News* 15, no. 7 (1934): 147. See also "Pancho's Goat," *Junior Red Cross News* 14, no. 3 (1932): 51–53.

17. Beals, "Those Mexicans," 80.

18. Carleton Beals, "Going to School in Mexico," *Junior Red Cross Journal* 9, no. 9 (1932): 198.

19. Anna Milo Upjohn, "Manuel of Mexico," *Junior Red Cross Journal* 7, no. 2 (1930): 38.

20. Pérez Montfort, "Una región inventada desde el centro," in *Estampas de nacionalismo popular mexicano*, 134.

21. "About a Next Door Neighbor," *Junior Red Cross News* 10, no. 3 (1928): 46–47.

22. "A Letter from Mexico," *Junior Red Cross News* (February 1941): 167. See also "A Children's Fiesta," *Junior Red Cross News* (January 1942): 136–37,

and accompanying photos of young children dressed up in indigenous "costume."

23. Sánchez-Eppler describes the process of creating friendship albums in the nineteenth-century United States as a conscious way for children to reproduce and create a version of self-conscious identity, in the context of the literary and artistic conventions available to them at the time, in "Copying and Conversion."

24. Photo, *Junior Red Cross News* (May 1938): n.p.

25. *The Three Caballeros*, directed by Norman Ferguson (Walt Disney Productions, 1944).

26. "Working Together," *Junior Red Cross News* (April 1941): 218–19.

27. *El Universal*, May 18, 1931.

28. Charlotte Kett, *The World's Health* (November 1925), in Sackett, *Administration of the International School Correspondence*, 81.

29. Recommendation of the First Pan-American Red Cross Conference in Buenos Aires, 1923. AHSEP, Serie Subsecretaría de Educación Pública, Subserie Unión Panamericana, Washington DC, Caja 6, Exp. 18, Folio 7, 1932.

30. *El Universal*, March 16, 1931.

31. *El Nacional*, April 15, 1939.

32. AHSRE, III-402-7, 1939.

33. José Vasconcelos, who famously served as minister of education in the 1920s, coined the term *cosmic race* in his 1925 essay "La raza cósmica." While he wrote specifically for a national audience, the idea of a common racial heritage advanced Pan-Hispanism in the twentieth century.

34. "Serenidad de América," *El Nacional*, August 13, 1937; "Celebración escolar del 12 de octubre," *El Nacional*, October 3, 1937.

35. "Primer concierto infantil con motivo del Día de la Raza," Centro Nacional de las Artes, Programas de mano, GP-MF01545, 1938.

36. AHSRE, L-E 274 (III), 1934.

37. *Semillita: Para la Educadora y el Niño* 1, no. 2 (October 1, 1944), Fondo Xochitl Medina.

38. AHSRE, L-E 274 (III), 1934.

39. AHSRE, L-E 274 (III), 1934.

40. AHSEP, Departamento Escolar, Caja 4, Exp. 35, 1922.

41. "Sois vosotros, compañeritos, los futuros hombres de la gran nación azteca; en vuestras manos está el porvenir de vuestra patria, y nuestro mayor deseo es el de que aprovechéis hoy los consejos y lecciones de vuestras maestras, para que cuando llegue el día de ser los dirigentes, tengáis una inteligencia clara al servicio de un noble corazón." AHSEP, Departamento de Escuelas Rurales, Dirección General, Caja 21, Exp. 32, 1934.

42. Prof. Lupe Jiménez Posadas, "La Cruz Roja de la Juventud de la Escuela 'República Argentina,'" in *Memoria del VII Congreso Panamericano del Niño*,

1:918–21. For more about the child-driven nature of extracurricular organizations, see the previous chapter of this dissertation.

43. Sackett, *Administration of the International School Correspondence*, 23.

44. "Intercambio de Correspondencia Escolar entre México-Chile," AHSRE, III-1704-4, 1938; "Intercambio o Acercamiento Escolar entre las Americas," AHSRE, III-172-23, 1938.

45. AHSRE, III-380-10, 1937.

46. AHSRE, III-220-12, 1933.

47. The National Bureau of Educational Correspondence at George Peabody College was first designed to organize correspondence between schoolchildren in the United States and France. The program soon expanded to Spanish-speaking countries. The emphasis of the program became almost entirely Latin American with the advent of the Roosevelt administration and the Good Neighbor Policy for hemispheric solidarity, although educators affiliated with the program emphasized its nonpolitical character. By 1942 the official goals of consolidating Western Hemispheric neighborliness and defense were more transparent. See Oliver, "National Peabody Foundation"; and Roehm, "National Bureau of Educational Correspondence" and "Learning Foreign Languages."

48. Roehm, "Learning Foreign Languages," 227.

49. AHSEP, Subsecretaría de Educación Pública, Unión Panamericana, Washington DC, Caja 6, Expediente 18, Folio 1, 1932.

50. Junior Red Cross officials acknowledged that children alone could not forge international peace but noted that international correspondence between children was a step in the right direction, making citizens of different nations more interested in international questions, more conscious of human similarities in different races, and more friendly toward each other. Sackett, *Administration of the International School Correspondence*, 44, 48, 81.

51. "La Cruz Roja de la Juventud no es una institución arbitraria, individualizante, de caridad o de pasatiempo. La Cruz Roja de la Juventud es una institución necesaria, socializante, de servicio social y de función educativa." Dr. Alfonso Priani, "La Cruz Roja de la Juventud y su cooperación permanente en la protección a la infancia," in *Memoria del VII Congreso Panamericano del Niño*, 1:907–13.

52. "Mensaje de buena voluntad de los escolares australianos a los de México," *El Maestro Rural*, July 1, 1934, 3.

53. *El Maestro Rural*, May 15, 1935, 8.

54. AHSEP, Departamento de Escuelas Rurales, Dirección General, Caja 26, Exp. 19, 1935.

55. W. Benjamin, "The Cultural History of Toys," in *Walter Benjamin, Selected Writings*, 114.

56. For a theoretical exploration of the possibilities and problems presented by toys in Latin America, especially as they conflate and confuse war and play, see Albarrán, "Guerrilla Warplay."

57. Fideicomiso Archivos Plutarco Elias Calles y Fernando Torreblanca (FAPECFT), APEC, Expediente 54: Elias, Arturo M., Legajo 8/17, Folios 302–10, Inventario 1718.

58. AHSEP, Departamento de Escuelas Rurales, Dirección General, Caja 26, Exp. 12, 1935; Caja 47, Exp. 19, 1933.

59. FAPECFT, APEC, Expediente 54: Elias, Arturo M., Legajo 8/17, Folios 302–10, Inventario 1718.

60. Pérez Montfort, "Una región inventada desde el centro," in *Estampas de nacionalismo popular mexicano*, 121–48.

61. "Habrá un concurso de juguetes en Detroit," *El Universal*, September 5, 1937.

62. "Boy Scouts," *Washington Post*, May 15, 1927, R12.

63. "Student Hikes to Washington from His Mexico City Home," *Washington Post*, September 2, 1928, M7; "Mexican Boy Scout Hiker Received by Mrs. Coolidge," *Washington Post*, September 15, 1928, 20.

64. Hillcourt, *Baden-Powell*.

65. The Mexican Boy Scouts took many forms and never consolidated under one official organization. All of the manifestations of the group followed the structure of the Boy Scouts, but the publication of various manuals and the existence of various directors suggest that many times they were divided into local and regional organizations. For example, one group was called the Tequihuas de México, another was the Amigos del Bosque (Friends of the Forest), and another was the Boy Scouts de México. At one point, many groups united under the name Consejo Nacional Escultista (National Scouting Organization). The Mexican Boy Scouts are most commonly referred to in Mexican literature and history as the Exploradores Mexicanos, or Mexican Explorers. For the sake of clarity, in this chapter I usually refer to the Mexican corps as Boy Scouts. "Ciencia del Explorador: Origen de los Exploradores," *El Univesal Gráfico*, October 3, 1941. Clarck was a professor of geography, national economy, and languages. He spoke eight languages. AGN, Ramo Presidenciales, O-C 816-E-17, 1921; Clarck, *El Explorador Mexicano*.

66. Two years earlier Explorer leaders hosted the First National Congress of Explorers (Primer Congreso Nacional de Exploradores), but the 1928 conference distinguished itself by its marked nationalism, established in part by the slight change of the name of the organization to include references to "tribes" and "Mexico." See *Tihui*, no. 1 (December 1926): 14–15; and Escobar, *Informe del Trabajo*, 5–6.

67. Escobar, *Informe del Trabajo*, 11.

68. AGN, O-C 816-E-17; "Oficina de Acción Social," *Memoria de la Secretaría de Educación Pública* (Mexico City) 2 (1938–39): 315–17.

69. Escobar, *Informe del Trabajo*, 10.

70. Of the twenty Mexico City "tribes" reported in 1928, thirteen were organized in the public schools, one in the Club Deportivo International,

three in the Asociación Cristiana de Jóvenes, and three were organized by private citizens (*jóvenes empleados*). José U. Escobar, "Informa del Trabajo de las Tribus de Exploradores Mexicanos," *Publicaciones de la Secretaría de Educación Pública* (Talleres Gráficos de la Nación, Mexico City) 16, no. 7 (1928).

71. José U. Escobar, "Tribus de Exploradores Mexicanos. Reglamento," *Publicaciones de la Secretaría de Educación Pública* (Talleres Gráficos de la Nación, Mexico City) 22, no. 6 (1929): 9.

72. José U. Escobar, "Vivac," *Tihui*, no. 1 (December 1926): 13.

73. AGN, O-C 816-E-17, 1921.

74. AGN, O-C 241-E-R-27, 1925.

75. AGN, O-C 241-E-R-27, 1925.

76. "Una Bella Idea," *El Universal Gráfico*, October 3, 1925; Profesor Alfredo Sánchez O., "Los Niños Legionarios Mexicanos," *El Universal Gráfico*, October 5, 1925; the article continues in installments in the same publication on October 6, 7, and 8.

77. Escobar, *Informe del Trabajo*, 5–6.

78. "¿Qué son las Tribus de Exploradores Mexicanos?" *Tihui*, no. 2 (January 1927): 15–16.

79. *Tribus de Exploradores Mexicanos: Semana del Explorador, del 20 al 27 de noviembre de 1929* (Mexico City: Secretaría de Educación Pública, 1929).

80. Clarck, *El Explorador Mexicano*, 191–92.

81. In fact, the Aztecs were only the last of many great and overlapping dynasties across the modern Mexican territory and were the group that held power—not uncontested by rival ethnic groups—upon the arrival of the Spanish. The linguistic and cultural diversity that characterizes the Mexican population is only marginally represented in most popular treatments of a romanticized, Aztec, past. Pérez Montfort, "El estereotipo del indio en la expresión popular urbana, 1920–1940," in *Estampas de nacionalismo popular mexicano*, 183.

82. Escobar, *Las tribus de exploradores mexicanos*.

83. Leila J. Rupp, cited in Alexander, "Girl Guide Movement," 49.

84. S. Miller, *Growing Girls*, 14–23.

85. "¿Qué son las Tribus de Exploradores Mexicanos?" *Tihui*, no. 2 (January 1927): 16.

86. "¿Qué son las Tribus de Exploradores Mexicanos?" *Tihui*, no. 2 (January 1927): 16.

87. "Charla de tecuthli [*sic*] cronista," *Tihui*, nos. 3–4 (March 1927): 28.

88. "Muchachos distinguidos," *Tihui* 2 (January 1927): 31.

89. Hershfield, *Imagining "la Chica Moderna,"* 11.

90. AHSEP, Subsecretaría de Educación Pública, Caja 22, Exp. 2, Folios 4–45, 1938.

91. Clarck, *El Explorador Mexicano*, 160.

92. Clarck, *El Explorador Mexicano*, 64.

93. Clarck, *El Explorador Mexicano*, 172.

94. Clarck, *El Explorador Mexicano*, 172.

95. In addition to the clothing, the equipment included a walking stick, a spear, a pickaxe, a hatch, a canteen, cooking utensils, a backpack (and the list itemizes the content of the backpack), a jackknife, five meters of cable, a section of a tent, two flags, a whistle, a compass, a watch, a pencil, a notebook, and a first-aid kit. Clarck, *El Explorador Mexicano*, 172–74.

96. I explore the phenomenon of the "proletarian child" as a national trope in Albarrán, "*El niño proletario.*"

97. AGN, O-C 816-E-17, 1921: 6.

98. "Charla del tecuthli [*sic*] cronista," *Tihui*, nos. 5–6 (June 1927): 34.

99. *Tihui*, nos. 5–6 (June 1927): 28.

100. Another inconsistency can be seen in that the Asociación de Exploradores Mexicanos boasted three "classes" of Scouts, based on experiences and requirements that boys had to achieve in order to pass to the next level. Far from being a socialist organization that minimized class distinction, the ADEM established a rather rigid hierarchy within its organization, based on the norms set by the international corps of the Boy Scouts. See "Las tres clases de Exploradores," in Clarck, *El Explorador Mexicano*, 165–68.

101. "Muchachos distinguidos," *Tihui*, no. 2 (January 1927): 30–31.

102. AHSRE, IV-276-28, 1933.

103. Professor Alfredo Sánchez O., "Los Niños Legionarios Mexicanos," *El Universal Gráfico*, October 5, 1925.

104. "Llegaron los Exploradores a Washington," *El Universal*, July 1, 1937. See also "Convención de 'Boys-Scouts' en los EE.UU," *El Nacional*, February 13, 1937.

105. San Luis Potosí was the first state to inaugurate an official section of the Junior Red Cross, and the capital and other regions followed shortly, drawing membership from student councils, Boy Scouts, and other student organizations. The Mexican Junior Red Cross first received international recognition on April 30, 1928. *La Cruz Roja Mexicana* 2, no. 4 (April 1928): 13; "El establecimiento de la Primera Rama de la Cruz Roja Juvenil," *La Cruz Roja Mexicana* 2, no. 6 (June 1928): 5.

106. Arthur W. Dunn, National Director, American Red Cross, "The American Junior Red Cross at Work," speech given at the Pan-American Red Cross Conference, Washington DC, National Archives and Records Administration (NARA), Records of the American National Red Cross (ARC) 1917–1934, Record Group (RG) 200, Stack 130, Row 77, Compartment 1, Shelf 7, Box 81, 102.1 Junior Red Cross—Statements & Tributes, 1921–1934.

107. NARA, Records of the ARC 1917–1934, RG 200, Stack 130, Row 77, Compartment 1, Shelf 7, Box 80, 102.1 Junior Red Cross—Organizations, Functions, Plans, Program.

108. Dunn, "American Junior Red Cross at Work."

109. Little has been published about the Mexican Girl Scouts. See *Boletín de la* SEP 4, no. 10 (1925): 213–14; and *Tihui*, no. 1 (December 1926): 14.

110. *Tihui*, no. 1 (December 1926): 14.

111. *Tihui*, no. 1 (December 1926): 15.

112. AHSRE, L-E 213, ca. 1932.

113. Priani, "La Cruz Roja," 1:910–11.

114. Other committees included Hygiene, Civics, First Aid, and International Friendship. Lupe Jiménez Posadas, "La Cruz Roja de la Juventud de la Escuela 'República Argentina,'" in *Memoria del VII Congreso Panamericano del Niño*, 1:918; Priani, "La Cruz Roja," 1:910–11.

115. *Asociación Mexicana de la Cruz Roja*, 9.

116. Roberto Solís Quiroga, "La Cruz Roja de la Juventud," *La Cruz Roja Mexicana* 2, no. 6 (1928): 8.

117. *La Cruz Roja Mexicana* 2, no. 8 (August 1928): 31.

118. *Coopera* 2, no. 3 (May 1927): 18, 24.

119. Jiménez Posadas, "La Cruz Roja," 918–21.

120. Jiménez Posadas, "La Cruz Roja," 919–20.

121. *Sexta Conferencia International Americana*, Habana, Cuba, January 16, 1928 (Washington DC: Pan-American Union, 1928), 121–23.

122. Jiménez Posadas, "La Cruz Roja," 920.

123. Jiménez Posadas, "La Cruz Roja," 920.

124. Olcott, Vaughan, and Cano, *Sex in Revolution*.

125. Sophie Wittemans, "The Double Concept of Citizen and Subject at the Heart of Guiding and Scouting," in *Scouting Frontiers*, edited by Block and Proctor, 56–71.

126. Pérez Montfort, *Estampas de nacionalismo popular mexicano*, 122.

Conclusion

1. Taibo, *Cárdenas de cerca*, 17.

2. See the interview with leftist leader Heberto Castillo Martínez in Gil, *Hope and Frustration*, 245–83.

3. Granados, *XEW*, 107–19.

4. Sosenski, "El niño consumidor."

5. Cuevas, "The Cactus Curtain [1956]," in *Readings in Latin American Modern Art*, edited by Frank, 187–93.

6. "Children of the Revolution," *Look*, July 18, 1961, 34–35; Cuevas and Foppa, *Confesiones de José Luis Cuevas*.

7. Albarrán, "En busca de la voz de los herederos de la Revolución."

BIBLIOGRAPHY

Archival Sources

Archivo General de la Nación (AGN)

Archivo Histórico de la Secretaría de Educación Pública (AHSEP)

Archivo Histórico de la Secretaría de Salubridad (AHSSA)

Archivo Histórico del Distrito Federal

Archivo Histórico "Genaro Estrada" de la Secretaría de Relaciones Exteriores (AHSRE)

Arizona Historical Society

Biblioteca Luis Guevara Ramírez

Biblioteca Miguel Lerdo de Tejada

Biblioteca Nacional

Centro de Estudios de la Historia de México—CONDUMEX/CARSA

Centro Nacional de las Artes (CNA)

    Fondo Reservado

    Fondo Xóchitl Medina

Dirección de Estudios Históricos, INAH

El Colegio de México

El Instituto de Investigaciones Dr. José María Luis Mora

    Archivo de la Palabra

Fideicomiso Archivos Plutarco Elías Calles y Fernando Torreblanca (FAPECFT)

    Archivo Fernando Torreblanca (AFT)

    Fondo Plutarco Elías Calles (FPEC)

    Archivo Plutarco Elías Calles (APEC)

    Fondo Álvaro Obregón (FAO)

Fondo Elías Calles (FEC)
Fondo Soledad González (FSG)
Hemeroteca Nacional
Library of Congress
National Archives at College Park MD
Universidad Nacional Autónoma de México (UNAM)
Universidad Pedagógica Nacional
University of Arizona
Walter Havighurst Special Collections, Miami University, Oxford OH
    Rodolfo Usigli Collection

Published Sources

Acevedo Rodrigo, Ariadna. "Struggles for Citizenship? Peasant Negotiation of Schooling in the Sierra Norte de Puebla, Mexico, 1921–1933." *Bulletin of Latin American Research* 23, no. 2 (2004): 181–97.

——, and Paula López Caballero, eds. *Ciudadanos inesperados: Espacios de formación de la ciudadanía ayer y hoy.* Mexico City: El Colegio de México / Centro de Investigación y Estudios Avanzados, Departamento de Investigaciones Educativas, 2012.

Ades, Dawn. *Art in Latin America.* New Haven CT: Yale University Press, 1989.

Agostoni, Claudia, ed. *Curar, sanar, y educar: Enfermedad y sociedad en México, siglos XIX y XX.* Mexico City: Universidad Nacional Autónoma de México, Instituto de Investigaciones Históricas / Benemérita Universidad Autónoma de Puebla, 2008.

——. "Las mensajeras de la salud: Enfermeras visitadoras en la ciudad de México durante la década de los 1920." *Estudios de Historia Moderna y Contemporánea de México* 33 (January–June 2007): 89–120.

Albarrán, Elena Jackson. "A Century of Childhood: Growing Up in Twentieth-Century Mexico." In *A Companion to Mexican History and Culture*, edited by William H. Beezley, 575–88. Malden MA: Wiley-Blackwell, 2011.

——. "*Comino vence al diablo* and Other Terrifying Episodes: Itinerant Children's Puppet Theater in 1930s Mexico." *Americas* 67, no. 3 (2011): 355–74.

——. "*El arte de la infancia*: Children and Childhood in New Spanish Art." Paper presented at the Art History Graduate Student Association's Sixteenth Annual Symposium, "The Seven Ages of Man," Tucson AZ, March 2005.

——. "*El niño proletario*: Poems for the New Revolutionary Redeemer, 1936." Paper presented at the Rocky Mountain Council for Latin American Studies, Santa Fe NM, April 2011.

——. "En busca de la voz de los herederos de la Revolución: Un análisis de los documentos producidos por los niños, 1921–1940." In "Infancia:

Un archipiélago por explorar." Special issue, *Relaciones, estudios de historia y sociedad* 33, no. 132 (2012): 17–52.

———. "Guerrilla Warplay: The Infantilization of War in Latin American Popular Culture." *Studies in Latin American Popular Culture* 24 (2005): 69–81.

———. "Los Exploradores, la Cruz Roja de la Juventud, y la expresión infantil de nacionalismo: México, 1920–1940." In *Nuevas miradas a la historia de la infancia en América Latina: Entre prácticas y representaciones*, edited by Susana Sosenski and Elena Jackson Albarrán, 259–92. Mexico City: Instituto de Investigaciones Históricas, Universidad Nacional Autónoma de México, 2012.

Alcubierre, Beatriz, and Tania Carreño King. *Los niños villistas: Una mirada a la historia de la infancia en México, 1900–1920*. Mexico City: INEHRM, 1997.

Alcubierre Moya, Beatriz. *Ciudadanos del futuro: Una historia de las publicaciones para niños en el siglo XIX mexicano*. Mexico City: El Colegio de México, Universidad Autónoma del Estado de Morelos, 2010.

———, and Rodrigo Bazán Bonfil. "*Lecturas clásicas para niños*: Contexto histórico y canon literario." Paper presented at the Canons of Children's Literature Conference, Berkeley CA, March 15, 2007.

Alexander, Kristine. "The Girl Guide Movement and Imperial Internationalism during the 1920s and 1930s." *Journal of the History of Childhood and Youth* 2, no. 1 (2009): 37–63.

Anderson, Benedict. *Imagined Communities: Reflections on the Origin and Spread of Nationalism*. 2nd ed. New York: Verso, 1991.

Applebaum, Nancy, Anne S. Macpherson, and Karin Alejandra Rosemblatt, eds. *Race and Nation in Modern Latin America*. Chapel Hill: University of North Carolina Press, 2003.

Arce Gurza, Francisco. "En busca de una educación revolucionaria, 1924–1934." In *Ensayos sobre historia de la educación en México*, edited by Josefina Zoraida Vázquez, Dorothy Tanck de Estrada, Anne Staples, and Francisco Arce Gurza, 145–87. Mexico City: El Colegio de México, 1981.

Aréchiga, Ernesto. "'Un niño sano no puede ser un niño malo': Entre la educación y la propaganda; La literatura higiénica infantil en México, 1930–1940." Paper presented at the Coloquio Internacional, "Sanar, curar y educar: Salud, enfermedad y sociedad en México, siglos XIX–XX," Instituto de Investigaciones Históricas, UNAM, April 2006.

Ariès, Philippe. *Centuries of Childhood: A Social History of Family Life*. New York: Alfred A. Knopf, 1962.

Asociación Mexicana de la Cruz Roja: Estatutos de la Sección de la Cruz Roja de la Juventud. Mexico City: Asociación Mexicana de la Cruz Roja, 1932.

Azuela de la Cueva, Alicia. *Arte y poder*. Zamora, Michoacán: El Colegio de Michoacán, 2005.

Bauer, Arnold J. *Goods, Power, History: Latin America's Material Culture.* Cambridge: Cambridge University Press, 2001.

Baxter, Jane Eva, ed. *The Archaeology of Childhood: Children, Gender, and Material Culture.* Walnut Creek CA: AltaMira Press, 2005.

———. *Children in Action: Perspectives on the Archaeology of Childhood.* Archaeological Papers of the American Anthropological Association, no. 15. Berkeley: University of California Press Journals, 2006.

Bazant, Mílada. *Historia de la educación durante el Porfiriato.* Mexico City: El Colegio de México, 1993.

Beezley, William H. "Cómo fue que El Negrito salvó a México de los franceses: Las fuentes populares de la identidad nacional." *Historia Mexicana* 226, no. 2 (2007): 405–44.

———. "Creating a Revolutionary Culture: Vasconcelos, Indians, Anthropologists, and Calendar Girls." In *A Companion to Mexican History and Culture,* edited by William H. Beezley, 420–38. Malden MA: Wiley-Blackwell, 2011.

———. *Mexican National Identity: Memory, Innuendo, and Popular Culture.* Tucson: University of Arizona Press, 2008.

———, Cheryl English Martin, and William E. French, eds. *Rituals of Rule, Rituals of Resistance: Public Celebrations and Popular Culture in Mexico.* Wilmington DE: SR Books, 1994.

Benjamin, Thomas. "The Leviathan on the Zócalo: Recent Historiography of the Postrevolutionary Mexican State." *Latin American Research Review* 20, no. 3 (1985): 195–217.

Benjamin, Walter. *Walter Benjamin: Selected Writings.* Vol. 2, *1927–1934.* Edited by Michael W. Jennings, Howard Eiland, and Gary Smith. Translated by Rodney Livingstone. Cambridge MA: Belknap Press of Harvard University Press, 1999.

Bennett, Susan. *Theatre Audiences: A Theory of Production and Reception.* London: Routledge, 1990.

Bergerson, Andrew Stuart. "Listening to the Radio in Hildesheim, 1923–53." *German Studies Review* 24, no. 1 (2001): 83–113.

Best Maugard, Adolfo. *Método de Dibujo: Tradición, resurgimiento y evolución del arte Mexicano.* 2nd ed. 1923. Reprint, Mexico City: Editorial Viñeta, 1964.

Best Pontones, Fernando. "El método 'Best Maugard' para la enseñanza del dibujo, y su aplicación a los trabajos manuales." *Boletín de la SEP* 1, no. 2 (1922).

Bliss, Katherine Elaine. *Compromised Positions: Prostitution, Public Health, and Gender Politics in Revolutionary Mexico.* University Park: Pennsylvania State University Press, 2001.

———, and Ann S. Blum. "Dangerous Driving: Adolescence, Sex, and the Gendered Experience of Public Space in Early-Twentieth-Century Mexico City." In *Gender, Sexuality, and Power in Latin America since Inde-*

pendence, edited by William E. French and Katherine Elaine Bliss, 163–86. Lanham MD: Rowman and Littlefield, 2007.

Block, Nelson R., and Tammy M. Proctor, eds. *Scouting Frontiers: Youth and the Scout Movement's First Century.* Newcastle upon Tyne: Cambridge Scholars, 2009.

Blum, Ann S. "Children without Parents: Law, Charity, and Social Practice, Mexico City, 1867–1940." PhD diss., University of California, Berkeley, 1998.

———. *Domestic Economies: Family, Work, and Welfare in Mexico City, 1884–1943.* Lincoln: University of Nebraska Press, 2009.

———. "Making and Breaking Families: Adoption and Public Welfare, Mexico City, 1938–1942." In *Sex and Revolution: Gender, Politics, and Power in Modern Mexico,* edited by Jocelyn Olcott, Mary Kay Vaughan, and Gabriela Cano, 127–44. Durham NC: Duke University Press, 2006.

———. "The Picture of Health: Baby Portraits, Eugenics, and the Illustrated Press in 1920s Mexico City." Paper presented at the XXVII International Congress of the Latin American Studies Association, Montreal, September 2007.

———. "Public Welfare and Child Circulation, Mexico City, 1877–1925." *Journal of Family History* 23, no. 3 (July 1998): 240–72.

Boemer, Marilyn Lawrence. *The Children's Hour: Radio Programs for Children, 1929–1956.* Metuchen NJ: Scarecrow Press, 1989.

Booth, George C. "Socialist Secondary Education in Mexico." *School Review* 47, no. 8 (1939): 602–9.

Buchenau, Jürgen. *Plutarco Elías Calles and the Mexican Revolution.* Lanham MD: Rowman and Littlefield, 2007.

Buck, Sarah A. "The Meaning of the Women's Vote in Mexico, 1917–1953." Paper presented at "Las Olvidadas: Gender and Women's History in Postrevolutionary Mexico," Yale Center for International and Area Studies, New Haven CT, May 2001.

Butler, Matthew, ed. *Faith and Impiety in Revolutionary Mexico.* New York: Palgrave Macmillan, 2007.

———. *Popular Piety and Political Identity in Mexico's Cristero Rebellion: Michoacán, 1927–1929.* Oxford: Oxford University Press, 2004.

Caplow, Deborah. *Leopoldo Méndez: Revolutionary Art and the Mexican Print.* Austin: University of Texas Press, 2007.

Características biológicas de los escolares proletarios. Mexico City: DAPP; SEP, Departamento de Psicopedagogía Médico Escolar, 1937.

Cárdenas, Lázaro. *Apuntes.* Vol. 1. Mexico City: UNAM, 1972.

Carretta Beltrán, Claudia. "La mediación de la inteligencia de los mexicanos: Construcciones de normalidad y anormalidad (1920–1940)." Paper presented at the XXVII International Congress of the Latin American Studies Association, Montreal, September 2007.

Castro, Justin. "Wireless: Radio, Revolution, and State Formation in Mexico, 1897–1935." PhD diss., University of Oklahoma, 2013.

Chaoul Pereyra, María Eugenia. "Escuelas de primera, segunda y tercera clase . . . y niños también: La educación primaria porfiriana." Paper presented at the Coloquio Internacional "Sanar, curar y educar: Salud, enfermedad y sociedad en México, siglos XIX–XX," Instituto de Investigaciones Históricas, UNAM, April 2006.

Chasteen, John Charles. *Born in Blood and Fire: A Concise History of Latin America.* 2nd ed. New York: W. W. Norton, 2005.

———. "Introduction: Beyond Imagined Communities." In *Beyond Imagined Communities: Reading and Writing the Nation in Nineteenth-Century Latin America,* edited by Sara Castro-Klaren and John Charles Chasteen, ix–xxv. Washington DC: Woodrow Wilson Center Press, 2003.

Civera Cerecedo, Alicia. "Del calzón de manta al overol: La misión cultural de Tenería, Estado de México, en 1934." In *Escuela y sociedad en el periodo cardenista,* edited by Susana Quintanilla and Mary Kay Vaughan, 251–62. Mexico City: Fondo de Cultura Económica, 1997.

Clarck, Federico. *El Explorador Mexicano.* Mexico City: n.p., n.d.

Cline, Sarah. "A Century of Childhood: Casta Children in Eighteenth-Century Mexico." Paper presented at the Fifty-Fifth Annual Rocky Mountain Council for Latin American Studies Conference, Flagstaff AZ, April 2008.

Coffey, Mary. *How Revolutionary Art Became Official Culture.* Durham NC: Duke University Press, 2012.

Coles, Robert. *The Political Life of Children.* Boston: Atlantic Monthly Press, 1986.

Contribución del Departamento de Psicopedagogía e Higiene de la Secretaría de Educación Pública al 6° Congreso Panamericano del Niño [Lima, Peru, June 1930]. Mexico City: SEP, 1930.

Cook, Daniel Thomas. *The Commodification of Childhood: The Children's Clothing Industry and the Rise of the Child Consumer.* Durham NC: Duke University Press, 2004.

Cordero Reiman, Karen. "The Best Maugard Drawing Method: A Common Ground for Modern Mexicanist Aesthetics." *Journal of Decorative and Propaganda Arts (Mexico),* no. 26 (2010): 44–79.

———. "Modern Mexican Art: Visions and Revisions." In *Mexican Modern Painting from the Andrés Blaisten Collection,* 23–27. Mexico City: Universidad Nacional Autónoma de México, 2011.

Corona Berkin, Sarah, and Arnulfo Uriel Santiago Gómez. *Para la infancia: Ediciones de la SEP, 1921–1993.* Mexico City: n.p., 1995.

Craven, David. *Art and Revolution in Latin America, 1910–1990.* New Haven CT: Yale University Press, 2002.

Cuevas, José Luis. "The Cactus Curtain." In *Readings in Latin American Modern Art*, edited by Patrick Frank, 111–20. New Haven CT: Yale University Press, 2004.

——, and Alaíde Foppa. *Confesiones de José Luis Cuevas*. Mexico City: Fondo de Cultura Económica, 1975.

Cunningham, Hugh. *The Invention of Childhood*. London: BBC Books, 2006.

Curiel, Gustavo, et al. *Pintura y vida cotidiana en Mexico, 1650–1950*. Mexico City: Fomento Cultural Banamex, AC, 1999.

Dávila, Jerry. *Diploma of Whiteness: Race and Social Policy in Brazil, 1919–1945*. Durham NC: Duke University Press, 2003.

Davis, Diane E. *Urban Leviathan: Mexico City in the Twentieth Century*. Philadelphia: Temple University Press, 1994.

Dean, Carolyn. "Sketches of Childhood: Children in Colonial Andean Art and Society." In *Minor Omissions: Children in Latin American History and Society*, edited by Tobias Hecht, 21–51. Madison: University of Wisconsin Press, 2002.

Deering, Freemont B. *Border Boys with the Mexican Rangers*. Border Boys Series. New York: A. L. Burt, n.d.

De la Luz Mena, José. *Escuela Racionalista: Doctrina y método*. 2nd ed. Mexico City: n.p., 1936.

Del Castillo Troncoso, Alberto. *Conceptos, imágenes y representaciones de la niñez en la Ciudad de México, 1880–1920*. Mexico City: El Colegio de México / Instituto Mora, 2006.

——. "La invención de un concepto moderno de niñez en México en el cambio del siglo XIX al XX." In *Los niños: Su imagen en la historia*, edited by María Eugenia Sanchez Calleja and Delia Salazar Anaya, 101–16. Mexico City: Instituto Nacional de Antropología e Historia, 2006.

Deloria, Philip J. *Playing Indian*. New Haven CT: Yale University Press, 1998.

De Mause, Lloyd, ed. *The History of Childhood*. New York: Psychohistory Press, 1974.

Dewey, John. *Impressions of Soviet Russia and the Revolutionary World: Mexico—China—Turkey*. New York: New Republic, 1929.

Díaz Cárdenas, León. *Literatura Revolucionaria para Niños*. Mexico City: Ediciones DAPP, 1937.

Diccionario Porrúa. 6th ed. Mexico City: Editorial Porrúa, SA, 1995.

Dowler, Wayne. *Classroom and Empire: The Politics of Schooling Russia's Eastern Nationalities, 1860–1917*. Montreal: McGill-Queen's University Press, 2001.

Eineigel, Susanne Karin. "Distinction, Culture, and Politics in Mexico City's Middle Class, 1890–1940." PhD diss., University of Maryland, 2011.

Eklof, Ben. *Russian Peasant Schools: Officialdom, Village Culture, and Popular Pedagogy, 1861–1914.* Berkeley: University of California Press, 1986.

Elias, Norbert. *The Civilizing Process: Sociogenetic and Psychogenetic Investigations.* Translated by Edmund Jephcott. Rev. ed. Malden MA: Blackwell, 2000.

Época de oro del Teatro Guiñol de Bellas Artes, 1932–1965 [CD-ROM]. Mexico City: Instituto Nacional de Bellas Artes, 2005.

Escobar, José U. *Informe del Trabajo de las Tribus de Exploradores Mexicanos.* Mexico City: Talleres Gráficos de la Nación, 1928.

———. *Las tribus de exploradores mexicanos.* Mexico City: Silbarios de la SEP, 1929.

Fass, Paula. *Children of a New World: Society, Culture, and Globalization.* New York: New York University Press, 2006.

Fell, Claude. *José Vasconcelos: Los años del águila (1920–1925).* Mexico City: UNAM, 1989.

Fernández, Justino. *El arte del siglo XIX en México.* Mexico City: UNAM, Instituto de Investigaciones Estéticas, 1983.

Flores A., Manuel. *Alcoholismo.* Mexico City: DAPP, n.d.

Frank, Patrick, ed. *Readings in Latin American Modern Art.* New Haven CT: Yale University Press, 2004.

Freire, Paulo. *Pedagogy of the Oppressed.* Rev. ed. New York: Continuum, 1993.

Gallo, Rubén. *Mexican Modernity: The Avant-Garde and the Technological Revolution.* Cambridge: MIT Press, 2005.

Galván Lafarga, Luz Elena. "Del ocio a la instrucción en *La Niñez Ilustrada*: Un periódico infantil del siglo XIX." *Estudios del Hombre* 20 (2005): 201–33.

Gamio, Manuel. *Forjando Patria: Pro-nacionalismo [Forging a Nation].* Translated by Fernando Armstrong-Fumero. 1916. Reprint, Boulder: University Press of Colorado, 2010.

García, Genaro. *Una vuelta a la República Mexicana por dos niños: Libro de geografía nacional y lectura corriente adaptado a las Escuelas Primarias de México.* Mexico City: Sociedad de Edición y Librería Franco-Americana, SA, 1926.

Gil, Carlos, ed. *Hope and Frustration: Interviews with Leaders of Mexico's Political Opposition.* Wilmington DE: SR Books, 1992.

Giménez Cacho, Marisa, et al., eds. *El Teatro Guiñol de Bellas Artes: Época de oro en México / The Puppetry of the Institute of Fine Arts: Golden Age in Mexico.* Mexico City: Instituto Nacional de Bellas Artes / Editorial RM, 2010.

Glusker, Susana Joel, ed. *Avant-Garde Art & Artists in Mexico: Anita Brenner's Journals of the Roaring Twenties.* Austin: University of Texas Press, 2010.

Gombrich, E. H. *Myth and Reality in German Wartime Broadcasts*. London: University of London / Athlone Press, 1970.

Gonzalbo Aizpuru, Pilar. "De familias y 'calidades' en el México colonial." Special issue, *Saber/ver* (June 1994).

———. *Familia y orden colonial*. Mexico City: El Colegio de México, 1998.

Gonzáles, Michael J. "Imagining Mexico in 1921: Visions of the Revolutionary State and Society in the Centennial Celebration in Mexico City." *Mexican Studies / Estudios Mexicanos* 25, no. 2 (2009): 247–70.

Granados, Pável. XEW: *70 años en el aire*. Mexico City: Editorial Clío Libros y Videos, SA de CV, 2000.

Guerra, François-Xavier. "Forms of Communication, Political Spaces, and Cultural Identities in the Creation of Spanish American Nations." In *Beyond Imagined Communities: Reading and Writing the Nation in Nineteenth-Century Latin America*, edited by Sara Castro-Klaren and John Charles Chasteen, 3–32. Washington DC: Woodrow Wilson Center Press, 2003.

Guía de la Sección Asistencia del Fondo Beneficencia Pública en el Distrito Federal, no. 6. Mexico City: Centro de Documentación y Archivo, Archivo Histórico de la Secretaría de Salud, 1988.

Gutiérrez del Olmo, José Félix Alonso. "Introducción." In vol. 6 of *Guía de la Sección Asistencia del Fondo Beneficencia Pública en el Distrito Federal*. Mexico City: Centro de Documentación y Archivo, Archivo Histórico de la Secretaría de Salud, 1988.

Gutman, Marta, and Ning de Coninck-Smith, eds. *Designing Modern Childhoods: History, Space, and the Material Culture of Children*. New Brunswick NJ: Rutgers University Press, 2008.

Guy, Donna J. "The Pan American Child Congresses, 1916 to 1942: Pan Americanism, Child Reform, and the Welfare State in Latin America." *Journal of Family History* 23, no. 3 (1998): 272–92.

———. *White Slavery and Mothers Alive and Dead: The Troubled Meeting of Sex, Gender, Public Health, and Progress in Latin America*. Lincoln: University of Nebraska Press, 2000.

Habermas, Jürgen. *The Structural Transformation of the Public Sphere: Studies in Contemporary German Social Thought*. Translated by Thomas Burger. 1962. Reprint, Cambridge: MIT Press, 1991.

Halbwachs, Maurice. *On Collective Memory*. Edited and translated by Lewis A. Coser. Chicago: University of Chicago Press, 1992.

Hayes, Joy Elizabeth. "National Imaginings on the Air: Radio in Mexico, 1920–1950." In *The Eagle and the Virgin: National and Cultural Revolution in Mexico, 1920–1940*, edited by Mary Kay Vaughan and Stephen E. Lewis, 243–58. Durham NC: Duke University Press, 2006.

———. *Radio Nation: Communication, Popular Culture, and Nationalism in Mexico, 1920–1950*. Tucson: University of Arizona Press, 2000.

Hecht, Tobias, ed. *Minor Omissions: Children in Latin American History and Society*. Madison: University of Wisconsin Press, 2002.

Henderson, Timothy J. *The Mexican Wars for Independence*. New York: Hill and Wang, 2009.

Herrera Feria, María de Lourdes, ed. *Estudios sociales sobre la infancia en México*. Puebla: Benemérita Universidad Autónoma de Puebla, Dirección de Fomento Editorial, 2007.

Hershfield, Joanne. *Imagining "la Chica Moderna": Women, Nation, and Visual Culture*. Durham NC: Duke University Press, 2008.

———. "Race and Ethnicity in Classical Cinema." In *Mexico's Cinema: A Century of Film and Filmmakers*, edited by Joanne Hershfield and David Maciel. Wilmington DE: SR Books, 1999.

Heywood, Colin. "*Centuries of Childhood*: An Anniversary—and an Epitaph." *Journal of the History of Childhood and Youth* 3, no. 3 (2010): 343–65.

Hillcourt, William. *Baden-Powell: The Two Lives of a Hero*. New York: Gilwellian Press, 1992.

Hobsbawm, Eric. *The Invention of Tradition*. New York: Cambridge University Press, 1983.

Holguín, Sandy. *Creating Spaniards: Culture and National Identity in Republican Spain*. Madison: University of Wisconsin Press, 2002.

Informe de la Secretaría de Educación Pública [Conferencia Panamericana, Montevideo, Uruguay]. Mexico City: SRE, 1933.

Informe sobre los trabajos de la Unión Panamericana, 1923–1927. Washington DC: Gobierno de los Estados Unidos de América, 1927.

Jackson, Elena K. "Order in the Nursery: Eva Sámano de López Mateos and the Institutionalization of Child Welfare." Master's thesis, University of Arizona, 2002.

James, Allison, and Adrian L. James. *Constructing Childhood: Theory, Policy, and Social Practice*. New York: Palgrave Macmillan, 2004.

Jensen, Erik N. *Body by Weimar: Athletes, Gender, and German Modernity*. New York: Oxford University Press, 2010.

Johnson, Greg. "The Mobilization of American Childhood during World War I." Paper presented at "In the Name of the Child," Social and Cultural History of Children and Youth Conference, Norköpping, Sweden, June 2007.

Joseph, Gilbert M., and Daniel Nugent, eds. *Everyday Forms of State Formation: Revolution and the Negotiation of Rule in Modern Mexico*. Durham NC: Duke University Press, 1994.

Kaplan, Wendy. *"The Art That Is Life": The Arts & Crafts Movement in America, 1875–1920*. New York: Little, Brown, 1987.

Katzew, Ilona. *Casta Painting: Images of Race in Eighteenth-Century Mexico*. New Haven CT: Yale University Press, 2004.

Kelly, Catriona. *Children's World: Growing Up in Russia, 1890–1991*. New Haven CT: Yale University Press, 2007.

———. "'Thank You for the Wonderful Book': Soviet Child Readers and the Management of Children's Reading, 1950–75." In *The Global History of Childhood Reader*, edited by Heidi Morrison, 278–304. New York: Routledge, 2012.

Kozlovsky, Roy. "Adventure Playgrounds and Postwar Reconstruction." In *Designing Modern Childhoods: History, Space, and the Material Culture of Children*, edited by Marta Gutman and Ning de Coninck-Smith, 171–90. New Brunswick NJ: Rutgers University Press, 2008.

Kunzer, Edward J. "'Education' under Hitler." *Journal of Educational Sociology* 13, no. 3 (1939): 140–47.

Kwong, Julia. *Cultural Revolution in China's Schools, May 1966–April 1969*. Stanford CA: Hoover Institution Press, 1988.

Lago, Roberto. *Teatro Guignol Mexicano*. 3rd ed. Mexico City: Federación Editorial Mexicana, SA, 1987.

Lassonde, Stephen. "Age and Authority: Adult-Child Relations during the Twentieth Century in the United States." *Journal of the History of Childhood and Youth* 1, no. 1 (2008): 95–105.

Lavrín, Asunción. "Mexico." In *Children in Historical and Comparative Perspective: An International Handbook and Research Guide*, edited by Joseph M. Hawes and N. Ray Hiner, 421–45. New York: Greenwood Press, 1991.

Lear, John. "La brocha y el martillo: State-Sponsored Educational Projects for Workers and Artists in Mexico City in the 1920s." Paper presented at the Fifty-Fifth Annual Conference of the Rocky Mountain Council for Latin American Studies, Flagstaff AZ, April 2008.

———. *Workers, Neighbors, and Citizens: The Revolution in Mexico City*. Lincoln: University of Nebraska Press, 2001.

Lerner, Victoria. *Historia de la Revolución Mexicana*. Vol. 17, *La educación socialista*. 2nd ed. 1979. Reprint, Mexico City: El Colegio de México, 1982.

Levine, Robert M. *Images of History: Nineteenth and Early Twentieth Century Latin American Photographs as Documents*. Durham NC: Duke University Press, 1989.

Lewis, Stephen E. "Modernizing Message, Mystical Messenger: The Appropriation of the Teatro Petul in the Chiapas Highlands, 1954–1974." Paper presented at the Fifty-Fourth Annual Conference of the Rocky Mountain Council for Latin American Studies, Santa Fe NM, January 2007.

———. "Modernizing Message, Mystical Messenger: The Teatro Petul in the Chiapas Highlands, 1954–1974." *Americas* 67, no. 3 (2011): 375–97.

Lewis, Tom. "'A Godlike Presence': The Impact of Radio on the 1920s and 1930s." In "Communication in History: The Key to Understanding." Special issue, *OAH Magazine of History* 6, no. 4 (1992): 23–33.

Lindemeyer, Kriste. *"A Right to Childhood": The U.S. Children's Bureau and Child Welfare, 1912–1946.* Urbana: University of Illinois Press, 1997.

Lipsett-Rivera, Sonya. "Model Children and Models for Children in Early Mexico." In *Minor Omissions: Children in Latin American History and Society*, edited by Tobias Hecht, 52–71. Madison: University of Wisconsin Press, 2002.

List Arzubide, Germán. "Petroleo para las Lámparas de México." *El Maestro Rural* 11, no. 7 (1938): 20–22.

———. *Teatro guiñol.* Mexico City: UNAM, 1997.

———. *Tres comedias infantiles para Teatro Guignol.* Mexico City: Departamento de Bellas Artes, 1936.

———. *Troka el Poderoso.* Mexico City: El Nacional, 1939.

Lombardo García, Irma, and María Teresa Camarillo Carbajal, eds. *La prensa infantil de México (1839–1984).* Mexico City: Instituto de Investigaciones Bibliográficas, Hemeroteca Nacional, Universidad Nacional Autónoma de México, 1984.

Lomnitz, Claudio. "Final Reflections: What Was Mexico's Cultural Revolution?" In *The Eagle and the Virgin: Nation and Cultural Revolution in Mexico, 1920–1940*, edited by Mary Kay Vaughan and Stephen E. Lewis, 335–49. Durham NC: Duke University Press, 2006.

López, Rick Anthony. *Crafting Mexico: Intellectuals, Artisans, and the State after the Revolution.* Durham NC: Duke University Press, 2010.

———. "The Noche Mexicana and the Exhibition of Popular Arts: Two Ways of Exalting Indianness." In *The Eagle and the Virgin: Nation and Cultural Revolution in Mexico, 1920–1940*, edited by Mary Kay Vaughan and Stephen Lewis, 23–42. Durham NC: Duke University Press, 2006.

Los mejores de la SEP. Vols. 1–13. Mexico City: SEP, 1990.

Los niños mexicanos de Diego Rivera [Consejo Nacional para la Cultura y las Artes, Instituto Nacional de Bellas Artes, Fondo de las Naciones Unidas para la Infancia–UNICEF, Museo Casa Estudio Diego Rivera y Frida Kahlo, April 28–August 30, 1998]. Mexico City: Instituto Nacional de Bellas Artes, 1998.

Loyo B., Engracia. "En el aula y la parcela: Vida escolar en el medio rural (1921–1940)." In *Historia de la vida cotidiana en México*, edited by Pilar Gonzalbo Aizpuru, vol. 5, pt. 1, *Siglo XX: Campo y ciudad*, edited by Aurelio de los Reyes, 273–312. Mexico City: El Colegio de México/ Fondo de Cultura Económica, 2006.

MacGregor, Josefina. *México de su puño y letra: El sentir de un pueblo en las cartas al presidente.* Mexico City: Editorial Diana, 1993.

Malvido, Elsa. "International Trends: The Role of the Female Body in the Mexican Colonial Period." Translated by Joan M. Hoffman. *Journal of Women's History* 4, no. 1 (1992): 119–32.

Marten, James, ed. *Childhood and Child Welfare in the Progressive Era: A Brief History with Documents*. Boston and New York: Bedford / St. Martin's, 2005.

Martínez Moctezuma, Lucía. "Lecturas recreativas para pequeños lectores a finales del siglo XIX en México." *Estudios del Hombre* 20 (2005): 235–57.

Matesanz, José Antonio. *Las raíces del exilio: México ante la guerra civil española, 1936–1939*. Mexico City: El Colegio de México, 1999.

Matthews, Michael. "*De Viaje*: Elite Views of Modernity and the Porfirian Railway Boom." *Mexican Studies/Estudios Mexicanos* 26, no. 2 (2010): 251–89.

Mechling, Jay. *On My Honor: Boy Scouts and the Making of American Youth*. Chicago: University of Chicago Press, 2001.

Mehlman, Jeffrey. *Walter Benjamin for Children: An Essay on His Radio Years*. Chicago: University of Chicago Press, 1993.

Memoria del Primer Congreso Mexicano del Niño. Mexico City: El Universal, 1921.

Memoria del VII Congreso Panamericano del Niño [Mexico City, October 12–19, 1935]. Mexico City: Talleres Gráficos de la Nación, 1937.

Meneses Morales, Ernesto. *Tendencias educativas oficiales en México, 1911–1934: La problemática de la educación mexicana durante la Revolución y los primeros lustros de la época posrevolucionaria*. Mexico City: Centro de Estudios Educativos, Instituto Iberoamericano, 1998.

Mickenberg, Julia L. *Learning from the Left: Children's Literature, the Cold War, and Radical Politics in the United States*. Oxford: Oxford University Press, 2006.

Milanich, Nara. *Children of Fate: Childhood, Class, and the State in Chile, 1850–1930*. Durham NC: Duke University Press, 2009.

Miller, Mary, and Karl Taube, eds. *The Gods and Symbols of Ancient Mexico and the Maya: An Illustrated Dictionary of Mesoamerican Religion*. London: Thames and Hudson, 1993.

Miller, Susan A. *Growing Girls: The Natural Origins of Girls' Organizations in America*. New Brunswick NJ: Rutgers University Press, 2007.

Mintz, Steven. *Huck's Raft: A History of American Childhood*. Cambridge MA: Harvard University Press, 2004.

———. "Reflections on Age as a Category of Historical Analysis." *Journal of the History of Childhood and Youth* 1, no. 1 (2008): 91–94.

———. "Teaching the History of Childhood." *SHCY Newsletter* 11 (Winter 2008).

Miranda Silva, Francisca, and William H. Beezley. "The Rosete Aranda Puppets: A Century and a Half of an Entertainment Enterprise." *Americas* 67, no. 3 (2011): 331–54.

Monografía de las escuelas de pintura al aire libre. Mexico City: Secretaría de Educación Pública, Editorial "CVLTVRA" México, 1926.

Monroy Nasr, Rebeca. "Fotografías de la educación cotidiana en la posrevolución." In *Historia de la vida cotidiana en México*, edited by Pilar Gonzalbo Aizpuru, vol. 5, pt. 2, *Siglo XX: La imagen ¿espejó de la verdad?* edited by Aurelio de los Reyes. Mexico City: El Colegio de México / Fondo de Cultura Económica, 2006.

Monroy Padilla, Heriberto. *Civismo.* 11th ed. Mexico City: Publicaciones "Monroy Padilla," n.d.

Monsiváis, Carlos. *¡Quietecito por favor!* Mexico City: Grupo Carso, 2005.

Morales Muñoz, Noé. "Troka el Poderoso." *La Jornada Semanal* (July 30, 2006).

Muñoz Cota, José. "Introducción." In *Tres comedias infantiles para Teatro Guignol.* Mexico City: Departamento de Bellas Artes, 1936.

Nava, Carmen. "Forging Future Citizens in Brazilian Public Schools, 1937–1945." In *Brazil in the Making: Facets of National Identity*, edited by Carmen Nava and Ludwig Lauerhass Jr., 95–117. Lanham MD: Rowman and Littlefield, 2006.

Nava Nava, María del Carmen. *Los abajo firmantes: Cartas a los presidentes.* Mexico City: SEP, Unidad de Publicaciones Educativas / Editorial Patria, 1994.

Olcott, Jocelyn, Mary Kay Vaughan, and Gabriela Cano, eds. *Sex in Revolution: Gender, Politics, and Power in Modern Mexico.* Durham NC: Duke University Press, 2006.

Olguín Alvarado, Patricia, and Rosalba Tena Villeda. "Los niños en el Manicomio General de México, 1910–1935." *Cuadernos para la Historia de la Salud* (2003).

Oliver, Thomas Edward. "The National Peabody Foundation for International Educational Correspondence." *Modern Language Journal* 4, no. 2 (1919): 73–76.

Ornelas Herrera, Roberto. "Radio y cotidianidad en México (1900–1930)." In *Historia de la vida cotidiana en México*, edited by Pilar Gonzalbo Aizpuru, vol. 5, pt. 1, *Siglo XX: Campo y ciudad*, edited by Aurelio de los Reyes, 127–69. Mexico City: El Colegio de México; Fondo de Cultura Económica, 2006.

Ortíz Monasterio, Pablo, ed. *Mexico: The Revolution and Beyond; Photographs by Agustín Víctor Casasola, 1900–1940.* New York: Aperture Foundation, 2003.

Palacios, Guillermo. *La Pluma y el Arado: Los intelectuales pedagogos y la construcción socio-cultural del "problema campesino" en México, 1930–1934.* Mexico City: El Colegio de México/ Centro de Investigaciones y Docencia Económicas, 1999.

———. "Postrevolutionary Intellectuals, Rural Readings, and the Shaping of the 'Peasant Problem' in Mexico: El Maestro Rural, 1932–1934." *Journal of Latin American Studies* 30, no. 2 (1998): 309–39.

Paris, Leslie. "Through the Looking Glass: Age, Stages, and Historical Analysis." *Journal of the History of Childhood and Youth* 1, no. 1 (2008): 106–13.

Parsons, Timothy H. *Race, Resistance, and the Boy Scout Movement in British Colonial Africa*. Athens: Ohio University Press, 2004.

Payá Valero, Emeterio. *Los niños españoles de Morelia (El exilio infantil en México)*. Mexico City: Edamex, 1985.

Payson, Lieut. Howard. *The Boy Scouts under Fire in Mexico*. New York: A. L. Burt, 1914.

Paz, Octavio. "Sons of La Malinche." In *The Labyrinth of Solitude: Life and Thought in Mexico*, translated by Lysander Kemp. 1959. Reprint, New York: Grove Press, 1962.

Pérez Montfort, Ricardo. *Avatares del nacionalismo cultural: Cinco ensayos*. Mexico City: Centro de Investigación y Docencia en Humanidades del Estado de Morelos / Centro de Investigaciones y Estudios Superiores en Antropología Social, 2000.

———. *Estampas de nacionalismo popular mexicano: Diez ensayos sobre cultura popular y nacionalismo*. 2nd ed. Mexico City: Centro de Investigaciones y Estudios Superiores de Antropología Social / Centro de Investigación y Docencia en Humanidades del Estado de Morelos, 2003.

Piaget, Jean. *The Child's Conception of the World*. 2nd ed. 1929. Reprint, New York: Humanities Press, 1951.

Piccato, Pablo. "De la ciudadanía a los ciudadanos: Notas sobre la contingencia en la historia política." Epilogue to *Ciudadanos inesperados: Espacios de formación de la ciudadanía ayer y hoy*, edited by Ariadna Acevedo Rodrigo and Paula López Caballero, 315–32. Mexico City: El Colegio de México / Centro de Investigación y Estudios Avanzados, Departamento de Investigaciones Educativas, 2012.

Pierce, Gretchen. "Fighting Bacteria, the Bible, and the Bottle: Projects to Create New Men, Women, and Children, 1910–1940." In *A Companion to Mexican History and Culture*, edited by William H. Beezley, 505–17. Malden MA: Wiley-Blackwell, 2011.

———. "Sobering the Revolution: Mexico's Anti-Alcohol Campaigns and the State-Building Process, 1910–1940." PhD diss., University of Arizona, 2008.

Pilotti, Francisco. "Crise e perspectives da assistência à infância na América Latina." In *A arte de governar crianças: A história das políticas sociais, da legislação e da assistência à infância no Brasil*, edited by Francisco Pilotti and Irene Rizzini. Rio de Janeiro: Instituto Interamericano del Niño, 1995.

Pla Brugat, Dolores. *Los niños de Morelia*. Mexico City: Instituto Nacional de Antropología e Historia, 1985.

Plotkin, Mariano Ben. *Mañana es San Perón: A Cultural History of Perón's Argentina*. Translated by Keith Zahnhiser. Wilmington DE: SR Books, 2003.

Pons Prades, Eduardo. *Los niños repúblicanos en la guerra de España.* Madrid: Oberon, 2004.

Premo, Bianca. "How Latin America's History of Childhood Came of Age." *Journal of the History of Childhood and Youth* 1, no. 1 (2008): 63–76.

Programa de visitas "Los niños a la SEP: Descripción de los siete talleres de producción artística y científica." Mexico City: SEP, 1999.

Puig Casauranc, J. M. *De nuestro México: Cosas sociales y aspectos políticos.* Mexico City: n.p., 1926.

———. *La educación pública en México a través de los mensajes presidenciales.* Mexico City: Publicaciones de la Secretaría de Educación, 1926.

Ramos Escobar, Norma. "Niños redactores e ilustradores de periódicos escolares: Un acercamiento a las producciones escolares en la escuela nuevoleonesa posrevolucionaria." *Relaciones, estudios de historia y sociedad* 33, no. 132 (2012): 53–93.

Rankin, Monica A. *Mexico, la Patria: Propaganda and Production during World War II.* Lincoln: University of Nebraska Press, 2010.

Rashkin, Elissa. *The Stridentist Movement in Mexico: The Avant-Garde and Cultural Change in the 1920s.* Lanham MD: Lexington Books, 2009.

Reyes Pérez, Roberto. *La vida de los niños iberos en la patria de Lázaro Cárdenas: Treinta relatos.* Mexico City: Editorial América, 1940.

Richards, Irmagarde, and Elena Landazuri. *Children of Mexico: Their Land and Its Story.* San Francisco: Harr Wagner, 1935.

Rochfort, Desmond. "The Sickle, the Serpent, and the Soil: History, Revolution, Nationhood, and Modernity in the Murals of Diego Rivera, José Clemente Orozco, and David Alfaro Siqueiros." In *The Eagle and the Virgin: Nation and Cultural Revolution in Mexico, 1920–1940,* edited by Mary Kay Vaughan and Stephen E. Lewis, 43–57. Durham NC: Duke University Press, 2006.

Rockwell, Elsie. *Hacer escuela, hacer estado: La educación posrevolucionaria vista desde Tlaxcala.* Zamora, Michoacán: El Colegio de Michoacán, CIESAS, CINVESTAV, 2007.

———. "Schools of the Revolution: Enacting and Contesting State Forms in Tlaxcala, 1910–1930." In *Everyday Forms of State Formation: Revolution and the Negotiation of Rule in Modern Mexico,* edited by Gilbert M. Joseph and Daniel Nugent, 170–208. Durham NC: Duke University Press, 1994.

Rodríguez, Pablo, and María Emma Mannarelli, eds. *Historia de la infancia en América Latina.* Bogotá, Colombia: Universidad Externado de Colombia, 2007.

Roehm, A. I. "Learning Foreign Languages and Life by New Techniques Including International Educational Pupil-Correspondence." *Peabody Journal of Education* 19, no. 4 (1942): 227–29.

———. "The National Bureau of Educational Correspondence." *Modern Language Journal* 10, no. 1 (1925): 39–41.

Rubenstein, Anne. "Nahui Olín: The General's Daughter Disrobes." In *The Human Tradition in Mexico*, edited by Jeffrey M. Pilcher, 149–64. Wilmington DE: SR Books, 2003.

Sackett, Everett Baxter. *The Administration of the International School Correspondence of the Junior Red Cross.* Paris: Secretariat of the League of Red Cross Societies, 1929.

Sánchez, George I. *Mexico: A Revolution by Education.* New York: Viking Press, 1936.

Sánchez Calleja, María Eugenia, and Delia Salazar Anaya, eds. *Los niños: Su imagen en la historia.* Mexico City: Instituto Nacional de Antropología e Historia, 2006.

Sánchez-Eppler, Karen. "Copying and Conversion: An 1824 Friendship Album 'from a Chinese Youth.'" In *Asian Americans in New England: Culture and Community*, edited by Monica Chiu, 1–41. Durham: University of New Hampshire Press, 2009.

———. *Dependent States: The Child's Part in Nineteenth-Century American Culture.* Chicago: University of Chicago Press, 2005.

———. "Practicing for Print: The Hale Children's Manuscript Libraries." *Journal of the History of Childhood and Youth* 1, no. 2 (2008): 188–209.

Sanders, Nichole. *Gender and Welfare in Mexico: The Consolidation of a Postrevolutionary State.* University Park: Pennsylvania State University Press, 2011.

Sansón Flores, Jesús. *El niño proletario: Poemas clasistas.* Mexico City: Ediciones Ala Izquierda, 1936.

Schafer, R. Murray. *The Tuning of the World.* New York: Alfred A. Knopf, 1977.

Schell, Patience. *Church and State Education in Revolutionary Mexico City.* Tucson: University of Arizona Press, 2003.

———. "Nationalizing Children through Schools and Hygiene: Porfirian and Revolutionary Mexico City." *Americas* 60, no. 4 (2004): 559–87.

Schwarcz, Lilia Moritz. *The Spectacle of the Races: Scientists, Institutions, and the Race Question in Brazil, 1870–1930.* Translated by Leland Guyer. New York: Hill and Wang, 1999.

Scott, James C. *Seeing Like a State: How Certain Schemes to Improve the Human Condition Have Failed.* New Haven CT: Yale University Press, 1998.

Sealander, Judith. *The Failed Century of the Child: Governing America's Young in the Twentieth Century.* Cambridge: Cambridge University Press, 2003.

Siepmann, C. A. "Can Radio Educate?" *Journal of Educational Sociology* 14, no. 6 (1941): 346–57.

Skabelund, Aaron. "Mobilizing All Creatures Great and Small: Dogs, Children, and the Second World War." Paper presented at "In the Name of the Child," Social and Cultural History of Children and Youth Conference, Norköping, Sweden, June 2007.

Sluis, Ageeth. *City of Spectacles: Gender Performance, Revolutionary Reform, and the Creation of Public Space in Mexico City, 1915–1939.* Tucson: University of Arizona Press, 2006.

Smith, Benjamin T. *Pistoleros and Popular Movements: The Politics of State Formation in Postrevolutionary Oaxaca.* Lincoln: University of Nebraska Press, 2009.

Smith, Bruce R. *The Acoustic World of Early Modern England: Attending to the O-Factor.* Chicago: University of Chicago Press, 1999.

Smith, Dennis. "*The Civilizing Process* and *The History of Sexuality*: Comparing Norbert Elias and Michel Foucault." *Theory & Society* 28 (1999): 79–100.

Snodgrass, Michael. "'We Are All Mexicans Here': Workers, Patriotism, and Union Struggles in Monterrey." In *The Eagle and the Virgin: Nation and Cultural Revolution in Mexico, 1920–1940*, edited by Mary Kay Vaughan and Stephen E. Lewis, 314–34. Durham NC: Duke University Press, 2006.

Sosenski, Susana. "Diversiones malsanas: El cine y la infancia en la ciudad de México en la década de 1920." *Secuencia: Revista de historia y ciencias sociales* 66 (September–December 2006): 37–64.

———. "El niño consumidor: Una construcción publicitaria de la prensa mexicana en la década de 1950." In *Ciudadanos inesperados: Espacios de formación de la ciudadanía ayer y hoy*, edited by Ariadna Acevedo Rodrigo and Paula López Caballero, 191–222. Mexico City: El Colegio de México, 2012.

———. *Niños en acción: El trabajo infantil en la ciudad de México, 1920–1934.* Mexico City: El Colegio de México, Centro de Estudios Históricos, 2010.

———. "Niños limpios y trabajadores: El teatro guiñol posrevolucionario en la construcción de la infancia mexicana." *Anuario de Estudios Americanos* 67, no. 2 (2010): 493–518.

———, and Elena Jackson Albarrán, eds. *Nuevas miradas a la historia de la infancia en América Latina: Entre prácticas y representaciones.* Mexico City: Instituto de Investigaciones Históricas, Universidad Nacional Autónoma de México, 2012.

Spenser, Daniela. "Encounter of Two Revolutions: Mexican Radical Elites in Communist Russia during the 1920s." In *Strange Pilgrimages: Exile, Travel, and National Identity in Latin America, 1800–1990s*, edited by Ingrid E. Fey and Karen Racine, 147–62. Wilmington DE: Scholarly Resources, 2000.

Staples, Anne. "Primeros pasos de la higiene escolar decimonónica." Paper presented at the Coloquio Internacional, "Sanar, curar y educar: Salud, enfermedad y sociedad en México, siglos XIX–XX," Instituto de Investigaciones Históricas, UNAM, April 2006.

Stearns, Peter. *Childhood in World History*. Themes in World History Series. New York and London: Routledge, 2006.

Stepan, Nancy Leys. *"The Hour of Eugenics": Race, Gender, and Nation in Latin America*. Ithaca NY: Cornell University Press, 1991.

Stern, Alexandra Minna. "Responsible Mothers and Normal Children: Eugenics, Nationalism, and Welfare in Post-revolutionary Mexico, 1920–1940." *Journal of Historical Sociology* 12, no. 4 (1999): 369–97.

Stone, Lawrence. *The Family, Sex, and Marriage in England, 1500–1800*. New York: Harper & Row, 1977.

Szir, Sandra M. *Infancia y cultura visual: Los periódicos ilustrados para niños (1880–1910)*. Buenos Aires: Miño y Dávila Editores, 2007.

Taibo, Paco Ignacio, II. *Cárdenas de cerca: Una entrevista biográfica*. Mexico City: Grupo Editorial Planeta, 1994.

Tannenbaum, Frank. "The Miracle School." *Century*, August 1923, 499–506.

Taylor, Lucy, and Fiona Wilson. "The Messiness of Everyday Life: Exploring Key Themes in Latin American Citizenship Studies, Introduction." *Bulletin of Latin American Research* 23, no. 2 (2004): 154–64.

Tenorio Trillo, Mauricio. "Stereophonic Scientific Modernisms: Social Science between Mexico and the United States, 1880s–1930s." In "The Nation and Beyond: Transnational Perspectives on United States History." Special issue, *Journal of American History* 86, no. 3 (1999): 1156–87.

Tomkins, Richard. "Sweet Child of Mine." *Financial Times Weekend*, June 24, 2006, W1–W2.

Tsivian, Yuri. *Early Cinema in Russia and Its Cultural Reception*. Translated by Alan Bodger. London: Routledge, 1994.

Twinam, Ann. *Public Lives, Private Secrets: Gender, Honor, Sexuality, and Illegitimacy in Colonial Spanish America*. Stanford CA: Stanford University Press, 1999.

Una historia hecha de sonidos, Radio Educación: La innovación en el cuadrante. Mexico City: Secretaría de Educación Pública / Radio Educación, 2004.

Utopia—No Utopia: La arquitectura, la enseñanza y la planificación del deseo. Mexico City: Museo Casa Estudio Diego Rivera y Frida Kahlo / INBA, 2005.

Vasconcelos, José. *La raza cósmica*. Spanish ed. 1925. Reprint, Madrid: Aguilar, 1966.

———. *Lecturas clásicas para niños*. 1924. Reprint, Mexico City: Departamento Editorial Secretaría de Educación Pública, 1984.

Vásquez, Josefina. *Nacionalismo y educación*. 2nd ed. Mexico City: El Colegio de México, 1975.

Vaughan, Mary Kay. "Cambio ideológico en la política educativa de la SEP: Programas y libros de texto." In *Escuela y sociedad en el periodo cardenista*, edited by Susana Quintanilla and Mary Kay Vaughan, 77–108. Mexico City: Fondo de Cultura Económica, 1997.

———. "Cri-Cri: A Pedagogy of Propriety and Promise." Paper presented at the Fifty-Fifth Annual Conference of the Rocky Mountain Council for Latin American Studies, Flagstaff AZ, April 2008.

———. *Cultural Politics in Revolution: Teachers, Peasants, and Schools in Mexico, 1930–1940.* Tucson: University of Arizona Press, 1997.

———. "The Educational Project of the Mexican Revolution: The Response of Local Societies (1934–1940)." In *Molding the Hearts and Minds: Education, Communications, and Social Change in Latin America,* edited by John A. Britton, 105–27. Lanham MD: Rowman and Littlefield, 1994.

———. "Modernizing Patriarchy: State Policies, Rural Households, and Women in Mexico, 1930–1940." In *Hidden Histories of Gender and the State in Latin America,* edited by Elizabeth Dore and Maxine Molyneux, 194–214. Durham NC: Duke University Press, 2000.

———. "Pepe and Nico in the Vecindades, 1943–1960." Paper presented at the XII Congress of Mexican, United States, and Canadian Historians, Vancouver BC, October 2006.

———. *The State, Education, and Social Class in Mexico, 1880–1928.* DeKalb: Northern Illinois University Press, 1982.

———, and Stephen Lewis, eds. *The Eagle and the Virgin: Nation and Cultural Revolution in Mexico, 1920–1940.* Durham NC: Duke University Press, 2006.

Velasco Ceballos, Rómulo. *El niño mexicano ante la caridad y el Estado: Apuntes históricos que comprenden desde la época precortesiana hasta nuestros días.* Mexico City: Beneficencia Pública en el Distrito Federal, 1938.

Velázquez Andrade, Manuel. *Fermin Lee: Llibro para enseñar a leer a los niños de las escuelas rurales.* Illustrated by Diego Rivera and Agustín Velázquez. Mexico City: n.p., 1928.

Vinson, Ben, III, and Matthew Restall. *Black Mexico: Race and Society from Colonial to Modern Times.* Albuquerque: University of New Mexico Press, 2009.

Wakild, Emily. "Resources, Communities, and Conservation: The Creation of National Parks in Revolutionary Mexico under President Lázaro Cárdenas, 1934–1940." PhD diss., University of Arizona, 2007.

———. *An Unexpected Environment: National Park Creation, Resource Custodianship, and the Mexican Revolution.* Tucson: University of Arizona Press, 2011.

Walsh, Andrea N. "Healthy Bodies, Strong Citizens: Okanagan Children's Drawings and the Canadian Junior Red Cross." In *Depicting Canada's Children,* edited by Loren Lerner, 279–304. Waterloo, Ontario: Wilfred Laurier University Press, 2009.

Waters, Wendy. "Remapping Identities: Road Construction and Nation Building in Postrevolutionary Mexico." In *The Eagle and the Virgin: Nation and Cultural Revolution in Mexico, 1920–1940*, edited by Mary Kay Vaughan and Stephen E. Lewis, 221–42. Durham NC: Duke University Press, 2006.

———. "Revolutionizing Childhood: Schools, Roads, and the Revolutionary Generation Gap in Tepoztlán, Mexico, 1928 to 1944." *Journal of Family History* 23, no. 3 (1998): 292–311.

Weber, Eugen. *Peasants into Frenchmen: The Modernization of Rural France, 1870–1914*. Stanford CA: Stanford University Press, 1976.

Whetten, Nathan. *Rural Mexico*. Chicago: University of Chicago Press, 1948.

Wilkie, James W. *The Mexican Revolution: Federal Expenditure and Social Change since 1910*. Rev. ed. Berkeley: University of California Press, 1970.

Wright-Ríos, Edward. "A Revolution in Local Catholicism? Oaxaca, 1928–34." In *Faith and Impiety in Revolutionary Mexico*, edited by Matthew Butler, 243–60. New York: Palgrave Macmillan, 2007.

Zang, Xiaowei. *Children of the Cultural Revolution: Family Life and Political Behavior in Mao's China*. Boulder CO: Westview Press, 2000.

Zelizer, V. A. *Pricing the Priceless Child: The Changing Social Value of Children*. New York: Basic Books, 1985.

Zepeda, Beatriz. *Enseñar la nación: La educación y la institucionalización de la idea de la nación en el México de la Reforma (1855–1876)*. Mexico City: Fondo de Cultura Económica / Consejo Nacional para la Cultura y las Artes, 2012.

Zolov, Eric. *Refried Elvis: The Rise of the Mexican Counterculture*. Berkeley: University of California Press, 1999.

Zumbano Altman, Raquel. "Brincando na história." In *História das crianças no Brasil*, edited by Mary del Priore. São Paulo: Contexto, 1999.

INDEX

technology, 22, 23, 26, 129–31, 133–35; as propaganda, 131–32; reception statistics, 134. *See also* Office of Cultural Radiotelephony

Rationalist School, 177–78, 214, 348n6

Red Cross, 308. *See also* Junior Red Cross, American; Junior Red Cross, Mexican

Regional Confederation of Mexican Workers, 15

Revolutionary Family, 9, 21, 62, 65–66, 135, 137, 216, 222–23, 297, 322

Revolutionary Writers and Artists' League (LEAR), 188

Revueltas, Fermín, 184

Revueltas, Silvestre, 160, 187, 349n37

Rivera, Diego, 70–72, 76–77, 79–81, 108, 122, 123, 165, 184, 337n83, 338n8

Rodríguez, Abelardo, 63–65

Rodríguez, Aída, 45, 286

Ross, María Luisa, 133, 144

Sáenz, Moisés, 214, 251, 295

Sansón Flores, Jesús, 68

Santamarina, Rafael, 39–40

Secretaría de Educación Pública (SEP). *See* Ministry of Public Education (SEP)

Secretaría de Relaciones Exteriores (SRE). *See* Ministry of Foreign Relations (SRE)

Secretaría de Salubridad Pública (SSP). *See* Ministry of Public Health (SSP)

Siqueiros, David Alfaro, 76–77, 79

socialist education, 9, 34, 50, 68, 137, 175–78, 182–84, 199, 214, 250, 252–57, 261–63, 265, 273, 287, 317, 320, 330n17

Society for the Protection of Children, 44

Spanish Civil War, 267–69

Stridentist Movement, 129, 158–59, 165, 174, 346n77

student government, 223, *223*, 225–29, 232, 251

Teatro Guiñol. *See* puppet theater

television, 133

textbooks, 4, 8–9, 17, 71, 216, 218–19, 235–36, 243, 254, 324; *historia patria* in, 218, 352n15

Troka el Poderoso, 129–30, 159–70, *171*, 174, 321, 323

typewriters, 163–64, 346n77

Vasconcelos, José, 7, 12–13, 31–32, 37, 59, 61, 66, 71–72, 79–82, 84, 87–88, 112, 154, 213–14, 217, 234, 321, 351n1, 360n33

Velasco, José María, 107–8

volcanoes, 26, 78, 102, 106–11, 122, 297

Wilson, Woodrow, 308

World War I, 36, 40, 264, 282–83, 308, 355n62

Young Men's Christian Association (YMCA), 13, 295, 334n35

Zapata, Rosaura, 41, 194–95, 333n25

Pistoleros and Popular Movements: The Politics of State Formation in Postrevolutionary Oaxaca
Benjamin T. Smith

To order or obtain more information on these or other University of Nebraska Press titles, visit nebraskapress.unl.edu.